Islam, Peace and Social Justice

Islam, Peace and
Social Justice

A Christian Perspective

A. Christian van Gorder

James Clarke & Co

James Clarke & Co
P.O. Box 60
Cambridge
CB1 2NT
United Kingdom

www.jamesclarke.co
publishing@jamesclarke.co

ISBN: 978 0 227 17422 7

British Library Cataloguing in Publication Data
A record is available from the British Library

Contents

A frustrated man went to a Sufi and said: "My neighbor makes my life a misery by visiting me at all hours, hanging about the house and constantly asking all kinds of questions."

The Sufi advised: "Nothing is easier than the cure for this. All you have to do is to ask the man for money every time you see him, and he will soon start avoiding you."

"But supposing he then goes about the town telling everyone that I am a beggar?"

"Ahh", said the wise man, "I see that you are hoping to control the thoughts of mankind, not trying to stop your neighbor from annoying you. Do you often imagine that you want one thing when you really want another?"

— Idris Shah

Christ is the population of the world, and every object as well.
There is no room for hypocrisy.
Why use bitter soup for healing
when sweet water is everywhere?

— Jalal al-din Rumi

Acknowledgments and Dedication

Gratitude is the heart's memory.

— French Proverb

First and foremost, I would like to thank the excellent and professional editorial assistance of Bethany Churchard, chief editor Adrian Brink, and the entire staff at James Clarke & Co. It has been a delightful process working with this fine publisher. I have been deeply humbled and warmly impressed by their clear dedication to careful excellence and service to their readership. Through our interactions within this past year, I have become deeply honored to now have become part of the James Clarke & Co family of authors and editors.

Sukhran to my dear friends of the Masjid al-Siddiq — the Islamic Society of Central Texas — for their support in this research. Mohammed Bahamdun, Muhammad Alhendawi, Ricky Dnani, David Oualaalou, Warraq Khan, and Abzul (al) Siddiq have made invaluable contributions to this book through frequent discussion (many over meals) about how these ideas can promote greater mutuality. I would also like to thank Dr Arif Shaykh, Jamaal Chebli, Ali Datee, and especially my dear friend Mr Saif Saify of the Al Sabreen Islamic Society of Central Pennsylvania. Thanks to Dr Howard Kenig of the Harrisburg Jewish Community Relations Council who helped me in this research while I was at Messiah College. Thanks to Ramzy Kilic of the Council of American Islamic Relations in Tampa who aided me immensely while I was teaching at the University of South Florida. Thanks to Ibrahim Kalinin who shared numerous energetic conversations while we attended a seminar at Loyola Marymont University on "War and Peace in the Bible and the Qur'an" directed by Daniel Smith-Christopher and Dr Mustansir Mir. Thanks also to my dear Muslim friends during my years of work and study in the United Kingdom.

I am grateful for the assistance of my mentor A.H.M. Zahniser and to the input I received from beloved teachers Bishop Kenneth Cragg and Andrew Walls. Thanks to Morris Dowling of the Queen's University of Belfast. Thanks also to my best friends Artyom Tonoyan and Tibra Ail and also to Abjar Bakhou, Gordon Nickel, George Gawyrch, Charles McDaniels, Glenn Sanders, Kurt Werthmuller, and many others. Thanks to David W. Shenk for providing the foreword to this book. Thanks also to Jonathan Warner and Jon Hoover for assisting me with hours of careful proofreading. Special thanks go to Brandon Morgan, who worked diligently on the text. Thanks to friends in my hometown of Pittsburgh (a city named after the British Abolitionist William Pitt, the Elder). Most of all, I appreciate the loving support I have received from my Biafran Queen Vivian Ndudi Ezeife who, since the first day that we met, has been my rock and refuge. I am grateful for my brother Peter; and for the joy I know in the bright smiles of my seven beautiful children, Patrick Xavier, Brendan Daniel, Keegan, Sean Michael, Tatijiana Erika Ezeife, Andrew Johannes Ojukwu, and Gretchen Michele Ngozi.

A German Proverb states, "Where there are sisters there are riches." Special thanks to my sister, Gretchen Elise van Gorder. There is nobody in the world like you, sis, and your patient care for Stephen and Josh is an inspiration. I dedicate this work to you in thanks for your kindness in these dark years since we lost Erika Helena Lutsch of Bliesransbach, Saarland. Mom filled our home with her art and warm conversation as well as the smell of freshly cut flowers and freshly ground coffee. Your warmth brings to mind the line in Seamus Heaney's poem *At the Wellhead* (1996) in reference to his blind neighbor Rosie Keelan: "Being with her was intimate and helpful like a cure you didn't know was happenin'." Thanks, dear Gretchen, for your steady encouragement and timely and thoughtful sensitivity. May God give you a long and restful life of peaceful serenity!

Foreword by David W. Shenk

"Islam is peace!" declared President George W. Bush shortly after the destruction of the World Trade Center. "In compliance with God's order . . . kill the Americans and their allies", commanded Osama bin Laden. These quotes from the opening sentences of the chapter 'Islamic *Jihad* and the Path of Peace' demonstrate the engaging relevance of this book *Islam, Peace, and Social Justice: A Christian Perspective*. Each page and chapter is an immersion within the Qur'an, the traditions, and the history of the historic Muslim movement that is most captivating and instructive. Dr van Gorder's Christian perspective enlivens each chapter with explorations of convergence and divergence between Christian faith and practice and that of Islam. Our modern situation is penetratingly presented.

This book is not one of those soft irenic tomes that portray the Muslim way as the highest ideal. Neither is it ruthlessly critical, accenting themes such as the "sword" verses in the Qur'an, which has been much in vogue among some Western writers especially since 2001. Van Gorder seeks to present the realities of Islam in a balanced way, while remaining faithful to what the Qur'an and traditions say. Van Gorder gives a keen insight into the wide variety of ways that Muslims interpret these scriptures and traditions. Interwoven are the descriptions of ways in which these themes actually unfold within the real world; sometimes in horrible ways, as in the genocidal wars of Sudan, and sometimes in an edifying manner as in giving to the poor as an act of true piety and worship.

Van Gorder demonstrates a genuine commitment to portraying Islam authentically. As an author, he writes from a Christian perspective. And, while it is difficult for a person outside a movement to fully appreciate the inner soul of those who live within the movement, Muslims themselves will assess to what extent van Gorder's perspective has accurately portrayed the themes of social justice and peacemaking in Islam. Only Muslims will know to what extent this book is a true reflection of the soul of the Muslim community. Nevertheless, regardless of any number of possible Muslim assessments of van Gorder's work, it can be instructive for Muslims to hear the way the issues look to a non-Muslim who is sympathetic to the Muslim aspiration to be a people of justice and peace. The gift of this book to the Muslim world is that the author's description of peace and social justice themes in Islam is written by a friend of Muslims.

This book demonstrates that it is urgent for both Muslims and Christians to address the hermeneutical challenges of violence and expressions of injustice within their respective scriptures and the history of violence and injustice within their traditions. Van Gorder has opened the door for that process to commence. In these captivating chapters he boldly explores key themes within the Muslim tradition and within the Qur'an that are powerfully relevant to the challenges of social justice and peacemaking. He also weaves into the text Christian perspectives and realities. He does not mince words in his critique of both Muslim and Christian failures to be peoples of peace and justice, and he does not whitewash ways in which exegesis of their scriptures has justified or formed injustice and violence. On the other hand he also highlights social justice and peacemaking themes within these same scriptures.

Of course, all "Christians" and all "Muslims" claim to be committed to peacemaking. For example, both American Presidents and al-Qaeda terrorists have perceived themselves as pre-eminently people of God who are committed to the eventual advance of social justice and peace. Both the Muslim movement and the Christian movement claim to be committed to submission to the rule of God. This book explores the contours of that rule when the Qur'an and the traditions are faithfully interpreted and applied by the vast majority of Muslims. Van Gorder describes how that rule is actually expressed, and the enormous diversities within the Muslim movement in the interpretation and practice of the rule of God. Christians are also caught in the same quandary of diverse and inconsistent understandings of the rule of God. What does it mean to participate faithfully in the kingdom of God in times like these? That is, obviously, a question for both Muslims and Christians.

There is a distinctive Christian contribution to the engagement with Muslims with regard to social justice and peace that merits special emphasis. That is the centrality of Jesus Christ to the Christian faith. Christians confess that Jesus is the One in whom the Word became human (John 1:14). Christians confess that Jesus is the fullness of God in bodily form (Col. 1:19) and that he is the fullness of the presence of the kingdom of God among us (Luke 4:17–21). Therefore, we confess that Jesus has the last word, not the Qur'an, or the Muslim traditions, or the Torah, or Christian tradition.

A Christ-centered hermeneutic confesses, "In the past God spoke to our forefathers through the prophets at many times and in various ways, but in these last days he has spoken to us by his Son, whom he appointed heir of all things, and through whom he made the universe" (Heb. 1:1, 2). A Christ-centered hermeneutic provides a firm foundation to evaluate all other foundations. For example, a Christ-centered kingdom blesses the Qur'anic command to care for the orphans, but it challenges the command to slay the oppressors. A Christ-centered kingdom affirms the Mosaic year of Jubilee, wherein all debts are forgiven, but it challenges the Torah's condoning of slavery for foreigners. A Christian perspective that is truly Christ-centered relativizes both the Muslim and Christian experience. Christ enables authentic critique and evaluation of both the Muslim and Christian journeys.

Muslims respect Jews and Christians as the "people of the book". That respect can provide an open door for engaging Muslims in the common commitment to social justice and peacemaking. From a Christian perspective, a Christ-centered contribution to that conversation invites repentance for both Muslims and Christians, for indeed we have all fallen short of the kingdom that Jesus incarnated. The high respect that Muslims have for Jesus as the prophet who is a "sign" may open the way for authentic dialogue on matters of great concern to both Muslims and Christians. We enter those conversations in repentance, humility, and prayer beseeching the One who is the Wounded Healer to touch both communities with his healing grace, forgiveness, reconciliation, transforming power, and the revelation of truth.

— David W. Shenk

Introduction

Re-chisel then your ancient frame and build up a new being — Such
being, being real being — or else your ego is a mere ring of smoke.
— Muhammad Iqbal

Meeting Muslims

The Islamic *ummah* and the Christian Church are the two fastest
growing religious movements in our world: perhaps 60% of humanity
claims to be either a Muslim or a Christian. Given these dynamics, it
is incumbent upon adherents of these faiths to assume the posture of
intentionality in learning about each other to gain increased knowledge
(Q. 12:76) and wisdom (Q. 18:60–62). This wisdom and knowledge will
help Muslims, Jews, and Christians learn how to best honor God in their
inter-religious interactions. All three traditions teach that God loves all
within the beautiful creation (Q. 30:22). The people of God should be
tolerant; never striving against each other (Q. 22:67) because Allah is
ultimately responsible for the rich diversity of cultures worldwide.

All of us should be inspired by the vivid example of the Prophet
Muhammad who asked God in exemplary humility for the continual
development of his knowledge (Q. 20:114). All of us should follow
the clear example of Jesus Christ who called upon God to be glorified
through love, humility, and acts of service for others — even one's
enemies. As Muslims, Jews, and Christians begin to study each other's
traditions they will come to appreciate that their distinct traditions hold
"vast areas of agreement" about God's work and share in common many
ethical and moral standards.[1] The Ten Commandments (a distinctly
Christian term), and in Judaism, the Decalogue, for example, are largely
repeated in some variant form within the Qur'an.[2] As Muslims and non-
Muslims interact with increasing regularity, it would be ideal if both
communities could gain a deeper appreciation for how the faiths of
others confront the pressing social justice issues of our times.

Sadly, many people of faith only learn about each other through
biased lenses, which, at best, are incomplete and, at worst, are unfair
and inaccurate. Simplifications and incorrect assertions have often been
assertively broadcast as indisputable fact. Muslim imams, Jewish rabbis,
and Christian clergy have often been at the forefront of advancing a

host of negative, simplistic views about each other. Some Evangelical critics, for example, have even argued that the Arabic term *Allah* is actually a reference to an ancient moon-deity and not comparable to the God of Jewish and Christian revelation. Such an absurd claim is easily refuted by the millions of dedicated Arabic-speaking Christians who also lovingly refer to God using the Arabic term *Allah*. Other Christian and Jewish critics have berated the life and example of the Prophet Muhammad as a paradigm of violence, deceit, or debauchery. Florida-based internet preacher Bill Keller calls Islam a "1,400-year-old lie from the pits of hell" organized by "a murdering pedophile".[3] The early twentieth-century Protestant missionary Samuel Zwemer (1867–1952) derisively called the Prophet a "clever imposter from the first day of his message to the day of his death" and suggested that Muhammad was a pedophile and womanizer. Protestant missionary Duncan Black MacDonald (1863–1943) assured other Christians that Islam would invariably "collapse" as soon as the distorted "legend of Muhammad crumbles and his character is seen in its true light".[4]

Among many Jewish and Christian communities, "Islamophobia" (or "Crusadeaphobia") has been increasing since the tragic events of 9/11. European and North American media sources have often castigated Islam in generalized pasquinades that emphasize the denial of human rights, the promotion of violence against innocents, and the harsh oppression of women.[5] An entirely different view of these social justice concerns emerges from the pages of the Islamic tradition. This book, written to aid non-Muslims in better appreciating their Muslim neighbors, focuses on how Muslims actually address a host of specific, pressing social justice issues.

This is a critical lens for inter-religious dialogue because the ideals of social justice are at the heart of Christianity, Judaism, and Islam. Justice is a central keyword that that is also often found at the foundation of how many Muslims worldwide view their faiths. The Qur'an commands all believers to "Be just" (4:134; 6:153). The elusive term "social justice", however, can mean many different things to different people. Some have argued that the term can be used as a blunt "instrument of ideological intimidation", when evocation of its absence is used to advance a given political agenda.[6] The advance of social justice is ultimately foundational for almost all religious sensibilities because the transforming power of faith is not only directed towards the realization of one's own individual salvation (or satisfaction) but also towards the progressive enhancement of all humanity. The work of social justice, in its broadest sense, is a calling that unites all of us — no matter our spiritual or cultural background — to work with hopeful effort to make our fragile world a better place to live in for our cherished children and grandchildren.

The Torah, the Bible and the Qur'an instruct Jews, Christians, and Muslims to learn from God's call to Abraham chosen to become a blessing to all of humanity (Gen. 12:3). The sweeping inclusivity of this divine intention reminds believers that a day will eventually become reality when the "whole earth will be filled with the glory of the Lord as the waters cover the sea" (Habk 2:14). While the cold shadows of our uncertain world seem to offer scant glimpses of such a remote ideal, people of faith are nonetheless called to press forward to bring such visions into the reality of our shared experiences. Jews, Christians, and Muslims speak of God's promised kingdom, which will provide all of humanity with a living hope — even those who are oppressed. At the same time, these three visions of faith offer little promise to believers that such a realm of shared social justice will arrive anytime soon or that it will be realized without great effort. Jesus lamented that God's Kingdom would remain "hidden from our eyes" (Luke 19:42) until the "final days". Faith traditions worldwide call adherents to work for social justice even though many observable facts foretell that our world seems intractably destined to seethe as a brimming cauldron of nightmarish injustices.

The very idea of moral holiness — central within many spirituality traditions — anticipates that the pure lives of the faithful will have to be lived out in contexts of careening unsteadiness marked by ethical impurities. The apostle Peter called Christians a "holy nation" (1 Pet. 2:9) amidst a world abrim with evil; Christ commanded the faithful to go into the midst of all hurting cultures worldwide (Matt. 28:19–20) in order to serve others as a unique community of "salt and light" (Matt. 5:13–16). Anabaptist scholar David W. Shenk describes the Kingdom of God mission of Christ directly in terms of social justice:

> Jesus was committed to justice. Wherever His kingdom comes there is hope for the poor and the oppressed. The church is called to be an extension in our communities and around the world of the Messiah's commitment to justice and peace. . . . Broken bread and crushed grapes are the signs of the covenant established by Jesus, a covenant of repentance, of being crushed in sacrificial love for one another and for our enemies and of self-giving service.[7]

In this all-consuming work of nurturing social justice within our world, there can be little room — or time — for efforts dedicated to attacking people of other faiths or focusing on the many historic failures of some within those traditions. The teachings of Moses, Jesus, and Muhammad never asserted that those outside their folds were somehow morally deficient or inevitably beyond the scope of God's redeeming grace. Each believer has ample opportunity to find fault in others, or to work with others for improvements within our shared societies. There is nothing constructive in focusing on what others lack or how others fail. Instead, each of us can focus on how we can live out the full implications of our own convictions, including in our relationships with people of other faiths. This basic principle was expressed with clarity when Christ warned against harboring a dismissive spirit and judgmental attitude when he told his followers to look at the "mote in their own eye before pointing out the speck in their brothers' eye" (Matt. 7:3–5).

Before non-Muslims portray Islam simplistically as a religion of intolerance and injustice — based on pervasive media caricatures — they should carefully examine both the teachings of Islam and at their own community's culpability in a host of contexts in which injustice thrives worldwide. A sobering sense of spiritual self-examination will probably remove any remaining vestiges of arrogant self-assertion and condescending dismissal from the inter-religious equation. For a number of reasons, the long march of history shows that individuals and communities tend to view their own traditions in a charitable light, while highlighting the abundant weaknesses within their neighbors' traditions. Shabbir Akthar (b. 1960) warns that Christians who are quick to cast the first stones over the extent of Islamic intolerance should keep in mind that "Christianity's own moral record in such matters as pluralism, toleration, and coercion, judged by modern, internal Christian standards is, as some church-men now concede, utterly deplorable."[8] When we criticize individuals of other faiths we invariably invite the same standards of judgment to ourselves and our own faith communities.

Media Portrayals

Contemporary media portrayals often fail to emphasize that Muslims see Islam as, first and foremost, a faith that vitally promotes social justice. For many non-Muslims, reductive ignorance, based on fear, has joined pervasive media bias to foster a deeply rooted host of negative views about Muslims (and particularly Arab Muslims).[9] Lawrence Davidson (b. 1945) warns that there is a "consistent tendency among Americans to portray the peoples of the region [Arabs] as primitive and aggressive".[10] In one odd incident during the 2008 Presidential electoral campaign one woman during a John McCain rally even expressed that she did not trust Obama because he was "an Arab". Instead of clarifying this misconception in terms of ethnicity, McCain chose to clarify it in terms of moral values: "No, ma'am, no ma'am, he is a decent family man, [a] citizen that I just happen to disagree with."[11]

The "Ground Zero Mosque" debate in the United States illustrated the harsh realities of media bias against almost everything related to Islam and Muslims. In 2009, Imam Feisal Abdul Rauf (b. 1948) launched an initiative to locate a Muslim community center at the 13-story Park

51 Manhattan property; a few blocks away from the World Trade Center. In response, Fox News invited 47 different guests to attack the center over a 3-month period (May–August 2012) with rhetoric such as that expressed by the American talk show host, author and political commentator, Laura Ingraham: "I say the terrorists have won the way this has gone down. Six hundred feet from where thousands of our fellow Americans were incinerated in the name of political Islam and we're supposed to be considered intolerant if we are not cheering for this?"[12] Media portrayals are alarmist and often warn of Islam as a faith dedicated to "domination and injustice".[13] Terms such as "militant", "radical", "extremist", join with frequent mentions of "jihad" and "shariah" to portray Islam as a violent and threatening religion. One Fox News guest, Mike Gallagher, even suggested an "all Muslim checkpoint line at American airports".[14]

Another example is an article for London's *Sunday Express* by Robert Kilroy-Silk (b. 1942) which suggested that all Muslims were latent "suicide bombers, limb-amputators", and "women repressors".[15] For Kilroy-Silk it would seem that even the most noble of Muslims was only waiting to shed such virtues to take on inherently dark cloaks of hateful vituperation. Edward Said (1935–2003) thought that many "Western" media views presented Islam as a "resurgent atavism", which sought to plunge the entire world back into the primeval grip of the Middle Ages.[16] Stark black-and-white paradigms promote the questionable notion that the secular and Judeo-Christian West are the sole luminous forces of progressive modernity, while the vast and swarthy hordes that make up huge and uneducated Muslim societies are armed with obedient religious slaves who are blinded by evil religious leaders intent upon harshly oppressing women (and all non-Muslims) along their unwavering march towards world domination.

Jack Shaheen observes four basic myths that the media seems to reaffirm about Arab Muslims. They are "fabulously wealthy", "barbaric and uncultured"; "sex maniacs", who "revel in acts of terrorism".[17] Hollywood images reinforce these stark notions, abundant as they are absurd. Elvis Presley, for example, starred in a comedy entitled *Harum Scarum* (1965), in which he was captured by fez and sunglass-wearing Arab assassins who sported black "goatee" beards and screeched in guttural and nonsensical commands. These trends continue into our modern era: Children can watch a gaggle of Saturday-morning cartoon caricatures, in which the "bad guys" display the stock set of "cultural traits generally considered being those of Muslims".[18] One North American toy company even created an action figure named "Nomad" who wore a headdress with Arabic script and was described (on the packaging) as "unreliable as the sand, as cold as the nights, and as dangerous as the deadly scorpions from where he lives." Nomad's obviously Arab family is a gang of assassins and wandering thieves. They are, in the words of the toy's promotion: "Men without honor . . . using their knowledge of the desert to attack innocent villages."[19] One could cite other lamentable examples *ad infinitum* across the spectrum of North American and European popular culture.

The Primacy of Social Justice

In contrast to media renderings, social justice (*al-'adala al-ijtima 'iyyah*) is central to the practice of Islam; it is at the heart of all Islamic moral and ethical teachings. According to Islamic scriptures, righteousness is not only belief in God; it is also to help orphans and widows, the poor, and travelers, and to liberate the enslaved (Q. 2:177). One's *iman* (in the sense of one's commitment to Allah) is based on one's beliefs as well as one's actions (*'amal*). The *ummah* exists not only for its own benefit but also has a God-given responsibility (Q. 17:15) to be a generous blessing to all other nations (Q. 3:110). The *da'wah* (invitation) of God's *ummah* is that individuals should embrace Islam as a faith for the down-trodden, because advocacy for social justice is at the heart of God's divine revelation as received through the Prophet.

Qur'an chapter three describes Allah as creating Adam and Eve for a life of harmony in the gardens of the Edenic paradise; it is only after the first two humans are deceived by the wiles of Satan (*Iblis*) that God sends out humanity to populate the earth and serve as God's faithful representatives (*khalifa* or caliph) among the created order. God alone holds all worldly authority (Q. 2:115; 5:40); the divine plan is to return humanity to an inevitable, eternal destiny of Edenic blessing and the harmonies of paradise through the clear revelatory guidance of Islam. There is no other refuge for humanity besides the generous mercy of Allah (Q. 94:1) and divine guidance (Q. 17:9). This earthly life is only a fleeting test that humanity experiences before returning to Allah. The Qur'an promises that God will help us to pass every test in this world through the blessings that will flow to those who obey the divinely-inspired messengers.

Allah commands, first and foremost, that believers live a life opposed to all forms of injustice (Q. 7:181). The rights of women, for example, are to be championed (Q. 9:71), even when many cultures choose to defy God's commands and embrace sexist and chauvinistic practices that harm women. Believers are called to follow the straight pathway of God's revelation, which eternally elevates and temporally blesses individuals on the basis of their piety expressed as righteousness (Q. 49:13). God blesses individuals because of their moral actions and not on the basis of their sex, race, language, status, or economic wealth. Islam emphatically forbids all forms of economic injustice and class-systems, which have given rise to poverty and malnutrition, and, concurrently, to bribery and corruption. The wealthy cannot live in proud and dismissive vanity (Q. 4:29) but must share their resources with the poor and graciously forgive their debts (Q. 9:60). Muslims have always cherished the rule of law; one cannot call oneself a devout believer without being committed to the enactment of Islamic law as a social protection against any possible form of legalized injustice. While the arrogant may turn to weapons, or brute force; the righteous are duty-bound (Q. 5:1; 6:153) to rely upon the power of God's all-encompassing law. For example, those who "lend to Allah a godly loan" (Q. 11:245) by intervening against evils are promised to inherit an eternal reward (Q. 4:85). God promises to protect the weak; those who attack the weak will face divine wrath (Q. 4:75). Those who claim to be believers, yet support injustice will be judged on the Final Day as those who have betrayed Allah and disregarded the divine message of the rightly-guided Prophet (Q. 8:27).

This book is intended to help non-Muslims better appreciate the social justice emphasis that rings out through the many and varied historic expressions of the Islamic tradition (in contrast to the reductionistic idea of a trans-historic "Islamic civilization"). I am convinced that the theme of a shared commitment to social justice can serve as a constructive bridge for improved interaction between different faiths around the world. Usually a week does not pass without North American, British, and European newspapers lamenting the grim actions of Islamists; the articles carry the unstated assumption that such terrorists, in some way, represent the latent intentions of a billion Muslims throughout the entire house of Islam. These few extremists are, indeed, agents for social change, but do not represent anything that even remotely approaches a majority sentiment. Further, the greatest inroads that these non-orthodox extremists are making to advance their cause occur in the ranks of the battered poor and unheeded oppressed. It is those who are in the greatest need for justice who have most often responded to the shrill and assertive Islamist declarations that they alone have God-ordained solutions to the multivalent social, economic, and political problems of our time.

When media sources present the actions of extremists as representative of all Muslims they also compromise hopes for improved interfaith interactions. Sensationalist media portrayals reveal little of what is actually happening among Muslims worldwide, while, at the same time, resurrecting long-standing colonialist and orientalist assumptions about the inherently violent nature of Islam.[20] Media portrayals support those critics who selectively choose Qur'anic passages about war and take them out of context to attempt to prove that Islam is a violent religion. Many of these same critics, from Christian or Jewish perspectives, emphasize verses from the Bible that promote peace, as if to suggest that these three religions are unilaterally opposed. While some Islamists do take certain Qur'anic verses as a literal mandate to wage war on all non-Muslims, the vast majority of Muslims are able to appreciate the specific and historic context of these references to understand that the major thrust of their faith is the mandate to bring peace and justice to all of humanity for Allah's greater glory.

This view is exemplified by the life of the Prophet Muhammad, the historical context of the modern Muslim *ummah*, and centuries of learned reflection on the meaning of oft-recited Qur'anic verses. Among Muslims, there are, of course, numerous views about many of these contentious issues. In this book, I will introduce a few of these viewpoints, drawing from the Qur'an, Hadith (or traditions), and the perspectives of Muslim intellectuals across the vast spectrum of over 1,400 years of Islamic history. Even a cursory survey of this history will expose as false the simplistic view that Islam is only a force of demonic evil.

I do not claim to represent the more than 2.2 billion people worldwide who call themselves Christians. Whatever I say about the broad categories of "Christianity", "Judaism", or "Islam" cannot possibly parallel the varied experiences of adherents from diverse places and distinct times. Any commentator on multifaith dynamics begins from a limited and specific point of orientation; I write as a Euro-American Christian of German-Catholic ancestry, who attends a predominantly African-American church. This research has presented a number of specific challenges, not the least of which has been the issue of transliterating and translating terms from Arabic, Persian, or Urdu into English. In this effort I have sought to both minimize confusion and be true to sources being cited.[21] Further, the broad themes of social justice in Islam are amazingly multifaceted; I appreciate that understanding all of the nuances of any one of these subjects alone would require lifetimes of detailed analysis, and that any book on this topic will invariably fail to cover important issues and examples for consideration. Further, there is considerable room for amicable disagreement about the topics presented in these chapters. Because people of faith should work to improve our interactions, however, I offer this research as one perspective on a few of the major social justice issues that confront our changing world.

The Prophet taught that Allah's ways are filled with beauty (*al-jamal*). Humanity lives in a resplendent world under God's overarching control. In this beautiful world, however, a loving God has chosen to test humanity with a host of injustices that need to be confronted and overcome. The revealed message of God should motivate the faithful to action on behalf of their sisters and brothers worldwide who are suffering. While pain and injustice assaults humanity, God Almighty calls people of faith not to remain idle but to work to usher in the divine will into situations of injustice. Believers are committed to justice (*al-'adl*) because God, in very nature, is a righteous and loving God of justice.

The word for "justice" in Arabic is closely related to the word for "equilibrium" (*al-tawazun*), because without justice there can be no balance within our lives or within our societies. On the Final Day the "scales" of God will measure the weight of every soul in relation to their acts of justice (Q. 99:7; 101:5). This is underscored by the fact that the term for "injustice" is synonymous with the word "inequality" (*zulm*). Any form of injustice "disrupts" the work of God and will ultimately be rectified through the outworking of the divine will.

In Islam there is no such thing as justice that is not rooted in social action. A well-known Hadith states that "to know but not to act is not to know."[22] Further, one cannot confuse the Muslim concept of justice with the "Western" ideal of individual rights founded on an emphasis on individual freedoms, which is free of any inter-relational responsibility. Islamic justice is rooted in an understanding of God's plan as clearly expressed in Islam. Justice is not a natural phenomenon, but one that must be established in the world by God's people. To carry out the divine purpose in the world, everyone is obligated to oppose any and all social injustices or transgressions (*zulm, fitna, fassad*).

Partnerships for Social Justice

Abraham Joshua Heschel postulates: "No religion is an island. We are all involved with one another. . . . The religions of the world are no more self-sufficient, nor more independent, and no more isolated than individuals or nations."[23] In the case of social justice, the adherents of most religions share with Muslims the conviction that any struggle to aid the oppressed takes place in an "ocean of unjust forces that are very difficult for the oppressor to understand".[24] Some religious commentators have struggled to prove that societal injustices are actually also related to historic religious tensions. Others have argued that the world is primarily divided by economic or political forces into those who are being oppressed and those who oppress others. Whatever the case, it is clear that injustice occurs irrespective of religious boundaries and people of all faiths equally face its pervasive wrath. The harsh edge of this shared experience offers a helpful foundation for meaningful interaction between people of faith who share a desire to confront social injustice in the advance of honoring God's glory.

Non-Muslims will benefit from an understanding of the many ways in which Muslim communities worldwide believe that God's revelation mandates that all believers should be active agents for social justice. This book introduces various social justice themes articulated in the Qur'an (and Hadith), but will also look at the practice of how these distinct social justice values are expressed in a host of specific localities. A number of questions will be explored: what does Islam teach about peace in this age of war?

What guidance does Islam offer in confronting oppression and various forms of injustice? How and why have injustices flourished in certain Muslim-majority social contexts? What specific resources in the texts (or in the tradition) have Muslim agents for social justice found particularly effective? What are some specific examples of situations in which Muslims and people of other faiths have worked together to advance social justice? How can such examples become more common or more widely effective?

These questions are important for a number of reasons: first, our ability to appreciate Muslim views about social justice has the capacity to anchor our interfaith conversations in something beyond a frustrating, and often circular focus on seemingly intractable theological and soteriological arguments. An interfaith interaction along the lines of social justice has the potential to deepen a sense of mutual appreciation at a relational level, which then can become increasingly beneficial as theological issues emerge during our interactions. People of all faiths can find common ground in shared affirmations that social justice work is at the heart of God's work in our world. It is hoped that this book might also be able to serve as a beneficial catalyst for meaningful multifaith partnerships, which can be developed into practical joint efforts to confront a broad range of specific social injustices. Substantial multifaith partnerships should be relational before they are theoretical; based on shared experiences and commitments instead of simply on ideological agreement or shared platitudes.

There are many multifaith pathways that one could pursue in reaching this stated objective. I have no interest in advocating a generic overarching Frankenstein-like dream that will wistfully promise to heal all the world's problems through *kumbayah* programs and discussions. Those who engage in such work are not to be dismissed, because, as one Irish proverb wisely reminds us: "there is plenty of sky for plenty of birds." Maybe it will be the case somehow that love and imagination will magically resolve all of the world's problems overnight. It is my hunch, however, that it is much more likely that concrete and concerted efforts will be required. Have you ever seen one of those mile-marker signposts with arrows pointing to dozens of different directions all at once: New York, Kampala, Cardiff, Sao Paulo, or Tokyo? In contrast to a wide-angle and scatter-shot approach, this book begins with one trajectory towards one key, specific interfaith point of reference: social justice.

Confronting Misconceptions

One objective in writing this book has been to address critics of Islam who disseminate the seeds of inaccurate misrepresentations of what the Qur'an says about a host of issues pertaining to social justice. Another has been to illustrate for non-Muslims how the Muslim world has tried to carry out those mandates. For whatever reason, European and North American media sources, politicians, and religious leaders have often led the way in promoting a host of inaccurate portrayals about Islam and how Muslims view various peace and social justice issues. Muslim readers may well wonder what my underlying motive is; why someone like me would feel obligated to undertake this effort. The answer is simple: the tasks we face in our modern social morass are far too demanding for any one group of individuals to assert it as their own province. On the other side of the equation, Muslims should be challenged by adherents of other faiths to re-examine a host of compelling non-Muslim understandings of social justice concerns. As a Christian, my hope is that this task will assist fellow believers to appreciate better the ways that we, as both individuals and as communities, can best serve the God of Christ and the God of Moses in the context of meaningful interactions with our sincere and progressive Muslim neighbors.

John Esposito (b. 1940) rightly warns against non-Muslims "viewing the Muslim world and Islamic movements as a monolith".[25] Any faith tradition is far more than set of solitary, descriptive categories; faiths are living, dynamic traditions that are practiced by millions of people across a wide range of cultural contexts. While George Bernard Shaw was right in warning that "to generalize is to be an idiot", there are admittedly certain advantages to "intellectual shorthand" just as long as one keeps in mind that the individual trees of certain comments do not make up the entire forest of a given issue.

Sociologist Pierre Bourdieu (1930–2002) reminds us about the power of a given term: "Islam, Islamic, Islamist — is the headscarf Islamic or Islamist?"[26] According to Bourdieu, the term "Islamism" is the quintessence of "all Oriental fanaticism, designed to give racist contempt the impeccable alibi of ethical and secular legitimacy."[27] In this book, I will use the term "Islam" to refer to the normative and conservative Islamic heritage as understood by centuries of tradition and scholarship and use the widely contested and problematic term "Islamist" to refer to the recent reformist and authoritarian militant movements that are sometimes (inaccurately) labeled Islamic fundamentalism, Salafism, jihadism, Islamo-facism, or radical Islamic extremism. The term "fundamentalist" is problematic because it does not aptly express those Muslims (or "believers") who have actually turned away from historic, fundamental revelations and practices even though they claim to have returned to such foundations. I hope to distinguish between the ancient religious tradition and a modernist re-casting of Islam, which has generated so many of the misconceptions about the faith as an intolerant, violent religion. As our multifaith conversations continue to mature, it is hoped that they will also become more constructive. When it comes to terminology, for example, there are a number of equally acceptable ways to accentuate a basic distinction between Muslims who embrace a tolerant, traditional view of the world and those who are more militant and extreme. Khaled Abou El-Fadl (b. 1963), for example, does not use the term "Islamist" but speaks instead of "Islamic Puritanism" or "authoritarianism", because he feels that it is vital to underline that Islamist movements are not fundamental to the faith. While I appreciate El-Fadl's concern about the term "Islamist"; the use of the term in this book is intended to provide a clear contrast with normative "Islam".

Extremism

Islamist groups share a common modern heritage; they are "bottom-feeders" in a lake of murky disenfranchisement and widespread marginalization. Islamists have only really existed since the end of the eighteenth century: early revisionists, in an era of colonial oppression, it should be emphasized, were initially driven by genuine motives and a commendable desire to improve the lot of oppressed Muslims worldwide. These revisionists believed Islam offered the best hope for humanity and explored what methods they had in order to realize their social vision that were often more pragmatic than historically "Islamic".

During the long (and generally oppressive) march of colonialism some secular elitists — known by their critics as the *Munafiqs* — turned to embrace Western ideals such as socialism, nationalism, communism, and specifically Western constructs of democracy. Critics called these advocates "pseudo-Muslims" and suspected that they were under the blinding spell of what Iranian scholar Jalal Ahmad (1923–1969) called "West-struckness" (*harb-zadegi*).[28] Even in the present, certain Muslim communities have become increasingly polarized by a debate between those who have drawn stark lines between what they perceive to be two distinct polarities: the "West" and "Islam". While the stated intent of many early Islamists was to preserve the health and welfare of their communities, in their efforts, they launched out on a new path that broke from centuries of hermeneutic and communitarian agreement.

Islamists, such as the first Wahhabist puritans (who use the term *Salafism* to describe their views) or nineteenth- and twentieth-century groups, such as Hamas, did not (and do not) employ traditional, normative Islamic legal methods in the advance of their arguments. Such movements have often gained traction in response to the many obvious evils of European colonialism and the many frustrations and difficulties that people face as they confront the complex demands of modernity. These movements are not traditional, as they would like to suggest, but actually modernist and revisionist in both character and origin. They challenge the authority of the *ummah* when they argue that the sacred boundaries of authority lie with the message of the Qur'an alone as an eternal guide. Extremists disregard a historic posture of humility before the text as well as centuries of a rich and variegated Islamic intellectual heritage about the many possible meanings of the text in favor of their claim that their beliefs and actions alone are based on the Qur'an and are designed to return their specific view of the House of Islam, rooted in their own version of fundamentalist purity.

These questions are not theoretical or remote: as I write this section, the world is remembering the anniversary of the tragic massacres of 156 people in Mumbai, India at the hands of ten fanatics from the Pakistani extremist group *Lashkar e-Taiba*. The intention of this group was to kill and maim as many individuals as possible and to gain as much publicity for their sordid acts as possible. Such actions have no viable link to the core of an ancient and normative Islamic faith. Linking a group like *Lashkar e-Taiba* to Islam would be similar to linking the virulent actions of the Ku Klux Klan or Sinn Fein to the widely-accepted teachings of historic Christianity.

While militants are correct that any true believer should be willing to die for God at any moment (Q. 2:154), they are wrong in disregarding centuries of carefully crafted tradition to promote violent new strategies while claiming to serve God (see Q. 4:76). While extremists frequently evoke idyllic images of glorious centuries past, when Islam was the dominant force in the world — and call fellow Muslims to return to those glories by embracing their version of an "authentic Islam" — extremist ideologues are actually revisionists who are outside the vast mainstream of Islam's rich intellectual traditions.

Orthodox Islamic social and religious institutions are deeply ingrained framing traditions, committed to preserving the order and balance of a given Muslim community. In contrast, extremists are working towards a fundamentally militant and rapid transformation of the *status quo* among fellow Muslims. They question, what Katherine Gittes calls, the "structural elasticity" of Islamic communities rooted in culturally sensitive adaptations in favor of a more categorical view of the world, which leaves little room for open-ended variance.[29] According to Asaf Hussein, the creative power of historic Islam is grounded in the power of the family (*usrah*), the school (*madrassah*) and the masjid.[30] In contrast, Islamists promote blind acceptance (*al-qubul al-a'ma'*) of their bold assertions that are confined to their own emphatic interpretations (*ijtihad*); not in the centuries of careful scholarly consideration. They caricaturize any measure of doubt as a form of unbelief, and see doubt as "flirtation with the unknown" that is ultimately "destructive of social order".[31] Extremists promote aggressive versions of impatient fanaticism and non-Qur'anic intolerance. Their approach is ahistorical and disrespectful to centuries of studious Qur'anic interpretation and deeply rooted communitarian traditions.

Globalization and Multifaith Engagement

People around our world are interacting with each other as never before. The term "globalization" can be defined in many different ways and merits careful consideration in its use. Pierre Bourdieu argues the term is often used as a suffocating blanket to describe "the imposition on the entire world of the neoliberal tyranny of the market and the undisputed rule of the economy and of economic powers, within which the United States occupies a dominant position."[32] For Bourdieu, the world has become "commodified" by a dominating and generalized vision in which "globalization" is seen as an uncontested fact of a constructed and economically exploitative universalism.

Here, "globalization" refers to the wide-ranging process in which social institutions are forced (for a host of technological and political reasons) to respond to one world (a "global village") and thus, to create globalized strategies in a context of inter-engagement, which is increasingly cross-referential, inter-aware, and interdependent. The concept of an increasingly globalized village mandates that individuals are called upon to interact with each other in ways that were unimaginable just a few decades ago. This globalizing, internationalizing, transcultural, and transnational process is continuing through communication and technological advances and through economic, political, and cultural forces. Cultural and geographic categories, such as "East" and "West", are increasingly blurred by the realities of our shared experiences. It remains to be seen if globalization can ultimately become a source for peace and justice, or if it will simply remain a dynamic force for continued economic, military, and political oppression.

Given the forces of globalization, traditional religious leaders are less able than ever to "control" or "define" adherents of various faith traditions or to contain those within their community who are spreading their virulent ideas in God's name. Social networking tools such as the internet (and other potentially democratizing forces) have set in motion powerfully new communication synergisms, which seemingly mutate into countless new forms by the minute. Travel, technology, and communication bridges are increasing all over the world faster than one can evaluate the implications of such changes. For example, Western television programs (such as *Baywatch*, 1989–1999) and industry giants such as Disney or Viacom spout forth glossy images on television screens around the world that become part of a globalized conversation of expectations and assumptions. A number of contemporary Muslim intellectuals (such as El-Fadl, Sardur, Esack, and Engineer) have talked about how traditional Islamic societies are facing a host of challenges due to these shifting forces.[33] Religious adaptation in the face of globalization will also mean that social, political, and economic pressures will continue to assault social norms, traditions, and beliefs.

Non-Muslims should promote views about contemporary Islam that are not simply confined to theoretical questions about broad-brush religious ideals (in the context of competing national interests). As stated earlier, multifaith interactions should be relational and local before they are theoretical and remote. There are, for example, between five and eight million Muslims living within North America today. Almost none of these Muslims, it should be emphasized, have any connections at all to the extremist views of Islamism. They are upstanding citizens who pay their taxes and participate in elections.[34] Islam is also growing at a steady pace in the UK and in almost every European country. In some countries such as France — even as a minority presence — Islam is the most visible, verbal expression of socially practiced religious conviction.

Globalizing forces are particularly visible on the metastage of political concerns. For many, the focus is on advancing a "human rights agenda" around the world and regardless of local considerations that might nuance, or even curtail, what others view as fundamentally God-given human rights. In frequently repeated political arguments, there is an assumption that liberal, tolerant democratic governments will protect personal freedoms, while also making economic resources more accessible to an ever-widening group of citizens. Liberal democracies (in their various incarnations) look askance at governments formed around religious authoritarianism (such as Iran) because it is assumed that such nations will be inherently discriminatory against other religions or competing views. Critics of such views see in globalizing forces a new (and more subtle) form of colonialism, which gains control through a hegemonic economic oppression. Some Muslims argue that a belief system is foundational to globalizing forces, which are decidedly un-Islamic because they reject any notion that Islam is a universal truth.

Focusing on competing ideologies, however interesting they are, may not be very constructive in the larger agenda of promoting the relational dynamics at the heart of contemporary multifaith and multicultural mutuality. In contrast, a multifaith discussion that centers on social justice themes is, at the same time, both theoretical in its scope as well as practical in its specific application. It is a hopeful focus that offers the prospect of moving away from some of the conversational and conceptual dead-end streets, which many non-Muslims find themselves trapped in as they try to deal with the differences that they perceive with their Muslim neighbors. Ironically, because historic and normative Islam, and even Islamist revisionist movements, both assert to promote social justice, the latitude that such a fulcrum provides is rich and varied. To state this another way, a multifaith conversation about social justice is capable not only of bringing in the normative expressions of modern Muslim communities, but also of engaging those who would be described as extremists; on the angry or assertive fringes of the larger Muslim *ummah*.

The Centrality of Justice

Any unchecked injustice will invariably lead to increased dehumanization and to swirling currents of chaos that drag individuals further away from all that a loving God intends for creation. The unambiguous message of the Qur'an is that Allah has shared a divine plan for humanity. Islam is intended to support a community that is committed to enacting that plan and to serve as the foundation for God's work — social justice activism — within the world. Those who faithfully follow the necessary mandates and relevant messages of the Qur'an will never be led into error. According to the Kurdish Turkish theologian and mystic "Bediuzzaman" Said Nursi (1878–1960), the worst enemies of the Qur'an are "ignorance, poverty, and disunion": the powerful message of the Qur'an, however, is "much stronger than the sword used in battle" to defeat such forces of injustice.[35]

How does the revelation of the Qur'an explain and, then, address social injustice? The heart of the Qur'anic message calls individuals to integrate their beliefs into the challenging arena of their daily lives by works of ethical action. A traditional Islamic worldview emphasizes the synthesizing unity (*tawhid*) of everything within God's creation, while also guarding against the possible heresies of divisions (*shirk*), innovations (*bid'ah*), bifurcations, compartmentalization, and godless, secularizing influences. A comprehensive Islamic worldview, rooted in divine revelation, is beyond contestation. Allah commands that believers should practice a comprehensive faith in the midst of life's variegated challenges; what Fazlur Rahman (1919–1988) describes as a daily lived experience of an "integrated *tawhidi* existence".[36]

God's revelation calls for complete allegiance from every believer. At the same time, this lofty path is not forbidding but provides followers with generous allocations of encouragement as they confront social injustices. The social justice work that the believer is called to do, it is promised, will be supported by a God of mercy who will bring to the faithful eternal rewards as well as earthly benefits. The concept of daily accountability lifts Islam from the realm of the theoretical into the lived realities of practical experience. Because the truths of Islam can only be known in the practice of daily life and cannot be embraced as remote conceptualities, there is little reward to be found in theoretical arguments, which can often degenerate into either ornate idealism or reductionistic platitudes. The God-pleasing life of genuine faith will be expressed at all times; in shadowy flecks of morning-prayer times before sunrise, as well as in the twilight; in the cold of night as well as the garish glare of a strong midday sun.

How does this focus on faithful practice relate to how believers worldwide are dealing with emerging tensions between orthodox

Muslim and extremist perspectives? Anyone who has been paying attention can appreciate that the House of Islam is presently engaged in what Farid Esack (b. 1959) calls a "path between dehumanizing fundamentalism and fossilized traditionalism".[37] Esack calls for believers worldwide to embrace a "radical Islam committed to social justice, to individual liberties and the quest for the Transcendent who is beyond all institutional, religious and dogmatic constructions."[38]

Consistent with the orthodox heritage of the faith, Esack's vision is rooted in the Qur'anic mandate to apply truth in the practice of a faithful life. From this foundation, believers can confront social injustices with the confidence that their faith is capable of providing a viable paradigm that addresses these challenges. An individual believer has a responsibility before Allah to be faithful: but the individual is also responsible to a corporate community and, as such, has a duty to uphold the cohesiveness of the *ummah*. This tension is as old as the Islam first lived by the Prophet Muhammad: the Prophet attained the highest of spiritual experiences in a glorious ascension (*mi'raj*) to paradise but was called by God to return to the messy challenges of humanity, in order to live out a divine call to fight injustice. The Prophet's example calls believers to embrace both the lofty glories of God's amazing greatness along with the pedestrian mandate to carry out the demanding work for social justice.

Orthodox Islamic devotion has always existed to undergird ethical action. Allah has revealed that true faith cannot exist independently of the actual conscious participation of the adherents (Q. 4:43). The Qur'an links devotion with moral action when it notes that "prayer prevents lewdness and evil" (Q. 29:45). The very pillars of the historic faith present clear ethical commands that infuse ideals with a corresponding commitment to a shared responsibility to glorify God by working for social justice. The centrality of this dynamic connection will be examined in further detail in Chapter One. In an academic context, in which it is probably true that "theological musings bleed into works that apparently claim to be critical and scholarly studies", I make no claim to be without an agenda in this research.[39] It is my hope to both accurately relate what I have gleaned are Muslim perspectives on issues of social justice, and also to offer a few reflections as a Christian about how these explorations can advance multifaith interactions and partnerships for social justice in a constructive direction. Going forward, I welcome any corrections or helpful addenda that readers might offer about the various themes of this research.

1. Islam's Divine Mandate for
Ethical Action against Social Injustice

God delegated to Muslims a moral trust. At no point in history can Muslims ignore their unending obligations to appropriately discharge this moral trust. The basic and invaluable point is that all Muslims — and non-Muslims — must understand that it is in the power and is in fact the duty of Muslims of every generation to answer the question: What Islam? The response must not be left in the hands of the bin Ladens of the world.
— Khaled Abou El-Fadl

The Relation of Islamic Theology to Islamic Ethics

What evidence supports the claim that social justice is central to Islam? How do ethical values relate to Islamic theological foundations? How does the theme of social justice relate to Islam's fundamental mandate that a believer should submit to the will of Allah? This chapter will explore the dynamic relationship between ethics and Islamic "theology" (*kalam*). Appreciating the conceptual *rationale* that supports believers in their work for justice will significantly aid those attempting to support interfaith social justice partnerships.

One's view of God's nature and attributes has a dramatic effect on one's view of the world. Islamic mandates for social justice spring from the Muslim understanding of God's revelation. Believers claim that God Almighty is at work in the world through the community of the faithful. Allah is self-sufficient (Q. 96:6–7), while all humans are dependent upon the divine for life itself. Although God is clearly beyond the limitations of human understandings, Islam reveals that God loves justice. To follow Allah is to obligate one to work for justice among the created order. One cannot conclude that any injustice comes from God or is an expression of the divine will (Q. 39:30).

Since God has provided clear revelation to humanity, individuals are expected to follow the straight path of righteous action. One cannot only believe in a transcendent and unitary God; one is also accountable to worship Allah and to express that worship through acts of service. The fact of God's authority is the foundation for our actions and attitudes. Those who do not work for social justice are not grateful to God and have forgotten the facts of the coming Day of Judgment (Q. 76:3; 74:55–

56). We should be ever mindful of the fact that death, at the end of this brief life, becomes the gateway and provides the beginning of eternal life. The vertical quest for right relationship with God relates integrally with the horizontal responsibilities of an individual's daily interactions. In Islam, there are no monasteries or calls for the faithful to serve Allah in remote and isolated corners of the world: true faith in this temporal and fleeting dimension must be engaged within our daily lives.

Muslim teachers note that one of God's Ninety-nine Magnificent Names is *al-Rabb*, which means "the nurturing and the sustaining". God sustains and nurtures us so that we can serve the divine will. This explains why the Prophet defined piety in terms of ethical conscience. Nothing is hidden from God and God promises to reward every single act of charity (Q. 2:271) performed within the community (*ummah*) of believers (see Q. 10:19; 11:118; 16:93; 42:8; 43:3). Allah has revealed only one religion that has been given equally to all of the Prophets (Q. 21:92; 23:52); this one truth teaches that believers have both an inward and an outward obligation to divine decrees.

Atkhar writes, "The God of Islam is an educator."[1] Despite the rhetoric of some anti-Islamic apologists, God is not indifferent to the injustices that individuals experience in their daily lives. This critique clearly says more about the plaintiff than it does about the defendant. Farid Esack observes of some Christians who make this claim: "Much of this talk of a God of love has become little more than Western conservative Christianity avoiding fundamental issues of structural social injustice and poverty in a society that prevents the love of Allah from being experienced in concrete terms in the daily lives of ordinary people."[2] Believers, in contrast, are forbidden to follow any unengaged path of an escapist idealism, which sidesteps the evils of the world in the name of serving God.

A Distant God?

Critics have argued that Islamic philosophy, influenced by Greek thought, has promoted narrow and legalistic interpretations that have perpetrated the pervasive notion of a remote God. It is imperative to distinguish between the nearness of God and the historically Jewish or Christian idea of the personality of God. A static — and usually critical — view of Islam may try to take into account questions about the nature of God; these renderings often fail to consider the dynamic portrayal in Islam of a compassionate and merciful God who calls the faithful to work for ethical justice.

It is difficult to disprove the claim that the Qur'an and Hadith describe God's loving nurture and compassionate graciousness toward the created order. While this is true throughout Islamic religious and devotional sources, it is particularly visible in the Sufi tradition, the warm and smiling face of Islamic theology. Sufism stresses an individualized, ongoing experience of the divine in everyday life and underscores what all Muslims believe — that an awareness of God's presence should fill every expression of life. The Qur'an explains: "And when my servant questions you concerning me then surely I am near" (Q. 2:186).

The active nearness of Allah within our daily lives does not contradict the truth of divine greatness or God's over-arching uniqueness; in fact, it underscores the pervasive reality of Allah's authority as Lord over all. While God is above and beyond, the call to follow God is pressing and immediate. The eternal God is worshiped in the present tense through lives of obedient righteousness. The Qur'an teaches a message that must be embodied in the daily lives of the Muslim community. It is God's nearness and the promise of God's active, engaged participation in the everyday events of the world that calls the faithful to work tirelessly for causes of social justice.

This nearness is expressed in Muslim responses to the question of theodicy (why Allah allows evil). Islamic teachers have often reframed the theoretical problem of evil by assuring believers that God knows all about their daily lives and, with justice, will ultimately answer every perplexing question and resolve every experienced evil. Humility and submission before Allah frees an individual from trying to ascertain why, for example, a child might die with an illness, and allows them still to accept that God is both loving and all-powerful (to use the paradigm popularized by Rabbi Harold Kushner, b. 1935). This is not to say that believers cannot ask these perplexing philosophical questions, but that they should be asked in the spirit of exploration, not in the hope of finding simple conclusions. Engaged faith in Allah is not compromised by such probing questions. On the contrary, the absence of such doubts might characterize the experience of a superficial believer who has never really fully subjected their faith to the gritty tests and tumults of daily life. Those who submit in obedience to Allah will find, on the Final Day, that all mysteries will be revealed and that all doubts will be silenced.

The Day of Judgment and Social Justice

Critics have claimed that Islam teaches that God has no moral responsibility to humanity and that He can be capricious, because, as God (by definition), He is somehow beyond the pale of any kind of moral responsibility.[3] In actual fact, God's greatness reaffirms the justice message of Islam. One cannot say that Allah is capricious or callously allows for humanity to suffer. One text reminds the believer,

"God desires ease for us and does not wish us discomfort" (Q. 2:185). Coming to terms with the transcendence of God forces us to go beyond the confines of ourselves. The constantly repeated refrain *Allahu Akbar* is often translated as "God is Great" but it can also be translated as "God is Greater" (as in, greater than anything at all). God's transcendence demands from each individual complete humility and radical obedience. There is no room for any form of dishonesty in God's presence. Because Allah is "the light of heaven and earth" (Q. 24:35), there is always a way on this earth to live out the revealed will of heaven.

The Qur'an repeatedly reminds believers that the Day of Judgment is fore-ordained to demonstrate God's eternal justice and to end oppression through the outworking of divine power: only God Almighty has the authority to judge every individual's actions and prescribe an eternal reward or punishment. The very notion of a Day of Judgment is, in itself, a statement about ethical morality and the inevitability of accountability to the highest authority. This revelation is about more than simply instilling fear and terror in the minds of believers; it is about gaining an accurate perspective on what is truly important in life and about our fundamental dependence on God. Qur'an 112:1–3 asserts that there is none like Allah; Qur'an 83:4–6 reveals that every individual will eventually face a Divine Judge: "Do they not think that they will be called to account? On a Mighty Day, a Day when all humanity will stand before the Lord of the Worlds?" It is a day of "sorting" (Q. 30:14–16), which is so horrific that even a "mother will forget her suckling babe" (Surah 22) because the power of Allah will be on full display and those who have promoted injustice will be called to give a full account.

God's revelation through Islam is incontrovertible; all individuals will be rewarded in heaven for their earthly actions. Allah is the giver of both merited punishment and unmerited mercy (see Q. 33:17). Those who have disregarded their obligations to promote social justice will find that they have chosen to place themselves outside of God's merciful path to abundant blessings, the path of Islam. The fires of hell can even be viewed as a loving gift to motivate the faithful in this life; the ample warnings of the Qur'an give no doubt about how righteousness or unrighteousness will be regarded by the Great Judge of the world. Of this theme, Daud Rahbar explains: "the reminders of the Judgment Day are invariably there throughout [the Qur'an], which again is the most obvious evidence of the fact that the central theme, in light of which the character of the Qur'anic doctrine of God is to be determined is God's strict justice."[4]

Qur'an 30:14–16 warns that on the Day of Judgment, oppressors will cower before their divine interrogator and give account for their vile misdeeds. While it is God's abundant mercy, and not the sum of one's charitable deeds, which ultimately causes a person to enter paradise, an individual should never forget that God's mercy should not be assumed upon; Allah cannot be mocked. There is a direct relationship between what one has done and whether one will be considered either acceptable or unacceptable; to think otherwise would make moot the very notion of our ethical accountability.

Islamic *kalam* teaches that if God simply forgave all misdeeds by divine fiat, this would be the ultimate expression of a capricious being; such actions would devalue the significance of living a life of faithful obedience to Islam. It is this view, which many Muslims contrast with certain Christian views of God's grace, which are seen to make irrelevant the need for righteous living because an individual can simply live a sinful life and then expect God to forgive all of their sins because of the salvific work of Christ. In contrast, one Hadith warns that all souls will be required to cross a narrow bridge, and oppressors, the unrighteous, and non-believers, will invariably fall off into the hellfire while the righteous are promised to enter into an eternal garden of amazing delight. Sinful Muslims may also fall into the fire for a time, other Hadith explain, but these errant believers will probably and eventually be rescued by the intercessions of faithful family members, friends, and the Prophet Muhammad. Many Islamic theologians — most notably Ibn Taymiyyah (1263–1328) — have concluded that even the flames of hell will only be temporary because the logic and wisdom of God suggests that there would be no place for a loving God to punish for countless eons those who had been rebellious.[5] In contrast, paradise is the just reward for those who have endured trials and lived noble lives that have advanced Allah's will. Only those who practice justice in their lives are promised to gain the right in heaven to have intercessory powers on behalf of others.[6]

The fear of Allah is clearly a prime motivation for all believers to work for social justice. Over and over again this theme resonates from the pages of divine revelation; some have asserted that at least one in ten verses in the Qur'an urges believers to avoid the possibility of divine punishment.[7] The Creator God knows the nature of humanity, and these warnings are to be seen as blessings of God's grace and not some primitivistic form of divine terrorism. It is for their own benefit — and not for God's self-satisfaction — that believers are repeatedly encouraged to fear Allah (see Q. 22:1–2 and Q. 27:87–90). God's revelation is unambiguous about the need for moral obedience. Rahbar explains: "It is a fact well-recognized in scientific scholarship that the fear of God is the dominant sentiment in Qur'anic morality. The roots of this conviction are in God's stern justice."[8] An example of this recurring prophetic theme is found in Qur'an 2:264, which declares: "do not perform charity for your own glory but for the fear of Allah on the Last Day."

Social Justice Work as Worship

Gratitude for God's goodness is another vital motivating reason that Muslims are called to strive for social justice in this world of evil. Because Allah has been merciful to each person, individuals should graciously extend compassion to those around them. Qur'an 93:6–9 calls Prophet Muhammad to be generous: "Did He not find thee an orphan and give thee shelter. And He found thee wandering and He gave thee guidance. And He found thee in need and made thee independent. Therefore treat not the orphan with harshness, or repulse the petitioner (unheard); and the bounty of the Lord — proclaim." Merciful acts that foster social justice are the works of an ethical warrior in a world of injustice; such actions are of far more value than pious acts of devotion which do nothing to address injustice.

Islamist cleric Sayyid Qutb (1906–1966) cites a Hadith, which announces: "The one who helps widows and the poor is like the one who participates in *jihad* or the one who watches all night (in prayer) and fasts all day."[9] Qutb recounts another Hadith about a devout person of prayer who possesses many spiritual powers — not because of his prayers, but because of the acts of mercy and generosity practiced by his older brother. When Muhammad was asked about the spirituality of this devoted man of prayer, the Prophet confirmed: "Surely his brother worships better than he."[10] Allah is pleased by those who compassionately invest their lives in others with a bountiful heart of genuine thankfulness. Gratitude may be the best motivation to labor for justice and to help others, but it is not the only impetus. Individuals who work for social justice will also bring eternal benefit to their souls (see Q. 57:7). Qur'an 64:16 challenges all believers to "spend in charity for the benefit of your own souls. And those saved from covetousness of their own souls — they are the ones that achieve prosperity."

A Message for All People

Allah loves the entire created order without partiality; the message of Islam is democratic in its scope. Because God is egalitarian in responding to humanity, the faithful should be careful not to favor the wealthy or the powerful above the poor and the oppressed. Each individual comes before their Creator with their hearts and souls and not with their ledger sheets or their resumes. Islam is adamant in asserting the equality of all peoples because worldly success is meaningless when an individual stands before the throne of Almighty God. The mightiest of kings and the poorest of beggars will stand side by side on equal footing at the Final Day to be held accountable for their obedience to God. Individuals should never trust in the saving-power of their riches or come to think that they can gain material wealth on this earth that will carry into the ethereal halls of eternity.

The message of Islam makes clear that Allah is pleased by piety expressed through righteous actions and not by a person's economic, material, or political status. During the yearly pilgrimage to Mecca everyone is mandated to join the prayer line as an equal before God Almighty, wearing white robes without adornment to illustrate their equal standing before Allah. While it is consequential to do *salat* for one's own benefit, blame will be ascribed to "those who oppress men and revolt in the earth unjustly and they shall have a painful punishment" (Q. 42:41–42). The practice of *zakat* is one of the foundational "pillars of Islam" and it calls the faithful to give financially to the needy because of God's greatness (Q. 9:60).

This should explain why, through the centuries, Muslims who have been faithful to the Qur'anic teaching have sought to undertake social justice causes in God's name. Yaacov Lev describes the *ribats* of Medieval Islam, which were homes (or fortresses) for outcasts and widows who had no family.[11] Food and shelter were provided along with spiritual nourishment. One *ribat* built in Cairo (around 1285) even provided facilities for divorced (or separated) women until they either remarried or returned to their husbands.

The Oneness of God and Social Justice

There is a clear link in historic Islamic *kalam* between worshipping God and ministries of social concern. God's "Ninety-nine Beautiful Names" (or the "Most Comely Names") cite characteristics of God's will and actions among humanity. God is called the Merciful (*al-Rahman*), the Compassionate (*al-Rahim*), the Loving (*al-Wadud*), and many other similarly positive names reflecting God's virtuous actions. Qur'an 59:22–24 describes an awareness of these attributes as a way to worship Allah, which also obligates individuals to act in their lives with ever-increasing ethical consideration. The balance of the created universe reveals that God has created everything to live in harmony with divine decrees for social justice (see Q. 49:13).

God's unity is the foundation upon which Islam builds its vision for social justice. The relationship between the doctrine of God's oneness (*tawhid*) and social justice is rarely fully appreciated by non-Muslims. Because individuals have been liberated in their souls from the bondages of selfish idolatry or hedonistic darkness (*jahiliyya*), they are free to create a unified society before the one God rooted in singular justice and solidarity. Freedom from divisive polytheism (or other distorted caricatures of monotheism) allows individuals to live their lives with greater clarity and moral singularity. Believers are called to "imitate" the unity of Allah's attributes of goodness, unity, peace, forgiveness, mercy, wisdom, and justice. God's "beautiful names" are not only descriptions of God's will in the world, but they also form the well-spring source for how believers are to practice justice. The Qur'an shows that when individuals submit (*islam*) to the divinely established path they will foster human-to-human interactions that can construct a comprehensive and unified "world house" before the one true God. In one of the most striking verses in the Qur'an (2:177), God summarizes the way that humanity is called to work for social justice in light of the oneness of the divine character:

> It is not righteousness that you turn your faces toward the East or the West, but it is righteousness to believe in Allah, the Last Days, the Book and the Messengers; to spend your substance out of love for Him for your kin, for orphans, for the needy, the wayfarer, for those who ask, and for the ransom of slaves; to be steadfast in prayer and to practice regular charity, to fulfill the contracts that you have made and to be firm and patient, in pain or in suffering and adversity, and throughout all periods of panic. Such are the people of truth, the God-fearing.

2. Islamic *Jihad* and the Path of Peace

All ye who believe! Enter fully into peace.

— Qur'an 2:208

If the strivings for inter-religious dialogue are expected to yield world peace, the authority of sacred texts must first be secured from all kinds of politics of violence and function in the form of symbolic texts. As long as the authority of a sacred text can lead its followers to produce something good by strengthening mutual understanding, both among themselves and with the people of other faiths there can be an emancipating authority. Otherwise, such authority can easily be the source of legitimization behind the politics of violence due to some ideological confinements put on it. A sacred text that functions as the basis of a politics of violence is already subjected to the same politics of violence. The duty of people of faith who long for a peaceful world is to secure their sacred texts from this paradoxical situation.

— Burhanettin Tatar

A Peaceful or Violent Religion?

"Islam is peace", declared President George W. Bush shortly after 9/11 when he visited the Islamic Center of Washington DC.[1] President Barack Obama, in 2009, went to great lengths in his Cairo Address to reiterate this claim. In contrast, the former leader of al-Qaeda, Osama bin Laden (1957–2011) contended, "In compliance with Allah's order, we issue the following *fatwa* to all Muslims: the ruling to kill the Americans and their allies — civilian and military — is an individual duty for every Muslim who can do it in any country in which it is possible to do it."[2]

There seem to be two fundamentally oppositional views that many non-Muslims have about Islam when it comes to issues of peace and violence. The statements by President Bush, President Obama, and Osama bin Laden (and the uneven reactions to these variant claims of the populations of North America and Europe) underscore the follies of such essentializing reductionism. Questions about the many ways that Islam views issues of war and peace merit thorough consideration by those seeking to promote interfaith social justice partnerships. An examination of these issues will reveal that the vast majority of Muslims oppose terrorism and shun violence: believers aspire to *salaam* (peace).

Many non-Muslims, however, are more familiar with the instrumentalist ideas of Islamist *jihad* than they are with the foundational message of Islamic *salaam*. James Beverley reminds Christians to look at these complexities with great caution: "We hear so many differing accounts of Islam today precisely because Muslims are in the midst of a struggle for the soul of Islam. We would be wise as Christians, humbled by our own past, to remember that as we seek to understand and engage Muslims today out of love for Christ."[3]

Peacemaking in a World of Injustice

The goal of Islam is personal and social peace (*salaam*). Peace in communities, it is taught, will not be realized until secular individuals and the faithful first learn to live together in harmony. The attainment of a substantial peace at the national level may, however, require short periods of conflict and war (*jihad*). Peace cannot be imposed upon other people (see Q. 3:21). Majid Khadduri (1909–2007) explains that "the ultimate objective of Islam is the ultimate establishment of peace."[4] It would be more accurate to say that Islam is a religion committed to realism and ultimate ends. The Islamic *ummah* has been faced with countless grave threats from its inception. The divinely-inspired concept of peace is an ideal and demands the concrete efforts of those committed to working as peacemakers in often very demanding situations.

   A Muslim realist may have no other option but to resort, from time to time, to the short-term use of weapons in order to bring much-needed peace and to oppose great injustices. Sometimes some lives will have to be taken so that many more lives will be spared. Because the *ummah* should be protected at all costs, some Muslims adhere to a "just-war theory", which explains that there may be situations when war becomes inevitable as a last resort. For Muslims, this sense of dynamic engagement with the "world-as-it-is" as opposed to the "world-as-it-should-be" is one of the compelling strengths of the tradition. Above all else, and in honor to Allah, a believer should carry out an active struggle against injustice and refuse to let injustices stand against their fellow humanity. Working within the parameters of diplomacy and social civil engagement, Islam (as is true of most major faith traditions) is committed to fostering a peaceful environment of mutual social stability. But a temporal peace is not the ultimate goal: God's will is the final determinant. No truce can be made with godless forces of evil injustice or defiant oppression. The Qur'anic narrative (as well as Islamic history) shows conclusively that there could be many situations in which war is an unfortunate necessity, as the lesser of two evils. In these situations, the Qur'an gives believers clear parameters with which to fight in order to overcome the unrepentant enemies of Allah.

Perceptions of Islam as a Violent Faith

Critics view Islam as an inherently violent religion that springs from an aggressive and confrontational way of relating to others. Their monolithic Islam is a constructed and imagined religion that drips with blood and allows for mass-killings. Ahmidayyan Hazrat Mirza Tahir Ahmad (1928–2003) mourned that "Islam is as closely related to terrorism as light is to darkness or life is to death or peace is to war."[5] Clinton Bennett and Geros Kunkel assert that, in the West today, "terrorism . . . appears to have an Islamic face."[6]

After the 1979 Iranian hostage crisis, the declaration by Osama bin Laden of *jihad* against the non-Muslim West (1998), and the tragic events of September 11, 2001, many non-Muslims have tried to understand Islamic views about war and peace. Some have claimed that violence is encouraged by the revelation of the Qur'an and the life of the Prophet, while others have refused to bring religion into the equation at all. Harold Ellens asks of these Islamist terrorists the direct question which typifies the views of many critics: "Are they [Muslims] bad theologians or is this a bad book?"[7]

Muslim clerics, vividly aware of pejorative misconceptions, have called on fellow Muslims to address such criticisms as well as to apologize for instances of violence within their own communities. In June, 2009, Iran was rocked by a series of political protests that devolved into riots as the police and Special Forces (*basmaji*) sought to intimidate the protesters. One of the leading clerics in Iran, the Grand Ayatollah Hussein Ali Montazeri (1922–2009) argued that such acts were un-Islamic and would result in God's judgment upon the nation. Immediately after a 23-year-old music student, Neda Agha-Soltan was murdered by the *basmaji* (June 20, 2009), the Grand Ayatollah wrote this response: "A political system based on force, oppression, changing people's votes, killing, closure, arresting and using Stalinist and Medieval torture, creating repression, censorship of newspapers, interruption of the means of mass communications, jailing the enlightened and the elite of the society for false reasons, and forcing them to make false confessions in jail is condemned and illegitimate."[8]

There are many other Muslim voices that agree with the Grand Ayatollah Montazeri and who have spoken out against all forms of violence. These messengers, however, are ignored by anti-Muslim critics, or are dismissed away as tangential, while more strident and authoritarian assertions are often underlined, italicized, and re-recorded in bold print. As many in the Western media have focused on the global threat of Islamist movements, many non-Muslims have fallen prey to reinforcing the notion that historic and orthodox Islam is an inherently violent religion that promotes terrorism. Some within an agenda-driven Western media have chosen (for whatever reason) to blur the lines between historic Islamic teachings about self-defense and those extremist revisionist teachings that promote tactics of terror for Allah's glory.

The Meaning of *Jihad*

Many of the problems non-Muslims have when it comes to understanding Islamic views tend to revolve around the meaning of the Arabic term *jihad*. The word has always been in the orthodox Islamic lexicon, but has gained increased significance since Islamic countries have been forced to confront European and American military powers during the last three centuries. Arguably, *jihad* is of "central significance to Muslim self-understanding and mobilization" when it comes to political and military issues.[9] S.M. Farid Mirbagheri states: "It is a religious term that represents a belief in purity and justice and in humanity's efforts to achieve these goals."[10] There are a number of nuanced and historically bound meanings that can be ascribed to this oft-misunderstood term.

The Qur'an is not unique among the texts of the world's religions in dealing with the issues of war and violence. The Bhagavad Gita and the Bible are just a few of the many scriptures that confront issues relating to combat. In the Book of Judges, for example, it is impossible to ignore the fact that God repeatedly calls for the genocide of all who live in the land that is about to be conquered by the chosen people of Israel (see also 1 Sam. 15). Previously, this same God had also incinerated entire cities with fire from heaven (Gen. 19) and had drowned all but a handful of His children through a divinely-mandated flood. Modern redactors often emphasize that these Biblical stories, like those in the Qur'an, that summon the faithful to war are situated at a specific point in time when the emerging community of faith was still in the process of establishing its own destiny among rival factions who sought their destruction.

While most Jews and Christians are quick to underline the historic context of these stories (and, obviously, do not retell such stories to encourage violence), these narratives cannot be ignored. Indeed, across history these very stories have sometimes been appropriated by Christian advocates of violent actions (for example, the Puritans who arrived in New England saw the Native Americans whom they displaced as "Canaanites"). Christian crusaders used these Biblical stories to justify the massacre of Jews and Muslims whom they attacked during their holy wars.[11] In one metaphorical statement Christ, the "Prince of Peace" announced: "Do not suppose that I have come to bring peace to the earth. I did not come to bring peace but a sword" (Matt. 10:34).

Muslims, throughout history, have also utilized context-specific violent passages in the Qur'an to suit their own particular and political situations in ways that are "mysterious and highly complex".[12] In recent years, Sohail H. Hashmz noted that "virtually every" Muslim writing "produced in the past century is to some degree responses to Western apprehensions of *jihad*".[13] There are countless views about the role that warfare should play in the life of the community, and Muslim history, like most histories, has often been filled with violence in God's name. After the death of the Prophet, the first Caliph, Abu Bakr (573–634), led an army to conquer an enormous empire in the name of *jihad* and the term has been used repeatedly throughout the Muslim world across time to justify a wide range of military actions. Because of its widespread and various uses, it is important for non-Muslims to approach this term with caution; paying close attention to the multivalent specifics of a given textual and historical *sitz-im-leben*.

Is it adequate to translate the Arabic word *jihad* as "holy war"? The term "holy war" is actually a Christian term, which was coined in reference to the Crusades and does not convey the way that Muslims view the necessity of war. In spite of this fact, some Muslims have used this historically context-loaded term in recent generations.[14]

The Qur'an uses the term *jihad* in different ways in over 150 citations. Many of these passages refer to the struggles of earlier prophets of God such as Noah (7:60), Abraham (6:75–79), Lot (26:166–168), Elias (37:126–127), Moses (7:105–106), and even Jesus (3:52–6; 5:118; 19:37). According to Ella Landau-Tasseron only ten of the Qur'anic references to *jihad* actually refer to physical violence and warfare.[15] The most direct translation of *jihad* is "striving" or "exertion" for God's will. Chaiwat Satha-Anand's definition roots *jihad* in a larger vision for social justice: "An effort, a striving for justice and truth that need not be violent" and existing for the larger purpose of "ending structural violence (that is conditions that are characterized by deep inequity, preventable human suffering, and an inequitable distribution of life chances). . . . Muslims have no choice but to oppose injustice — combatting tumult and oppression with determination."[16] David Dakake explains that *jihad* can take any number of forms that advance social justice:

> The exertion of *jihad* can be in an infinite number of ways, from giving charity and feeding the poor, to concentrating intently on one's prayers, to controlling oneself and showing patience and forgiveness in the face of offenses, to gaining authentic knowledge to physical fighting to stopping oppression and injustice.[17]

The greatest foes in battle are Satan (Q. 35:6) and the evil aberrations of our own human nature. Many Muslims stress the personal nature of *jihad* with reference to spiritual piety. Qur'an 2:218 teaches that some have "suffered exile and struggled [*jihad*] in the Path of God" through holy effort. Qur'an 5:54 speaks of the *jihad* of speech; Qur'an 5:19 tells of Muhammad making effective *jihad* through the force of his fiery sermons.

Most Muslims speak of a "lesser" and "greater" *jihad*, with the greatest of challenges being a struggle for justice (see Q. 25:52, which implies non-violent effort). The idea of a spiritual *jihad* became widespread in the early tenth century (after the establishment of an Islamic empire) and was promoted by Sufi interpreters of the Qur'an. It relates to the Prophet's message to his followers, while they were still living in Mecca, in which he asked them to focus on prayer and piety instead of on warfare (Q. 4:77). A frequently cited Hadith tells of Muhammad returning from the hellish stresses of a battle and saying to his comrades, "we are returning from a lesser *jihad* to the greater *jihad*."[18] Farid Esack, however, questions the use of this particular Hadith noting that, although it has been "elevated to canonical status", it is of questionable authority.[19]

Muslim writers understandably present an Islam that promotes peace and discourages war. Tamil Sufi Bawa Muhaiyaddeen (d. 1986) claims that, during battles, Muhammad did not take an active part but instead "spent the entire time praying for the fighting to stop. He remained alone, hands outstretched praying to Allah. Every second his heart was crying."[20] In this rendering, the Prophet is carrying on the "greater" *jihad*. This is an internal struggle against "one's animal tendencies."[21] The great Persian theologian Abu Hamid al-Ghazali (1058–1111) supported this more pacific interpretation, and the renowned Persian poet Jalal al-Din Rumi (1207–1273) described the "greater" *jihad* as the daily and ongoing "abandonment of personal wishes and sensual desires".[22]

The *jihad* of the spirit can be carried out on both an individual as well as a corporate level. This encompasses a wide range of possibilities; an individual struggling for social justice can be involved in a *jihad* for righteousness, as can an educator who is trying to convey an important idea. Believers are commanded to struggle for the cause of Islam with the preaching of the "heart, by the tongue, by the hands and by the sword" if necessary.[23] Some non-Muslim scholars think, however, that while the Qur'an is clear that there is a "greater" and "lesser" *jihad* (*al-jihad al-ashgar*), Muslims today only focus on the greater *jihad* (*al-jihad al-akbar*) as a way to reinterpret the aggressive intent of the Qur'anic revelation and to distance modern Islam from its various militant expressions.[24]

Because Qur'anic references to *jihad* that are based in history cover such a wide range of meaning, some Muslims have summarized that it simply means the "striving to do God's will" in the context of individual effort.[25] Efforts of striving can take many forms including, in extreme cases, physical force. Initiating violence against others is strictly prohibited (Q. 2:39–40) but those who oppose God must be opposed by God's people (Q. 2:190–193). There is never any allowance for any forms of unnecessary violence.

Extreme revisionists, in contrast, have developed an ahistorical hermeneutic, which approaches apparent contradictions about *jihad* by explaining that certain verses have been abrogated (or superseded) by later revelations. Allah has provided revelation progressively throughout history, meaning that the revelations of Abraham or Jesus, for example, are consistent with later revelation but are not as complete. In contrast, most traditional Muslims have maintained that none (or only a very few verses) of the Qur'an has ever been abrogated. This is called "assignation" because, instead of dismissing a text, the reader is encouraged to assign to the reference a more accurate understanding. Varying interpretations within Islamic history should be given careful consideration, but a general guideline would be to gain, as far as is possible, an appreciation of the specific context of the Muslim *ummah* at the time of a given revelation. All revelations from God are universally "true" even if they are not universally "applicable".

War and Peace in the Life of the Prophet

Because Muhammad provides Muslims with an ideal paradigm for "all Islamic movements in their struggle to reform society and the world", his actions merit careful consideration.[26] In one Hadith the Prophet explained: "My fate is under the shadow of my spear."[27] Islamic tradition recounts that in 624 C.E. the Prophet led 300 Muslims in the raid of a Meccan trade caravan, then led troops to victory in a clash at Badr against Meccans who retaliated against this raid, and finally, fought a series of battles over the next three years that culminated in a victory at the so-called Battle of the Trench (627).

Some claim that the Prophet actively participated in 27 military campaigns and organized 59 others during these years.[28] In none of these incidents, Muslims assert, was the Prophet the aggressor or an instigator of violence. Victories that were won in fierce battles were seen as a clear sign of God's blessing, while defeats were God's way of testing the faithfulness of the believers (Q. 3:140–142, 152–154). In every instance, the Prophet turned to warfare as a last resort. He was a community leader and spiritual pilgrim, who participated in an unending search for peace. One might note that this hesitance contrasts with the Bible, in which God specifically mandates that followers initiate combat against a number of unsuspecting enemies.

John Esposito claims that extremists have used the Prophet's military actions as their starting point because "the Prophet's precedent prevails over his preachments . . . behavior speaks so loudly that verbal messages can hardly be heard. . . . Instead of *jihad* as warfare being the exception to the rule, as it is in the Holy Qur'an, it tends today to function as a rule itself."[29] Muhammad was the first to call for *jihad* in the sense of military struggle, but before he had done that, he encouraged followers to a "peaceful *jihad*." This is underscored by the fact that the Prophet received verses about *jihad* while living peacefully in Mecca. These revelations came within specific situations. One example is found in Qur'an 2:218, which teaches that "those who have believed and those who have . . . fought and labored with great vigor and diligence in the cause of Allah — those should expect the mercy of Allah." Other passages (see Q. 3:142–146 and 5:54) promise mercy to those who "strive in the cause of Allah". These texts speak of *jihad* in the general sense of being an obligation for all believers as they struggle against unrighteousness in this world of evil.

Other verses in the Qur'an are more specific: while in Mecca, Muhammad received a number of revelations encouraging him to strive for the promotion of peace. The way that believers were to struggle against unbelief was by warning the doubters of their errors and calling them to repentance (see Q. 5:19 and Q. 11:12). These verses parallel the role that the Hebrew Prophets play in their divinely-mandated relationship with their communities. In one passage (Q. 16:125), the faithful are called to strive by inviting "all to the way of the Lord with wisdom and beautiful preaching and arguing with them in ways that are best and most gracious." Believers should win over enemies by acts of kindness: "nor can goodness and evil be equal. Repel evil with what is better and those who were your enemies will be as your friends." (Q. 41:34)

Revelations promoting defense, revealed to Muhammad while the fledgling community was taking root in Medina, underscore a very different rendering of the term. Medina at the time of the Prophet was a typical Arabian city that was in need of defense from political and military foes. At this time the world was "steeped in oppressive social relations and caught up in vicious cycles of violence".[30] These revelations encouraging the Prophet to defend himself and the community of believers in the face of attack came only after the *ummah* had already lived for 13 years in Mecca, without ever once resorting to any form of violence. Medina provided new challenges to the Muslim community. It was a time for civil governance, which also meant defensive warfare.

Allah commanded Muhammad to use force against his enemies in order to defend the fledgling *ummah*: "Fight in the way of Allah those who fight you, but do not provoke hostility — God does not love aggressors" (Q. 2:190). One cannot begin a fight, but once believers are attacked they must protect themselves: "To those against whom war is made permission is given to fight, because they have been wronged" (Q. 22:39–40). If there is an opportunity for an end to a military conflict, however, God's servants should work toward that result: "And if they incline to make peace, incline thou to it" (Q. 8:61–63; see also 2:193). Muhammad was ultimately a peacemaker who showed a clear "commitment to nonviolent resistance in his early years in Mecca" and only a "reluctant endorsement of limited warfare after his move to Medina" because war was only "permissible if there was no other way to resist aggression against the faith".[31]

Yusuf Ali's (1872–1953) interpretation of Q. 22:40 expostulates: "Permission to take up arms is given to those against whom war is made because they have been wronged and Allah, indeed, has power to help them." This verse promises that God's aid will always be with the oppressed, never with the oppressor. Oppression is worse, in God's sight, than the slaughter of the oppressor. The essential fact to remember is that Islam might well have been destroyed at its inception had it not defended itself against aggressive military attacks. Pre-Islamic Arabia was steeped in pervasive violence and unending oppression. Karen Armstrong observes that the Prophet was not fortunate enough to have been born into a world of peace: "Muhammad and the first Muslims were fighting for their lives and they had to undertake the project in which violence was inevitable."[32]

Sword Verses

Some of the most controversial passages in the Qur'an, the so-called "sword verses", are also the most oft-misunderstood texts dealing with *jihad*. These passages were revealed to the "Commander of the Faithful" in Medina as Muhammad was returning to Mecca with an army to recapture the city.[33] The war that the Prophet initiated was brutal and took numerous lives.[34] Qur'an 9:5–6 announces: "But when the forbidden months are past, then fight and slay the Pagans wherever you find them and seize them, beleaguer them, and lie in wait for them in every strategy of war." Another "sword verse" that is often quoted is Qur'an 9:123, which seems to condone the slaughter of non-believers even outside the scope of battle: "O you who believe, fight those adjacent to you of the disbelievers and let them find your harshness. And you know that Allah is with the righteous."

One passage, some suggest, promotes the idea that war is sometimes God's will is Q. 61:11: "It is that you believe in Allah and His messenger and strive in the cause of Allah with your wealth and your lives." One of the most militant of the "sword verses" is Q. 66:9: "O Prophet, strive against the disbelievers and the hypocrites and be harsh on them. And their refuge is hell and wretched is their destination." It is the duty of Muslims to carry out *jihad* against unbelievers: "And kill them whenever you overtake them and expel them from wherever they have expelled you, and *fitnah* (disbelief) is worse than killing. . . . If they fight you, then kill them" (Q. 2:191). Extremists often fail to cite this reference in the context of the immediately-preceding verse (Q. 2:190), which mandates specific limitations in warfare. The Qur'an, in fact, forbids all killings unless done in the due process of law or "with the truth" (*bi'l haqq*).

Extremists emphasize that those who refuse to participate in the blessings of *jihad* will be punished by God (Q. 48:16), while those who are active in battle will be amply rewarded for their faithfulness (Q. 4:74; 94). Any martyr who dies for the cause of the truth will arise to the bliss of paradise: "Those who die in the path of God are not dead. Nay, rather they live (Q. 2:154; 3:169–171)." These verses have led to a number of Hadith that promise eternal rewards for dedicated martyrs (*shuhada'a*) of the faith. One Hadith states that once a jihadist enters paradise and finds all of the blessings awaiting him/her, he/she will be so blissful that his/her desire will be to return to the earth to "get killed again".[35] Martyrs will "never be touched by the fires of hell" because their cause is linked to God's command, thus they will receive a divine reward.[36]

Suicide Bombers

Moderates assert that a distinction should be made between righteous martyrs who die in the certain cause of God and the misguided terrorist acts of suicide bombers who harm innocent victims. Moderates base this distinction on their reading of scripture and their deep aversion to Islamist terrorists who, obviously, are convinced that those of their number who die are also "righteous martyrs". Allah has a destiny for all individuals (Q. 24:21; 57:22) and is merciful in granting salvation but the Qur'an is clear about the eternal fate of those who kill themselves for whatever misguided reason: "And do not kill yourselves. Surely God is most merciful to you. And whoever commits that through aggression and injustice, we shall cast him into the Fire, and that is easy for God" (Q. 4:29–30). Moderates claim that this verse affirms the sanctity of life as a sacred trust and authoritatively "trumps" all other revelations about the fate of combatants who claim to do God's work. Life is a sacred trust; foolishly taking away what Allah has given is forbidden in all circumstances, including warfare. A number of strong Hadith confirm this unambiguous prohibition. One tradition warns: "Whoever kills himself with an iron tool, then his tool will be in his hand and he will be stabbing himself with it in the Fire of Hell forever and ever."[37]

Extremists claim that those who give their lives in the path of martyrdom will find eternal salvation on the Day of Judgment. There is no lesser path than that of absolute obedience to the commands of political and religious leaders, as if those leaders spoke for God Almighty. Carl Raschke explains: "Commitment must be complete and the glorification of God must be total, including even the annihilation of the self."[38] Osama bin Laden promoted an extremist "death-cult" draped in religious language even though it focused on temporal political agendas. Bin Laden referred to those who gave their lives in "martyrdom operations" as those who had given the ultimate gift to the *ummah*. Given the clear message of the Qur'an against suicide, one sees set in motion by extremists a highly distorted socio-religious vision, which plays on the misguided hopes of young zealots who feel that they have no other reason to live in an unjust world. Those who accept this bankrupt logic believe that they are paying the highest price of a sacrifice to become martyrs (*shahid*), who love both Allah and their communities. Of course, far more than debased religious sentiment is behind such decisions, but instrumentalist religious language is unconscionably generated in order to allow suicide-killers to clothe their murderous acts in a confident piety.

Anthropologist Lawrence Rosen asserts that "faith and politics alone do not explain why terrorists engage in self-destruction" because these terrorist actions are rooted in an Arab regard for social cohesion that is more important than individual survival.[39] Such actions stress the compelling priority of the eternal over the temporary. Those who perform such acts show a level of sacrifice — based in their actions of love for the community — which marks them as those who are truly mature in faith. On the Final Day, extremists affirm, God will erase all of the misdeeds of the martyrs and assure them a place in paradise. If an "innocent person" dies in an act of martyrdom then Allah will also allow such a victim to share in the portion of the blessing that the martyrs will receive. Their deaths will be richly rewarded by a God who cares for each individual.

Moderates respond that this kind of rhetoric blurs the clear revelation of the Qur'an that the murder of one innocent person can be equated with the killing of all those who are innocent (Q. 5:32). Only those "necessary" killings, which occur in the course of fulfilling God's will to bring justice, are not regarded as murder (Q. 6:151; 17:33; 25:68). The killing of non-combatants is forbidden under *every* circumstance without exception (Q. 2:190). Various traditions detail that those who are always to be seen as innocent in battle include all "women and children", "the people in cloisters" (monks), the infirm, and old men and women.[40] Those responsible for the killing of any innocent will certainly face a stern judgment on the Final Day.

Limitations in Warfare

Islamic tradition has placed specific boundaries on who can become a "jihadist". Warriors can never fight for fame, glory, or wealth, but only for the advancement of God's will. One must never fight when filled with rage. Warriors must be believers who are mature and of sound mind and they must have their family's permission to fight. A warrior must be an able-bodied person who is independent economically (meaning that they is either debt free or excused by their debtor). The Qur'an also provides specifics about exactly what could be done in the field of battle (Q. 2:190). The chaotic realities of a battlefield do not give warriors permission to be freed of their obligations to act in the path of righteousness. God's revelation explains that when believers fight they cannot "transgress limits" (Q. 2:190); believers cannot define how (and when) fighting is permitted. One Hadith instructs, for instance, that combatants cannot be burned alive or tortured by fire: "Punishment by fire does not behoove anyone except the Master of the Fire."[41]

The Qur'an also lays out a series of safeguards for prisoners who are captured during the course of a battle. Any adversary who surrenders should be protected by his/her captors in the hope that they will eventually convert to Islam because of the mercy that they have been shown (Q. 9:6). Qur'an 47:4 teaches that after the war is over, prisoners should receive "either grace or ransom" (see also Q. 8:67). Captives should be taken care of out of love for Allah and in hopes of eternal rewards (Q. 76:8). They should be treated with brotherly/sisterly care and be protected from harsh weather. According to some Muslims, however, prisoners can be executed if it serves the military interests of righteous Muslim forces (or if it weakens their enemies). Executing prisoners should be avoided if possible; it is better to ransom prisoners back to their families, set them free, or consign them to a period of slavery.[42] A Hadith relates that, after the Battle of Badr, the Prophet fed his prisoners-of-war delicious ripe dates while he and his own soldiers ate only bread. He told his followers: "Take heed of these recommendations and treat the prisoners fairly."[43]

One famous Qur'anic passage affirms that non-combatants and the wounded are to be protected: "if anyone kills a person — unless it is for murder or for the spreading of mischief in the land — it would be as if he kills the whole people; and if anyone saved a life, it would be as if he saved the whole people" (Q. 5:32). The exceptions to this rule of not killing non-combatants might include those, such as one 100-year-old man, who advised others to fight against Muslims.[44] Another exception is when the innocent die by accident if a necessary weapon must be used in a generalized assault against the city or fortifications of one's enemy.[45] Extremists have used these few legal precedents as justification for their tactic of suicide bombings and murdering of innocents. Such claims fly in the face of countless injunctions, both in the Qur'an and in Muslim intellectual history, which mandate that innocents must be protected at all costs.

The lands of an enemy combatant should not be destroyed; if possible, the dead bodies of combatants should be returned to the ranks of the enemy. The lands of battle "should not be corrupted" and crops should not suffer because of war (Q. 2:204–205). Treaties should be carefully honored and any act of war must be declared openly (Q. 8:58). Only enemy combatants should be killed: Qur'an 17:33 mandates, "And do not kill any one whom Allah has forbidden, except for a just cause, and whoever is slain unjustly, we have indeed given to his heir authority, so let him not exceed the just limits in slaying; surely he is aided." This passage parallels the Hebrew Bible statute that nothing more than an equitable "eye for an eye and a tooth for a tooth" (Ex. 21:24; Lev. 24:20; Deut. 19:21) should be extracted in order to promote justice. One Hadith teaches that it is consequential to check one's motivation for fighting: "A person, whose intent is glory, spoils, or a female, has no ties to God, and only God knows who does *jihad* for His sake." Just as in Christianity, a righteous martyr of Islam is someone whose heart and actions are pure and whose deeds are unblemished by sinful self-interest or temporal benefits. David Oualaalou notes that Hadith relate that one can also be considered a true martyr for a number of other reasons: "Martyrdom is seven things besides being killed for the sake of Allah. The one who dies by plague is a martyr, the one who is drowned, the one who dies of pleurisy, the one who dies of a stomach disease, the one who dies in a fire or who dies beneath a collapsed building, and the woman who dies in pregnancy is a martyr."[46]

Fighting Non-Muslims

There is one other significant limitation that has been imposed upon believers who find themselves in the midst of war: throughout history, scholars such as Abu Hanifa (d. 768) and Shaybani (d. 804) have asserted that believers are forbidden to go to war against non-believers simply because they are not believers. These teachers have explained that tolerance should be shown to non-believers, "especially the People of the Book (though not idolaters or polytheists) and advised fellow believers to wage war only when the inhabitants of the *dar al-harb* came into conflict with Islam."[47]

This prohibition against killing non-believers raises a thought-provoking question: Islam teaches implicitly (see Q. 3:193) that the world is divided into two fundamental groups of people, those who live within the "house of Islam" or "house of peace" (*dar al-Islam* or *dar-al salaam*) and those who are in what can be translated as the "house of war" (*dar al-harb*). After the revelation of the Qur'an, this theme came into even sharper focus and was given a stronger emphasis: it became the duty of every believer to work for the transformation of the "house of war" into the "house of Islam".[48] This dualism is the primary reason why some Muslims have misunderstood their relations to non-Muslims in a combative (and sometimes lethal) manner. According to this logic, all non-believers are enemies and should be obliterated (according to extremist readings of Qur'an 3:141). Another passage, Qur'an 4:115 has been interpreted to mean that all non-believers will go to hell: "If anyone contends with the Messenger even after guidance has been plainly conveyed to him, and follows a path other than that becoming to men of Faith, God shall leave him in the path he has chosen, and land him in hell — what an evil refuge." Other verses such as Qur'an 8:39, 23:27, 7:72, 9:52, 11:68, 7:84, 7:137 and 4:75, are cited as proof of this mandate to war against those destined to burn in hell for opposing God.

Extremists teach that life in this world has no value (Q. 9:38) and should be readily given to the cause of Allah in battle. It is an honorable action to give one's temporal life to advance God's eternal glory. Further, the very presence of non-believers is reason enough to wage war because those who are not believers are fundamentally in opposition to Allah. Faithful warriors who oppose God's enemies — even by giving their lives — will be rewarded with the pleasures of paradise. Some militants argue that all who are not Muslims are not fit to live either in this life or in the world to come. The Egyptian-born British writer Bat Ye'or states: "*Jihad* is the normal and permanent state of war between the Muslims and the *dar al-harb*, a war that can only end with the final domination over unbelievers and the absolute supremacy of Islam throughout the world."[49] A pure state ruled by Muslims, God's ultimate design, brokers no room for competing authorities. In this ultimate sense, some extremists have argued that Allah wills the death of all non-Muslims who continue to rebel against revealed truth. The Egyptian al-Qaeda jihadist Saif al-din al Ansari al-Adel, responsible for the death of journalist Daniel Pearl (1963–2002) and the American embassy bombing in Kenya (1998), preached that "Allah made annihilating the infidels one of His steadfast decrees."[50] On May 22, 2013, two converts to Islam murdered British soldier Lee Rigby in cold blood on the streets of London with a meat-cleaver and knives after running him over from behind. One of the assailants, Michael Adebolajo claimed that he was fulfilling a religious duty and was seeking retaliation for those Muslims who died at the hands of British soldiers in Aghanistan and Iraq: "I am a soldier of Allah in a war. I remain certain about my deeds being *hallal* (permissible). Only Allah can judge me."[51]

Extremist *Jihad*

In contrast to moderates, who argue that wars are exceptional (and acts of defense of the faith are uncommon), militant preaching asserts that the *ummah* is under perpetual threat in this modern, godless era. The entire corrupted non-Muslim world is at "war" with the righteous truth of a pure Islam; there is no viable alternative but unending conflict against non-Muslim agents of Satan. Extremists attack the West, often referring to Islamophobic Westerners as "Crusaders", while reserving particular vituperation for "Zionist Jews" and the "Zionist State of Israel".

It is not only non-Muslims who merit their self-righteous scorn: extremists also criticize errant Shi'a and lackadaisical Sunnis who do not embrace their zealous enthusiasm. Particular scorn is reserved for Sufi Muslims because it is felt that their other-worldly notions are misplaced; Sufis are seen to have abdicated their Islamic duty to oppose evil and defend the *ummah*. Scorn is also reserved for those believers living in the lands of the "crusaders" who maintain their allegiance to those nations instead of obeying *fatwas*, which command Muslims within any and every army to subvert the efforts of non-Muslim governments.[52]

Extremists preach that the world is a threatening black-and-white chessboard-like battlefield, which is filled with pagan idol-worshippers. Neutrality toward non-Muslims is only a temporary, strategic expediency. According to Majid Khadduri, "Sooner or later the *jihad* must be enforced on all people, regardless of their racial character or the physical nature of their country. . . . No country has ever been declared immune from the *jihad* in the authoritative sources of Islamic law."[53] Either a person is a believer or an enemy of the truth. When there are two worlds wrapped within one world, the idea that people are the marginalized and discredited "other" becomes underlined. At the same time, the authority of those who claim assertively to be in the right can also often result in people giving in to a sense of blind hatred rooted in an unwavering arrogance about the shortcomings of the marginalized "other".

Those who emphasize intolerant views use them as the basis for terrorist attacks or for going to war in order to bring outsiders within the house of Islam. Extremists are universalists in that they believe that the world will continue to live in strife until all people submit themselves to Islam. Sayyid Qutb writes that "there are two parties in the world: the Party of Allah and the party of Satan — which includes every community, race, and individual that does not stand under the banner of Allah."[54] Moderates have asked militants to consider the term *dar al-harb* to mean the "house of innovation" instead of the "house of war" and have encouraged other Muslims to seek to influence others by kindness, instead of presumptuous confrontation.[55]

Moderates have argued about whether or not *jihad* is a major duty for Muslims in the modern age and how violence fits into this equation. Classical jurists and theologians have consistently condemned all instances of terrorism and aspire to live in peace. In contrast, extremists quote the "sword verses" as proof that it is a sacred duty for all Muslims to wage perpetual war against all godless non-Muslims. Their argument is that, because these texts come in the last revelations of the Prophet, they abrogate the previous, earlier passages. Noted spokespeople of this argument include Abdul al-Mawdudi (1903–1979) and Sayyid Qutb (1906–1966).

Abdul al-Mawdudi was one of the earliest proponents of Islamist perspectives. Mawdudi was a religious journalist and activist in a political party called the *Jaamat-e-Islam* on the Indian subcontinent. In 1930, he published *Jihad in Islam*, a collection of articles, which had been previously published in an Indian newspaper (he also addressed the issue in a Qur'anic commentary written between 1950 and 1973). In addition to defensive warfare, Mawdudi preached the need for a "reformative war" wherever the safety of the *ummah* was under threat. In order to prepare for these threats, Muslims were obligated to possess every type of weapon available (Mawdudi cited Qur'an 8:60 as his rationale for this view). Generally, Mawdudi supported traditional ideas about protecting prisoners of war.[56] He scorned, however, a tentative approach to war and claimed that any non-combatant male could be seen as a combatant and killed because they have the "capacity" to eventually fight.[57]

Once Muslims came to power it was essential that they rule with "authoritarian control".[58] Because the Prophet always had success it was incumbent upon all believers to also never settle for anything less than total victory over anyone who was a *kafir* (*kufr*) — anyone who was not a Muslim. Islam was the only cure for humanity's ills and a completely perfect revelation that must be accepted with total submission and without any compromise. There is only one God and only one way to follow that God. In a time of crisis and fearful degradation for the Muslim world, Mawdudi saw the willingness of a believer to engage in acts of *jihad* as a litmus test, which ultimately validated the depth of their truest convictions. Mawdudi dismisses as soft the notion that *jihad* can refer to something bloodless (able to be accomplished only through the use of one's pen or one's mouth).[59] He claims these views blur the inarguable facts that anyone who is not a Muslim is an enemy of Islam.

Egyptian cleric Sayyid Qutb agrees with Mawdudi that there is no room for moderation during our present era of *jahiliyya* (darkness), in which Islam is being threatened as never before. Qutb inveighs against those who look for grounds to justify a non-violent *jihad*. It is a holy duty to be initiated by the faithful devout:

The establishing of the dominion of Allah on earth, the abolishing of the dominion of man, the taking away of sovereignty from the usurper to revert it to Allah, and the bringing about and the enforcement of the divine law (*shariah*) and the abolition of man-made laws cannot be achieved only through preaching.[60]

Jihad is the only path for the righteous because, in this unambiguously evil world, "one is a true believer or an infidel, saved or damned, a friend or an enemy of God. The army of Allah is locked in a battle, or holy war, with the followers of Satan."[61] Not surprisingly, Qutb's critics are legion. Karen Armstrong wrote: "By making *jihad* central to the Muslim vision, Qutb had, in fact, distorted the Prophet's life. Traditional biographies make it clear that even though the first *ummah* had to fight in order to survive, Muhammad did not achieve victory by the sword but by a creative and ingenious policy of non-violence."[62]

Extremist activists in Palestine agree with the worldview espoused by Mawdudi and Qutb but confine their application to their own military confrontations against, what they perceive as, the provocative intransigence of the State of Israel. Instead of quoting these writers, however, the military and political forces in the Palestinian *Intifada* frequently cite passages from the Qur'an and Hadith to justify terrorist actions, including suicide-bombing and the killing of unarmed Israeli women and children. Their God-ordained uprising, which began among Palestinian Arabs of the Gaza Strip and West Bank (1987), is centered on the goal of obtaining a just Palestinian state for its citizens with a foundation of Islamic principles.

The founder of the Islamic Center in the Gaza Strip, Shaykh Ahmed Ismail Hassan Yasmin (1937–2004) worked with members of the Society of the Muslim Brothers to form a new organization called The Islamic Resistance Movement (known by its Arabic acronym as *Hamas*). Critics claim that Yasmin's theocratic and militant organization "emerged from the cobwebs of Medieval times".[63] Supporters, however, argue that Hamas emerged in Palestine because there was a vital need for the oppressed people of Gaza to be adequately represented. Hamas felt that the Palestinian Liberation Organization (PLO) was too accommodating to the influence of Western political ideas. Hamas framed its work of "community salvation" in terms of a religious — rather than a purely political — vision. The "Hamas Covenant" calls on all Islamic nations to confront the insidious power of Zionism. One of the most repeated slogans of Hamas declares that, "Allah is our goal, the Messenger is our leader, the Qur'an is our constitution, *jihad* is our methodology, and death for the sake of Allah is the most coveted desire."[64] All of these declarations, it must be remembered, continue to be generated as a way to browbeat supporters into embracing their path and to advance their political agendas.

Former PLO leader Yasser Arafat (and others) frequently cited passages such as Qur'an 2:190–193 and 61:10–14, which promise that an individual will be blessed if they fight for God (see also Q. 4:75–76). Chairman Arafat (1929–2004) often quoted a Hadith from *Tafsir al-Jalalayn* and depicted the Palestinians as the promised people and the State of Israel as the evil and tyrannical Pharaoh, who will not allow justice for the oppressed people of God. The former Palestinian Minister of Communication, Imad Faluji, frequently railed against the Zionist Jews and cited the Qur'an to justify his vituperation.[65]

These militant views, however, are less characteristic of historic Islam — and tried and true dispute-resolution methods (arbitration, mediation, reconciliation) based on traditional laws — than they are of national liberationist ideologies and the anti-colonialist views of the nineteenth and twentieth centuries. While extremists frame their views in Muslim terms, they also rely on a number of non-Qur'anic terms such as *hizb* (party), *harakah* (movement) and *harb muqaddasa* (struggle against darkness).

Voices of Moderation

Moderates worldwide accept the more balanced position that Islam allows war only in the unavoidable case of responding to attack and for fundamentally defensive purposes. For the mainstream, *jihad* is a corporate duty of the community as a whole (*fard kifaya*), and never an individual duty, when it comes to actual warfare. Individual duties (*fard 'ayn*), such as fasting and prayer, are quite distinct from one person's decision (on his/her own) to begin a war against God's enemies. Moderates note that the theme of community must be central to understanding this doctrine: "In the West, conflict is often defined as between individuals acting as individuals — acting as free agents to pursue their own goals and interests" but all activities of righteous believers have to be viewed in terms of the context and needs of the larger Islamic *ummah*.[66] This is the reason why extremists have frequently issued a *fatwa* in order to advance their positions, calling upon the Islamist *ummah* to take a specific action. The legitimacy of these *fatwas* have been vigorously contested by orthodox scholars who claim that they alone have traditionally had this power to issue *fatwas*, using it only in extreme circumstances.

Recent scholars who have written in defense of upholding centuries of moderate, mainstream positions include Mahmud Shaltut (1898–1963), Muhammad Talbi (b. 1921), and Mahmud Taha (1909–1985). Within Islam's intellectual history, it has been juristic, and not philosophical (or ethical) issues that have defined discourses on war and peace. One reason for this is that there is no clear distinction between "masjid and state" within Islamic *kalam*. There is little philosophical discussion within early Islam about issues of when war is justified. The Qur'an is clear: fighting is permitted only in response to an attack — tolerated but never encouraged. Qur'an 2:216 explains, "Fighting is prescribed for you and you will dislike it." No individual should relish or promote warfare. Allah desires peace for the created order; war is allowable only when absolutely necessary.

Mahmud Taha argued that using the doctrine of abrogation in the context of justifying acts of war exposes Muslims to other potential errors. Further, he claims that every verse — including controversial ones — is an applicable element of divine revelation because the Qur'an operates on two levels — the natural and the spiritual — because God's ways are far beyond human comprehension. Every passage can have "a distinct meaning with the Lord, and a nearer meaning that comes down to the slave".[67] Muslims should maintain a posture of humility as they continue toward the goal of a "completed religion" (Q. 5:3), which will finally result in all being "with Allah" (Q. 3:19). If any texts are to be placed in a primary position, it should be the Meccan Surahs, which present Islam in its most idealized form. Taha claims that the "second message of Islam" is the conviction that all should live in peace and pursue egalitarian democracy and true freedom for individuals to worship Allah.[68] The basis of hope for the dawn of this social peace is confidence in God's power and belief that the divine will shall triumph.

Progressive and moderate Muslims maintain that the peace-verses of the Qur'an represent the truest rendering of God's revealed will. They claim that the early revelations that condoned violence were limited to specific, contextual instances within the early *ummah*. This assertion means that Muslims actually have no justification for engaging in any form of warfare in God's name. Progressives and moderates call believers to work toward the final ideal goal of establishing social justice through openness and becoming free of all sexist, intolerant, and de-humanizing practices.

Farid Esack calls on Muslims to worship the God of Qur'anic revelation with reason instead of slavishly bowing to a confining and myopic literalism. It is not fair, Esack claims, for non-Muslims to cast the tragic events of September 11 in categorically religious terms simply because the lunatics who carried out these atrocities claimed to be devout Muslims. Esack trumpets: "I can use Islam and its text, the Qur'an, to reinforce all my prejudices, to shed them or to rework them. . . . Interpreters are people who carry all the inescapable baggage of their human condition."[69] Esack attacks all forms of blind fundamentalism (whether they are in the name of Islam or free-market capitalism) because all fundamentalisms place cold ideals over warm human needs. Esack is not advocating for relativism but for humility and mutual respect. He is open in expressing his convictions but argues that only Allah (and not any human) is the Final Judge. "All fundamentalisms", Esack warns, share "an obsession with a single truth as understood by me or my group, the demonizing of all others who refuse to get behind this 'truth,' the willingness — even desperation — to destroy those who offer alternatives in a holy war."[70] The modern world consists of a vast plurality of cultures, contested opinions, and various religions, whether we agree with them or not, and Esack writes, "Because we refuse to risk a full life of knowledge of the other, we die behind our fears and prejudices."[71] For Esack, this means that religious differences are not as significant as the more pressing need to defend our common desire for social justice and a life of peace.

The diversity of opinion concerning war and peace within the Muslim tradition should not be hijacked by self-serving militant assertions espoused as simplistic conclusions. The Qur'an says much more than one thing about the many issues relating to war and peace. Mainstream Muslims throughout the centuries have accepted these various views by concluding that God's wisdom is greater than the human potential to make sense of apparent contradictions. This consensus is now under attack from extremists who claim that they alone have the correct interpretation of these verses, in spite of centuries of scholarship which has called for mature humility before Allah. Of course, Islamists — like all types of extremists — are not usually interested in building consensus with others, but in advancing their own particular holy agenda. The failure or success of their efforts is largely in the hands of the vast majority of Muslims worldwide who promote moderate views about *jihad* as a last resort and who are committed to the daily promotion of increasing intercultural toleration.

Christian Holy War

Every faith tradition balances its ideals with the actual practice of its adherents. Deepa Kumar writes: "Looking at Christianity's brutal history today, one might well advance an argument that all Catholics are bloodthirsty fanatics. Indeed, this logic would be analogous to the argument that Islam is inherently violent and that Muslims have a predisposition toward violence."[72] It is in that spirit of appropriate humility that this brief section is included in the larger discussion of how Muslims view issues of war and peace.

Christianity ideally teaches us to "love our neighbor as ourselves" (Mark 12:31). Christ said that those who made peace would be called "the children of God" (Matt. 5:9), and told His disciples to "put your swords away" because "those who lived by the sword will die by the sword" (Matt. 26:59). Such clear injunctions, however, have not stopped countless Christians from advocating numberless acts of violence against their neighbors. Ferguson wrote that, in its early history, "Christianity and war were incompatible. Christians were charged with undermining the Roman Empire by refusing military service and public office."[73]

Christian jurists throughout centuries of European history, beginning with Augustine of Hippo (354–430), have discussed questions about when war is justified and how it should be conducted (*jus ad bellum* and *jus en bello*). Rules and rulers were to be obeyed and God's will, even if violent or militant, was not to be questioned even when it seemed to be wrong by the standards of human reason. As Christianity expanded across Europe, so did the use of force to convert resistant pagan tribesman to the true faith. These freshly-minted converts failed to appreciate the heart of the Christian message as being one of tolerant love and gentle peace. Some of these warriors insisted on being baptized with their right arm — which was used to wield their weapons — being held above the sanctifying water so that they could continue to fight without fearing that religious convictions might interfere with their murderous work. When King Clovis of the Franks was asked to comment on the crucifixion, he bellowed with fiery passion: "If I and my Franks had been there, we would have made sure that it never would have happened!"[74]

Charlemagne fought with a Papal blessing and, in March 1095, Pope Urban II launched a full-scale war against the Muslim realm that was to become the First Crusade. The Pope told his warriors: "It is our duty to pray. It is yours to fight against the Amalekites [Muslims]."[75] This war, instigated by the church, began with Crusaders massacring (as if to practice) large number of Jews before they left their homes in Europe. Those Crusaders who finally arrived in Jerusalem (July 15, 1099) set the Great Synagogue on fire and "rode up to their knees and bridle reigns" in the blood of those who had surrendered.[76] Raymond of Agiles summarized the day by saying, "Indeed, it was a just and splendid judgment of God that this place should be filled with the blood of unbelievers, when it had suffered so long from their blasphemies."[77]

Christians have to ask if Christ's mandate that we should "do unto others what we would have them do unto us" should be the guiding principle in our interactions. Is this a theoretically abstract notion or a genuine way of living our lives? While we may not reach the promise of universal peace within our own lifetimes, is it appropriate to strive for such ideals given all that we have learned from the grim annals of human history? Real problems call for pragmatic solutions: while this real world remains abrim with socio-political contexts such as Iraq, Afghanistan,

Northern Nigeria, Syria, and the Sudan, each of these contexts can be personalized in order to help us remember that the legacies of war touch the lives of countless grieving mothers and heartbroken fathers at bus stations and airports who are waving goodbye to their sons and daughters as they go off to fight in bitter, intractable wars.

Active Peacemaking

Aalia Sohail Khan argues emphatically that, in its ideal form and in its fundamental meaning, "Islam is intrinsically a religion of peace, tolerance, and universal brotherhood."[78] There is more than one way to interpret the relationship between war and peace within Islam's intellectual tradition. Throughout history, there have been countless wars, yet there have also been countless Muslims who have been active and engaged peacemakers. These wars and conflicts may not expose the failure of the Islamic revelation as much as they underscore the failure of disobedient believers to live out their peaceful ideals. One scholar lamented simply that "some Muslims have not exercised the *greater jihad*."[79] Many Muslims agree with the conclusion that, in recent years, extremists have misused and instrumentalized the term *jihad* in such a way as to suit their own skewed political agendas. In this sense, these extremists have done nothing less than dishonor Allah and pervert the gentle heart of their own religious tradition.

According to one Muslim scholar, A.G. Noorani (b. 1930), "the crimes which Muslim extremists advocate or commit in the name of Islam are not exercises in *jihad*."[80] Rather, they are promoting nihilism and calling it Islam by quoting a number of scriptures to support their crimes. Noorani continues: "The simplistic visions of paradise for suicide bombers preached by militant jihadist clerics defy over 1,400 years of Islamic history and wisdom."[81] Noorani argues that extremists demonstrate their lack of connectedness with the larger, and more normative, tradition. When believers return to the dynamic truths of their own faith as revealed in the Holy Qur'an, they will set aside ungodly strategies involving violence and pursue paths of peace.

When Islam is fully practiced there will be peace. Believers must first begin to become peacemakers in their own lives, communities, and nations. The problem is that individuals are flawed and there are times in the world we live in when war is necessary. One famous Hadith preaches: "Do not desire an encounter with the enemy; but when you encounter them be firm."[82] The primary belief that Islam is a religion of peace springs from the fact that Islam recognizes the precious value of all humanity. *Jihad* is to be seen primarily as an internal struggle and only a military option as a last resort. The primary task of believers is to fight against injustice.

War is to be avoided and peace is to be pursued. Voices advocating violent solutions need to be silenced through the efforts of active peacemakers. The serious challenges that face our generation mandate that all people of faith should strive with maximum effort to resist evil and to develop the bright holiness of their own spirituality. It is hoped that one's enemies can eventually be turned into one's friends (Q. 41:34). All individuals should be cherished as equal before God (Q. 7:11), and all human life is to be protected (Q. 5:32). The Qur'an states that non-believers should be invited to embrace Islam through the tools of "wisdom and beautiful preaching" (Q. 16:125), not with aggressive confrontation and reckless violence. Allah does not love aggressors (Q. 2:190); the destiny of the violent is hell-fire.

Islam advocates numerous non-violent, peace-building values and expects believers to live by these cherished, eternal principles. Qur'an 2:256 is clear: "Let there be no compulsion in religion. Truth stands clear from error." Peace is personal, social, spiritual and physical (Q. 5:64). While militants argue that they alone possess the truth, they represent only a tiny percentage of the entire breadth of the Muslim community. While extremists may be correct that early Islam might not have even existed without the "blessing of *jihad*", we are now living in a very different time.

The vast majorities of Muslims throughout history have no connection with bellicose and intolerant militants and want nothing to do with the violence that such extremists espouse. Grand Shaykh Muhammad Sayyid Tantawi (1928–2010) of the al-Azhar Masjid in Cairo argued that so-called "suicide bombers" were enemies of Islam: "Extremism is the enemy of Islam. Whereas *jihad* is allowed within Islam to defend one's land or to help the oppressed, the difference between this *jihad* and that of extremists is like the earth and the sky."[83] The Ahmidayyan Hazmat Mizra Tahir Ahmad (1928–2003) is correct that "no true religion, whatever its name, can sanction violence and the bloodshed of innocent men, women, and children in the name of God. God is love, God is peace! Love can never beget hatred and peace can never lead to war."[84] No one is more affected by Islamism than decent and average Muslims and it is the case, as Melody Moezzi asserts: "If anyone is to rescue Islam from the distortions and manipulations to which a small number of misinformed fanatics are subjecting it, it will be the logical, freethinking, and outspoken Muslims of the world."[85] Muslims worldwide are supporting numerous constructive peace building efforts and participating in discussions in search of fresh insights as to how make our world more just. In this *jihad* their greatest support are those traditional Islamic values that systematically empower and undergird the active work of peacemaking.

3. Islamic Responses to Poverty and Economic Oppression

Never had I bemoaned adversity; never had I felt troubled before the numerous cares that assailed me until the day I found myself shoeless and without a penny to buy a pair of babouches. Dejected, I entered the mosque at Kufa in order to unburden my heavy heart with prayer. And there I saw a man who had no feet. I therefore thanked God and patiently bore my lack of slippers.

— Musharraf al-din Sa'di

Faith in a World of Economic Injustices

Poverty, as defined by Youssef al-Abdin, is a "condition of life so characterized by malnutrition, illiteracy, and disease as to be beneath any reasonable definition of human decency".[1] Poverty is complex, debilitating, persistent, and extensive. Numerous gut-wrenching statistics can be cited to show the extent of poverty, famine, and the diseases that such problems engender worldwide. Al-Abdin asserts that there are over a billion individuals worldwide who fall below the poverty-line of making less than $370 a year and over 633 million of these are in extreme poverty (making less than $275 a year).[2] Saddest of all is that over fourteen million children perish every year because of diseases related to famine and malnutrition.[3]

Karen Lebacqz writes, "As a white, well-educated, middle-class American, my life connotes cocktail parties rather than slums. How different it is from the extreme poverty that affects our world."[4] Our modern world is awash in materialism, Farid Esack comments:

Looking at our lives today and the amount of time, love, and energy that we devote to our stone idol (the house), to our metal idol (the car), and to our paper gods (the share certificates), it is no longer so strange that the Israelites, whom Moses led out of the darkness of oppression to the light of liberation, should fall for gimmicks. . . . The idols of capitalism and consumerism today are created by a whole class of people whose lives rotate around little other than exploitation for profit.[5]

Forces of religion throughout history have sometimes been on the side of the oppressed but are usually found protecting the vested interests of the powerful elite. Christianity, for example, was a liberating force for the poor until it was co-opted by Rome's powerful ruling establishment, after which it often became a weapon of oppression in the hands of the wealthy.

The message of the biblical prophets is that God sides with those who are poor (Isa. 42:2–7; Amos 5), cares for their plight (Deut. 10:17–19), and is opposed to economic oppression (Ps. 82:3–4; Isa. 1:17). Christ explains that the purpose of stewardship is to aid those who are gripped by the curse of poverty (Matt. 25:31–46); the book of James (5:1–6) warns that the rich oppressors will suffer on the Day of Judgment. Those who seek their own wealth are "friends with the world" and enemies of God (James 4:1–12). In spite of these clear mandates from scripture, powerful Christians throughout history have stood on the sidelines as the poor have been oppressed while the privileged rich have lived in ease and comfort.

Economic injustice has, in spite of Islamic values, flourished in Islamic history. Religious leaders, sadly, have often paid more attention to the whims of the wealthy than to the cries of the impoverished. As a belief system, however, Islam is not to be blamed for this regrettable fact. Wilson observes that "central to Islam is the concept of awareness (al-wa'y)" and this includes being aware of the economic injustices being experienced in a given society.[6] Wilson claims that over 1,400 of the 6,226 verses in the Qur'an deal with economic issues; illustrating that faith and finances are clearly tied together.[7] The example of Muhammad provides the House of Islam with its best guide for virtuous economic activities, and in particular, in the action of calculating the devotee's economic righteous deeds for the sake of God (hisbah). The Prophet was equitable and generous in all of his business dealings (Q. 26:181–183). One of the stated goals of his life was "encouraging the rich to help the poor".[8] The Prophet taught that truest wealth was seen in those whose hearts were generous to those in greatest need.

A number of other scholars have explored a wide-range of economic questions throughout the long course of Islam's intellectual history. Ibn Taymiyyah, popular amongst extremists today for his strident assertions, wrote extensively about economic theory and advocated that any Islamic government was to take an active role in regulating financial policies for the benefit of the entire ummah.

Historic Opposition to Economic Injustice

Zaid bin Ali (695–740) and Abu Yusuf (d. 798) were early Islamic economic theorists who taught in the eighth century. They were followed by later thinkers such as Abu Ubaid and Jamaluddin al-Afghani (1838–1897), who sought to integrate the faith with economic challenges. Fourteenth-century philosopher and historian Ibn Khaldun (1332–1406) also wrote extensively about a number of challenging economic questions. A dutiful student of Aristotle, Ibn Khaldun was interested in how moral and ethical considerations affected economic realities. He thought that economic and political policies should be rooted in Islam and should be considered together when envisioning an *ummah* that cultivated social stability and social justice. Ibn Khaldun's economic ideas have greatly influenced modern Muslim economic thinkers such as the Iranian Abul Hasan Bani Sadr (b. 1933), Syed Naqvi of Pakistan, and Fahim Khan and Kurshid Ahmed of Bangladesh (b. 1932). Ibn Khaldun stressed that Muslims should ensure that any society gives resources to those citizens who were less fortunate. For Ibn Khaldun, the economic welfare of each person was interrelated and those who were wealthy could not bury their heads in the sand and plead ignorance about those who were poor. Ibn Khaldun stressed that action must be taken on behalf of the poor because the Islamic faith is proven in action and expressed through economic and social justice. As the message of Islam flourished in the world the plight of the poor would be eased until all were Muslims and none were impoverished. Ibn Khaldun believed that it was the duty of the Muslim state to "avail the opportunity to work to all of its able persons by promoting economic development and by educating and training people for the various vocations required in the labor market."[9] The poor must not only be helped but also helped in such a way that they were respected, which explains why the Universal Islamic Declaration of Human Rights states that "the poor have the right to a prescribed share in the wealth of the rich, as fixed by *zakat* levied and collected in accordance with the Law."[10]

While Allah entrusts some with a measure of wealth (*amanah*), what is done with those resources is the responsibility of the individual. Those believers who spend their God-given blessings on themselves will be judged accordingly on the Final Day. All economic blessings come from God and all will eventually return to God, and those who live as if this were not the case are living in a heightened state of delusion and ignorance. Those who have turned away from the poor have turned away from God's righteousness. Those who are wealthy face great temptations to become selfish and unspiritual. Greed will lead to destruction: As one Hadith explains, "Two hungry wolves let loose among a flock of sheep do not commit more damage than is caused by a person's greed for wealth and prestige to his faith."[11]

Muhammad began his own life within the throes of deep poverty. This illiterate orphan knew poverty firsthand; this experience helped him to gain a high level of sympathy for those who were poor. As a youth he did tough manual work on the caravan routes and eventually became a successful entrepreneur. In all of his business dealings the

Prophet was honest, generous and resourceful in his finances. One Hadith (metaphorically) enthused that after he married the wealthy Khadija he eventually might drive her from wealth into poverty because of his extensive generosity.[12] There is even a Hadith that says that on the Day of Judgment the Prophet will be raised "among the poor" because his open-handedness to the needy made Muhammad poor himself.[13] Many poor believers went to the Prophet's masjid where there was a dining table (*sufrah*), and were fed there by his generosity (these friends were known as "the companions of the table").[14] Many of the warriors who defended the Prophet in Medina came from the ranks of those who were poor, and their valor had a significant role in protecting the entire Muslim community at its vulnerable inception.

During the Medieval period, poverty came to be seen by some (especially the Sufi brotherhoods) as a religious ideal, and those who were devout were assumed to be more impoverished because their focus was on spiritual rewards and not on temporal benefits. Sabra writes, "For many Medieval Muslims, scholars, soldiers, and commoners, poverty was an indication of extreme piety, even a sign of being chosen by God."[15] During the Medieval era, Islamic devotional literature (almost certainly influenced by Christian sources) underscored the chosen poverty of Jesus and revealed him as an ideal to be followed by all pious Muslims because Jesus did not allow himself to be burdened down and snared by the crass, golden chains of temporary, material wealth.

Charity in Islam

The issue of poverty is central to Muslims and is discussed in the Qur'an far more than issues relating to fasting, pilgrimage, or prayer. This is because poverty fundamentally attacks the dignity of an individual: poverty dehumanizes. Because "the believers are brethren" (Q. 49:10) poverty destroys the health of a community and causes some to turn away from God.

The most frequent way that poverty is discussed in reference to Islam is in one of the five pillars of Islam — the *zakat* (or *zakah*), or wealth tax. It is a duty that all "whose hearts are being reconciled with Islam" (*muallafa al-quluh*) are required to pay if they are able to fulfill this requirement. Paying *zakat* brings one closer to Allah and to the promise of paradise, which will be bestowed on all who are generous and pious. Giving charity means that a person is making an "eternal investment" (see Q. 107:3), which will keep an individual from becoming a blind "slave of gold, silver, linen, and silk".[16] Motive is important and it is not enough to be merely sentimental or filled with pity when one gives to the poor. Charity should be given "from the heart" (*ala hubbihi*) and the practice should be encouraged among Muslim children from about the age of seven, certainly before the age of ten. An individual who does not give is seen to be immature because they are avoiding their religious and civic responsibilities.

The amount expected of each member of the community is at least 2.5% of the annual amount that one is able to save (it is not an income tax but a savings tax). Qur'an 2:177 teaches that all believers must "spend from your own wealth, in spite of your love for it, for your kin, for orphans, and for ransom of slaves, to be steadfast in prayer and practice regular charity (*zakat*)." Qur'an 2:215 confirms this command: "They asked you what they should spend in charity. Say: Whatever you spend is good, it must be for parents and relatives, and orphans, for those in want, and for wayfarers."

During the life of the Prophet, there were many individuals in Mecca and Medina who were completely destitute (*miskin*) of all economic resources. Even though the impoverished did not have regular meals or homes to live in (or even went blind from malnutrition), it was preached that they were to be seen as individuals who had been created by Allah and who were worthy of honor and dignity. Some (within the Prophet's own extended family) would even "tie stones to their stomachs to lessen the pains of hunger" so that they could give their last pieces of bread to help those who were poor.[17] This is the historical context of God's revelation to help the poor and to redistribute the wealth of those who enjoyed abundance. God called the faithful not to sell or trade their excess, but to give it away to others in need. Those who do not have any wealth actually enjoy a God-given right to share in the abundance that God has given to others (Q. 51:19; 70:24).

Generosity came to be seen as the hallmark of the faithful. The Qur'an states that those who feed the destitute (*miskin*) are "companions of the Right Hand" of God (Q. 90:13–20) and those who do not feed the poor will be confronted for their greed on the Day of Judgment (Q. 107:3; 69:34). The assertion is that many individuals do not feed the poor because they do not love the community: rather, it is money that is dearest to them. Allah in His kindness is lavishly generous to us, and when we are generous to others we advance the glory of the divine light in this dark world. Obedience to our generous and loving God is the basis for social altruism, and giving is a form of worship that honors Allah and strengthens the community. Amy Singer explains that charity in Islam is meant to be "directed toward God in intent".[18]

For a believer, duties toward the poor are not completed even when the *zakat* has been paid. The divine call to serve others in giving is intended to help create a stronger community in which mutuality is normative. Generosity builds bridges among individuals and fosters a sense of collective harmony. The act of giving a gift to another person should be handled with relational sensitivity so as not to allow those who are giving to feel that they are somehow better than those who are receiving their tokens of charity. One should be sensitive to others' needs in a giving way that may or not be monetary. A believer is encouraged to give of their resources with a generous spirit, beyond the minimum that is required. The best charity has an ongoing, as opposed to sporadic, social benefit.

Zakat differs from charity or voluntary giving (*sadaqah*) because the word itself means purification; those who are generous to the poor do not aid the poor from a position of superiority but out of an equitable sense of mutual respect. The generous person receives more from acts of kindness than those who are the recipients of generosity. Resources are to be redistributed amongst the poor as a way of cleansing the effects of economic injustice from the entire community. The motivations for alleviating the problems of the poor are fundamental to the egalitarian view of all individuals who stand on this earth equal before God. No one should become proud and, to avoid pride, Muslims are encouraged to give their gifts privately and secretly. Qur'an 2:271 explains, "If you publish your free-will offerings, it is excellent. But if you conceal your offerings, and give them to the poor, it is better for you, and will acquit you of your evil deeds; Allah is aware of the things that you do" (see also Q. 2:260–264).

Zakat is collected in some countries by the government as part of a designated tax. These countries include Yemen, Saudi Arabia, Libya, Sudan, Pakistan, and Malaysia. Seven other nations (Egypt, Jordan, Kuwait, Iran, Bangladesh, Bahrain, and Iraq) have governmental mechanisms to collect *zakat* from their citizens but it is paid on a voluntary basis. In those nations where charity is collected there also seems to be a correlative commitment on the part of those governments to take responsibility for alleviating income disparities. In Pakistan, the government redistributes funds among various local governments so that these funds can be used more effectively. Other officials, in the "National Accountability Bureau" work to ensure that the funds are not lost through corrupt misappropriations.[19] Some funds are directed to the Khushhal Pakistan Program (KPP), which was launched in the year 2000 and was designed to utilize surplus labor in rural and low-income urban areas. Still other funds are directed to microfinance programs to help small business start-ups. Among Muslims in Africa (such as Gambia and Sierra Leone), *zakat* is distributed privately to avoid opportunities for instances of corruption or nepotism.[20]

The idea of *zakat* is that the wealthy should share their resources with the poor but it is also expected that even the poorest member of society should pay a small percentage of whatever they do have, in order to help others. Only those with mental infirmities or with no resources at all do not need to pay *zakat*. One of the key reasons that everyone should pay is that each person should receive the purifying spiritual benefits that come from charity. In contrast, severe penalties will come from God for those who are greedy. Even greater reward will go to those who do not have to pay or who overpay.

Charity cannot just be given to anyone: one cannot give *zakat* to those who are rich, those to whom one is related, the family members of the Prophet, enemies of Islam, or those who are able to work through their own efforts. Allah has instituted *zakat* as a divine plan to lessen the extent of poverty among the community. Poverty is an "enormous weight" on the shoulders of the poor that should be removed from eligible recipients who are asking God for help with their dire economic circumstances.[21] One beautiful Hadith of the Prophet proclaims that the poor should guard against hellfire by their giving "even half a date", or, if one does not have even that, then at least they should "give a kind word".[22] Sometimes poor believers will donate their time to a worthy civic building project, or to some other social program, as a way of paying their offering to God and expressing their devotion and thanks to Him.

When the government collects these monies, they are often designated in many countries not only to alleviate poverty but also to assist those deeply in debt and to build masjids. Some governments have established "*zakat*" houses" to distribute the monies in a way that protects the dignity of recipients. Monies are sometimes directed to recent converts as compensation for their sufferings or even to prospective converts (*al-muallafa qulubuhum*). *Zakat* must be paid at least once a year and its payment is a prerequisite for going to the bliss of paradise.[23] In addition to paying one's alms, believers are encouraged to give additional charity (*sadaqah*) to the beggars who often congregate around houses of prayer before and after times of worship.[24] Hopfe writes that, because of the emphasis in Islam on the obligation of alms-giving, believers have never looked upon beggars as being dishonorable individuals. Beggars have an accepted function to play in society because the "receiving as well as the giving of alms is considered a source of God's blessing."

One of the largest Muslim charities worldwide is the International Red Crescent Society (IRCS). This non-sectarian relief organization was founded in 1932 in conjunction with the efforts of the International Red Cross. The IRCS has often worked closely with numerous United Nations charitable efforts (e.g., WHO, UNICEF, UNHCR) in a wide range of efforts, from providing artificial limbs and wheelchairs to drilling wells and helping refugees in wars or local ethnic conflicts.

Muslims in the United Kingdom, for example, often support the efforts of Islamic Relief Worldwide (IRW), which is based in Birmingham (since 1984) but active worldwide. The IRW has been at the forefront of a number of relief efforts after a series of devastating earthquakes (such as the October 5, 2005, 7.6 magnitude earthquake in Kashmir) destroyed countless villages across South Asia.[25] The IRW has also worked to help those caught in the northern Malian Civil War (1990–2013) even though their efforts have brought their staff into contexts of great personal danger.

Charity for Orphans

Orphans (*yatim*) are mentioned 23 times in the Qur'an. Although they are the most economically dependent individuals within any community, Allah, in infinite wisdom, chose the Prophet from among the ranks of those who had been orphaned (Q. 93:6–9). First, Muhammad's paternal grandfather, the leader of the Hashim clan, took responsibility for the youth. Later this guardianship was passed on to his uncle Abu Talib. Later in life, the Prophet adopted (*tabana* — a fictive relationship) an orphan named Zayd ibn Haritha (changed from ibn Muhammad after his divorce, see Q. 33:37).[26]

A wide array of circumstances led to children becoming orphans, with many children being orphaned during times of war. Children orphaned because of the battles of Badr and Uhud merited particular attention in the Qur'an. All references to orphans in the Qur'an refer to fatherless children below the age of puberty and not to parentless children because ancient cultural concepts do not completely correlate with modern understandings.[27] The expectation would be that defenseless children would be cared for by relatives and would in turn be seen as equal to any other child, with identical rights of inheritance and responsibilities to care for their elderly parents as well as all financial benefits (Q. 8:41; 59:7). If no family was available then the child would be entrusted to the "foster care" (Islamic tutelage, *kafala*) of a guardian who would not claim, as was the case in pre-Islamic Arabia, that the child was an actual relation through a fictitious bond.[28] Those who fail to take financial care of the orphans in their charge risk the fires of hell (Q. 4:2–10; also 2:220 and 17:34).

Early Islamic understandings of adoption mirrored the practices of Jews and Christians.[29] Over time, institutions were created that presage the modern concept of an orphanage. The first Muslim "orphanages" were actually primary schools. In our modern era of social systemization and centralized governance, more frequently Muslim states have taken on responsibilities for orphan care. In Egypt, for example, the Regional Foster Care Committee under the direction of the Administration for Children and Families finds foster parents and provides financial support for orphans until some familial connections can be identified. Generally speaking, these same nation states tend to scorn international adoption programs because of the conviction that Muslim children should, first and foremost, be raised by fellow believers.

There are also many informal and cultural alternatives to adoption such as "gifting" children to infertile couples or "secret adoptions" of abandoned children. Sadly, some abandoned children become vulnerable to abusive exploitation as cheap labor or sex slaves, while other orphans avoid these oppressions by choosing to live on the streets. The problems that many orphans face are identical with the problems of others who live in abject poverty. There is a direct correlation between the level of poverty in an area with the number of orphaned children. While the Muslim tradition has done much to protect orphans, there are also many injustices against these children that remain unresolved.

Wealth in Islam

Some of the wealthiest nations on the earth are those Muslim-majority nations, such as Qatar, that are rich with oil resources. Qatar, with an average income of $67,000 (2011), has the fifth highest per-capita income in the world. Saudi Arabia, well known in the world for its opulent palaces and lavishly-spending princely rulers, has a per-capita income ($21,062), which is only a third of that of Qatar.[30] These wealthy realms dramatically contrast with Muslim-majority nations such as Somalia, Bangladesh, and Afghanistan, which are some of the world's poorest countries.

What is the Islamic view of wealth (*mal*, plural *amwal*)? Allah is wealthy (*ghina*) beyond compare and graciously dispenses the bounties of heavenly wealth to humanity. Humans desperately need God, while God does not need us (Q. 35:15); Allah is independent of the created order (Q. 29:6). God combines bestowed wealth with mercy (Q. 6:133) to satisfy human needs (Q. 53:48). Those who "loan to Allah" will find it doubled to their credit (Q. 64:15–17). God gives wealth to individuals from the divine surplus, but wealth can turn people away from God (Q. 8:36; 10:88; 17:18). This is the implication of the Hadith: "Ruined is the slave of the silver coin." Wealth has the power to corrupt and must be "cleansed" by giving *zakat*. Further, individuals should never squander their wealth (Q. 2:188; 4:29). It should be used for God's glory. Wealth is useless on the Day of Judgment (Q. 15:84; 69:28; 92:11; 111:1–2). In eternity, it will be people of piety who will be regarded as having great wealth.

Muhammad spent many years of his life as a prosperous and successful businessman. The Prophet was a man who always worked hard and honorably, receiving a just economic reward for his labors (Q. 39:10). This focus on economics in the life of the Prophet is sometimes presented in contrast to the abject poverty of Jesus. The Islamic tradition notes that Muhammad, like Jesus, came into this world in poverty and "will be raised on the Day of Judgment among the poor."[31] Before his teaching ministry, Jesus was a skilled craftsman who worked in a small Palestinian carpentry business. For Muslims, the example of both Muhammad and Jesus is a call to be diligent in work but also to be frugal with one's earnings. One Hadith recounts the simple lifestyle of the Prophet and his desire to seek wealth in the world to come. This contrasts with the widespread pejorative view of some non-Muslim critics that Muslim cultures encourage economic oppression.

Globalized Economic Injustice

Islam is able to cut with scythe-like precision through the specter of contemporary global materialism. The faith offers an alternative to the frightening, indifferent coldness of our calculating and impersonal, dog-eat-dog economic *milieu*. Farid Esack argues that "modern capitalism is born from entrenched selfishness . . . our struggle to establish it (Islam) is as much a struggle against uncaring and unjust socio-economic systems as it is a struggle against *nafs* (lower self)."[32] Islam is able to identify the alienation inherent in unjust economic structures and direct these urges toward a God-ordained solution. The Islamic message provides a secure harbor from economic oppression. It not only affirms the widespread nature of the problem, but also offers a series of concrete solutions (such as *zakat*), which address issues relating to economic injustice.

Islam asks of believers the salient questions: "How do we become witness bearers for Allah in an economically unjust society? How do we strengthen ourselves in a common commitment to establish a just economic order on earth?"[33] Qur'an 59:9 preaches: "They (Muslims) prefer others above themselves, though poverty becomes their lot." Each of us should choose to suffer ourselves, if, in so doing, we can ease the poverty of another brother or sister. One noted Hadith confirms this priority: once, a person came to Muhammad complaining of hunger. A follower of the Prophet stepped forward and offered to take the man to his house for dinner even though he barely had any food in his own home. When he came home he took his wife aside and explained to her their problem: "Look, I have invited this man to come to our home as a guest of the Prophet. We must entertain him as best as we can and not spare anything in doing so." The wife was perplexed because she had no food in the house except for a small portion for each of her children. They couple decided to lull their children to sleep without feeding them and then sit with the guest and provide him with the best meal possible, given their resources. They planned that, when they sat with the guest, they would dim the lights of the room so that the guest would not be able to see that the host and the wife were not actually eating with him. Their plan worked as hoped: the children went to sleep hungry and the guest was able to eat a satisfying meal.[34]

One of the lessons of this story is that we should completely identify with those among us who are suffering in poverty. Empathy brings empowerment to the plight of the poor and helps to ease their many problems. As long as one of us has something to give we cannot be content that another brother or sister has nothing to eat. Addressing poverty, then, is not heroic but obligatory and appropriate for every believer. It is one way for a devout believer to make sane the insane and unjust economic realities of our age.

Economic Inequalities

Class divisions are evident throughout the modern world and one can see their presence clearly in a host of cultural practices and even in daily greetings. Some Arabs, for example, will feel free to cut into a line of people instead of queuing because they feel that their status gives them this privilege. All of these practices, however, have no connection to Islam, which repeatedly stresses that all believers should see each other as equal in the eyes of God (Q. 6:155). Allah shows special favor to all who act equitably (Q.60:8; 4:127).

Islamic tradition does not have a parallel with the phrase of Jesus: "the poor you will have with you always" (Mark 14:7), a verse which some have taken out of context from the book of Deuteronomy in which there are many clear injunctions to aid the poor. Some Christians have used such passages about the poor to convince themselves that the economic state of the poor is God's will and should not be contested. For Islam, poverty is not reasonable, or something to be accepted, without contestation. There can be no ambivalence or acceptance regarding the presence of poverty within a given Muslim community.

When making a pilgrimage to the holy cities, the devout believer wears the simple *ihram*, a loose fitting cotton wrapping worn by rich and poor alike. The choice of these clothes communicates, in vivid clarity, the fact that, before Allah, all men and women are equal in worth and status. Qur'an 107 states that an individual who rejects the faith will probably also be one who is "rough to the orphan" and who "does not encourage the feeding of the poor". One cannot claim to be a devout believer while at the same time ignoring the plight of those who are facing financial misfortune.

Ideals are not realities: government policies throughout many Muslim-majority nations, sadly, often foster increased poverty. Many businesses are not required by law to pay a fair wage for the labor of their workers. This is a form of robbery that occurs with the consent of a given political process. Individuals battling poverty often feel powerless and vulnerable in society. The poor are at the margins of the social order: lacking good health care and decent homes, they lead lives which may often spiral into crippling devastation. Disease and starvation sometimes take root and prematurely rob individuals of their lives. God's revelation is that poverty is not something to be accepted as inevitable but a man-made tragedy to be eliminated. It is not God's will and will not exist in paradise: the very social structures that create (and then foster) poverty are not of God. In fact, because all material wealth belongs to Allah, we must be stewards of all that we have and will be judged for our use of our material wealth (Q. 2:276–282; 2:129). The "end" will never justify unjust "means". There is no path that a person can live in life that will please Allah if it does not include charity towards those who are poor (Q. 3:92).

Islamic Economic Practices

The broad ethics and values of Islam provide believers with both general and specific guidelines for their business practices. In addition to the teachings of the Qur'an and the Hadith of the Prophet there are also a host of commentaries (such as the *Kitab al-Kasb* or "Book of Acquisition") on Islamic economic life that are often discussed in relation to the development of legal codes within various countries. Most importantly, Islam gives complete freedom to almost all forms of righteous economic enterprise. Any individual is free to start, manage, organize, and run any kind of business that is moral and lawful. Even though Islam encourages free markets it has also developed certain restraints in order to check malpractices and unjust efforts that do not promote fairness and civility.

A central tenet of Islamic economic philosophy is the prohibition against interest (*riba*) or extra sums that moneylenders might charge borrowers for deferred payments, usury. Throughout history and in various contexts, however, there have been widely differing views about how this prohibition should be interpreted. What often happens is that a borrower is charged a straightforward flat fee and not a percentage rate. Some Muslims have felt that this historic system disadvantages them in international speculative markets (*al-gharar* — a commodity which is not present at hand), price-fixing, and other practices, which sometimes cause business people to miss certain short-term economic opportunities. All Muslims, however, are in agreement that these guidelines are clearly designed by Allah to protect the community and especially the poorest of the poor.

Business dealings must be carried out by trustworthy people who do not lie to each other. Those who are unjust forfeit eternal blessings for temporary profit and will be judged by God for their misdeeds. All contracts and promises must be fulfilled. One person cannot take advantage of the ignorance of a buyer or partner through efforts of "trickery" (*al-najsh*) or fraud of any kind. Weights and measures must be fair and stolen goods cannot be knowingly resold. Employers must be fair to their employees and provide good working conditions. People are often exploited in morally dubious situations by opportunistic economic predators (Q. 2:275). It is forbidden, for example, to charge a higher price to a person who is in a vulnerable situation. The assumption is that the poor will become victims of those who have the ability to charge interest, as they are able to lend surplus capital. Those in debt should be treated with leniency (Q. 2:280).

What is interesting to a non-Muslim is how these micro-economic issues are considered to be connected to macro-economic realities. Macro-economic issues are usually the concerns of governments, but Islam teaches that the larger community will not succeed if individuals do not honor Allah at the grassroots level. There is a Keynesian ring, for example, to the Qur'anic admonition against hoarding finances (Q. 9:34). Believers are encouraged to spend their money and, thus, distribute their wealth into the community (Q. 2:254). Believers should recognize that they have a duty to be generous (Q. 2:267) and discreet or secretive in their giving (Q. 2:271).

Since gambling (*qimar*) is forbidden, it follows that all speculative economic ventures such as stock-trading are also prohibited. Risk-sharing (insurance, *murabahah*) instead of risk-taking is the Islamic economic ideal. If economic policies such as the prohibition against usury, the giving of *zakat*, and the honoring of those who experience poverty are enacted, then entire economic pictures will brighten. It is as if God will reward those who are "faithful with a little" with greater rewards on a larger scale.

Poverty in Pakistan

Pakistan is a country in which poverty is endemic and which is cursed with a volatile economic situation marked by a very high annual inflation rate (15% in 2013). Even though many are poor in the nation, the government continues to build its nuclear arsenal and strengthen the ranks of its huge military. Vast political and ethno-religious tensions in the country seem to dwarf issues of poverty. On the bright side, the government has sponsored a number of programs designed to help those suffering in poverty but the Pakistani government itself is limited as to what it can do because it is crippled with huge debts. Meritorious government "poverty reduction strategies" include public work programs, micro-financing to generate loans, and governmental reform to guard against corruption ("misappropriation") and bribery.[35] The Pakistani government has also launched a number of job programs in numerous poor villages where there is little industrial production. Commendable efforts have been made to reform legal systems by "creating greater checks and balances to put an end to the often reported cases of police harassment of the poor and less influential people."[36]

In rural Pakistan, there are a number of developmental relief organizations, such as the (previously mentioned) Islamic Relief Worldwide (IRW), which are working among the poorest people. This development agency has been active since an earthquake led to the deaths of over 70,000 Pakistanis on October 5, 2005. Since 2008, the IRW has launched a number of water-development projects designed to help drought-afflicted regions such as Baluchistan. Until economic programs, which are designed to address economic injustices in Pakistan, begin to take root, the attraction to militant organizations such as *Lashkar e-Taiba* will continue to grow among impoverished villagers. Worldwide, as well as in contexts such as Pakistan, it is essential to appreciate how these kinds of economic development programs — framed by Islamic social ideals — relate to contexts in which religious and political voices are becoming increasingly polarizing and strident.

Rampant Poverty

Social structures that create and institutionalize poverty breed deeply-felt alienation. Capitalist structures that emphasize self-interests (according to Sayyid Qutb and others) also increase the growing gap between the rich and the poor. Those bound in the heavy chains of poverty cannot easily lift themselves into any kind of stability because their daily struggles demand so much. Many of the impoverished within Muslim countries ultimately find solace in various emphatic militant organizations. Those battling poverty feel frustrated when they realize that they are receiving no help from those who are more privileged within their societies. In Palestine, for example, the desperate living conditions in refugee camps, urban slums, and economically lethargic villages have become dynamic contexts which "easily foster suicide bombers", because poverty-stricken families are offered financial support after one of their family members chooses to serve God in holy martyrdom.[37]

This raises an oft-repeated question: "What is the connection between poverty and militant movements?" Islamism has been described as, "in essence a revolt of the poor."[38] The oppressed find solace in the purposefulness and promise of a militant, self-reflexive extremist identity. Noorani explains that "the poverty belts around the big cities became a natural breeding ground for militant, anti-elitist, anti-Western views of Islam."[39] The former President of Turkey, Suleyman Demirel (b. 1924), warned that "as long as there is poverty, injustice, and repressive political systems, militant Islamic tendencies will grow in the world."[40] One Hamas leader in Gaza, Mahmoud al-Zahar (b. 1945), stated: "It is enough to see the poverty stricken outskirts of Algiers or the refugee camps in Gaza to understand the factors that nurture the strength of the Islamic Resistance Movement."[41] These leaders note that many of the early Muslim soldiers who defended the Prophet at the Battle of Badr (and in other points of crisis) came from poor villages and were able to defeat the "self-inflated and rich" soldiers of commercially-wealthy Mecca.[42] Both domestic policies and international aid organizations should make the rectification of economic injustice the highest priority that they have in the larger war of supporting moderate influences that are seeking to blunt the strident voices of extremism.

Partnerships for Economic Justice

Faith-based communities can effectively address economic injustice with faith-based solutions and the promotion of a socially-popular, God-centered perspective. Muslims look to the generous example of Muhammad, who championed the sufferings of those who were impoverished. Jews note that their scriptures have abundant references to God's call that the entire community should see themselves as responsible to care for those who are unfortunate within their midst. Christians can embrace the poverty of Jesus and the communitarian example of the early Christian church, about which it was said that "all the believers were together and held everything in common" (Acts 2:44). Each tradition equates the fostering of vibrant communities with the practice of sensitive generosity toward those who are confronting poverty. When individuals in these traditions follow God with piety, they will not be able to tolerate poverty in any measure.

While non-Muslim and Muslim understandings of human development differ, all faith traditions share a great deal of common ground in addressing the many related issues of poverty. This means that both Muslims and non-Muslims should be able to partner together to reduce poverty. Sub-Saharan Africa, for example, is an urgent context in which joint-action between Muslim and non-Muslim development agencies can make a vital difference. Catastrophic poverty is so widespread in many sub-Saharan African settings that it is assumed by many to be an inevitable fact of life. In Northern Nigeria, for example, some Muslims fear that partnering with Christian-based aid organizations will threaten the social cohesion and specifically Islamic quality of their communities. Even though poverty has no respect for persons or religious identity, the issue of "who gets the credit or who gets the blame" means that there are, at present, very few Muslim and non-Muslim partnerships in Northern Nigeria that jointly address economic injustices.

In Islam, as in other faith traditions, Allah calls followers to address the plight of the poor and to remember that all individuals have an inherent dignity and will stand as equals on the Final Day. The dream of alleviating poverty — birthed by the revelation of the Qur'an and exemplified by the efforts of the Prophet — must ultimately be brought to fruition at every local level of the *ummah*. It is un-Islamic to see poverty and not to respond with charity (Q. 4:8; 107:4–7; 42:39; 4:135). Vibrant economic policies rooted in Islamic values will address the cultivation of "spiritual needs alongside of material needs".[43]

Believers are encouraged to modestly and progressively increase wealth for themselves and for their families, while not forgetting others who are less fortunate. Islam teaches that the over-riding goal of local and national economic policy should be a fundamental sense of fairness. Moderate economic inequities may be seen as inevitable, but extreme disparities in wealth cannot be accepted as God's intention. Muslims and non-Muslims should continue to prioritize the local, national, and international fight against poverty and work together to find new ways to alleviate economic injustice. While some positive efforts have been launched, they are far too infrequent. Al-Ghazali defined poverty as the "absence of what is needed"; there are still many believers who lack basic financial security and economic justice.[44] Ashgar Ali Engineer states that at the heart of the Islamic vision is the "concept of a society which is free of exploitation, oppression, domination, and economic injustice in any form".[45] It is still the case, as Jewish, Muslim, and Christian Liberationist theologians remind us, that people of faith must "choose solidarity" with the marginalized as a reflection of spiritual integrity.[46]

4. Islamic Responses to Political Oppression

If there is a failing of Islamic societies much more centrally relevant to the theme of tolerance than some offending verses in the Qur'an, it is this sustained absence of democratic mobilization; and at least some of the responsibility for this failing lies with the historical and contemporary influence of Europe and the United States, first by their colonial and then by their corporate presence in these Muslim nations.

— Akeel Bilgrami

The oppressor will not be helped by God.

— Moroccan Proverb

"Help your brother whether he is an oppressor or whether he is oppressed." *People asked, "it is right if we help one who is oppressed but how shall we help him if he is an oppressor?" The Prophet answered, "By preventing him from oppressing others".*

— Hadith, Sahih al-Bukhari

Confronting Political Oppression

Political oppression can be defined as subjugating, limiting, persecuting, or restricting any individual by any unjust use of force for political reasons, particularly for the purposes of restricting or preventing their ability to take part in political life.[1] For example, African-Americans after the American Civil War faced a plethora of unjust ("Jim Crow") laws that limited their political freedoms; leaving them vulnerable to further oppression; without viable representation in civic society. There are also countless examples of political oppression that one can observe throughout the Muslim world.

The first Muslim community came into existence at a time when most political organizations were ruthlessly cruel, yet the message of the Prophet Muhammad actively opposed political oppression. Qur'an 49:9 challenges that governments should rule with justice and equality for all individuals — whether they are slave or free, man or woman, orphaned or wealthy. Whenever the Prophet faced political opponents, he dealt with them with mercy and patience (see Q. 21:107) because he was beholden to a vision of social justice that incorporated every strand of civic society under God's rule. The Prophet's warm and gracious openness towards those who differed with him (or even opposed him) contrasts vividly with those extremists who issue *fatwas* and curse their opponents, praying for their destruction with no regard for the overarching maintenance of civic unity and the fostering of a socially cohesive harmony.

Political oppression assumes many insidious forms and is rarely blatant or easily identifiable. Individuals frequently find themselves denied due process of law and faced with no other promising option but to deal with political corruption and nepotism. Government policies and programs can also be agents that — directly or indirectly — engender countless forms of social injustice. In South Africa, for example, money was historically allocated for the education of Afrikaner or English children but was denied to dark-skinned African children. The pious and privileged often observe those who are politically oppressed from the comfortable vantage point of societal influence. Christians in Europe and North America and Muslims in many Middle Eastern nations constitute majority populations who live within societies that cater to their own preferences, assumed perspectives, and comforting inclinations. Adherents of these traditions, then, ought to force their constituencies to confront the broad extent of political oppression wherever it is found.

The Political Dimensions of Islam

Muslim communities are conversant with a foundational conviction inherent in the Qur'an and the example of the Prophet that the practice of one's faith has clear societal and political ramifications. Civic powers exist within the context of a higher spiritual duty to obey God's commands and to submit to the divine Lordship as the highest authority. When a community is united in a desire to submit to Allah's perfect will in their lives, oppression will not be able to take root and flourish. Political oppression can never be accepted as an expression of God's perfect will. Islam supports a theocratic form of democracy that promotes consultation (*shurah*) as the way to foster a balance between individual (or minority) needs and the wishes of the ruling majority. Political oppression arises from the greed and insecurity of those who rebel against Allah's revelation and deny the clear commands of God's perfect will. The Qur'an explains that it can never be stated that it is God's will that any soul should be wronged (Q. 45:22).

Social cohesion "is the paramount political goal of Islam".[2] This is a basic starting point for understanding political rights and for appreciating how these rights relate to curbing instances of political oppression. The community (*ummah*) is the collective cultural and religious identity, which determines the shape of political life for every individual within the Muslim world. Rights are dynamically linked to responsibilities (duties) and the corporate interests of any Muslim society are always more compelling than any individual claim to some autonomous right or privilege. This helps to clarify (but not to justify) why there are often a significant number of political prisoners in a number of Islamic states. The vision for an ideal political state reflects the oneness (*tawhid*) of God. Political action is the outworking of Allah's perfect will on the earth and among the faithful. Of course, this ideal is rarely (if ever) put into actual practice due to the selfish ambitions of those who reject God's truth.

The term "consultation" (*shurah*) is a key phrase that should be appreciated by those seeking to grasp the foundational ideals of many Islamic political views about democracy. The widespread usage of the term implies that it is consultation specifically with Muslim leaders, scholars and clerics (*ulama*, Persian *ulema*). In Saudi Arabia, for example, the royal family has turned to the *ulama* repeatedly through consultation to reassert their own political authority. Since there is no "secular" law within Saudi Arabia, these same religious figures are called upon to serve as the functionaries of the judicial branch of government. A consultative council called the *Majlis ash-Shura* functions as a pseudo-parliamentary body in Saudi Arabia that advises the King, but is fundamentally different from the religious consultative council (*shurah*).

Individual Rights and Corporate Harmony

One factor that has complicated Islamic response to political oppression is the strong conviction (advocated in the Qur'an) that individuals should never presume to rebel against their political and religious leaders. Muslims are called to unerringly "obey Allah and obey the Apostle and those charged with authority among you" (Q. 4:59). It assumed in most (if not all) cases that God has established every state and each leader. In an ideal situation, an individual Muslim should be loyal to the God-ordained state without question. Throughout history, those who have wanted to frame unquestioning political and religious loyalty in the power of God's word have cited Qur'an 10:59: "Did you note how God sends down to you all kinds of provisions, then you render some of them lawful and some of them unlawful? Say, did God give you permission to do this? Or do you fabricate lies and attribute them to God?" Those who diligently follow Allah's revealed law cannot arbitrarily pick and choose those divine laws that they intend to obey.

God is the source of the law and all authorities (Q. 6:114). An individual living in a non-Muslim State must obey Allah's laws above the mandates of those who are not enlightened by the truth of Islam (see Q. 6:114; 1:2; 7:185; 17:36). Those individuals who are rebellious should expect divine punishment (Q. 85:10). Those who willingly submit to their God-appointed Muslim rulers will receive a heavenly reward (Q.

33:35). Those rulers who are unjust and corrupt will ultimately be dealt with by Allah's certain justice on the Final Day. The right to rebuke a political leader, some have argued from scripture, is reserved for God alone, even if a ruler is extremely unjust (see Q. 58:8–9).[3]

The *ummah* anchors individuals in support, affirmation, and inspiration. Prayers and rituals that support the *ummah* are recited in unison. Every believer who meets another believer is actually meeting their God-given sister or brother. As in a family (*al-nas*), brothers and sisters are obligated to share one another's burdens and joys. This need not be (as often presented in the Western media) a controlling, stifling, or suffocating dynamic. The family of faith — at its best — is a place of mutual nurture and helpful, sensitive encouragement, and is able to transcend economic or cultural limitations. When one feels lost or doubtful within the *dar al-Islam*, all one need do is look around oneself and draw on the readily available and supportive strength from the caring family of faith.

Dealing with Dissent

Some leaders within the Muslim world, beginning with the Umayyad Dynasty, have promoted a quietist approach (of submitting without question) by citing the Islamic doctrine of "compulsion" (*jabr*). God created humanity and knows what is best for human beings within any given situation. Since Allah is sovereign, the status quo is an expression of the divine will and, in this regard, "the question of human responsibility is irrelevant."[4] Tenth-century Hanbali jurist and scholar Ibn Battah (916–997) preached: "You must therefore abstain and refrain from sedition (*fitnah*). You must not rise in arms against Imams even if they be unjust.... If he oppresses you, be patient; if he dispossesses you then be patient."[5]

There are also noted critics of this view: Muslims throughout history have contested quietist, passive views and have advocated for an activist approach to dealing with unjust rulers. Ibn Tayib al-Baqelani (d. 1013) preached that it was the duty of the *ummah* to depose from power any leader who was godless and wicked.[6] Instead of the doctrine of "compulsion" (*jabr*), some scholars and political commentators have promoted the idea of spiritual and holy power (*qadar*), which is able to trump all forms of political injustice. Allah gave humanity power and expects it to be used in a proper way, as a means of stewardship within society that promotes equanimity and justice. One of the passages supporting this view is Qur'an 42:41–42, which calls on Muslims to "defend themselves after a wrong done to them". One Hadith further underlines this view when it asserts: "It is obligatory for a Muslim that he should listen to the ruler appointed over him and obey him, whether he likes it or not, except that he is ordered to do a sinful thing. If he is ordered to do a sinful act, a Muslim should neither listen to him nor should he obey his orders."[7] For activist Muslims, political legitimacy springs from faithfulness to the Qur'anic revelation (and other traditions) and is not simply based on title or position.

Islamists and Wahhabist/Salafist fundamentalists have described *shurah* as the ideal understanding of politics and governance amongst Muslims. They refer to the views of Ibn Taymiyyah (1260–1327) who taught that, while the leader is bound to respond to "consultation" in order to implement the divine law, the community is responsible to support the government in upholding the divine law. This is the quietist position, according to which Muslims owe obedience to any state if that state institutes *shariah*, but the position should revert to one of activism whenever Islamic law is being challenged.

Cynics say that politics is fundamentally a dirty game that eventually devolves into some form of oppression. This is not the view of Islamic revelation: Islam cannot stand on the sidelines and watch oppression develop. Islam has always been both a religion and a polity. The Qur'an tells numerous stories in which oppressive leaders, such as Pharaoh (who is challenged by Moses), are confronted by the truth of God's way. Implicit within Islam's historical political tradition is the idea that individuals can know their role and proper function within an orderly political society. Both ruler and subject are completely able to grasp their specific and distinct social responsibilities. Any ruler in a Muslim society who does not publicly reject Islamic law should be assumed to be legitimate.[8] This, unfortunately, may open the doors for some oppressive leaders to flourish without being aggressively challenged as long as they claim to be Muslims.

The Qur'an proclaims that rulers are obligated to deal justly and should never be harsh or insensitive to their subjects (Q. 2:270, see also Q. 3:159). God, however, is responsible for addressing injustices and will do just that on the Final Day of Judgment. On that day, rulers will be judged as to whether or not they have always spoken the truth with directness. This is key because political oppression is often based on manipulative language and phraseology — a kind of abusive verbal injustice — which is particularly reprehensible in Islam. The tool of deceptive rhetoric, including the use of deliberate falsehoods to advance political aims, is completely unacceptable within a pious Muslim context.

Political instability invariably creates a wide range of problems. Rampant anarchy increases tensions and anguish for all citizens. The group dynamics of widespread fear and crippling suspicion thrive in the deep soil of unchallenged political oppression. Order and peace are required to help individuals and communities carry out their lives of faithful worship and consistent obedience to Allah as mandated. The *ummah* should be a place of clarity and safety, acceptance, and toleration, within the context of a shared unity of faith and vision. The *ummah* expresses and reinforces Islamic unity on a social plane, and its ultimate civic goal is widespread social justice for the greater glory of God.

Democracy and Islam

How do such fundamental social values relate to the prospects for the promotion of democracy within a Muslim context? In this discussion we need to be clear, as Joseph R. Gusfield proved decades ago, that the so-called "traditional societies" of the Muslim world have never been static societies.[9] In the past, orientalist perspectives on Islamic cultures have glossed over various social particulars in the creation of a skewed metanarrative, which presents a despotic Islam as inherently and inevitably undemocratic. Bernard Lewis, for example, speaking of the Arab world explained to an American audience: "They are simply not ready for free and fair elections." In response to this statement Deepa Kumar sighed: "Even in the twenty-first century, the natives, the unwashed masses still don't know better. Their systematic organizing and Twitter-based publicity for free elections, more political parties, and greater political freedom are best ignored."[10] Issues of modernity and hierarchical tradition are sometimes presented by orientalists as polar opposites instead of as prismatic and mutually inter-related dynamics across a wide range of ever-changing and distinct social contexts. Tunisian scholar Labri Sadiki asserts that, actually, "modernization can be said to reify the more traditional social forces. The resilience of Islam is not necessarily the result of incongruence with modernization so much as it is of interaction with it."[11]

Democracy is a widely contested term that is variously defined by both Muslims and non-Muslims who are trying to make sense of what they regard as the widespread extent of political oppression among a number of Muslim-majority nations. There are, of course, many different, contextualized forms of democratic systems. Reduced to its most basic sense, Europeans and North Americans usually use the term "democracy" to describe the representative-facilitated rule of the people — the majority and not only the elite.

Extremists sometimes challenge the foundational assumption of this definition. Does the democratic promotion of toleration conflict with the conviction that a Muslim state should be ruled by Muslims and with distinctly Muslim laws? Or, to frame the question another way: do democratic values shift the sphere of political influence from the religious to the secular? Militants allege that all forms of democracy are inherently secular. It is their claim that the very concept of democracy rules out the theocratic reign of God and God-ordained leaders and functions as a secular religion in its own right. The Jordanian-born Salafist Abu Muhammad al-Maqdisi (b. 1959) wrote: "Democracy is denying Allah the Almighty, associating other deities with Allah and is contrary to the religion of unity. . . . Democracy is legislated by the masses or the regime of tyrants and is not instituted by Allah. . . . Democracy is the vile fruit and the illegitimate daughter of secularism."[12] Extremists assert that there can ultimately be no such thing as an Islamic democracy.

One of the reasons that the legitimacy of democracy is so bitterly contested among extremists is that Islamic history has shown that distinct political standards should apply unevenly to various groups of people, as they believe with God's blessing. Believers under Muslim rule; believers under non-Muslim rule; and non-believers under Muslim rule, are all treated separately within the divine revelation and this has ramifications for political theory and practice. The very notion that religious preference should so dramatically affect social standing runs counter to most European and North American views about democracy, which stress individual (and minority) equality instead of social equanimity in spite of religious affiliation.

Toleration and Plurality

The first Arab Muslim community sprang up in a very distinct tribal context. The formation of the Islamic *ummah* was actually the gradual creation of an entirely new tribal group. How does this tribalistic foundation relate to the modern search for fresh political models that are both Islamic and democratic? One of the most compelling values of a democratic society, it is widely assumed, is a high degree of toleration for political and cultural difference. On this front, it is helpful to stress that there is no inherent reason why a Muslim society should be less amenable to promoting civic tolerance than any other kind of political framework. Speaking of efforts to promote democracy in Indonesia, Pramano U. Tanthhowi underscored the importance of toleration by stating:

> Sustainable democracy can develop only within a fully tolerant society where harmonious interfaith relationships become the groundwork for the people's own existence. Within an extremely pluralistic nation like Indonesia, real democracy will be able to survive only if pluralism becomes a *raison d'etre* for an imagined community called the nation of Indonesia.[13]

Advocates for democracy within a Muslim context do not believe that a society governed by values of toleration and plurality conflict with fundamental Islamic values. Islamic democracy, as it is envisioned in contexts such as modern Indonesia, is capable of promoting the plural interests of a diverse community even as it also submits to God's rule and promotes divine law (*shariah*). In fact, democracy may be the best political path in the promotion of the Islamic vision to work to enhance mercy to all humanity (*rahmatilil alamin*), free from any forms of unjust exclusion. It can be argued that because Islam teaches that Allah expects governments to care for their citizens and confront injustices, a democratic model becomes an Islamic ideal. Without justice, in the Islamic vision, there can be no genuine democracy. As the word *Muslim* means one who submits to God's ways, an unjust tyrant is in opposition to God's perfect will. All believers, including political leaders, are accountable and must "submit" (give up) their own will before God's perfect will in order to create a truly Islamic democracy.

The Rights of Non-Muslims

In every expression of political concern within any given Muslim context, the *ummah* is seen to be affirmed as central. This raises obvious questions about the role of Muslims under non-Muslim governments. In effect, according to extremists, the faithful are obligated to rebel against any political authority until *shariah* is established. Mawdudi (or Maududi), whom we have already discussed, holds to these views as the basis for his call for *jihad* against all non-Muslim states. The President of the *Middle East Forum* and editor of the *Middle East Journal*, Daniel Pipes (b. 1949), who is often accused of stressing to his readers the most strident view imaginable as normative, claims that "Muslims living in *dar al-harb* can either break away from their rulers or overthrow them."[14] For the good of all humanity, extremists believe, there is no option for accommodation. All believers are required to actively resist the "modern *jahiliyya* of the West".[15] Sayyid Qutb adds that even Muslim governments that are not enforcing *shariah* are, by definition, practising rakish political oppression and should be overthrown for God's greater glory.

Qur'anic Leadership Principles

One of the central issues related to political oppression is the fact that citizens are not treated with dignity and respect under authoritarian rule. The social equality that all humans share as brothers and sisters is a sign of Allah's work within the world (Q. 30:22). The Qur'an teaches that even the angels of heaven bow down before human beings (Q. 2:30–33), and, thus, all human beings should be free from any form of political oppression. The Qur'an mandates that when this respect is withheld, it is incumbent upon an individual to correct the situation him/herself: "For each one human there are angels one following another, before and behind him: they guard him by the command of Allah. Surely Allah will not change the condition of a people until they change it themselves. But when Allah wills a punishment for a people there is no holding back; nor will they find any other than Him to protect them" (Q. 13:11). The politically oppressed should first demonstrate a determination to seek justice from God. As Qur'an 42:39 explains, "those who, when grave wrong is inflicted on them, are not afraid but defend themselves" will see God's assistance. Qur'an 4:75 wonders, "What is wrong with you believers? Why do you not fight in the cause of Allah, for those fellow-believers who are weak, the ill-treated and the oppressed?" Believers are required without question to defend other oppressed believers from the tentacled scourges of political oppression.

The Qur'an rings clear: only those who are devout believers should serve as leaders (*khalifa*) over the affairs of the community (Q. 18:28) and the leaders in turn should not seek their own interests, but are required to attend first and foremost to the needs of the entire *ummah*. These leaders will promote freedom because God opposes "force or compulsion in religion" (Q. 2:256, see also 18:29). Qur'an 6:114 explains, "Shall I try to find a judge other than Allah? When it is He who sent you the book and explained in detail." Because Allah has provided the transforming gift of the Holy Qur'an as a divine revelation, it is to be followed without question as the highest and purest law.

Contrasting Views about Islam and Governance

Does the Qur'an advocate one specific form of government? Is it not more accurate to say that God's revelation actually only provides ethical guidelines that can relate to any form of government? This was the view of the Egyptian reformist scholar Ali Abd al-Raziq (1887–1966) who was strongly influenced by the writings of the great intellectual Muhammad Abduh (1849–1905) and the Syrian Muhammad Rashid Rida (1865–1935). Al-Raziq was a controversial writer and teacher who is sometimes called the father of Islamic political secularism. It was his argument that all governments should be seen to be rooted (*asala*) in the pedestrian imaginations of human beings; there was no specific divine imperative as to what kind of government should rule over a Muslim community. There was no need to restore a Caliphate to rule over all believers. Al-Raziq declared in 1925 that "Islam is a religion, not a state; a message, not a government."[16] The Prophet was not sent to the earth only to be a political ruler in one small corner of the world but a messenger of a religion (*din*), which revealed a far more pressing universal spiritual truth (Q. 24:54). Critics saw that his views were rooted in Western secular legacies but al-Raziq argued that a more secular understanding of the political process would actually safeguard the pure message of Islam from the invariable corruptions and compromises that take place when any government confronts day-to-day challenges. Al-Raziq himself carefully rooted his contentions in the framework of the Qur'an and Hadith as well as the vast and compelling record of Islamic political and intellectual history.

In contrast to al-Raziq's secularized political vision, the rise of extremists has been marked by their claim that Islam is not only a religion but a comprehensive political structure that provides no room for variance or difference. Far from being a neutral model, or one acceptable option among many others, the extremist political vision only raises the prospect of further political oppression throughout the Muslim world. Even from a traditionalist and historical perspective, it would appear that extremist views are actually more connected with modernist (*hadatha*) assumptions about the relationship between individuals and a specific political state than the communitarian ideas of the Qur'an, which emphasize the role of the believer's relationship with God and the shared ethical responsibilities of the entire Muslim community.

Two Case Studies: Saudi Arabia and Egypt

Saudi Arabia, the "Land of the Two Holy Mosques", is a nation that is often linked in the Western media to various government-sponsored human rights abuses. The nation, like other Muslim countries (Iran, the Afghanistan of the *Taliban*, etc.) has established an organization, "The Committee for the Promotion of Virtue and the Prevention of Vice", which employs about 3,500 religious police officers. These *mutaween* (their official name is *hayaa*, which means "commissioner") are charged with the task of strictly enforcing *shariah* (since 1992) and often carry out their charge with extreme zeal. Suspects accused of prostitution, fornication, homosexuality, proselytization, and theft can be arrested. Other punishable offences include socializing between unrelated men and women; those who use alcohol; people who own, sell or buy, cats or dogs; owners of banned products; critics of the government; women who are not properly wearing Islamic dress; people who own depictions of animals or people; and shop-keepers who are open during times of prayer.

While justice is swift, it is not always certain. For example, one 75-year-old woman was arrested and sentenced to four months in prison and many lashes after two men (who were not her immediate relations) helped her lift some packages in public. Foreign business-people celebrating Christmas in their enclosed compound had their gifts confiscated and the food on their table destroyed when a native Saudi reported their unrighteous celebrations. In 2007, a man was accused and then beaten to death, while under arrest for consuming alcohol, although the neighbor who accused him had no evidence and held a bitter grudge. In 2008, a Saudi Christian had her tongue cut out and was set on fire after being accused of proselytizing, even though no evidence was forthcoming that such accusations were accurate. Famously (also in 2008), an American businesswoman was arrested at a Starbucks after sitting with a male colleague. During her subsequent arrest she was beaten until she agreed to sign a "confession" and was released. The tragic deaths of 15 teenage girls during a raging fire at an all-girls school in 2002 was also laid at the feet of the *mutaween,* who stubbornly refused to allow the fire department to intervene (this incident is discussed in the next chapter).

Some reforms at the level of the national government have begun to address these issues, but the role of Saudi Arabia's vigilante religious police force remains largely unchecked and unchallenged. It should go without saying that many of their actions have produced extensive ill-will among much of the Saudi citizenry and there are increasing calls for their free reign of terrorizing local communities with religious zeal to be controlled.

In contrast to the reign of the religious police of Saudi Arabia, the rise of the Muslim Brotherhood to political ascendance in Egypt in 2012, followed by its sudden fall through a military coup in 2013, has been marked by very few immediate social changes. The Muslim Brotherhood of Egypt is an often misunderstood political movement, which has often been described by unsympathetic Westerners as a radicalizing force for social upheaval. In fact, the Muslim Brotherhood — launched in 1928 by Hassan al-Banna (1906–1949) — has within its original premise statements that affirm political pluralism, social reform, and non-violent means to change. It is far from the most extreme political group in Egypt. Problems have arisen because of "secret" splinter-organizations (such as those once led by Sayyid Qutb), which promote violent strategies for social change.

When the Muslim Brotherhood's Muhammad Morsi became the duly elected President of Egypt in 2012, many worried — based on inaccurate views — that Morsi's leadership would suddenly lurch the country towards the fundamentalist social policies of Saudi Arabia: such concerns seem to be unfounded. While Morsi and the Muslim Brotherhood are unapologetically Muslim in their faith and orientation, their political commitment before they were deposed was to gradually win over the support of the entire Egyptian citizenry. The fact that they failed miserably to do this combined with fears about their rule from outside the country led to massive street protests against their democratically elected authority. Their rise in Egypt was seen as part of a larger trend throughout North Africa (and the Middle East) towards an increasingly unstoppable "Salifization" of local politics as new generations challenge the hegemony of authoritarian powers long supported by Britain, Europe, and the United States. The primary focus of these new political movements (especially when not in power) has been localized and has been expressed through ongoing efforts to forge social welfare networks in order to open madrassas, masjids, clinics, and hospitals in small villages across the nation. Immediately after the deadly earthquake of 1992, for example, it was workers from the Muslim Brotherhood who often responded with aid far more effectively than government agents. It must be noted, however, that Morsi's attempt to implement a new constitution clearly extended the powers of the state to an unreasonable degree. This trend toward autocracy, along with the fact that those who disagreed with the Muslim Brotherhood (once in power) were often marginalized or attacked, only emboldened those who asserted that the organization had cynically forsaken its earlier lofty claims to moral authority and its self-righteous contentions that it strongly supported the cause of social justice in Egypt.

Social justice initiatives were first rewarded in the 2005 elections, in which the Muslim Brotherhood won 88 seats (20% of the total), and finally in the successes at the polls in 2012. While some have carried out violent deeds claiming inspiration from the Muslim Brotherhood, most Egyptians realize that the previous Mubarak Regime and present Western and Royalist governments are those who are most active in seeking to discredit the organization with fear-mongering rumors. One spokesman explained: "Our only weapons are honest and truthful words and selfless dedication to social work. We invite all those who are involved in acts of violence to remember the advice of our Messenger (PBUH) in the farewell pilgrimage speech when he commanded us to protect the sanctity of blood and property of every Muslim."[17] It is too early to tell after the 2013 coup against Morsi if the Muslim Brotherhood will be able to recover from this catastrophe. What began in the deposition of Mubarak as a return to prominence after 80 years in the shadows now languishes as the Muslim Brotherhood are again forced underground and senior leaders face extended prison sentences. Given such rapidly changing political dynamics, it is difficult to predict whether or not the Muslim Brotherhood will be able to return again from the margins of Egyptian political influence.

Conclusion

Religion has long served as a smokescreen for political oppression, and Islamic responses to political oppression are multivalent. Different standards apply based on who is governing whom. In many contexts, certain Qur'anic verses are applied in different ways in order to serve diverse political agendas (either quietist or activist). Many extremists emphatically assert that any society will be fundamentally unjust as long as it is un-Islamic and does not establish pure *shariah* law.[18] One should take seriously, however, the argument that many Islamist movements across the Arab world are gaining popular support because of economic disparities and social marginalization that were unaddressed by previous leaders. Dictators, rulers, and others share in common that they have succeeded in installing their own oppressive power structures after decades of colonial injustice.

Extremist forces worldwide are becoming increasingly assertive, which is why it is incumbent upon reasonable people to appreciate how militant advocates justify decisions to commit acts of terror by appealing to a commitment to social justice in God's Name.[19] South Africa's Archbishop Desmond Tutu (b. 1931) is right that "what is legally right is not necessarily morally right".[20] Moderate voices from all traditions should support those Muslims who confront fellow religionists who misuse scripture in order to advance their strident extremist agendas. Oppressive solutions should be replaced by existing traditions, morals, and ethical ideals that are amply able to advance justice, stability, and peace. Khaled Abou El-Fadl writes that Muslims have sometimes looked for a "theology of power" to advance their own political and oppressive self-interests.[21] Others, such as Samuel Huntington (1927–2008), have predicted an inevitable "clash of civilizations" to explain why political oppression is more widely exposed in the West and, in their minds, more likely to be tolerated within the Muslim world. Huntington's views are orientalist, Islamaphobic, and reductionistic. The cruelty and moral depravity of those "Muslims", who have promoted political oppression, do not reflect Islamic values any more than the Crusades, the Inquisition, or the Ku Klux Klan mirror the peace and justice-advancing message of Jesus Christ. Acts of violent political oppression reflect a deep alienation from a rich and broad Islamic tradition of respect and tolerance, the predominant values of which unambiguously support the dignity of all human beings.

5. Islamic Civil Rights and Individual Human Rights

While human rights in the West are based on individualism, human rights in classical and Medieval Islamic thought were based on the general interests of society. Not that Medieval Islamic thought denied individual rights, but it stressed that proper human rights had to be socially contextualized, or else individuals and societies would clash head on. Justice was seen as concomitant to freedom. Individual freedom that did not take into account the community's general interests was perceived as being unjust.

— Ahmad S. Moussalli

Human Rights in Islam

A few questions confront non-Muslims seeking to appreciate how Islam addresses civil rights and individual human rights. Many of these challenges result from profound cultural, as well as religious, differences. What individuals in one part of the world perceive to be an injustice may not be viewed the same way in another distinct political or religious context. One significant difference relates to the way that Europeans and North Americans generally look at issues of individuality compared to pervasive views held by some in other parts of the world. Social equivalence in the *ummah*, for example, is far more important than any notion of a compartmentalized individual who is entitled to equality with all other individuals. Lawrence Rosen suggests that, in Islam, "it is not equality that constitutes the basis for justice but equivalence — a recognition that people are not all the same, that to treat others true to their nature is fairer than to treat them as if they were identical."[1] The modern notion of a universalized code of human rights stems from the idealistic and individualistic values of the European Enlightenment. One need only read the opening lines of the American Declaration of Independence to see how such views are expressed as universal assumptions.

Long before the European Enlightenment, however, while Europe floundered in Medieval cultural systems that gave no regard to individual rights, the Muslim heritage endowed women and minorities with extensive individual rights that were unparalleled in the existing European cultures of the Prophet's time. Roger Garaudy (1913–2012) notes that while the American Declaration of Independence and the French Revolution's Declaration of the Rights of Man and Citizen proclaimed equality, hypocrisy typified their actual implementation, because the "former was to retain the slavery of blacks [*sic*] for a century and the latter was to deprive more than half the French nation of the right to vote as passive citizens because they had no property."[2] Democracy claims to promote the idea of governance by the general will, but the idea, since its inception, has been fraught with racist and sexist exceptions and convenient oversights. Strangely, even the word "democracy" originates from the oligarchy of Pericles, in which 20,000 "free" people had the power to rule over 100,000 enslaved citizens.

The Qur'an forbids favoring those with land and wealth (Q. 27:16) but has always been unapologetic in its allowance for slavery. Allah alone was to be the ruler over all, and God alone holds each and every citizen accountable on the final Day of Judgment. Bernard Lewis (b. 1916) claims:

> There was to be no castes or estates to flaw the unity of the believers; no privileges save the self-evident superiority of those who accept to those who willfully reject the true faith. . . . A slave was no longer chattel but a human being with recognized legal and moral rights and women, though still subject to polygamy and concubinage, acquired property rights not equaled in the West until modern times. . . . [E]ven the non-Muslim enjoyed a tolerance and security in sharp contrast with the lot of the non-Christian in Medieval — and sometimes modern — Christendom.[3]

Non-Muslim critics of the faith frequently claim that Muslims rarely enjoy freedom of speech. A legion of sequential protests against perceived insults to the Prophet Muhammad have provoked deep tensions and have been frequently detailed in the British, European, and North American media as (implicit) proof that the Muslim world is generally intolerant. Muslims who observed such effrontories being tolerated in Europe and North America have responded that a number of media-amplified incidents were Islamaphobic and noted that many governments also do not tolerate certain kinds of speech (such as that which fuels racial hatred or holocaust denials). Indeed, freedom of speech is an issue that many Muslim nations are repeatedly forced to confront.

There are numerous passages in the Qur'an and Hadith that could lead one to conclude that intolerance against differing views is not Islamic. The Qur'an reveals that God is the creator of all peoples and knows that they will have diverse views: "If the Lord had willed, He would have made humankind into a single nation, but they will not cease to be diverse. . . . And for this Allah created them (Q. 11:118–119). Because there is no "compulsion in matters of faith" (Q. 2:256) there should also be room for differences of opinion.

While freedom of speech is generally allowed, there is a different view concerning defamations of the Prophet Muhammad. This is based on Qur'an 33:57: "Those who annoy [mock, harm, curse] Allah and His Messenger; Allah has cursed them in this world and in the Next, and has prepared for them a humiliating punishment." Importantly, it is God that should curse these people and not those human beings who feel obligated to defend an all-sovereign God (Q. 54:55), who actually needs no defense. Differing points of view, even heretical views, can be seen as a divine test (Q. 5:49) to see if a person can continue to trust God. God will surely judge (Q. 5:50) those who mock the Divine will.

For many modern believers, issues of free speech are uniquely challenging because conservative and tradition-based communities are often confronted with radical ideals and values, which seem to hark back to the "times of darkness" (jahiliyya) that existed before the revelation of the Qur'an. Offensive views can be perceived as intellectually or culturally poisonous; weakening the strength of faith in society. It certainly demands a tremendous amount of sensitivity (al-riqa), tenderness (al-ta'attuf), and forgiveness (al-maghifira) toward those who espouse views that clearly confront traditional values. Should believers sacrifice peace in their society in order to tolerate views and ideas, which are perceived as agenda-driven, harmful, and un-Islamic? Fatima Mernissi concludes that such issues must be "managed" with sensitivity, in order to maintain both the rights of dissenters to speak and the fragile equilibrium of the ummah.[4] When believers argue or disagree with others, even about difficult issues, it should be done thoughtfully; "in ways that are best and most gracious" (Qur'an 16:25).

Islam is committed to supporting individuals in their personal spiritual reflection. It is not a faith of automatons and those who are blindly obedient without any thought or reason. The Qur'an frequently calls believers to studied consideration and quiet meditation. It is also true that, within Islam, individuality cannot exist apart from a communitarian identity: there is no room for a "me-first" mindset. Islam teaches that each individual is an amanah, a trust, from Allah to us as well as to each other. Islamic understandings of human rights can only exist "in the context of the community of Islam".[5] Sisk observes that most believers are "communitarians and not individualists" in that they "emphasize more the right of the community rather than the right of individuals".[6] Freedom of speech in Islam, then, should be understood in terms of one's social duties. Larger social justice issues are presented within the context of individuals being asked by their faith to reflect on their own responsibility. This is the genius of Judaism and Christianity as well as Islam. All three faiths teach that one cannot separate the authenticity of one's inner being from one's participation within the larger tradition.

As Islam seeks expression, it is often presented in the Western media as being a confining and rigid structure of oppression. This is because of an inability to understand the differences between Muslim and Western, classical and liberal understandings of freedom. For believers, freedom is not an inherent human right and "human rights exist only in relation to human obligations."[7] There is no true freedom apart from God's will and strict commandments. Believers within the *ummah* are not free to carelessly do whatever they want without regard for the needs of others. Those who promote blameworthy "innovations" (*bid'a*), as opposed to those who promote helpful and healing "innovations" (*bid'a hasana*), are held accountable for hurting or misguiding people.

Governments are ultimately responsible to Allah to carry out rules and regulations established by divine revelation. Submission to Allah is the source of individual freedom (see Q. 7:157), which is rooted in a communitarian responsibility to serve God. In this sense, there can never be "absolute freedom" in the libertarian European sense of the term. While many in Muslim-majority contexts speak highly of the freedom of speech rights in many non-Muslim nations, there are necessarily limits to these freedoms.[8] As Sardar and Davies say: "there is always some limit set beyond which free expression will be deemed a transgression, an infringement of the rights or freedoms of other people or the public interest in general."[9]

A Faith of Pilgrimages

Islam calls believers to a series of intellectual pilgrimages throughout their lives, all of which end in the great oneness (*tawhid*) of the divine but via variant paths and experiences. Year one of the Muslim calendar marks the journey (*hijrah*) of the Prophet into exile and away from all that he had known and found familiar. This first journey is a reminder to all believers that their faith may often keep them on the move and forbids them from the dulling comforts of stasis. When a believer participates in a pilgrimage they find themselves in the midst of a stressful and demanding process. Believers are called to a series of seven *tawafs*, or circumambulations, around the Ka'abah as if to say that one must methodically, persistently, and intentionally carry out duties with mind and heart as well as with outward form and ritual. Mecca is cited in the Qur'an as the *ma'ad* or "place of return" (Q. 28:85), which parallels the assured finality of conclusion within the often complex work of interpretation. An individual believer is grounded securely within the *ummah* just as a sturdy tree is rooted in the earth (Q. 14:24–26).

The rituals of Islamic devotion are invested with meaning and with constant reminders that life itself is a journey or search, which requires constant individual reflection. Ramadan is designed for the benefit of the *ummah* as a time of introspection. Fasting itself is a form of emphatic identification with those who lack the sustenance to meet their daily needs. Ramadan links meditation and revelation with intentional action. Before receiving revelation, it was the custom of the Prophet to retreat into the mountains around Mecca. It was on one of these forays of reflection that he was able to begin receiving divine revelation at the Cave of Hira. At the beginning of Ramadan, the faithful are called to "retreat" into the masjid (*i'tikaf*) for the purposes of devotion, but the month concludes with these same followers commanded to perform charity (*sadaqah al-fitrah*), which gives validation to the intensity of their devotion. The fruit of this yearly devotional journey is celebrated in a ritual social distribution of wealth.

Individual Freedoms in a Communitarian Context

The social and individual freedoms that Islam grants are based on a shared commitment and responsibility to the *ummah*. Allah guides all individuals (Q. 91:7–10), and, they in turn, must develop their spiritual freedom from the weaknesses of their flesh (Q. 70:19–20). The basis of freedom is a common agreement within the *ummah* that together the people will be guided by God (Q. 2:2, 5). Allah can only guide believers, not unbelievers (Q. 3:8) because they have chosen a different path. Freedom comes in a communal context because the people are "one nation under God" (Q. 2:213) that should flow together in a beautiful symphony of unity and harmony. One cannot exercise freedom of choice without accepting social responsibility for one's choices; one cannot rebel against the guidance of God as understood by the vast majority of a given community. On the other hand, individuals are not blind slaves; while there is no real freedom of choice without responsibility, there also can be no genuine sense of responsibility where freedom is absent. Culture determines perspective to such a degree that Leonard Rosen claims that "most Arabs see themselves as far more free (to build relationships) than we who are constrained by material objects and impersonal institutions."[10] Commitment to *ummah* and individual responsibility form an integral chain in the ways that believers understand the relationship between social and political freedoms.

Apostasy and Religious Freedom

It is only in that context (and, not as it often happens, in a vacuum) that non-Muslims can discuss issues of how the Muslim *ummah* relates to those "Muslims" who have become apostate (see Q. 2:217; 3:90–91; 8:55–56; 9:11–

2; 16:106) and blasphemers (Q. 33:57, 60–61). Apostasy is "turning away from Islam" or "severing ties with Islam".[11] Most Muslim jurists agree that "once a person becomes a Muslim, it is not permissible to change religion."[12] It would be the same as embracing a lie after knowing the truth or accepting ignorance after having gained knowledge. Apostasy violates communitarian expectations and threatens to undermine social stability; the example of the apostate sends a harmful message to the weak and the young within the believing community. It is not an act of religious freedom (Q. 9:29; 123) but an act of civic rebellion and repudiation aimed at challenging social stability. Tolerating apostasy is seen to be the same as tolerating a chaotic and willful evil. Saaed, speaking from a perspective that many find difficult to fathom, asks: "to which religion does the apostate convert?" because Islam is the truth and explains that "anyone who penetrates beneath the surface to the inner essence of Islam is bound to recognize its superiority over the other religions."[13]

Because of these foundational worldview assumptions, religious freedoms cannot be understood in the Muslim world in the same ways that they are described among non-Muslims. Many tenets of *shariah* regarding apostasy (*ridah*) seem to "contradict any supposed right which an individual has to exercise freedom of choice in his or her religious beliefs."[14] Apostasy is mentioned 13 times in the Qur'an. All of these verses assure eternal punishment for the apostate in the afterlife (see Qur'an 39:41, 72:23, and 3:176).

Throughout Islamic history, and in the formation of Islamic law, conservative, orthodox clerics and jurists have called for death in the case of blasphemy or conversions to religions other than Islam (see Q. 4:89; 91). Some have cited Surah 5:54 in support of this, but there is no specific injunction in this verse that apostates should be killed. More specific is one Hadith that supports executing heretics (*zindiq*): "The Prophet (Peace Be Upon Him) said, The blood of a Muslim who confesses *shahadah* cannot be shed except in three cases: a life for a life, a married person who commits illegal sexual intercourse, and the one who turns renegade from Islam and leaves the community of Muslims."[15]

There are Muslim scholars, however, who argue that apostasy should be viewed in a much more limited light. Since the ultimate punishment should be left to God in the afterlife, most of the community's reactions should be calm and measured — with the singular exception of those cases in which such decisions have put the lives of others at peril or have been cases of betrayal of the political *ummah* (treason). Proponents of toleration of differing religious views cite Qur'an 18:30, which declares, "This is the truth from your Lord; let him who will, believe, and let him who will, disbelieve." The Qur'an is clear that there is no compulsion in religion; God's revelation clearly ascribes penalties that are less harsh than a number of Islamic *shariah* codes that are now in place.

There have been some recent, widely-documented cases of apostasy in the Muslim world. These include Abdul Rahman, an Afghan who converted to Christianity and who now lives in Germany, Dr Nawal el-Saadawi, an Egyptian feminist who was called an apostate for questioning the wearing of the *hijab* as a cultural practice, Hashem Aghajari, an Iranian journalist and academic who was executed in Iran in 2002, and the British Indian author Salman Rushdie (b. 1947).

Generally speaking, insulting the Prophet (*saab al-rasul*) is not a punishable offense because, in theory, believers are forbidden from harming those who are peaceful in their religious practices. Allah will punish the blasphemer in the afterlife, and there should be no earthly punishment meted out by the civil authorities (see Q. 5:41). Modern extremists claim that this is enough and, as McGill scholar Forough Jahanbakhsh explains, "Peaceful conversions to another religion should only result in the death penalty if the person is also a danger to Muslim society."[16] This is a circular argument from a non-Muslim perspective, however, because any conversion could be viewed as an "act of rebellion against the Islamic social order" as well as God's divine truth.[17]

Limits to Individual Freedoms

There cannot be, however, independent freedom of speech in the Western Enlightenment sense when it comes to blasphemy (*sabb al-rasul*) or foul language, which is described usually as anything that belittles Allah, the holy books, the angels, proscribed rituals, and the prophets. To allow such freedoms, extremists assert, would be to revert to the era of *jahiliyya* when heresy (*shirk*) predominated. There is also the fear that, because ideas that originate in the *jahiliyya* of Europe and North America do not stem from Islam, they are inevitably Islamaphobic. Militants also cite a Hadith that warns: "Beware of matters newly begun, for every matter newly begun is innovation (*bid'a*) and every innovation is misguidance and every misguidance is in hell."[18] It could be argued that the Prophet meant only to oppose innovations that are harmful and not those that are productive (*bid'a hasana*).

The extremist urge to repress freedoms extends not only to speech, but also to many other activities. In Egypt, some extremists have condemned any "Western" form of leisure, arts, or education. Attacks have been launched against tourist sites such as Luxor and Aswan since 1995. The 83-year-old Nobel Prize Laureate Naguib Mahfouz (1911– 2006) suffered a stabbing to his face in 1999 by an assailant who did not consider his writing to be "Islamic enough". Discothèques are perceived as lewd and reprobate centers of moral vice and spiritual corruption. Although belly-dancing has been practiced in Egypt for millennia, belly-dancing establishments have been bombed and dancers and their agents have been threatened with assassination. One Egyptian newspaper passionately explained: "Belly-dancing epitomizes the sickness of man's soul. By crushing it, we take the first step toward godliness."[19]

In limiting freedom of speech in issues of religious controversy, conservatives cite Surah 33:57: "Those who annoy (mock or harm) Allah and His Messenger, Allah has cursed (*qatl*) them in this world and in the next and prepared them for a humiliating punishment." The use of the term *qatl* is important because it can be translated either as "to curse" or "to kill". A curse that is sometimes given is "May Allah kill him!" (*Qatalahu Allah*). This explains why some Muslims reacted so virulently to the publication of Salman Rushdie's *Satanic Verses* (1989) or to the 12 cartoons published in the largest Danish newspaper, the *Jyllands-Posten*, in September of 2005, which were viewed as defaming the Prophet Muhammad. These editorial cartoons were described as acts of intellectual terrorism, because they were deliberately provocative. When, months later, news of these cartoons reached grassroots media outlets throughout the Muslim world, bloody riots broke out in places such as Northern Nigeria and Indonesia, in which hundreds of people were senselessly killed.

At the core of this response was the general anger that Muslims feel about the disrespect they experience by European and North American societies, which they sense to be orientalist and Islamaphobic. Some claimed (inaccurately) that no church or government leaders rose up to criticize these insulting cartoons. Some Muslims noted that other topics — such as denials of the Holocaust or incitement to racial hatred — are not tolerated in Europe or North America, while attacks against the Prophet's honor are allowed to be voiced. The same argument was raised in 2012, when an amateurish American video attacking Muhammad was released on the internet and resulted in numerous riots and the deaths of many protestors. Anger, however, has not only been limited to attacks on the honor of the Prophet Muhammad. The films *The Last Temptation of Christ* and *The DaVinci Code* were banned in Egypt, Malaysia, and in other countries because they were seen to blaspheme the honor of the Prophet Jesus.

One response to those who cite Qur'an 33:57 as a rationale for attacking those who "insult Islam" is to remind those who are angry that it is God who does the cursing and that this is not the duty of believers. Qur'an 5:49 says that Allah "will resolve all matters in which you disagree" in the life to come. This makes it apparent that Allah does not expect the believers to conform to one belief or to allow disagreements to become violent.

The case of Salman Rushdie demands further consideration: it underscores the fundamental dilemma that Muslims face when a perceived assault on Islam conflicts with Islam's basic commitment to uphold freedom of speech. Rushdie, a non-practicing Muslim from India, became the object of a *fatwa* issued in 1989 by Iran's Ayatollah Khomeini that called for Rushdie's death on the charge of blasphemy. Rushdie was accused of blasphemy because (some claimed) he had insulted the honor of the Prophet. Anyone who reads Rushdie's book will easily see why such contentions have taken root.[20] In February, 2014, Senior Cleric Ahmad Khatami of Teheran announced to congregants that it was still their duty to seek Rushdie's death: "The historical *fatwa* is as fresh as ever."[21] Many Muslims, however, have suggested less draconian alternatives than a *fatwa*, such as the banning of the book and demanding an unconditional apology from the author. This case shows, among other things, that there is wide disagreement among Muslims about how to deal with such fiery issues. It also underscores the convictions of some extremists, who assert that the realms of art and literature are not entitled to the wide freedoms that they are usually ascribed in most of Europe and North America.

Tolerance of Diversity

Issues surrounding free speech relate to believers coming to terms with different points of view; this is often more of a cultural issue than a religious one. One survey, cited by John Esposito, noted that "when asked what they admired most about the West, both extremists and moderates" referred to technological advances, a strong work ethic, and a fair political system which promoted freedom of speech.[22] This citation notes that even extremists hold favorable views towards some dimensions of "Western" culture.

Believers have often been challenged by issues of diversity as they have interacted with non-believers (see Q. 3:113-114, 2:62, 5:68) who should never be the focus of combat or contention because of their different religious views. Islam is a faith that has always challenged its followers to embrace pluralism (Q. 3:64, 5:68-69) instead of the myopic and narrow centralism of many intolerant followers. As Islam spread throughout the world it continued to address these tensions as Muslims encountered a host of different cultures, ethnicities, and languages. Professor Abdulaziz Sachedina said that the ideal goal of Islamic society has always been to "develop a culture of restoration, just intra-religious and inter-religious relationships in a world of cultural and religious diversity."[23] At the heart of Islamic peacemaking is the great value within the tradition that is placed on difference (*ikhtilaf*) in many distinct forms. According to Abu-Nimer, "pluralism and diversity are among the core values of the Islamic religious and cultural traditions" based on gender (49:13; 53:45), skin color and language (30:23), and even belief, rank, and social status (64:2, 6:165).[24]

Tolerance is a sword with two sides. Believers and non-believers should work to express tolerance more fully than has been the case in either context. El-Fadl writes, "Externally, Muslims are among the most powerful, dominated, and abused people in the world. This makes the question of tolerance particularly troublesome. After all, isn't the real question whether non-Muslims are willing to tolerate Muslims instead of the other way around?"[25] Both believers and non-believers can diffuse tensions by avoiding unnecessary instances of cultural and religious insensitivity. Intolerance, violence, but also disrespect, should be eliminated. As Ziauddin Sardar (b. 1951) reminds "As Islam teaches and Muslims believe, argument, not abuse, is the basis for survival and progress. 'Argue and survive' could become a contemporary slogan for Muslims and secularists alike."[26] Protests should occur "in ways that are best and most gracious" (Q. 16:125) instead of being marked by either incendiary anti-Western or Islamphobic rhetoric.

The Rights of Non-Muslims

What rights do non-Muslims have while living in a Muslim community? The answer to this question seems to vary dramatically from one country to another. Ahmad S. Moussalli states that while the "Qur'an is clear that freedom of belief is guaranteed for all peoples, and while it disagreed with many beliefs of the Jews and Christians, it nonetheless did not call for their forcible conversion but for dialogue with them."[27] In the Qur'an, God commands the faithful to set a covenant of protection with the conquered "Peoples of the Book" (but not with "polytheists", *mushrikin*, in their midst). No harm can befall them and "anyone who kills a man under covenant (*dhimmi*) will not even smell the fragrance of paradise."[28]

The *dhimmi* includes Jews, Christians, Sabaeans, and sometimes Zoroastrians (and in some South Asian interpretations even extends to Hindus). The concept of *dhimmi* status, instituted during the life of the Prophet, establishes a sense of hierarchy among non-Muslims. *Dhimmi* enjoy a more recognized status than those who are not deemed "People of the Book". This system, for all of its obvious flaws, has functioned across a wide range of historical and cultural contexts. It has provided Muslims with a way of understanding their own superiority while also providing a way to accommodate and "accept" non-Muslims. Adult *dhimmi* were forced to pay a tax on their income and, in some instances, on their land as well. Ever-evolving restrictions on the freedom of non-Muslims — especially during centuries of the Ottoman Empire — included rules about where non-Muslims could live, what they could wear, whom they could marry, and what jobs they could perform. Before non-Muslims fly into a sense of self-righteous rebuke of such an exclusionary concept, they should be reminded that such categorizations are not unique to Islam. The so-called "Holy Roman Empire", for example, required non-Christians to pay a "common pfennig tax", stay within certain designated areas, and were restricted from participating within certain professions.

Non-believers and polytheists have the right to become faithful believers. God gives each person free-will, but, if they convert, *dhimmi* would gain the privileges, but also the responsibilities, of being a member of the *ummah*. Because of the viewpoint that the Qur'an is the final truth and is a law that pertains to all sectors of public and private life, there is no social benefit for individuals who voice political dissent against God's mandated social decrees. Since *dhimmi* are not willing to accept the benefits of being a Muslim, they should not be coerced into those benefits. All relationships with non-believers must be conducted in a manner that allows for the harmony of the believing community.

Christians in Turkey, Northern Nigeria, Uzbekistan, and a number of places in which they are in the minority among the *ummah*, note that they often have perplexing difficulties in gaining permission from their governments to build new churches or even to renovate or repair existing churches. Daniel Pipes claims that there are clearly demarcated restrictions for *dhimmi*: "They may not proselytize or build new buildings of worship; they may be subjected to petty and humiliating sumptuary regulations (such as prohibitions on certain clothes, the riding of horses or living in multi-storied dwellings). In court, *dhimmi* resemble slaves and Muslim women; the testimony of each of these counts about half of that of a free Muslim man."[29] There have also been restrictions against *dhimmi* participating in certain levels of the government or the military. These restrictions are not seen by Muslims as unjust, because they are mandated by Almighty God. The restrictions are viewed positively as a way for Muslims and non-Muslims to live together with tolerance. In return for paying the tax, which recognizes the ultimate superiority of Islam (*jizya*), the Muslim government is expected to protect them and provide good government with the same social services enjoyed by the Muslim community. *Dhimmi* are also free to "practice their rituals, follow their personal laws, and conduct their religious education".[30]

The enforcement or extent of these standards has varied widely throughout history. In Malaysia, for example, the ruling political party (*Party Islam of Se Malaysia*) has insisted that non-Muslims be protected and be given full liberty to practice their "inaccurate and polytheistic" beliefs without any interference from the government of the state. This means, in effect, there is no *dhimmi* status ascribed to non-Muslims in Malaysia even though it is a "Muslim State". Part of the multivalent situation in Malaysia might relate to the fact that many non-Muslims in that nation are not "People of the Book" but are Buddhists or Taoist-Confucianists. The Islamic State Document of Malaysia (PAS) states: "The Islamic State guarantees individual freedom; freedom of religious beliefs; freedom of speech; political association and assembly; freedom to private ownership; freedom of education; freedom of religion and right to cultural expression."[31] In the last fifty years, a number of Muslim-majority states have adopted legal codes; often loosely based upon Western legal standards. Many of these states now guarantee in writing that their citizens will be protected by the rule of law and will not suffer from repressive or vindictive injustices.

Christian Persecution

Christians, as *dhimmi* in the Arab Middle East, have faced a number of differing circumstances; it is not helpful when observers speak in blanket generalizations about the various communities of faith across a wide range of varying contexts. It is undeniable that some Christians have experienced significant human rights abuses and, while it is beyond the scope of this specific study to look at each of these situations, it is helpful to underscore how such problems generate ill-will in multifaith and intercultural dynamics. In Saudi Arabia and Iran, for example, an individual can be punished for simply displaying publicly a Cross or a Star of David. People have been imprisoned for praying in public, and Bibles have been confiscated at international Saudi airports. Converts to Christianity, in a number of countries, have also been executed for apostasy away from the undeniable truths of Islam.

In a series of particularly tragic cases a number of Iranian Christians were killed. The Reverend Mehdi Dibaj was sentenced to death on December 21, 1993, only to be released and then immediately killed in an orchestrated vigilante attack on July 5, 1994. The Reverend Haik Mehr of the Assemblies of God, who brought the Dibaj case to the world was found dead on January 20, 1994 (while Dibaj was still in prison), and, on July 2, 1994, the Reverend Tatavous Michaelian was assassinated shortly before Dibaj was released from prison. Lounes Matoub, a Berber musician living in Iran, was executed on July 7, 1998, for his preaching of the Christian message. Beyond the notable case of Iran, it is true that countless Christians in other Muslim nations have been killed, imprisoned, and harassed because of their belief that Jesus is the Son of God. Pope Francis (b. 1936) has reminded the world in some of his earliest public prayers that Christians in Muslim contexts merit prayers. This is because they are often a threatened minority community in cultures that often stress the centrality of Islamic religious authority in civic society.

In Iraq, since the fall of Saddam Hussein (1937–2006), more than 60 percent of Iraq's Christians have emigrated due to the severe difficulties they have faced.[32] Some churches have been bombed, some Christians have been fired from their jobs, and some individual Christians have even been dragged from their homes and killed in the streets. Christians are not the only individuals suffering waves of persecution resulting from the rampant relative lawlessness and fragmented political situation that is often characterizes modern Iraq. It is also the case that deadly Shi'ite–Sunni contentions and crass attacks against Sabeans and Mandeans are also major sectarian problems in the corrosive environment that is post-war Iraq. The situation in Iraq is so overwhelming and (it is hoped) transitory that one is foolish to suggest much with authority about the grave and multivalent problems of that turbulent nation.

The same is true in the cauldron that is contemporary Syria in the throes of civil war. In contrast to the situation of Christians in Iraq, however, the Christians of Syria have enjoyed tremendous support and protection during the rule of the Syrian Ba'athist government of President Bashar al-Assad (b. 1965) and his father Hafez (1930–2000), who each sought to benefit from political coalitions with various minority communities. Throughout the Ba'athist era, Syrian Christians were able to build churches and institutions for education without opposition — even with government assistance. The Assad government, on certain occasions, even provided churches with free water and electricity and televised church services on Christian holy days. During the Syrian Civil War, Syrian Christians have largely supported the government and President Assad. This is because, as Bailey and Bailey have explained, "Characterized as a tolerant land of friendly and generous people, Syria has become home to many who experienced religious persecution elsewhere: Armenians, Assyrians, Chaldeans, Suryanis and others."[33] The New Testament records the early history of the Syrian church by noting that "they were first called Christians at Antioch", and the Syrian Orthodox Church of Antioch, Turkey is the continuing legacy of those first believers. Large Christian communities in Lebanon (probably 1.5 million) and Syria (about 1.2 million) have had a much more favorable situation, and some Lebanese and Syrian Christians have even held office in their national governments. Syrian Christians, however, have been uneasy since the political upheavals since 2011, which vividly reminded them that their situation might change quickly if the political favor that they have long enjoyed is lifted.

Coptic, Catholic, Protestant, and Armenian Christians in Egypt have faced tremendous difficulties since the beginning of the Arab Spring. The 10–12 million Coptic Christians of Egypt have faced a systematic process of discrimination for centuries; these tensions have increased within recent years. Countless Coptic communities have felt that they have had no choice but to flee their ancestral homeland after countless murders and attacks on their churches. It should not be forgotten by North American readers that this large community of Christians has experienced blatant human rights abuses at the same time that Egypt has been a major recipient of American foreign aid.[34]

In addition to these problems, extremist paramilitary groups have often targeted the highly visible Christian communities in countries such as the Sudan and Pakistan. Many Southern Sudanese Christians have been consigned to slavery in the Muslim-majority north. All of these complexities explain why many Christians among Muslims have been emigrating from these nations to Europe and North America in record numbers. Christians and Muslims who are sincere in promoting social justice partnerships must confront the human rights abuses of Christians who live in the Muslim world.

Declarations on Human Rights

European and North American critics of human rights in Muslim-majority countries frequently focus on issues relating to freedom of speech. Contemporary Muslim-majority societies are still grappling with the issue as they seek to reconcile religious convictions with an increasingly secular world, which values promoting freedom of speech more than protecting religious sensitivities. This chapter has already shown that a number of so-called "freedoms" are suppressed in many Muslim-majority contexts.

Progressive Muslims assert that Islam should promote freedom of all speech. Moussalli writes that "the original view on pluralism in Islam rests on the premise that every opinion that results from the fullest use of reason (*ijtihad*) is correct."[35] Progressive believers base this on the conviction that Allah could have lumped all the people of the world into a single nation, but humanity "will not cease to be diverse" (Q. 11:118–119). They note that, since "there can be no compulsion in religion" (Q. 2:256), any form of coercion of religious speech runs counter to God's will. Muslims are free to express both positive and negative opinions. Allah commands all people to "enjoin what is proper and forbid what is improper" (Q. 9:71 see also Q. 22:41; 3:104, 110).

Human rights abuses vary from country to country throughout various Muslim-majority nations. A number of non-governmental organizations (NGOs), such as Human Rights Watch and Amnesty International, are monitoring situations in many different countries. As non-Muslims look at human rights in Muslim-majority countries, it is vital to remember that in any discussion there is the "need to ground and implement human rights within diverse global traditions, (in order) to attain cultural legitimacy for standards of human rights".[36]

The most widely accepted document on the topic is the United Nations Universal Declaration of Human Rights, written in 1948. The first article states that "all human beings are born free and equal in dignity and rights. They are endowed with reason and conscience and should act towards one another in a spirit of brotherhood."[37] The Muslim-majority nations of Saudi Arabia and Pakistan took issue with Article 18 in the document, which not only called for "freedom of conscience in the choice and practice of religious faith" but also for the "right to change one's religion."[38] This was unacceptable because *shariah* clearly forbids a Muslim from converting to another religion. In the final analysis, the Declaration was passed by a vote of 48–0 with 8 abstentions, including Saudi Arabia.

A group of Muslim scholars wrote a document called the Cairo Declaration of Human Rights in Islam. It is based on the revelations of the Qur'an and enshrines many of the same rights that are in the United Nations document. It assures, for example, that all Muslims have a right to participate in their governments and to be represented by their officials. The document also promises that, based on the command of the Qur'an, all Muslims have a right to a decent livelihood within their communities and enough of an income to provide for the needs of their family (Q. 51:19).

Many conservatives have rejected the Cairo Declaration, while, at the same time, claiming to uphold human rights. Some hesitance about the Cairo Declaration may flow from fears that it is too closely based on "Western" ideals, but such concerns seek to individualize human rights issues, placing them in a contemporary context, when, in fact, the Holy Qur'an has already assured these rights to all believers. Khaled Abou El-Fadl says that the discussion about human rights in Islam has become cloudy, while, at the same time:

> There has, in the contemporary era been a systematic undermining and devaluing of the humanistic tradition in Islam, and a process of what could be described as a vulgarization of Islamic normative doctrines and systems of belief. Therefore, exploring the relationships of Islam to the concept of human rights implicates the crucial issue of Islam's self-definition: what will Islam stand for and represent in the contemporary age?[39]

Crime and the Rights of Criminals

What legal rights do convicted criminals have in Islam? All believers are expected to enjoy the right of living in a society free of crime. Those accused of crime are given the right to a fair hearing with a judge (see Q. 4:58). All believers have the right to avoid committing a sin by

disobeying an unjust law. Rulers are not above the law and all believers
are to be treated equally before the law. Arbitrary imprisonment is
forbidden and no one can be imprisoned for the deeds of another (Q.
6:164).

Crime is a problem throughout the world and, while Muslim-majority
nations have lower reported crime rates than other countries, they also
struggle with how to maintain the civil rights of common people in
ways that protect them from criminals while also being humane to law-
breakers. There are several reasons why crime rates are often lower in
Muslim-majority countries. These nations tend to be less developed, to
be more homogeneous in their composition, and to have strong family
network structures. Another important reason for lower crime rates in
Muslim-majority countries, however, is that there tends to be very strict
penalties for criminals.[40] The penal law of *shariah* codes designate three
classifications of crime: crimes of prohibitions (*hadd*) established in the
Qur'an, such as unlawful intercourse, false accusations, drinking wine,
theft, or robbery (see Q. 5:41–42); crimes of retaliation (*qasas*), including
murder or bodily assault (see Q. 5:45); and civil crimes (*ta'zir*), which
are all crimes not mentioned in the Qur'an, such as usury, treason, and
cursing.[41]

Believers are guaranteed the right to security of life and property.
The state is ordained by Allah to control discord on earth (Q. 5:33–34).
This explains why thieves are treated with such force. A believer is
guaranteed the right to maintain and, if necessary, protect her/his honor.
Defamation is not allowed (Q. 49:11–12). The Qur'an also guarantees
the right of privacy — people cannot enter a home, or even look inside
the window of a believer's home, without the owner's permission (Q.
49:12 and 24:27). Such intrusions are seen as "thefts" of privacy.

Conclusion: An *Ummah* of Human Rights

While many Europeans and North Americans are willing to place the
right to individual free speech above widely-held expectations about
maintaining obedience to the moral values that are vital for social
cohesion; Muslims generally do not accept this individualized standard.
As Sardar and Davies say, "Freedom is not a holy belief, nor even a
supreme value. It is a contestable concept. How a free society marks the
limits of freedom will change with time."[42] On the contrary, Muslims
believe that their truths are unchanging and beyond question. While
Europeans and North Americans must constantly confront questions
about the meaning of freedom and its expression, there is no such debate
in regions where *shariah* has already established its clear guidelines.

These guidelines are specific: human opinions are debatable but
divine revelation is not for re-consideration or negotiation. God's law

is not man-made and cannot be curtailed or surrendered. Rebels are eligible to be tortured to death (Q. 5:33). Aside from flagrant criminal offenses — such as rebellion, apostasy, and blasphemy against the *ummah* (as well as some sexual practices that are not criminalized in many countries) — it is generally the case that the careful practice of Islam will lead to most believers being able to carry out their lives without the Islamic state infringing on their individual and civil rights.

One Hadith warns that "No one has the right to hinder the rights of other men."[43] The individual and his/her civil rights, are assumed within the Islamic tradition. Esack relays the beautiful Hasidic legend of the Rabbi Zusya, who shared shortly before his death that in the "world to come I shall not be asked: 'Why were you not Moses?' I shall be asked: 'Why were you not Zusya?'"[44] Esack chooses not to cite a Muslim story to parallel this legend; he instead claims that all Muslims should aspire to this Jewish value of respect for individuals.

The "Golden Rule" of Islam is, "Do not deal unjustly and you shall not be dealt with unjustly" (Q. 2:279). The "Great Commission" of Islam is summarized in Muhammad's words "do not oppress and do not be oppressed" (see also Q. 42:38–39). This will demand effort and struggle: there is a well-known Hadith of the Prophet that a person should "speak the truth, though it is bitter." [45]A person should provide the community in which he/she lives an opportunity to hear the truth about their situation, even though it might be difficult for them to accept, such as the Revd Dr Martin Luther King, Jr (1929–1968). Islam allows for the prophetic voice to function in society and encourages the *ummah* not to stifle freedom of speech, and especially dissent, because there is an underlying recognition that communities will only remain healthy if they have within themselves voices of correction, protest, and dissent.

The great Pakistani philosopher and poet Muhammad Iqbal (1877–1938) claims that the concept of Allah's oneness (*tawhid*) means that all human and civil rights apply equally to all. God is universal in essence and the Divine commands have universal applicability "encompassing solidarity and freedom" for all individuals.[46] While Iqbal criticized a "heartless European civilization — betraying the love of Christ — and producing World Wars, oppression and colonialism", he also felt that many Muslims had become "living corpses", blind to the urgent need for justice.[47] Our teachings about justice cannot remain locked within our books of revelation. Rather, they must be put to work in society for the sake of justice. Iqbal believes that the shared *ummah* of humanity has a bright future as it fuses together the best of Eastern and Western values, perspectives, and abilities.

This chapter has introduced a number of issues relating to civil and human rights within the Muslim *ummah*. Generally, Islamic social morality promotes freedom of speech except for those who are, in effect, traitors to the divinely-given standards of the *ummah*. For Islam, eternal responsibilities to Allah are more compelling than the defense of transitory freedoms or temporal human rights. Of course, the two are not mutually exclusive: there can be no freedom of speech and there are no guaranteed civil rights for those who would create confusion among the faithful about the core foundations of the faith.

Beyond this clear limitation, the Muslim tradition has, historically, had enough breadth to welcome a host of differing points of view. A community, like an individual, should be able to distinguish between that which is "hidden" by God from those who are casual or superficial observers of God's ways, and those who are careful to follow the truths of God's revelation in strict obedience. Everything mysterious and unknown will be made clear and understandable to everyone on the Final Day. Islam, like Christianity claims, that which has been "hidden" to the simple-minded and unaware will be fully revealed on the Judgment Day (see Matthew 10:26; Mark 4:22; Luke 8:17; I Corinthians 4:5).

The Final Day of Judgment will conclusively resolve all injustices. Allah is merciful but the Divine mercy cannot be flouted by oppressors (see Q. 3:159). In Islam, while individual freedoms are generally protected, they are always placed firmly within the context of communal needs and responsibilities. What is certain is that "Allah hears and knows all things" (Q. 2:256).

These normative and historically orthodox and conservative Muslim views are being ignored by militant extremists in today's world.[48] Whether or not political Islamism can come to promote individual freedoms and human rights is a sobering and complicated question. Progressive believers have the Qur'anic ideal on their side, while many radical extremists feel that pragmatic problems call for drastic, sweeping changes that lead to disregarding what they feel is the Westernized deception of "human rights". These two groups seem far apart on these issues. Governments in Iran and the Sudan tout "ultimate objectives" that mandate short-term expediencies, while moderate and progressive Muslim believers call for a process of supporting human rights on the grounds of Qur'anic revelation. In any event, discussions about human rights issues in the Muslim world need not be secular and have the potential to transcend the labels of "Islamist" and "progressive" to improve the lives of all Muslims. Islam is fundamentally not the cause, and thus not the solution to human rights issues in the Muslim world.

Perhaps it is too simplistic to conclude, using European and North American cultural guidelines as a rule, that the Muslim world is either incompatible or fully compatible with freedoms of speech and religion. The Qur'an establishes clear guidelines for civic society, which are unique to the larger objectives of the community. In the human rights debate between what Jean Bethke Elshtain calls the "universalists or the particularizers", Islam, Judaism, and Christianity offer a bold contention: human rights are God-given rights.[49] Religious scholars can argue over God's revelation (such as Q. 2:256–257; 16:90; 49:13) and the meaning of these revelations for the pragmatic challenges of pressing political realities. What cannot be disputed, however, is that a host of clearly egregious violations of human rights among most Muslim-majority countries clearly contradict Islamic ideals. These violations originate from political actors who have no regard for widely accepted standards (in the West) that support the moral and philosophical concept known as the "rule of law".[50] There can be no room for compromise or equivocation in response to the clear facts of those who suffer from any human rights abuse. Each abuse and each violation demands an answer. Lynn Hunt states: "The truths of human rights may be paradoxical but they are nevertheless still self-evident."[51] The challenge that confronts each of us is to continue to care, remembering and working for a world of peace, even when those in turmoil are far away from us. The Irish poet Mary O'Donnell in her poem *Lament for Babi Yar* (1998) speaks of this challenge, which we all face when we are far away from the trouble of others:

> When babies are split on stone
> solitude hovers like a cotton bomb.
> In circles where tea is sipped
> Homage paid to safety and righteousness.
> The relief of death from a distance.
> But the graves will not settle.
> Sobs thicken among the trees,
> Crackle on the frost at Babi Yar.
> I fume at this aloneness:
> Though redemption shines on every dawn,
> We dare not forgive ourselves.[52]

6. Genocide and Atrocity among Muslims

This is a simple photograph, a black and white picture of a child lying in the dust. She has no name. Call her Baby, Beauty, Unbeloved; she is the face of our time. She is thrown to the earth afraid, abandoned at the limit of word and note and brushstroke. Every poem pauses here. Important questions are decided: who will feed the child, the price of corn, what happens to the planets when they die; and how long do these doomed beauties last once the cameras are gone? . . . [S]he is most likely already dead.

— Mary O'Malley

Serbian Orthodox soldiers reportedly sang Christian hymns as they pillaged Bosnian towns and raped Muslim women. Extremist Jewish settlers invoke the Torah as they violate every sacred injunction against murder and hatred. Al-Qaeda terrorists, acting in the name of Islam, transgress prohibitions against the killing of innocents long established in Islamic law. The result is a tragic conflation of the law of the street with the law of the Gospel, the Torah, and the Qur'an.

— R. Scott Appleby

Centuries of Atrocity

The long march of human history has been repeatedly marked by a grim and ghoulish parade of unspeakable atrocities. Many of these violent evils were undertaken in God's Name and in the context of feverish religious communities. Religion, it can be observed, has promoted peace and justice, intolerance and violence. Martin Marty observes that "violence is not something alien to religion, but has been a feature of religion from its origins to the present day."[1] "Muslim" and "Christian" terrorists in recent years have relied on passionate religious convictions to justify horrific acts of violence with self-righteous confidence and a misplaced sense of moral virtue. The World Trade Center terrorists were convinced that they were doing God's will and gaining an eternal reward for their murderous actions. Charles Selengut believes that "religious violence is among the most pressing and dangerous issues facing the world community."[2]

The term "genocide" describes mass murder of a national, ethnic, political or religious group; an "atrocity" generally describes extreme cruelty, including acts of murder and torture.[3] Acts of atrocity and genocide have been used throughout history to assert the power of the dominant over the oppressed. What Americans did at Wounded Knee to the Lakota Sioux (1891), what the Ottoman Turks and Kurds did to the Armenians (1915–1917), what the Japanese military forces did to the defenseless women of Nanjing (1937), and what the Yoruba and Hausa did to the revolting Biafrans (1969–1971) are all acts of atrocity and genocide. Aside from Germany after the Second World War, nations rarely seem to readily admit to committing genocide. It is a term typically used by victims and not usually by perpetrators. The term "genocide" is a loaded term, either used sparingly by governments seeking to avoid taking action or frequently by victims who hope to stir others to an indignant response.

Biblical Violence

The Bible may well be one of the earliest holy books to describe full-blooded and God-ordained genocides: it is a violent book filled with bloodshed. The Bible is clear that some peoples are chosen and some are outside God's blessing and are a danger to those who are chosen. Those who are on the outside are seen as a threat to be feared. Lawrence Wills explains: "The Other has threatened in the past and will continue to threaten again in the future. . . . There is thus a continuing tension concerning the eternal Other. There is a command to destroy it finally, yet it will always endure to threaten again."[4]

Cain spontaneously killed his brother Abel due to his envy; God commanded Abraham to sacrifice his son Jacob and also decreed the complete massacre of all males amongst the Canaanite tribe of Shechem; God commanded the genocide of every man, woman, child, and animal in the city of Ai; the Pharaoh of Egypt ordered that all newborn Hebrew boys be killed, a command that God vengefully reiterated before the Exodus; King Herod issued the same decree to murder children at the time of Jesus. The New Testament portrayal of Christ culminates for Christians with the bloody and violent human sacrifice of God's only son, Jesus.

The Bible calls for violence and shows God, as is true in stories of other Near Eastern deities, to be a divine warrior (see Ex. 15:3; Jud. 5:19-20; Is. 24:21). Jubilant songs, which speak of God's military prowess, fill the Bible (Deut. 33:2-3; Num. 10:35-36; Ps. 24; Is. 35; Hab. 3:3-60). One such hymn glowingly exalts God's proclamation: "I will make mine arrows drunk with blood, and my sword shall devour flesh."[5]

The book of Exodus tells of how the Egyptian first-born were victims of a divine mass-killing on the night of Israel's departure from slavery (Ex. 12:29-30). When the armies of Pharaoh follow the slaves, they are lured by God into a deadly trap, which leads to their total annihilation (Ex. 14-15). Leo Lefebure is correct that "the concrete provisions of the holy war were gruesome."[6] When the Children of Israel finally arrive at their promised land they are ordered by Almighty God to execute every man (while women were to be kept as slaves or concubines). Joshua dutifully obeyed God and killed every person in Ai (Josh. 8:25–29) and in Jericho (Josh. 6:17-21) with the singular exception of Rahab the spy. No treaties were to be made with those who were living in their own homes and about to be invaded (Deut. 7:1-24) because God promises the Israelites that all of these people will eventually be destroyed. God ordered that every Amalekite be killed so that the holy people of Israel would not become corrupted by their paganism (1 Sam. 15:2–4); traitors and all native residents were to be massacred (Deut. 20:12–18); in Numbers 31:7, 17–18, God commands the massacre of all of the Midianites except for the young girls who were to be taken as concubines, prizes in warfare. Philip Jenkins is correct: "If the forces of Joshua and his successor judges had committed their acts in the modern world, observers would not hesitate to speak of war crimes, even of genocide, and they would draw comparisons with the notorious guerilla armies of Uganda and the Congo."[7] The biblical record is filled with dozens of other examples of slaughter, God-sent plagues and famines, and a host of other incomprehensible atrocities.

Eternal Punishment and a Terrorist God

Some versions of both Christianity and Islam claim that God will ultimately torture sinners for all eternity in a blazing hell-fire. The concept of a hell is not present in early Judaism, but seems to have been in place in some form by the time of Jesus who frequently warned of the punishments of hell. Even aside from the threat of hell, the Bible reveals God's destruction of humanity by flood (Gen. 11) and mandating the burning of populated cities (Gen. 18).

While also accepting the Biblical stories of God-sponsored lethal floods and consuming fires, Islam also teaches that a flaming fire awaits all non-believers and those Muslims who have rebelled (Q. 9:73). The message of hell is intended to "instill terror into the hearts of unbelievers" (Q. 8:12). Both the "unbelievers among the People of the Book and the pagans shall burn forever in the fire of Hell" (Q. 98:1–8, see also 43:74, 55:41–52 and 76:1–5).

The Qur'an preaches that "garments of fire have been prepared for the unbelievers (Q. 22:19–23) and the "wrong-doers" will live in "a fire which will encompass them like walls of a pavilion: when they cry out for help they shall be showered with water as hot as molten brass which will scald their faces" (Q. 18:28–30). Those who deny the truth of Islam "shall be dragged through scalding water and then burnt in the fire of Hell" by God (Q. 40: 67, 73). Unbelievers will eat "choking food" and undergo "harrowing torment" (Q. 73:12). Unbelievers are the "fuel of hell" (Q. 21:96–101) and the "heirs of hell" (Q. 5:10). There are many other passages like those cited above in the Holy Qur'an.[8]

Is there any relationship between the threat of eternal violence and the paralyzing fears of those who have abused other people in the name of Allah throughout history? Do threats of dreadful punishments in the afterlife encourage or discourage dreadful actions in this life? How can it be that religion, arguably the most powerful force in the world, could be so ineffective in bringing intercultural peace and mutual respect? In fact, until the advent of the twentieth century when Nazism and Stalinism changed the world forever, more people had arguably been killed in the name of religion (mostly by Christians and Muslims) than by any other multi-generational institutional force in the world.[9] Muslims and Christians alike have been on both the giving and receiving side of genocides and atrocities throughout their long histories. A few of the more recent atrocities that have affected the Muslim world will be briefly introduced toward the end of this chapter.

Torture

Torture, which is always an act of injustice, is forbidden in Islam. Torture blurs the line between necessity and morality and often results in murder. In the revelation of the Qur'an the same words are used for "to kill" and "to murder" (qatala). Premeditated murder is the second greatest sin after polytheism; Allah forbids the shedding of blood (Q. 2:30–39; 84). The Prophet spoke against the use of torture (muthla) as Muslims interacted with their enemies. He forbade the mistreatment and brutal killing of prisoners (Q. 2:208, 194). Allah is able to forgive those who have been captured (Q. 8:70–71) so believers should show them clemency (Q. 8:62); captives are to be fed (Q. 76:7–9). When one of the Prophet's warriors (Khalid) ordered that a prisoner should be killed, he was rebuked by Muhammad (Bukhari, 5, 59:628).

The Qur'an allows for war criminals to be maimed, exiled, executed, crucified, or have their hands and feet cut off (Q. 5:33–34). This passage refers to some Jewish traitors who were executed or exiled for their complicity in a plot against the Prophet in Medina during the "Battle of the Trench".[10] After this battle, the story of what happened with the Jewish betrayal at Banu Qurayaza (627) is complicated by the fact that it retells one of the most violent incidents in the life of the Prophet. Non-Muslims often cite the "Affair at Khaybar", in which Ibn Ishaq claims that the Prophet called for the torture of the thief Kinana bin al-Rabi, but this incident is denied by Muslims as coming from an unverifiable source.[11] Regardless, the main lesson of this story was that torture cannot be used to extract a confession from one's enemies. This ethical argument stands in contrast to the recent impression given by the international media that torture is permissible in Islam. Sadly, torture has been carried out over and over again in the history of Islam, against both fellow believers and non-believers.

Prisoner Abuse

Prisoner abuse, such as what has occurred in Iraq's Abu Ghraib — or as continues to occur at the detention centers of Guantanamo, is not permissible in Islam. In both prisons, those incarcerated were also humiliated and tortured. The intention of the abusive methods of Abu Ghraib and the Cuban island American enclave of Guantanamo is to shame an individual and attack his/her sense of personal dignity and honor (*haya*). From a Muslim perspective, one's dignity is the essence of one's humanity. This is the reason why issues of nakedness play such a prominent role in discussions of prisoner abuse. The Islamic tradition mandates that any person, including a prisoner, should be modestly covered (*hijab*) from the navel to the knees (according to the code of *satr*).

The extraordinary measures that the United States government adopted in its "War on Terror" in Iraq and Afghanistan (especially sending prisoners to Guantanamo or to other nations to be tortured), is of the gravest concern to Muslims worldwide. News of what happened in Abu Ghraib led to militant extremists beheading Nicholas Berg (an American civilian in Iraq) as well as killing several other American civilians. The reporting of these events among Muslim communities galvanized hatred against the United States, which continues to be an ongoing point of concern in the relations between Muslim-majority nations and the secular governments of Europe and North America. Particular anger was also leveled against citizens of the UK because of British involvement in the "War on Terror"; including the abuse of some prisoners at Abu Ghraib at the hands of British personnel.[12]

Such acts of injustice, as those which have occurred at Abu Ghraib and at the detention center in Guantanamo, are described by Muslims as *haram*. This Arabic term refers to a place of holiness and sacredness. For most Muslims, this usually refers to the *al-bait al-atiq*, the "ancient house" of Mecca, but the entire world is also to be cleansed from all impurities. It is a zeal for holiness that should motivate believers to react strongly against any form of injustice such as torture, atrocity, and genocide. While war may be inevitable, atrocity in war is strictly forbidden. Human beings are valuable to God and must therefore be honored. In one Hadith, the Prophet explains, "A pauper among my people is one who faces the Day of Judgment with a record of *salat*, fasts and *zakat*, but who will have abused this one, slandered that one, stolen from a third, shed the blood of the fourth and physically assaulted the fifth."[13]

Indiscriminate violence against innocent people happens around the world every day with numbing regularity. The most oft-cited examples of atrocities are the horrific Crusade Wars of the eleventh to the late-fourteenth centuries, which pitted Christians against Muslims. Such interfaith atrocities, however, are not only part of ancient history. Some modern atrocities are vast, such as the suffering of Armenian Christians at the hands of Turkish and Kurdish Muslims, and some are minor and rarely reported in the newspapers of the world. In September of 1998, for example, Dani Christians in the highlands of Indonesia burned a masjid to the ground and Muslims responded by burning down the home of a Christian pastor. There are countless other examples across the pages of time where violent tit-for-tat inter-religious conflicts have disfigured the nobility of a given faith community and challenged the legitimacy of religious idealism.

The Armenian Genocide

Any examination of genocide in the twentieth century should begin with what happened in Ottoman Turkey to their Armenian Christian minority between 1893 and 1918. These events are denied by the contemporary Turkish government, which refuses to admit that between one and a half and two million Armenians were killed as part of an organized governmental effort to wipe them out and to remove them from their ancestral homelands. Most of those who survived the murderous attacks were either exiled or emigrated; only a small number of Armenians remain in Turkey. Sadly, the United States government has officially overlooked the Turkish government's denial of the facts of their Ottoman-era history in the interest of modern-day military expediencies. As recently as 2013, President Obama has refused opportunities when meeting with Turkish officials to call these recorded acts of genocide by their accurate name. While campaigning for President, Senator Obama repeatedly promised to acknowledge the Armenian Genocide. Caving into pressure from Turkey, however, President Obama has not only failed to acknowledge these facts of history but has also actively blocked congressional efforts to rectify this egregious error.[14]

Fortunately, some Armenians have survived to tell the horrific story. Valiant Armenian survivors were even able to eventually create a homeland in the former Soviet Empire, while continuing to face stern opposition from their neighbors (especially an extensive war with Muslim Azerbaijan). The Caucasus region has become a contemporary cauldron of religious and ethnic tensions. Both the Armenians of Yerevan and the Azeri Turks of Baku claim that the hellish slaughter of innocents has gone on in the contested region of Nagorno-Karabakh. In a parade of continuing insults, one historic ruin of a sacred Armenian church in Van, modern-day Eastern Turkey, has been transformed into a dung-laden hayloft and storage facility for farm implements and animals.[15]

Muslim Turks and Armenian Christians had previously lived in relative peace with each other for centuries. Of course, there were problems from time to time, but these problems escalated to nightmarish heights in the 1890's and exploded again with venomous force between 1915 and 1918. Because some Ottoman Turks wanted to purge non-Turkish ethnicities from their midst, they violated the *dhimmi* status of Armenians and began to deport and slaughter them. A decree was issued on April 24, 1915, to commence these murders, beginning with the intellectuals and Armenians who were serving in the Ottoman military. The vast majorities of these innocent victims were neither nationalists nor involved in politics. Ottoman Turks inspired their citizens to mercilessly hunt down and slaughter any and all Armenians as an act of *jihad*; Muslim clerics piously sanctioned these brutal mass killings. Emphatic clerics issued *fatwas*, which assured those who carried out atrocities that they would have legal impunity and would be hailed as righteous defenders of the holy faith. Observers of the genocide have noted how frequently the rhetoric of religion was invoked to advance these mass killings.

In 1915, in the village of Yozgad, over 6,000 Armenian women and children were deported by the Turks. Vahakn Dadrian (b. 1924) tells what happened next: "To save shells and powder the gendarmerie commander in charge of the convoy gathered 10,000 to 12,000 Turkish peasants and other villagers armed with hatchets, meat cleavers, saddler's knives, cudgels, axes, pickaxes, and shovels" and sent them to murder the Armenians, which they did for the next four to five hours, shouting God's name as they wreaked their vengeance.[16] It is hard to imagine accurately the horror of such atrocities. One person who tried to personalize the horrors was the brilliant Armenian poet Siamanto (1878–1915), who was eventually executed in the Ottoman atrocities of 1915 simply because he was an Armenian intellectual. Before he was murdered by the State, he recounted in one of his poems what he witnessed: the mass rapes and burnings by gasoline fire of innocent Armenian women and girls of all ages in front of their defenseless men (before they were also executed):

I must tell you what I saw so people will understand the crimes men do to men — a dark crowd standing in a vineyard lashing twenty brides and singing dirty songs — with fury whips crashed on the naked flesh. . . . [A]n animal of a man shouted 'You must dance!' Dance they raved. Dance till you die infidel beauties. . . . Smile and don't complain. You're abandoned now, you're naked slaves. . . . Then someone brought a jug of kerosene. Human justice I spit in your face. The brides were anointed. Dance — they thundered. Here's a fragrance you can't get in Arabia. Then with a torch they set the naked brides on fire and the charred corpses rolled and tumbled to their deaths. . . .[17]

According to the writer Elie Wiesel, the final stage of genocide is the denial of the events that occurred. Milan Kundera has written that opposition against power often expresses itself as the struggle of memory against forgetting. Denial can be described as a "double-killing", because the guilty do not take responsibility and the victims cannot be properly mourned and remembered.

Some Muslims — and most Turkish people — deny that genocide occurred against the defenseless people of Armenia in the name of a holy religion. They argue that if atrocities did take place, they were provoked and were carried out for justifiable reasons on both sides and in the muddled fog of a very messy war. It is true that some Armenians were sympathetic to the efforts of those invading the Ottoman Empire and some of them even joined forces with the nation's opponents, but the number of rebels was small compared to the vast majority of Armenian civilians who were harmlessly trying to live their lives among their Muslim neighbors. The events of Armenia, 1915, a succession of Turkish governments have argued, cannot be described as "genocide" because the forced relocations that took place were not systematically carried out by the government. Turkish authorities admit that there was an initiative to remove citizens from their villages for their "protection" — as they were in the middle of a battleground — but claim that Armenians only died "accidentally" during the course of these "relocations". Clear facts, published documents, and reliable eye-witness accounts by non-participants are dismissed as propaganda or framed as unreliable historiography.

An organization called the Turkish-Armenian Reconciliation Commission (TARC) has joined with the International Center for Transitional Justice (ICTJ) to promote academic and legal studies to analyze the facts of history and legal issues, which relate to that history, in an objective way.[18] Facts are stubborn things, and the facts are that Ottoman forces were involved in the killings and that "death marches" were designed to incur as many Armenian deaths as was possible.

Turkish historian Taner Akcam observed that "under the pretext of searching for arms, of collecting war levies, or of tracking down deserters, there had already been an established practice of systematically carried out plunders, raids, and murders against the Armenians, which had become daily occurrences."[19]

Muslim Heroism in the Protection of Jewish People

During World War II, over six million Jews were murdered in dozens of Nazi concentration camps merely because they were Jewish. These camps were located throughout Germany and Eastern Europe, but there were also Nazi-operated forced labor concentration camps in occupied French provinces and in German-occupied North Africa. There were large and historic Jewish communities in North Africa; some of these even formed underground resistance units. Jews in Tunisia, Algeria, Libya, and Morocco were arrested and often deported to Nazi concentration camps in Europe. Robert Satloff reports that a number of North Africans such as Mohammad Chenik, Si Ali Sakkat, Si Kaddour Benghabrit, and Khaled Abdul-Wahab, valiantly worked to save some of their Jewish compatriots during the dangerous era of the Nazi Holocaust.[20]

Sadly, in the modern world, those who would blatantly deny the facts of the Nazi extermination of the Jews have found a listening ear among some Muslim communities. The claim is that the Holocaust simply did not happen. Some have even idolized Adolf Hitler; the state-owned Egyptian newspaper *Al-Akhbar* wrote: "Thanks to Hitler of blessed memory, who on behalf of the Palestinians revenged in advance, against the vilest criminals on the face of the earth."[21] The former President of Iran, Mahmoud Ahmadinejad, asserted of Hitler: "He is completely innocent of frying them (the Jews) in the hell of his false Holocaust."[22]

The denial of Holocaust and atrocity perpetrates the horror of these tragedies into the future. Peter Balakian (b. 1951) describes the denial of atrocities as being based on the "promotion of forgetting".[23] Those who deny atrocity actually blame the victims for the crimes visited upon them. Denial of the atrocities in Armenia and those during World War II is a form of murdering victims again by killing their memory. Denial and forgetting is a way to "absolve" any guilt or accountability against those who refuse to acknowledge atrocity; setting the stage for possible future occurrences of genocide.

Present generations should not feel blindly duty-bound to defend the honor of previous generations. Denial freezes any chance at eventual healing and reconciliation between victims and victimizers. Most tellingly, denying genocides clears the way for future genocides to take place. It is vital to remember such tragedies so that lessons can be learned and future can be wrongs avoided.

The Partition of India

Muslim-Hindu and Muslim-Sikh relations have been frequently marked with bloodshed since Muslims first arrived in the South Asian continent. Mass-killings of Hindus and Sikhs by Muslims have also escalated during times of repeated, bitter warfare. The Bahmani Sultans in Central India were particularly vicious.[24] Even the Mughal Sultanate (1526–1857), which was constrained in contrast to the Delhi Sultanate (1206–1526), carried out massacres of entire non-Muslim villages. A major Mughal victory in Vija in 1565 was "celebrated" with general murder and arson against any available unbelievers.

Once Mughal Muslim rule in India was firmly established, it was often the case that Hindus and Sikh subjects were humiliated and exploited by unjust laws and capricious government officials as a way to tighten social control and discourage attempts by non-Muslims to rebel against autocratic State power. Negationism, the denial of atrocity, is particularly strong amongst historians of Muslim-Hindu/Sikh relations in India. Contrary to historic hagiography (in Hindu, Sikh and Muslim sources in the interest of allaying further tensions), which often presented Mughal India as a benign and tolerant context (especially as portrayed by Muslim historians), Islamic rule in India was extremely violent and was marked by high taxes, appalling poverty, systematic terror, forced conversions, destruction of temples, summary executions, and deliberate impoverishment (such as in Jahangir).[25] In numerous long centuries of rule, many more Hindus and Sikhs were killed at the hands of their Muslim leaders than Jews were slaughtered in the Holocaust. Relatively small acts of terror added up over the centuries to create the present context of Hindu/Sikh-Muslim tensions: cruelty became the norm.

Horrific atrocities have also occurred to the Muslim communities of India. In 1947, India and Pakistan were given their independence from Great Britain but the hasty process of partition was poorly managed and resulted in massive confusion that lead to massacre and migration on an unimaginable scale. The problems of partition have remained even to our present day. For example, the majority Muslim state of Kashmir remains partly in India and partly in Pakistan as an unresolved legacy of this process. And in modern India, Muslims, Sikhs, and Hindus continue to fight over unresolved ancient legacies like the status of shrines in the northern Indian city of Ayodha. History, religion, culture, and politics have interwoven to create these systemic problems.

The Muslim politician Muhammad Ali Jinnah (1876–1948) called for a separate Muslim state (which became the Islamic Republic of Pakistan) for a number of reasons. Jinnah cited Qur'an 4:97–99 to assert that

Muslims would need to create their own Muslim government, which could ensure their own protection while also serving as a refuge for other South Asian Muslims facing persecution. When "Partition" came, tens of thousands of fearful Muslim refugees began to move northward into Pakistan while, at the same time, legions of anxious Hindu and Sikh refugees trekked southward from the Punjab. For many Hindus and Sikhs, the partition of their sacred motherland was a painfully unimaginable sacrilege.

When the mass killings began in 1947, the Hindu and Sikh communities in what is now called Pakistan were annihilated, excepting a few pockets in the Sindh and East Bengal. At least seven million Hindus and Sikhs moved south based on the ethnic cleansing strategy of "slaughtering one to expel a hundred". The Sikhs of the Punjab were the most frequent victims of these massacres, because they refused to be displaced from their cherished ancestral homes. In the coming months, hundreds of thousands of innocent women and children, and many unarmed men, were butchered by machete on both sides. Trains going in each direction arrived at their final stations with no one aboard left alive. These senseless massacres were especially shocking because, tragically, they came after centuries of relative harmony between the two faith communities. Of these events after his own village was destroyed the Punjabi poet Faiz Ahmad Faiz (1911–1984) wrote: "Today every instrument is forsaken by its melody and the singer's voice goes searching for a singer. Today the chords of every harp are shredded like a madman's shirt. Today the people beg each gust of wind to bring any sound at all, even a lamentation, even a scream of anguish, or the last trumpet crying the hour of doom."[26]

Bangladesh in 1971

In 1965, General Muhammad Ayoub Khan seized power in Pakistan and soon went to war with India. The progressive misfortunes of this war eventually led to a civil war, which resulted in East Pakistan becoming the new nation of Bangladesh after a series of atrocities exploded across the length and breadth of the land. As Bengalis struggled to gain independence from East Pakistan in 1971, they were invaded by an army from West Pakistan. West Pakistan showed particular disregard for the honor of Hindus living in the region.

The soldiers sought to terrorize their enemies into abject submission with sudden and overwhelming force. Racism also played a role in the hatred shown by Pakistani soldiers, who viewed their Bengali enemies as a soft, non-military and physically weak race, forever influenced by Hinduism and mysticism. The people of Bangladesh fell before the overwhelming weaponry and racist anger of the invaders, who felt that they were doing God's work. Soldiers particularly targeted the university and artistic communities of Dhaka as well as the slums and squatter camps known to house large numbers of Hindus. For over nine months, the West Pakistanis not only killed Hindus, but marauding soldiers "even killed *namazis* in mosques all across occupied Bangladesh."[27] People were slaughtered when they fled into the Bait-ul Mukarram masjid, and masjids in occupied territories had their pulpits filled by Jaamati extremists who were not afraid to promote violence in the name of religion.

Particular attention was reserved for the pockets of Hindu communities that had been long resident in Bangladesh. It is impossible to know how many were killed, but the number was approximately three million civilians; the vast proportion of those murdered was Hindu and Sufi non-combatants.[28] About 80% of all Hindus in East Bengal were killed or were forced to flee into India as refugees. As soldiers plundered, looted, and killed, they also began to rape many Hindu, and many Muslim, women. Incidents of mass-rape took place at the Razarbagh Police Line Prison and in police stations all along the Tripura border. The usual practice was to rape the women publicly, in front of their fathers and brothers, before the men of the home were executed. Specific rape-camps were also established near a number of army barracks.

On March 25, 1971, there was, according to Hasan "a selective massacre in Hindu populated areas where not even little children were spared."[29] It was on this same night that a sports field close to Dhaka University was designated to become a killing field for captured Hindus and resisting Muslims. Hasan relates, "They gathered a great number of Hindu men, women, and children from the vicinity. Before being shot, the high-priest of the age-old temple was forcibly compelled to recite Qur'anic verses. The men and children were put on the firing line while the women's lives were spared as they were whisked away to an unknown destination for rape."[30] According to Rounaq Jahan, as many as a quarter of a million women were victimized.[31] Perhaps these troops felt that they were justified in separating these Hindu and Muslim innocents "from night and day" as well as in raping countless thousands of innocent Hindu and Muslim women because these women were dismissively seen as the inevitable and necessary "spoils of war".

A further tragedy of the events of 1971 was that the resulting independence of the nation meant that the leaders of Bangladesh would remain largely quiet about these atrocities (until some legal cases were finally tried in 2013) in exchange for peaceful relations with Pakistan and other Muslim nations. In addition, the Pakistani government at the conclusion of the war began an almost immediate international campaign to deny any genocide and to wipe out any record of atrocities. This partially explains why what happened in Bangladesh in 1971 has remained largely hidden from history. While the international community, and the United Nations in particular, was very generous after the war in offering financial aid to Bangladesh, the support for war-crimes trials was virtually non-existent. Leaders of the new nation had little choice but to table their efforts to expose the truth, which resulted in a deep sense of betrayal and anger among the deeply abused and exhausted population. Do Bangladeshis still care about the events of 1971? The answer is yes: the truth about these crimes against humanity will never be resolved or forgotten until they are finally resolved through the power of truth and reconciliation.

Multifaith Tensions in South Asia

Tension between Muslims and Hindus (and also Sikhs) continues today in a number of contexts across South Asia. The situation in the Kashmir often explodes into violence. Kashmir is a peace-loving and culturally rich community with millennia of heritage and tradition. Most Kashmiris only want to live in peace, but political tensions between Pakistan and India have made that impossible since the 1947 Partition. There are many acts of injustice on both the Hindu and Muslim sides of this ongoing issue. The key flashpoints for terrorism have been the two Indian Provinces of Jumma and Kashmir. Because these two states have a majority Muslim population, it is felt that these states should rightfully belong to Pakistan. Some Hindus have been killed in the Kashmir Valley; many others have been threatened with death if they did not leave. Countless homes have been looted and burned, as have many ancient Hindu shrines.

Over 400,000 Kashmiri Pandit Hindus have been forced out of the Kashmir Valley by militant extremists within the last two decades. Hindu militants have responded by sadistically killing their innocent Muslim neighbors. Non-combatant Muslim villagers have been lynched at random, disemboweled, bled to death, and burned alive in Kashmir. Muslims claim that all of their brothers and sisters in Kashmir are under constant surveillance and experience unending harassment at the hands of the local police and government. Ethnic cleansing has occurred on both sides of Kashmir's unstable borders. International organizations such as Asia Watch, Human Rights Watch, and Amnesty International continue to monitor the situation, which has been marked by a series of ongoing offenses, including murders, in recent years.

A number of individuals have been massacred in the Indian state of Gujarat at the hands of both Hindu and Muslim militant fanatics. On February 27, 2002, for example, extremist Muslims torched and destroyed a train filled with Hindu activists near the town of Godhra.

In retaliation, members of the ruling Bharatiya Janata Party (BJP) and other groups led attacks against unarmed Muslim villagers in Gujarat. At least 3,000 non-combatant Muslims were killed; home and property damages exceeded 280 billion rupees.[32] Many Islamic-based schools have been closed and Muslim villagers frequently relate that they have become victims of indiscriminate police brutality. Some Muslims are afraid to enter the Indian government service or enroll in certain universities that are considered BJP strongholds. Most of those who were arrested by the police in these instances were not Hindus, but Muslims. Some progressive Hindus have tried to launch peace initiatives and have criticized the BJP for actions that they feel are anti-Islamic, but these tensions run very deep. Many minority communities live in fear today because these kinds of atrocities have largely gone unpunished.

Mumbai, India, the "New York of South Asia" was the scene of a series of nightmarish terror attacks in 2008. The horrific murders of at least 174 people and the wounding of 300 more innocent bystanders over a period of three days, which began on November 26, was carried out by 10 members of a Pakistani Muslim extremist group, the *Lashkar e-Taiba*. This terror group was probably founded with the assistance of the Pakistani national intelligence organization (the ISI). The stated objective of this terror group was to draw attention to the plight of Muslims suffering in Kashmir. The terrorists targeted a train station, a popular bar, two luxury hotels, and a Jewish Chabad House (about which, the director of the *Lashkar e-Taiba* said that killing 1 Jew was better than killing 50 Hindus). 6 Jews were killed, while the 2-year-old child of the director of the Chabad House, Moshe Holtzberg, was miraculously saved by his Indian nanny after the boy had been left for dead. Many other innocent men, women and children were not so fortunate. The waves of searing pain generated from these senseless bombings, fires, and killings cannot possibly be fathomed.

Muslim-Buddhist and Muslim-Christian relations have also been an issue in other parts of Asia. Many people do not realize that there were historically thousands of Muslim farmers in Cambodia before the arrival of the Pol Pot regime (1975–1979). During that time, the rural Muslims of Cambodia were targeted for murder and all Islamic schools were closed. Muslims were forced to step on the Holy Qur'an and publicly eat prohibited pork.[33] As was the case in other contexts, the perpetrators of these humiliations sought to torture their victims in order to destroy their powerful sense of personal dignity and socio-religious identity.

Fighting has also erupted in southern Thailand along the border with Malaysia as Muslim extremist terrorist bands have been forged to target teachers and education centers with the intent of ensuring that their Muslim-majority communities will only have madrassahs and not be infiltrated by non-Muslim Thai nationalistic ideas. Tensions between

Christian and Muslim communities have also resulted in violence on the island of Mindanao in the Philippines and in a number of areas of Indonesia, in which Christians have reacted against Muslim attempts to convert their neighbors to the Islamic faith.

Interventions in the Middle East

Warfare and a number of ethno-religious atrocities have gone on for decades in Palestine and the Arab Middle East. Many tensions have arisen out of the era of colonialism as new nations have sought to gain their own independence. In Iran, the Shah of Iran was placed in power in 1946, and one of his emerging opponents — the Iranian Prime Minister Muhammad Mossadegh (1882–1967) — was deposed by a CIA-backed coup in 1953. In 1957, the United States failed in an attempt to overthrow the Baathist government of Syria and, in 1958, President Eisenhower sent Marines into Beirut in order to support the autocratic and corrupt government in that nation, which was blindly pro-American. This trend was repeated again in 1983, when Ronald Reagan intervened in a Lebanese civil war on behalf of one of the minority Christian groups. It was at that time that a suicide bombing attack, known as the Beirut barracks bombing, killed over 200 Marines, which eventually forced President Reagan to withdraw all troops.

Civil Wars in Lebanon and Syria

The labyrinthine realities of politics in Lebanon defy easy description. The fact that the American government has sent troops into Lebanon twice since World War II parallels how other nations (specifically Syria and Israel) have shown little regard for the sovereignty of Lebanon. These facts have led to a number of extremist groups arising in Lebanon in the name of addressing decades of foreign interventions in their nation, which is divided so deeply along ethnic, cultural, and religious lines.

One of the most noted paramilitary extremist groups that took root in Lebanon in the 1980s is known as *Hezbollah*, or the "Party of God". The Shi'ites of southern Lebanon resented the fact that they had been dominated politically and economically by the Christians and Sunni Muslims of the nation. The Shi'ites' feelings of marginalization and victimization were aroused even further with the Iranian Islamic Revolution of 1979, which exemplified and fortified resistance to foreign intervention by deposing the US supported Pahlavi dynasty. Forces in the new Iranian Republic began to fund the efforts of those in Lebanon who sought justice for their communities. One of their founders was a former schoolteacher named Abbas al-Musawi, who began to forge a base of support in the Bekaa Valley and in the southern Lebanese city of Baalbek.

Hezbollah (or Hizballah) grew rapidly and "leadership became vested in young Shi'ite clerics who saw fundamentalist Islam as an alternative to the secular political systems of the capitalist West and the Communist East."[34] Hezbollah kidnapped a number of Westerners and hijacked TWA Flight 847 in Beirut in 1985. Their strong anti-Zionist stance led to the assassination of Abbas al-Musawi in 1992 and the invasion of southern Lebanon by Israeli soldiers (who did not leave the country until 1999). Fighting broke out again in 2006, when Israeli forces entered Lebanon and attacked Hezbollah forces. In one notable escalation of this conflict, with the assistance of Iran, Hezbollah was able to successfully launch a drone at least 35 miles into Israeli airspace in 2012.

A fully fledged civil war erupted in Syria in 2012 after the fall of Libyan, Tunisian, and Egyptian dictators, and continues at the time of this writing (2014). While the reasons for this war are primarily political and ethnic, they are often framed by rebel forces in terms of a religious war against the secular Ba'athist dictatorship of Bashir al-Assad (b. 1967) and his family, which has dealt with all forms of religio-political dissent with an iron hand. March 2014 marked the tragic third anniversary of the Syrian Civil War, which has resulted in the deaths of over 100,000 people and, according to the UNHCR, the displacement of over 9 million Syrians from their homes. Children have been particular victims of this unconscionable (and often ignored) humanitarian crisis with about 70% of them now unable to attend school. Infant mortality has soared and diseases like polio have returned. One refugee described their dire situation: "We have to drink from polluted wells and wash in the sewage. We eat leaves and rotten rice. We have no electricity. Our medical facilities lack basic sterile conditions and we must use expired medications." Another teenage refugee said simply: "I used to dream but those have all been blown away."[35] While a resolution of this conflict remains to be realized, what is tragic are the countless innocent non-combatants — largely women and children — who have been caught in the brutal crossfire of this civil war.

Palestine and Israel

After World War I, the French created Lebanon and Syria and the British invented Palestine and Jordan. In 1948, the United Nations called for the founding of the State of Israel and another state for Palestinians: this latter nation has yet to emerge. The militarization of this region has cost the lives of countless innocent people in its advance. Constant war has come at an extraordinary price.

North American newspapers frequently retell one-sided stories of so-called Palestinian "suicide bombers" who give their life and kill bystanders in the name of blinding love for their country. These actions have a disturbingly wide appeal. Mahmoud al-Zahar (b. 1945) of Hamas claims that a 2002 call for "martyrs" at the University of Alexandria in Egypt resulted in 2,000 students signing up to participate.[36] It is not fair to caricature all these young individuals as destitute and poor; many of them are educated and have families. Raed Abdel-Hamed Mesk, an Islamic studies teacher working on his Master's Degree (and the father of two young children) murdered 21 people on a public bus in Jerusalem on August 19, 2003. Hiba Daraghmeh was a student of English literature at the Al-Quds University in the West Bank before he murdered three people and wounded 48 bystanders at a shopping mall on May 19, 2003. Hanadi Jaradat was a young law school graduate who had her entire life ahead of her before she murdered 19 individuals and wounded 40 more by blowing herself up in a Haifa restaurant on October 5, 2003. Jaradat's two brothers (Fadi and Saleh) were members of the terrorist group Islamic Jihad. What all of these bombers have in common is a shared experience of a lifetime of going through hundreds of checkpoints to get anywhere (micro-aggressions) and a feeling that they were dispossessed within their own country. Jaradat's father said after his daughter's death: "I can tell you that our people believe that what Hanadi has done is justified. Imagine watching the Israelis kill your son, your nephew, destroying our house-they are pushing our people into a corner." None of these attackers feel that they are committing suicide or are attacking innocent victims. Islamists cite Qur'an 2:154, which promises them that they will live in eternal blessings, since they have died as martyrs in the cause of God.

Muslim and Christian communities in the West Bank and Gaza of Palestine have been struggling for their rights since 1948, when Israel became a country. Many individuals lost their homes and have lived in refugee camps (or in exile) for decades. When people talked about *jihad* in Palestine, attention was often focused on Hamas and the Palestinian Liberation Organization, but there has been a long history of war between Palestinian Muslims and immigrant Jews. The "First Great Jihad" in Palestine was led against the Byzantine Empire by Abu Bakr, the first Caliph, within two years of the Prophet Muhammad's death (634). Four thousand Jews, Christians, and Samaritans, who defended Gaza, were massacred. The villages of the Negev and towns such as Jerusalem, Jaffa, Caesarea, Beth Shan, and Nablus were pillaged. Sophronius, the Patriarch of Jerusalem, in his Sermon on the day of the Epiphany in 636, bewailed the destruction of churches, synagogues, monasteries, and towns and the people killed and tortured by the "Saracen invaders". Famine and plague followed; taxes levied against non-Muslims continued to rise until most villagers felt that they had no choice but to convert.

When violence erupted in Gaza at the end of 2012 and the beginning of 2013, many felt that the tensions between Israel and Palestine had the potential to escalate into a larger war as the two sides have become increasingly intransigent and aggressive. This has been the situation since the 1980s; there has been ample evidence of both Palestinian and Israeli aggression that has only added to overall tensions and threats of further hostilities.[37] In March, 2014 Gaza's most intense cross-border violence since 2012 flared when the militant group Islamic Jihad fired dozens of rockets into Israel which forced their retaliation. Economic and political pressure grew after the return of the Egyptian military government which has closed as many as 1,300 of the smuggling tunnels used between Egypt and Gaza. Hopes for successful peace talks resuming between Palestine and Israel seem dim at the time of this writing. Ahmed Yousuf, a pro-Hamas analyst, described the mood of many modern Palestinians: "The people are so angry, so upset, so frustrated. We are squeezed from every corner."[38] Once again, in this quagmire, as in all others, the primary victims of repeated rocket attacks from both camps were the innocent bystanders who had no place to run or hide in the face of the hellish warfare all around them. Any subsequent reprieve in the tensions between these two warring factions should compel the international community to work with determined alacrity to prevent future injustices.

Almost four years after that young Tunisian street vendor set himself on fire, the poverty, unemployment, and repressions that he was protesting have continued with dogged persistence. While Tunisia, for example has seen some political progress, economic problems continue to deepen. Egypt saw the overthrow of its dictator only to see its first democratically-elected President deposed by the military and his political party, the Muslim Brotherhood, banned once again as a terrorist organization. All across the region, deepening political divisions, economic stagnation, and seething public anger continue to characterize the unfulfilled hopes of the Arab Spring.

The Baha'i and other Minorities

Many religious minorities within Muslim-majority nations have faced cruel persecution at the hands of their own governments. The Baluchis of Pakistan and Iran and the Ismail'i of Iran have faced extensive persecution. The Baluchis follow a distinct sect in Islam that claims that a local holy saint named Nur Pak (Syed Mohamed Jaunpari) was a Prophet sent from God. While they may not have usually been murdered for their faith, they are considered "worthless" in society and are marginalized.[39]

Members of the Baha'i faith within Iran have also been severely persecuted as heretics since their origins in the middle of the nineteenth century.[40] The last Shah of Iran, however, loosened restrictions against the Baha'i, and they became highly successful and respected. When the Iranian revolution of 1979 transpired, the Baha'i were again legally considered to be heretics and traitors to Islam. Once more their lands began to be confiscated, and, when Baha'i protested, the police often deferred their attention while they were killed. Some Baha'i within Iran have been unable to obtain identity cards, which are essential in Iran to perform basic transactions for goods and services.

One of the most brutal expressions of the disrespect against Iran's peace-loving Baha'i concerns a number of young women who have been arrested and then brutally raped in prison before being executed as heretics. It seems that, since Iranian law forbids the killing of virgins, it became a religious "necessity" to rape these women in order for their executions to be legal. Although the Baha'i worldwide have spoken out in behalf of these sisters and their horrific shame, sadly, much of the world has turned away from this ongoing tragedy, or has not even realized that such unfathomable atrocities were still taking place in the modern age.

The Kurds of Iraq

There are 25 million Muslim Kurds in the world and they occupy a large area of over 200,000 square miles throughout Turkey, Iran, Syria, and Iraq. The Kurdish people throughout the region have suffered greatly, leading to the rise of a terrorist organization called the *peshmarga* ("Those who face death"), but the Kurds of Iraq have probably suffered more than any other Kurdish group. Between February and September of 1988, entire Kurdish villages were mercilessly gassed from the air by Governor Ali Hassan al-Majid (1941–2010, the cousin of Saddam Hussein). Kurds were terrorized by the Iraqi government and fled their homes. As many as 100,000 defenseless Kurds were murdered. The city of Halabja became known as the "Kurdish Hiroshima" because mustard gas was used on the village for three days beginning on March 16, 1988.[41] There were at least forty other chemical attacks on Kurdish villages. Since the United States backed Iraq in its war against Iran, they chose to remain silent although they knew exactly what was happening at the time. Al-Majid called this the *Anfal* (spoils) Campaign based on the eighth surah of the Qur'an, which says, "We said to them: Taste this! The scourge of Fire awaits the unbelievers."

Since the fall of Saddam Hussein in 2003, the people of Kurdistan have experienced a dramatically improved (if still politically tenuous) situation. At the same time, numerous communities are under the control of local authorities and have very little relationship to the national government. This present arrangement not only invites opportunities for human rights abuses but also makes it harder for international "watch-dog" organizations such as Human Rights Watch (HRW) to carefully monitor the claims of those who say they are being mistreated or abused. For many citizens of post-Saddam Hussein Kurdistan and Iraq, a continued state of war with extensive military activity and a weakened federal government means that basic civil rights are not securely protected.

American Wars in Iraq and Afghanistan

Many Muslims worldwide have asserted that not enough attention has been given in the West to the many troubling instances of innocent individuals being killed during the recent Iraqi and Afghani Wars with the United States. Atrocities against the Iraqi people actually began long before the war, as a series of draconian sanctions imposed by the West caused the unnecessary deaths by disease and malnourishment of many impoverished Iraqi citizens.

When the American war against Iraq began, it was not difficult for many to see the actions of America against their former ally as being connected to a larger antipathy that some Muslims felt that the United States had against Islam. One critic of the war Ahmed Omar, an Egyptian legal expert, condemned the American military offensives in Najaf and called the attack against Moqtada Sadr's Mehdi Army an unremitted "genocide". Omar has asked the United Nations General Assembly to cite the United States for violations of its agreements to ensure the protection of innocent civilians. Warplanes were used to assault Mehdi Army positions, which also led to a high non-combatant casualty toll. The Iraqi Ministry of Health claims that at least 165 Iraqis were killed and 594 were wounded during one specific attack, which took place on August 13, 2005.

Similar death-tolls among non-combatants in Afghanistan have deeply strained the credibility of American-led military actions in that nation. The United States entered Afghanistan immediately after 9/11 to oppose al-Qaeda led by the emphatic and elusive Osama bin Laden. Bin Laden had begun al-Qaeda by attacking Saudi Arabia and Egypt for their corruption and for the ways that they had accommodated Western interests. Bin Laden felt that it "was an act of heresy" to base non-Muslim American military forces "in the sacred land of Arabia". It was this motive that led to the 1993 truck bombing of the World Trade Center in New York, an attack in 1996 on the Khobar Towers in Saudi Arabia, the 1998 bombing of the American embassies in Kenya and Tanzania, an attack against the USS Cole in Yemen in 2000, and finally, the attacks of 9/11.

Bin Laden had previously been trained by the United States and supported in his war against the Soviet Union, which had invaded Afghanistan in 1979. Over one million Afghans perished in that war and over one third of the entire civilian population was displaced from their homes. Countless refugees, many of them were widows and orphans, fled to neighboring Pakistan where they eventually became players in the progressive destabilization of that nation. One group, the Taliban, was formed from the ashes of this war and trained countless youth to embrace their own fundamentalist version of Islam. Even though al-Qaeda and the Taliban have no support for their objectives and ideals among most Muslims, the fact that they are Muslims and the fact that they are being so violently opposed by American and European governments has raised their profile and status among many Muslims. This fact, and not their ideology, may explain why so many Muslims have joined forces with these two groups in a number of remote training camps in Yemen, Somalia, Afghanistan, and rural Pakistan.

There are many human rights violations and atrocities that take place during the fog of any war. On November 19, 2005, a roadside bomb placed by al-Qaeda in the Iraqi city of Haditha killed a Marine who had been driving his Humvee through the area. In retaliation, other Marines proceeded to enter the village and began to shoot people at random. The Marines killed 24 unprovoked and unarmed civilians while survivors of these atrocities received checks for $2500 in apology for their injuries and for the murder of their family members.[42] On September 16, 2007, security contractors from the Blackwater Corporation became enmeshed in an unprovoked firefight that left 11 civilians dead. No laws are yet in place to confront human rights abuses carried out by Private Military and Security Contractors (PMSCs). PMSCs have even been active in deeply abusive prisoner interrogations.[43] There have also been a number of reports of disproportionate violent actions by PMSCs at various checkpoints in both Iraq and Afghanistan.[44]

The Former Yugoslavia

The horrors of Bosnia and Kosovo include some of the most nightmarish events in Europe since the Holocaust of World War II. More than half a million Muslims were killed in Bosnia and Kosovo at the hands of Orthodox Serbian and Catholic Croat forces. Countless others were sent into exile or were placed in concentration camps.

From Prime Minister Gladstone's nineteenth-century atrocities in Bulgaria and the assassination that triggered the First World War, to the tribal slaughters of Serbia, Bosnia, Croatia, and Kosovo, the people of the Eastern European Balkans have faced one horrific tragedy after another. The region gives us a mirror to unprecedented barbarity in our time. Terrorism and genocide became state policies in these lands; international intervention was too little and came too late for villages such as Mostar and Srebrenica. One United Nations conference was interrupted by a young Bosnian protestor, Verdana Bozinovic, who shouted: "You are guilty for every single raped woman, for every single murdered man, woman, and child. . . . We think that you are guilty for our sufferings. What do you want before you will do something? How many more victims are needed before you act? Aren't 12,000 enough? Do you want 15,000 or 20,000? Will that be enough?"[45]

Before 1991, Yugoslavia was an uneasy federation composed of six republics. War ensued and the people of Kosovo in Albania (and before that in Bosnia and Herzegovina) were subject to years of atrocities, compulsory displacement, rape, and ethnic cleansings at the hands of Serbian and Croatian Christians (who did the same to each other).[46] One particularly grim incident took place, in the Bosnian city of Prijedor, in which Muslim prisoners were forced to bow as if facing Mecca before they were systematically clubbed to death one at a time.[47] Religion was used on all sides to identify people's fundamental ethnic allegiances, even though they spoke the same languages and had lived together side-by-side in Tito's secular, fascist Yugoslavia for decades.[48]

Atrocities took place in the name of God against Bosnian Muslims from 1992 to 1995. The Bosnian-Serbian government provided troops with weapons and ample truckloads of plum-brandy in order to help them to become more comfortable in carrying out the murders of women, children, and unarmed civilians.[49] Killing centers were set up where individuals were executed nightly by means of "sport atrocities", in which "victims would be tortured and thrown off the bridge and shot at as they fell down into the Drina River."[50]

Bosnian Serbs required Muslims to wear easily identifiable white arm-bands or paint white marks on their homes so that they could be marked for future violence. Before a town was "purified" (Serbian *cistiti*) of its non-Christians, religious leaders would often hold formal religious services for Bosnian Serbian troops.[51] Orthodox clergy uniformly and enthusiastically supported the war efforts against the Bosnian infidels. Priests often led the way in identifying the homes of their fellow villagers for destruction. The noted war criminal Zeljko "Arkan" Raznatovic related: "We are fighting for our faith, the Serbian Orthodox Church."[52]

The city of Banja Luka was "ethnically cleansed" of some 50,000 non-Serbians. 20,000 Muslim non-combatant men, women, and children from the town were used as slave laborers by Bosnian Serb nationalists. Bosnian Serb Christians who refused to participate in the killings (or who even protested the murders of their friends and neighbors) were also candidates to be executed. Michael Sells (b. 1949) observed that an "elitecide" took place, in which the first to be targeted by the Bosnian Serbs for death in these villages that were "cleansed" were teachers, lawyers, doctors, artists, poets, and musicians. Before being killed, many of them were forced to sing Serbian nationalist songs or Christian chants and hymns. Branimir Anzulovic claims that these Bosnian Serbs genuinely believed in a number of "myths and lies" about their religious and moral superiority and the holy duty of Bosnian Serbs to kill their Bosnian Muslim neighbors.[53]

Sells claimed that "gynocide" (the systematic rape and killing of women) took place throughout the conflict. Rape camps nicknamed *harems*, in which Muslim women and girls of all ages underwent continual rape and physical violence for months and even years without end, were set up in places such as Foca. Muslim men were forced to watch the rape of their wives, daughters, and neighbors before they had their throats cut. Serb militiamen "boasted about their gang rapes of Muslim women" and they sought to impregnate as many of these women as possible with "Serb seed".[54] Sadly, United Nations Peacekeepers were reported to also "patronize" these barbaric rape camps and joined in the de-humanizing rape of unprotected and captive Muslim women.[55]

Croatian and Serbian troops destroyed with dynamite over 600 masjids in the first months of the war with Bosnia. Some of these buildings, such as the Banja Luka Masjid (1551), were ancient monuments. Bosnian Serbian troops not only attacked people, but even waged war on books and libraries. On May 17, 1992, the Bosnian Serb army attacked the Oriental Research Institute, the largest collection of Islamic and Jewish manuscripts in southeast Europe. On August 25, 1992, the Serb army deliberately began shelling the National Library in Sarajevo.

The name of the village *Srebrenica* will forever linger in the memory of those who cherish peace and feel obligated to remember the victims of senseless atrocities. This small village was under the supposed "protection" of Dutch forces of the United Nations (UNPROFOR), but, beginning on July 12 and lasting until July 18, 1995, the Dutch freely allowed Bosnian Serbian forces to enter the camp and proceed to execute the Bosnian Muslims as they stood by at a distance to watch without any intention to intervene.[56]

Bosnian Serbs claim that the atrocities committed at Srebrenica were undertaken in revenge for previous killings that Muslims had carried out against fifty Serbian villages during the war. Bosnian Serbian soldiers were fed a frequent diet of descriptions and pictures of atrocities against their fellow Bosnian Serbs such as rape, mass murder and the desecrations of Serbian churches. General Ratko Mladic (b. 1942) had many devoted foot-soldiers, such as Nasir Oric, a 28-year-old brigadier who had already made a name for himself by ethnically cleansing the Drina Valley and slaughtering all civilians in the villages of Bijeljina, Zvornik, and Bratunac. But Mladic and Oric had more vile work to do. In July of 1995, over 8,400 Muslim boys and men were executed (often by their neighbors wearing ski masks) at the Srebrenica battery factory before their bodies were dumped into an open grave.[57] Their mothers, grandmothers, and daughters were set apart and taken to "rape rooms" where their honor was methodically destroyed. Although the Serbs denied these events, the careful record books citing each victim, the graves, and the videotapes that they took to document their work for their superiors stand as a living rebuttal of their attempts at denial. Thousands more were executed around Srebrenica on August 8, 1995.

On August 10, 1995, the United States Ambassador to the United Nations, Madeline Albright (b. 1937), released to the world the CIA proof of these mass executions. Airstrikes began and were carried out successfully without any significant opposition; only two NATO pilots died before the Dayton Peace Treaty ended this war a few months later (by the end of 1995). Tensions overflowed to other nations in the region, such as Montenegro, where Muslims who fled for protection were returned by the Montenegrin government to Bosnian Serbian forces to face their certain death.[58] Problems continue into the present in Kosovo where Albanian Muslims were persecuted by Bosnian Serbian troops until NATO forces intervened in 1999. Once again, the story in Kosovo is that atrocities have been carried out on both sides. Churches and masjids have both been defaced and even burned to the ground, and hundreds of thousands of innocent individuals have been barbarically massacred simply because of their ethno-religious identities.

Religion and Violence in the Sudan

In Africa, the Sudan is a context of incomprehensible genocide and atrocity. Echoes of the master-slave relations of the past have led to Southern Christians and Muslims from the Darfur region being enslaved. Ethnic cleansing, first against the Christians of the Southern Sudan and, more recently, against African Muslims in Darfur, has brought this backward nation to the forefront of world condemnation. It is easy to see the religious element at play in Northern Sudanese Muslims carrying out a genocidal war against Southern Christians; the situation in Darfur, however, is an intra-religious struggle, which is actually motivated by race and only thinly justified by misguided religious fervor.

Ethnic and religious conflicts have been going on in the Sudan for decades. The modern state of Sudan was established by the British in the 1950s, but northern and southern tensions were already in place at that time. In the 70s, 80s, and 90s, the West simply ignored incidents of widespread atrocity. In a coup in 1989, the National Islamic Front (NIF) came to power under the leadership of General Omar al-Bashir (b. 1944) and Hassan al-Turabi (b. 1932). They quickly called for a *jihad* against Christians in the South. Over one million Christian and animist southerners were killed and countless more were displaced.

There is almost no way to fathom the depths of the brutal atrocities that have swept across this impoverished nation for well over a decade. Political solutions remain frail and out of reach in Darfur, while the South has reached some agreements with the Islamists of Khartoum that continue to hold prospects for eventual peace. While leaders in the international community continue to raise words of protest, many villages in Darfur are razed to the ground with scores of men and women being killed on a routine basis. Finally, in September 2006, over 17,000 United Nations Peacekeepers entered Darfur, but their role, in a land the size of Texas, is, by necessity, quite limited.

Sudan is another Arab League member that is massacring its own minority populations through the agency of the Janjawid militia and with the full support of the government in Khartoum, which claims that it is helpless to intervene and stop the killings. These militia are armed and funded by the government and they claim to be fighting in a holy war against godless interlopers. The fact is, however, that those who are being killed are loyal Muslims who have lived in the region since time immemorial. At least two million ethnically African Muslims have been displaced into neighboring countries and their impoverished farms have been given over to ethnically Arab Muslims.

Interfaith Violence in Nigeria

Since 1979, in the West African country of Nigeria, over 70,000 Christians and Muslims have been killed in a series of interfaith riots and attacks. The demographics of the nation are probably almost evenly divided between Christian and Muslim, although census statistics vary in their conclusions based on who is doing the reporting; such records are either manipulated or contested. In the year 1999, *shariah* was imposed in a number of Northern Nigerian states — which led to thousands of people being killed as Christian crowds protested against its implementation and militants rose up to assert Muslim-majority hegemony. In September 2001, violence flared in Jos between Muslims and Christians, as many churches and masjids were set on fire after rallies celebrating the events of 9/11 spiraled into indiscriminate killing sprees. One report claimed that almost one thousand people died in these riots. In October 2001, over 200 Christians were butchered over two days of intense rioting in the city of Kano. In 2003, the government declared a state of emergency in Plateau State when about 600 Fulani Muslims were murdered by Christian militia in the central town of Yelwa. This led to further riots and reprisal killing sprees once again in Kano. Thirty thousand Christians were displaced from their homes in Kano while over 20,000 were displaced in East Central Nigeria; 57,000 Christians fled their homes in Northern and Central Nigeria.

Nigeria presents a particularly toxic mixture of politico-religious and ethnic rivalries that might erupt into full-scale genocidal sectarian violence at any moment. While the 1979 (reaffirmed in 1999) Federal Constitution of Nigeria promises a secular state, a number of Muslim states have insisted on adding *shariah* to existing legal structures. Since 2008, the terrorist organization Boko Haram has carried out an ever-increasing number of bombing attacks which have greatly disrupted the daily life of the country and underscored afresh the many ethno-religious tensions that remain unresolved within this passionately religious nation. Attacks against innocent villagers, both Christian and Muslim, have almost become a daily occurrence in the nation and sometimes these killings are not even mentioned in the news. For example, on July 29, 2013, 46 fishermen and traders were indiscriminately executed in two separate market incidents in Borno State.[59] The eventual hope is that reason will win out and Muslims and Christians can begin to enter into amicable dialogues that will restore a level of mutual trust and decrease the prospect of future sectarian violence. There are some bright spots and examples at the local level where Muslim and Christian clerics have met together to build bridges of civic reconciliation and mutual respect. Grassroots examples of carefully structured interfaith programs have helped to address local frustrations and have tried to channel deep currents of sectarian anger into constructive dialogues. The United States Institute of Peace, for example, has co-sponsored a series of conferences with the Interfaith Mediation Center in Kaduna since 2003 in the hope that Nigeria's future will increasingly be led by young people who learn to be tolerant and respectful of each other.

Atrocities in East Africa

There are other contexts in Africa where Muslim and non-Muslim relations have erupted in hellish waves of violence. One is a large community of Muslims in Kenya where, in 2003, the BBC reported that 11 Muslim boys were freed after being tortured at the Khadija Islamic Institute of Discipline and Education (an Islamic correctional center in Nairobi).[60] These children were held captive in chains and secured by padlocks in small rooms, and they were frequently beaten if they failed to recite the Holy Qur'an properly. Parents paid as much as US $1,500 to send their truant children to participate in this abusive religious education program. Some of the tribal tensions in Kenya are also related to interfaith assertions. Other conflicts have erupted between Muslims and Christians in Tanzania and Ethiopia, where Muslim and Christian missionaries have been active in seeking converts from each other's communities while also seeking to assert local political and economic influence.

In 1992, a horrific genocide in Rwanda accounted for the deaths of over 800,000 victims. Over an eight-month period of uninterrupted violence, the men of the Hutu majority massacred the men, women, and children of the nation's Tutsi minority with rough clubs and dull machetes. This onslaught took place even though many Tutsi and Hutu had, for centuries, intermarried and shared common lives as neighbors together in peace. Less known in the story of these atrocities, is the fact that Islam has become increasingly active in the region in the aftermath of these nightmares. Muslim missionaries have entered Rwanda from the Gulf States in large numbers and with ample economic resources. These missionaries have found success in helping Rwandans to appreciate that the senseless divisions between Hutu and Tutsi can be overcome by the unifying power of Islam.

It cannot be denied, as these Muslim missionaries remind us, that Catholic Hutu priests and Protestant ministers encouraged their congregations to kill Tutsis and that, for example, 7,000 Tutsis were massacred in a Benedictine monastery after they were betrayed by two Rwandan nuns. In contrast, when Tutsis went to Muslim homes they were often protected and rarely betrayed. Muslims in Rwanda were following the Qur'anic mandate: "If one amongst the pagans ask thee for asylum, grant it to him so that he may hear the word of Allah; and then escort him to where he can be secure" (Q. 9:6). This legacy of compassion left a major impression on many Rwandans. Today, Hutu and Tutsi are praying together in the same masjids. Since the genocide, "Rwandans have converted to Islam in huge numbers and Muslims now make up 14% of the 8.2 million people in Africa's most Catholic nation, twice as many as before the killings began."[61]

The Blood of the Innocent

Atrocity is particularly sordid when it is done with the organizational and moral support of religious leaders and institutions. There is a story in the Bible in which King Herod has all of the children in Judea under the age of two massacred because he fears prophecies about the rise of a future Messiah. The child Jesus was able to escape these events because his father took the family as political refugees (and illegal immigrants) into Africa; one wonders if the stain of such a memory did not linger in Christ's maturing consciousness as he ministered to the marginalized. Sadly, the story of innocents being killed in the name of God is not only an ancient story. Teófilo Cabestrero, in his book *Blood of the Innocent* (1985), recounts the following tale of those murdered during Guatemala's civil war: "They killed 11-year-old kids. I saw the atrocities. They murdered people and committed all sorts of abominations. And then they wear medals and crosses and carry a Bible! And then they say they pray before committing their evils and Jesus tells them that they are going to win!"[62]

Muslims in the Former Soviet Union

Muslim Central Asia provides another context of unresolved religious violence. In 2004, widespread torture and killings took place in Uzbekistan after the Uzbek government decided to crackdown against Islamist movements in the Ferghana Valley. Troops opened fire with machine guns against peaceful protesters. Thousands were killed and thousands more were rounded up and taken into prison. Human rights and freedom of speech were widely flouted in Islam Karimov's Uzbekistan. Those detained by the police continue to suffer physical and psychological abuse. Women who have been detained have also been raped in Uzbek jails. Many prisoners have been tortured by the police until they have died. The Uzbek government continues to deny the assertions of international human rights organizations that any torture is going on in their prisons.

Muslims in other parts of the former Soviet Union, including Ossetia, Ingushetia, and Dagestan, have reported persecution at the hands of their non-Muslim neighbors. Chechnya is yet another context in which Muslims have continued to struggle since Russian control came to the region at the beginning of the twentieth century. The North Caucuses is rich with oil and other resources, but historically most of the wealth generated by these local resources went to the central Soviet state. Chechnya remains one of the least developed areas of the Russian Federation, and the Chechens have continued to seek their independence after the collapse of the Soviet Union. In the failed Chechen war for independence, thousands were killed and the infrastructure of the society was ravaged. Chechen warriors have circulated reports that some Chechen women were publicly raped and that many innocent civilians were mutilated. Chechen rebels carried out a series of particularly violent terrorist attacks throughout Russia, including the capture and destruction of an elementary school in the village of Beslan, in which dozens of innocent children were murdered in cold blood.

Muslims in China

There are at least 60 million (some estimate as many as 80 million) Muslims in the People's Republic of China. Muslim communities have often confronted their secular leaders with calls for more freedoms and more opportunities to openly express their distinct, and often militant, views of how Islam should be practiced within their communities. Some of these issues came to the forefront in the summer of 2009 when bloody clashes between the military and local Muslim Uighurs of Western China exploded into violence, resulting in hundreds of deaths and the imposition of a state of martial law over the entire region.

China's Muslims are subdivided into at least ten ethnic groups and predominate in Northwest China, in the Xinjiang region (though there are also large numbers of Hui Chinese Muslims in Yunnan and Guizhou Provinces in the Southwest). Chinese Muslims have experienced unfathomable persecutions since the rise of Communism in 1949; some claim that as many as 500,000 Muslims were killed during the Cultural Revolution, simply because they were Muslims. Most Muslims were also not free to worship during that era. It is an old story in China: anti-Muslim sentiment took root in China during the Ch'ing Dynasty (1644–1911) and has waxed and waned since that time. Things have slowly improved for many Muslim communities in China since Chairman Mao's death in 1976, as long as Muslims have agreed to stay out of political concerns. In recent years Islamist terrorist organizations have become increasingly active in Northwest China. Their presence has caused a host of problems, and it was these groups that were at the heart of the violence that has erupted in Western China since 2009.

Conclusion

Prominent among all factors, one has to ask a basic question: how and why do interfaith and intercultural atrocities take place in the first place? Where was a loving and merciful God during all of these acts of horrendous evil? Such questions are capable of fostering a sense of shared humanity and common citizenship, what Seamus Heaney (1939–2013) calls the *Republic of Conscience*.[63] The human story, beginning with Cain murdering Abel, is one of deep animosity toward those who are different, but how and why are such atrocities able to take place on such a horrific scale? When these narratives are presented, however, we should remember that these are examples of faiths becoming captive to injustice and are deviating from their basic religious truths of universal love and forgiveness.

Religion has often been a tool of repression. However, it is also capable of becoming a pathway to defuse hostilities and to keep individuals from committing further atrocities. Almost all faiths teach a message of hope and healing, yet many religions have also been used throughout history to promote horrific pogroms of hatred. The Qur'an teaches that "if anyone kills a person — unless it be for murder — it would be as if he killed all people; and if anyone saves a life it will be as if he saved the lives of everyone in the world" (Q. 5:32). A Muslim is called to always resist evil (Q. 4:97). Ultimately, the fundamental compassion generating messages of the Bible and the Qur'an should be more powerful than the sword, but they have often become the brutish weight behind the sword of terror and atrocity.

7. Islamic Social Equality in Response to Racism and Slavery

Racism is man's gravest threat to man — the maximum of hatred for a minimum of reason.

— Abraham Joshua Heschel

The Qur'an asserts that diversity is part of the divine intent and purpose of creation. The classical commentators of the Qur'an did not fully explore the implications of this sanctioning of diversity, or the role of peaceful conflict resolution in perpetrating the type of social interaction that would result in people knowing each other.

— Khaled Abou El-Fadl

The Concept of Race

Racism, born from ethnocentric arrogance, has clear social, economic, and political implications. The extent of racism is far-reaching: we are all aware of the atrocities visited by the Nazis against Jews in Auschwitz or Birkenau, but there are countless other examples. Japanese-Americans, for example, who were interned in refugee camps during World War II, suffered in every aspect of their lives. The residual legacies of Apartheid in South Africa or slavery (and "Jim Crow" laws) in the United States, Brazil, and other nations are with us even to the present. While the world continues to cut primordial ties and move toward modernity, issues of race (and even slavery) continue to be a lingering problem.

Cultural injustice, bound with ethnocentric arrogance, has caused some to be removed from their ancestral lands, as was frequently the case in North and South America and Australasia. These "removals" are often violent and lead to chaos for generations: the number of victims is overwhelming. What can be easily forgotten in an avalanche of statistics is that each victim has a specific name and story that must be remembered. The Holocaust in all its horror, for example, is at its most basic level a series of stories of sons and daughters and mothers and fathers. This is vividly illustrated by Dutchman Henryk Zylberberg, he describes watching his only daughter being murdered during the Nazi occupation of the Netherlands: "Michaela gripped her mother's hand and screamed, 'Mummy! Mummy!' I saw Kneibel seize her by the arm and drag her away behind the line and got hold of her waist, and before my eyes, smashed her little head against the wall of the house."[1]

As a religious and ethical philosophy, Islam speaks with galvanizing intensity against attitudes that lead toward racism, or any form of ethnocentric injustice. In the same way that sexism or classism dehumanizes people, racism attacks a person's God-given dignity. All human beings are created and loved by Allah regardless of the color of their skin. Islam is a faith dedicated to the liberation of all humanity from such chains. In spite of this ideal, it remains a controversial question, open to continued debate, as to exactly how much prejudice (because of skin color) early Africans experienced at the hands of Muslim conquerors.

Edward W. Blyden (and others) taught that Islam provided a unique solution to the problems of American racism.[2] El Hajj Malik el-Shabazz Malcolm X (1925–1965) preached to his audiences that the truest Islam was color-blind in its original and purest form: "Americans need to understand Islam, because this is the one religion that erases from its society the race problem."[3] Many African-Americans who have become Muslims have noted that this message within Islam is of particular importance in their own decisions to convert ("revert"). Qur'an 15:28 declares: "I am going to create a human being from dry ringing clay formed from black mud." American Muslim Sanford Harper claims that this passage implies that the first humans were of African descent. He also asserts that "beyond a doubt all of the prophets including the Prophet Muhammad and Isa ibn Maryam were definitely Black (Nubian)."[4]

Whatever the skin color of the first humans, the Qur'an is clear that all of God's creation is of equal value (Q. 49:13; 30:22). Qur'an 2:213 states: "And humanity is naught but a single nation." Qur'an 3:103 (see also Q. 3:105) explains, "You should hold fast to the rope of God, all of you, and do not be divided." Muslims are taught in the *hajj* that all pilgrims are to unite equally before Allah; no one can look on another human being as inferior — which is the impetus at the heart of racism. A strong awareness of human equality is the inevitable result of a life of personal piety (*taqwa*) in devotion. Such a perspective is rooted in faith and is not based on Lockean ideas of social constructs — free of any element of God's work — which imply that individuals have "inalienable rights".

The Prophet experienced class-prejudice first-hand when he was opposed by the powerful elite of Mecca, which may have made him sensitive to the plight of those who were down-trodden. This may also explain why he fully supported the rise of the number of people of color to become a significant proportion of the first waves of the Muslim community. Many Muslims were of African descent and many of these boasted that their skin color was a wonderful gift from Allah. One ninth-century Muslim, al-Jahiz, proclaimed that his dark skin spoke of his physical strength and was strikingly beautiful because it was the color of "dates, ebony, gems, mountains, horses, lions" and, most of all, the sacred black stone of the *Ka'ba*.[5]

The Prophet taught that no individual should live in subservience (*ibadah*) to another person. The modern scourge of racism, with ancient expressions of prejudice, holds its foundation in the insecure, but human, need to dominate others, out of arrogance, misplaced privilege, or fear. People filled with prejudice are committing the sin of ingratitude, because they have failed to accept the gift that others have to offer — their own authentic selves created by Allah. A Hadith relayed by Bukhari says: "None of you truly believe until you love for your fellow what you love for yourself."[6]

Prejudice among Muslims

A Muslim community cannot be defined by the concept of a race or a culture, because Allah is the creator of all and has established the *ummah* around spiritual; not cultural nor ethnic, lines. This concept of an inclusive *ummah* has been challenged throughout Islamic history. One example is found in Algeria, which has a minority Berber population.[7] This people group feels that it has a need for self-determination and wants its diversity to be accentuated instead of diminished in the name of a unifying Islam. Similar challenges face Muslim minorities in the Arab States of the Persian Gulf (such as Kuwait and Bahrain), where thousands of Muslim Pakistanis and Indians are often treated poorly by Arab Muslim majorities on the basis of their cultural backgrounds. These foreign workers have very limited possibilities of participating in their adopted societies. Arab Muslim majorities have allowed these double standards to go on in the name of Arab social cohesion and their own economic and political self-interests.

Iraq is another country in which Arab Muslims have had difficulty accepting (and not persecuting) their Kurdish Muslim sisters and brothers even though the Qur'an forbids this kind of favoritism. In Iraq's setting of war, the challenges of creating an *ummah* of faith are complex given that Arab Muslims are further divided into Sunni and Shi'a Arabs and that sectarian and political agendas have often clouded a larger shared commitment to the one faith of Islam. Kurds in Turkey have also faced similar political and sectarian problems with their Turkish neighbors, who are also Muslims. When Kurds have immigrated to Europe, they have also experienced cultural animosities in a host of varied contexts. Their situation is particularly noteworthy because the Kurdish people remain the largest ethnic group in the world (about 25 million) who cannot lay claim to a distinct nation-state where they are the majority and are able to freely express their culture.

Immigrant Muslims among Non-Muslim Communities

Anti-immigrant "xeno-racism" in Europe (and to a lesser degree in North America) demonizes migratory communities from Muslim countries based on security concerns (inextricably linked to an infamous and scripted view of Islam). Using euphemisms such as "managed migration", specific policies have been enacted that target the "influx" or "swarm" of largely-Muslim North and West African migrants. Liz Fekete argues that many policies admit certain migrants based on "a socio-economic Social Darwinism that allows the rich First World to maintain its economic dominance by emptying the poorer worlds of their skilled workforces."[8]

Projections show that the number of Muslims in Europe will double, between 2005 and 2015, and may comprise as much as 20 percent of the entire population by 2050.[9] High birthrates and immigration are contributing to this rise. It cannot be confirmed by this author, but some sources have even claimed that the given name "Muhammad" is now the most frequently chosen name for newborn boys in modern London.[10] The Muslim community in North America is also growing at a rapid pace and this growth has led to extravagant fears by some non-Muslim Americans.[11] Moustafa Bayoumi says that, post 9/11, "Arabs and Muslims now hold the dubious distinction of being the first new communities of suspicion after the hard-won victories of the civil-rights era."[12] European and North American Arabs and Muslims in the foreseeable future will probably have to continue to deal with cultural prejudice against them in these new contexts.

While most Muslims are becoming citizens in these countries, they are not always adapting to their new environments. Savage observes that "younger Muslims are resisting assimilation into secular European societies even more steadfastly than the older generations did. They are willing to integrate and respect national norms as long as they can and, at the same time, maintain their distinct Islamic identity and practices."[13] Muslims in both Europe and North America are part of a critical discourse that is developing internally about appropriate ways for Muslims to adapt to cultural change while supporting religious identities in secular societies without aggravating prejudices. All of these issues of identification and accommodation are part of a global Muslim conversation about defining and supporting the *ummah*.

Slavery and Christianity

Before the American Civil War, Protestant preachers (initially the Puritans) relied upon the biblical accounts of slavery to legitimize the American slave trade. The story of Phinehas in the book of Numbers (25:1–15) was often cited as proof that God was displeased at any form of intercultural or inter-racial marriage.[14] When some Hebrews marry Moabites, God "furiously commands the Chiefs of Israel to be impaled in the sun as a means of quenching His anger."[15] Aaron, another biblical hero, saves the day by slaughtering a mixed-race couple; resulting in God's choice to end a plague on the land.

Slavery was widespread and accepted in Biblical times and religious authorities did not seem too concerned to address it as evil. Some North American and British Protestants found in the Bible a story that explained why slavery existed and how it could be accepted within an otherwise mercy-centered revelation. These Protestant slave masters claimed that the "curse of Canaan" (Gen. 9:18–25) justified their particular brand of dehumanizing slavery because God had cursed the ancestors of those enslaved. Their preachers were adept at using the Bible to challenge the claims of their religious rivals (in the case of the Abolitionist movement led in England by Pitt and Wilberforce) that slavery was an ungodly evil.[16] Controversy remains over whether the "Curse of Ham" idea was widely believed among Muslims or if Muslim retellings of this story were simply brazen attempts to find religious justifications (albeit from Jews and Christians) to support their extensive efforts to enslave Africans.

Slavery is described in the earliest sections of the Bible and is seen to be normative (Josh. 9:22–27; Ezra 8:20) but it was never based on racial (or ethnic) considerations. The Bible commands the kind treatment of slaves and gives them rights in the larger community (Ex. 21:2–11; Deut. 15:12–18; Lev. 25:44–46; Num. 3:25–47). In the New Testament, slavery is never mentioned by Jesus. He does not condemn, nor affirm, the institution of slavery. When it is mentioned, once by the apostle Peter (1 Pet. 2:18–25) and at least seven times in the writings of the apostle Paul (1 Cor. 7:20–24; 12:13; Col. 3:11, 22–25; Tit. 2:9–10 and Philemon) it is mentioned in a matter-of-fact way, which does not challenge the underlying logic of slavery. Philemon's story is especially trenchant because it tells of a Christian slave who fled his master only to be commanded by Paul to return again — voluntarily — to a life of slavery. Paul does say that Christians, whether they are slave or free, are one in Christ (Gal. 3:28) and equal before God. It is not surprising, however, that Howard Thurman (1899–1991), Martin King, and other African-American Christians found Paul's views on slavery abhorrent.[17]

Muslim Slave-Masters

A widespread acceptance of slavery is also part of the Islamic tradition. The revelation of the Prophet seemed more intent on softening the daily experience of those enslaved than transforming the institution of slavery, or explaining why slavery exists and whether or not it should exist. As Muslim empires expanded throughout the world, so did the curse of slavery with its concurrent rapes, beatings, killings, and other abuses. Muslim leaders justified the capture of slaves as a gift from Allah and the fruits of victory. The Ottoman Empire equated the owning of many slaves with wealth and social prestige.

William Gervase Clarence-Smith writes that "the foundations of slavery in the original texts of Islam were weak" and that this uncertainty led to a "permanent tension between religious belief and social realities."[18] One thing is certain; slavery in the European and Muslim contexts was quite different in many noticeable ways. In the Atlantic Slave Trade, it was generally the case that there were two men enslaved for every woman, while in the Islamic trade the opposite was the case. While slaves in North America were not usually regarded as humans, they had many rights among Muslim-majority nations.[19] In both contexts, slavery was accepted as an inevitable part of social life, but among many Muslims, its alleviation was also seen as an opportunity toward greater spiritual blessing.

The "death" that captives experience in slavery was not institutionalized by Islam. In fact, Islam "resorted to confronting this problem gradually, imposing at every chance the very principles which would bestow inner, then outer, freedom to slaves."[20] From the outset of Islam, there is an obvious tension that existed over slavery because the revelation was so clear that all individuals were equal before God (see Q. 2:178). As was the custom before Islam, slaves were taken in battle (Q. 8:67). According to tradition, the Prophet owned slaves but emancipated all of them before he died. In one mention of slavery, the Qur'an states that all people are slaves before God in the same way that a slave must always submit to the will of his master (Q. 30:28). The lowly status of a slave is seen to be acceptable to Allah and applicable for all humanity. The Qur'an affirms the reality of slavery, but it is equivocal whether or not it addresses the larger question of whether slavery is a direct result of divine will (Q. 30:38).

Slavery was widespread in class-stratified Arabia at the time of the Prophet; his message did much to alleviate the plight of slaves, while not eliminating slavery directly. While slavery was not abolished, it was dramatically changed by Islam. Muslims were encouraged to see slaves as Allah saw them and to actively work for their liberation. Qur'an 90:13 announces: "As for the steep and difficult path it is the path of the freeing of the slave." Manumission is a commendable act (Q. 24:33). Other passages state that sins can be forgiven readily when a person effects the freeing of a slave (Q. 4:92; 5:89, 2:177; 58:3). When an individual freed a slave, it was expected that the slave would be integrated into the family of the former owner and that the former slave would take the former owner as his/her patron. If a freed slave died without an heir, the former owner would become the inheritor of the emancipated slave's estate.

Slaves were captured in war, purchased, kidnapped, found abandoned, or were criminals and debtors, or those seeking shelter in
exchange for a term of slavery. The very fact that a person had been
vanquished in battle was enough reason for their victors to bring them
into slavery. In many cases, however, slaves only had to serve for a
specific number of years. Slaves born into a master's home were often
treated better than slaves bought in the market. They were seen as a
vital economic resource and a key commodity for the social security
and gradual advance of a family.

The slave markets of Algiers, Tunis, and Tripoli were filled with
Christian Europeans. Slave-raiding efforts combed the coastlands of
Europe and attacked European sailors without any provocation. It is
hard to ascertain exactly how many Europeans were enslaved, but
one popular saying in the sixteenth century was that one could "swap
a Christian for an onion".[21] Probably more than 500,000 Circassian
Europeans living in the Caucus Mountains were forcibly driven by
Russians into Ottoman enslavement. After the eighteenth century,
Muslims were less able to capture large numbers of European slaves;
this renewed earlier Muslim efforts to find available slaves in Africa.[22]

It was in the nineteenth century that Muslim slaving in Africa reached
its zenith with slave-traders being held in high esteem and winning
significant wealth for themselves and their sponsors. Certainly, the
impending efforts of Europeans to end the slave-trade altogether had
something to do with the dramatic increase of Muslim slave-selling
across Africa in the nineteenth century. As slaving increased, the
disregard that Arab Muslims had for people of African descent also
reached new heights. Africans came to be seen as indolent creatures
that were given by God to be exploited by the people of God. Initially,
the simple fact that Africans were not Muslims was a major reason why
they became the focus of the Islamic slave-trade. By the nineteenth
century, this became less important and Arab Muslims even began to
enslave Black Muslims without regard to their faith. Africans were seen
to make ideal slaves because they were believed to be strong physically
and weak culturally; without any "genealogy" and thus without any
praise-worthy identity. It was also widely assumed, in the words of
Muhammad al-Andalusi (b. 936), that the women of Africa were "highly
prized" as concubines, because they were "best for the pleasures of the
bed".[23] Women and children were often ideal targets to be taken as
slaves because they are easier to dominate.

As many as 20,000 Africans were taken every year from East Africa
(especially Ethiopia, just across the Red Sea from Arabia) to far flung
lands because these Africans were not Muslim and they were easier to
procure than others. There were also a number of Native Arab slaves as
well as European slaves throughout the "House of Islam". In fact, there

are instances in which European slaves were specifically treated more severely than African slaves.[24] European slaves, for example, were more often intentionally paraded about town before and after slave markets, with crowds lining the streets to jeer at the subjugation of these forlorn, defeated Christians. It was often recorded that many Arabs felt that Slavic and Eastern European slaves had "raw humors" because they lived far from the warmth of the Sun (while Africans, because they lived in climates where the Sun was at its zenith had "hot and fiery humors and lacked in self-control; overcome by fickleness, foolishness, and ignorance").[25]

The Fair Treatment of Slaves

No Muslim could be enslaved, while free non-Muslim members of society (*dhimmi*) were also not permitted to be enslaved. Pagans, criminals, debtors, prisoners, and *kafir*, on the other hand, were allowed to be enslaved. If an individual converted to Islam after they had been enslaved, they remained in slavery but often enjoyed some benefits for their conversion. Many were eventually freed, or their children were freed, "resurrected" from the "death" of slavery, to the life of liberty. The act of freeing a slave was regarded by the *ummah* as a wonderful act of piety and extraordinary generosity. One oft-recited Hadith states: "The man who frees a slave, God will free him from Hell, limb for limb."[26] Eventually, most freed slaves converted to Islam and entered the mainstream of society as full and equal members, often taking ownership of other slaves.

Most African slaves in the Arab world did menial labor or worked in their masters' businesses. Many who were sent to the Arabian Peninsula worked in the salt pits, on spice plantations, and in oasis communities in the harvesting of date palms. Many African slaves in Arabia also toiled as overburdened porters walking with the camel caravans across vast deserts. African women were often consigned to a life of sexual service and child-bearing. Some male slaves, especially small boys, were turned into eunuchs, while others were made to join the military or work as prostitutes.

All slaves were offered a degree of protection by Islamic legal codes. They were not allowed to be mutilated or killed (Q. 4:36). A number of Hadith show that beatings, when necessary, should be "humane".[27] This injunction was rarely observed, however, and most slaves suffered horrific beatings at the hands of their owners. Slaves were rarely educated and usually were not allowed to own land. If they converted, they were able to lead fellow Muslims in congregational prayers. What defines individuals was not whether they are slave or free, but whether they are believers or non-believers. At the same time, the Qur'an accepts that there is a difference between those enslaved and those free people (Q. 16:71). When a slave committed a crime, he/she only had to pay half the penalty that would be assigned to a free person (Q. 4:25). Slaves were property but they were also human and, ultimately, belonged to God. The Qur'an mandates the kind treatment of slaves (Q. 76:7–9). Qur'an 4:36 commands believers to be kind toward family, neighbors, the poor, the stranger, and, last of all, to slaves. Slave-masters should share a meal with the slave who has prepared the food, and the service of a slave is to be recognized as labor. Slaves could marry free people (Q. 4:24–25; 2:221), and it was better to marry a believing slave than a free non-believer (Q. 4:3). Because most African slaves were frequently abused and often beaten to the point of death, it was not uncommon for many of them to rise up in various rebellions. One of the most notable slave rebellions that took place in the Arab world happened in 869 CE.

There are many examples from the Hadith of the Prophet being kind to slaves. Qur'an 24:33 teaches: "If any of your slaves ask for a deed in writing, give them such a deed if you know any good in them; yea, give them something yourselves out of the means which Allah has given you." This shows that they had the hope for eventual freedom. Female slaves could be used for sexual purposes, but they must be cared for and not raped or abandoned (Q. 23:6; 33:50) because Allah is watching over them and will protect them from such evils. Qur'an 70:29–30 commands that any sexual activity with a slave should be as respectful as any sexual activity with a wife. This view of "chastity" was completely accepted within the formative era of Islamic culture.

Does Islam promote the idea of the abolition of slavery? Progressives have argued that the rules and restrictions and other positive protections for slaves show that Allah's intention was that the *ummah* gradually work toward a time when slavery would be abolished. It is a human idolatry that was never authorized by Allah and it must be abolished (Q. 42:2). Parwez argues, "Whatever happened in subsequent history was the responsibility of the Muslims and not of the Qur'an."[28] The reality, however, was quite different. Muslim-majority nations have long been a center for the proliferation of slavery. As political borders stabilized and wars came to an end after the rise of the Ottoman Empire, those seeking slaves turned their attention to sub-Saharan Africa and to the unstable social cauldron that was the Ottoman Empire Balkans.

Slavery among Modern Muslims

While the names of European and North American abolitionists are well-known to the world, less-known are the stories of Muslim abolitionists, such as the Algerian scholar Muhammad ibn Ali as-Senussi (1787–1859) and the Ottoman-era Libyan politician Pasha Mustafa Ahmad Rashim

(1800–1858), who fought to end the slave trade in the middle of the nineteenth century. Poets and playwrights such as the Ottoman Ahmed Midhat Effendi (1844–1913) were also active in efforts to stop slavery. For many jurists at the end of the nineteenth century, according to Shaun Marmon, the practice of slavery had to be abolished because it was an "affliction beyond the pale of Islam".[29]

Slavery, tragically, still exists in the modern world: according to one source there are still "an estimated 27 million slaves in the world today."[30] Women from Eastern Europe, Belarus, and Ukraine are still being kidnapped and forced into sexual slavery around the world.[31] In the *dar al-Islam*, both Sudan and Mauritania still sanction slavery based on race and echo past histories of master–slave relations that are based upon racism. Sudanese slavery is particularly well documented. In just the three months between December of 1998 and February of 1999, sources documented no less than 2,064 people enslaved and 181 people killed during slave-raids carried out by the Popular Defense Forces (PDF) of the Sudanese government.[32] Women and children are the most likely targets of these horrific attacks because they are most easily overpowered. Once enslaved, these victims face unbelievable abuse, beatings, malnourishment, dismemberments, rapes, and genital mutilations.

Even though the Mauritanian government continues to make denials, the practices of chattel slavery continue within the country. The role of skin-color is obvious in the region, where the word for dark colored people is often *abd* (slave). Segal explains:

> The survival of State-sanctioned black slavery in Mauritania and the Sudan today presents a series of crucial challenges. It is a challenge to Islam, in whose name and values the regimes of both states presume or pretend to act. It is a challenge to democratic governments which recognize and assert their own values are neither safe nor sounder in isolation from the rest of humanity. It is a challenge to the authority of the United Nations whose Universal Declaration of Human Rights is so blatantly being breached. And ultimately, it is a challenge to the redemptive force of experience and memory, without which we may as well not bother with history at all.[33]

The practice of slavery was legal in the Kingdom of Saudi Arabia until 1965. It still exists, but at a much more covert level, with migrant workers from the Philippines, India, Sri Lanka, and other nations being held captive against their will. Kidnapped women from around the world, it is reported, are still being held in Saudi Arabia as sex-slaves without any hope of release. Camel-drivers and jockeys in a number of Gulf States face a situation of "employment" that can only be described as a form of slavery, forced labor. As recently as 2003 Shaykh Saleh al-Fawzan warned that those who sought to end slavery among Muslims were "ignorant" because "Slavery is a part of Islam. It is part of *jihad* and *jihad* will remain as long as there is Islam."[34]

In the United Arab Emirates (UAE), the lucrative sport of camel-racing has been at the heart of repeated injustices. Children from Asia have often been trafficked into the UAE through kidnappings or through deception and direct payments to parents who are desperate to feed their families. Reports note that some South Asian children have been sold for as little as $75. In this sport, small children are often forcibly tied to the backs of camels which are able to run between 25 and 40 miles per hour. Many of the children fall off of their camels and are then trampled. In addition to these dangers, these children are often abused and mistreated.

Women have also been trafficked into Muslim nations to work as indentured servants or to work in prostitution. Lured with promising offers, it is often the case that their passports, visas, and other supporting documents are taken and held. Others are drugged in order to be enslaved. Although the such crimes are widespread within the UAE, accounts of cases have also been cited in Saudi Arabia, Iraq, Iran, Egypt, Syria, Jordan, Lebanon, Yemen, Kuwait, Qatar, and almost every other country throughout the Middle East.

It is not possible simply to read these facts without asking ourselves what we personally should do about these atrocities.[35] Fortunately, as slavery has become exposed, a number of organizations have worked to free slaves and confront this horror. UNICEF, Christian Solidarity International, CASMAS, and the American Anti-Slavery Group are just a few of the international organizations uncovering instances of slavery in the Sudan and around the world. While our hearts are touched and our minds are shocked, we need to translate these feelings into concrete action on behalf of those who are being enslaved during our own lifetime. These shocking facts should cause all Muslims, Jews, and Christians to see themselves as accountable and to be determined to find ways to work together in partnership for social justice that end such human rights abuses. The tragedies of the past continue into the present, but most of us turn away.

Conclusion

A host of puzzles remain in the ongoing exploration of how racism, prejudice, and slavery were able to flourish throughout the Muslim world for centuries. Depending on how one views the facts of history, it may seem that Muslims should have followed a faith that worked to end slavery instead of underpinning its carnivorous advance. The ugliness of slavery, from our modern vantage point, beggars our imaginations, and yet Christians, Jews, and Muslims, not that many centuries ago, allowed the platitudes of their faiths to advance this hellish institution. It is also notable that while the nightmares of the North Atlantic slave trade have received widespread academic consideration in the West, far less attention (both in the West and among Muslims) has been focused on the abuses of centuries of Muslim slaving throughout Africa and at the fringes of the European world.

Muhammad, Moses, and Jesus lived in a world where slavery was culturally acceptable. It is often recited by modern Muslims, Jews, and Christians that these men were dedicated to eventually altering the course of the arc of the social standard away from one in which slavery is taken for granted, to one in which slavery is seen not as God's ideal design for civic society but as an evil to be eliminated. Critics have responded to this view by stating that God's divine revelation should have been more directly combative instead of being so indirect in the face of such evil. Nonetheless, the gradualist approach can be seen as either realistic or problematic depending on one's vantage point. Martin Luther King, sensing that his critics were using delaying tactics instead of dealing with him in good faith, warned that "justice too long delayed is justice denied" and spoke against gradualism, a warning that remains a vivid challenge to all.[36]

8. Sexual Injustice, Sexism and Homophobia among Muslims

Within Muslim communities women are the primary victims. My own research on Qur'anic interpretation and implementation focuses on gender and the ways that exclusionary textual readings marginalize women's full agency within society. Not only are non-Muslims subjugated to sub-human standard and victimized by violent acts, but Muslim women are as well, as an outcome of practices that stem from the authoritarian voice of puritanical interpretations.

— Amina Wadud

A woman has only half a brain.

— Lebanese Proverb

Sexism within Islam

Sexism is often defined as behaviors and attitudes that foster stereotypes of social roles based on gender. Sexism is most often expressed as discrimination against women. Communities from all faiths and cultures often construct essentializing generalizations, which serve to limit people unnecessarily. Muslim women are often presented as those who "lead an essentially truncated life" in which they are "sexually constrained, ignorant, poor, tradition-bound, and religiously domesticated".[1]

Although the subject is complex, it is helpful to remember that situations are changing rapidly and feminist movements worldwide have gained momentum only within recent centuries. Labels and categories are only helpful in terms of beginning a general conversation, but, broadly speaking, Muslim communities are often described as belonging to one of two generalized groups — first, reformers, liberals, and moderates who often combine tradition with contemporary considerations, and second, fundamentalists or conservatives, who fear that the alteration or devaluation of any tradition will somehow weaken society. Conservatives often view reformers as apostates and secularists for seeking new paths of possibility in religious interpretation. In both camps, women are seen as the center of either reforming or preserving tradition. Again, these issues should be discussed in their own specific contexts and not become indicators to gauge how "Western" or "non-

Western" a given Muslim community has become in comparison with some external ideal. It is also instructive to remember that paternalistic concerns about the status of women in Islam is a relatively new phenomenon. Deepa Kumar reminds us:

> While sexually repressed Europe was fascinated and titillated by Muslim marriage customs even during Medieval times, there was no systematic discussion of women and Islam until the nineteenth century. . . . the dominant narrative that emerged was one that presented Muslim women as severely subjugated, oppressed, and little more than slaves. Just as Muslim despots tyrannized their subjects, it was argued, they also tyrannized their wives and daughters.[2]

In fact, there are many significant instances of Islamic feminism, but, as Ron Geaves underscores, Islamic feminists "do not show a united face to the world. There are competing variations to be noted."[3] Issues about the place of women within the *ummah* are complex, but Islam should not be blamed for sexism in the male-dominated Muslim world any more than Christianity or Judaism can be blamed for these same trends in Europe and North America. Here is the tension: Muslims, Jews, and Christians claim that their faiths can liberate women, while others look at the facts of history and conclude that the force of these traditions has supported patriarchal domination. If the assertion is being made that these religions are rooted in divine revelation, then why is it that so little has been done to change the second-class status of women in many societies? Muslims, Jews, and Christians should acknowledge that their received divine revelations, if not actually promoting sexism, have done little to interrupt its advance throughout history.

In questions of sexism (as is true of all other social justice issues), Muslims are commanded not to passively accept that which is evil. While it is true that we are as much products of our social setting as our social setting is a product of who we are, that does not exclude believing men and women from a sense of duty to correct injustices against women. Believers are called to be Allah's representatives on the earth: "Lo, We offered the trust unto the heavens and the earth and the hills, but they shirked from bearing it and were afraid of it. And then humankind assumed it" (Q. 33:72). If sexism is rampant throughout the Muslim *ummah*, then true believers are obligated to address these pressing problems.

Are women free within the *dar al-Islam*? The answer probably depends on whom you ask and how that individual defines freedom. If freedom means that women are equally as able as men to freely express their views, resist abuse, and choose their religion, careers, family arrangements, education (see Q. 86:5 and 17:36), and even the types of clothing they wear, then the answer would often be negative. In terms of religion, some claim that women are encouraged to pray at home with few exceptions.[4] Among extremists, women have been reported to read only the Holy Qur'an or Muslim books.[5] All believing women are encouraged to fast during Ramadan and to try to take a pilgrimage to Mecca, if they are physically and financially able, once within their lives.[6]

A patriarchal culture throughout many Muslim-majority countries that motivates and controls both men and women through shame has often kept women from even thinking that they are oppressed in any way for fear of bringing troubles to themselves and their families. "Western" definitions of sexism are often reframed in terms of the need for men to be self-controlled and to maintain tribal and cultural traditions. Because of variant understandings between cultures and religions, the issue of sexism often becomes an exercise in misunderstood inquiry. Some women in traditional Muslim societies, for example, have not been encouraged to think critically about their plight and have sometimes assumed that their situation is normal, adapting themselves and their expectations to tribalist mindsets. It is taught that their bodies assign their God-given role because, as the Algerian playwright Fatima Gallaire graphically writes, women come into the world with a "flower between our legs", while a man starts life with a "gun between his legs".[7] It is taught that a loving God has ordained these natural divisions, which explains why women in some countries live under strict patriarchal legal restrictions. Sexist contexts are supported by a lack of education and of the free flow of information, which keeps women from recognizing and articulating their oppression or from learning about how women are able to thrive in other situations around the world.

Of course, there are many "Islams" and the social status of women continues to undergo dramatic changes in a number of Muslim contexts. Changing marriage, divorce, and family laws often have a direct bearing on a number of key economic considerations relating to the social status of women. In Lebanon, for example, the government has recently come to recognize the validity of civil unions if these unions were arranged outside the country. Muslim and Christian religious leaders maintain firm control over the workings of family law, but their power has been weakened as those in recent generations have clamored for increased personal liberties, including the right to marry those of another religion or religious sect. Laws have also loosened within Indonesia, for example, allowing women to become more active in a broader range of economic spheres of influence. Islam can be a key factor in these social advances for women. One women's empowerment organization within Indonesia assumed the name "Aisha" in order to educate women in the faith and to celebrate the independence and confident nature of the Prophet's wife.[8] Female lawyers in Malaysia have formed the organization "Sisters in Islam", which confronts instances of patriarchy in the judiciary.

Muslim Women in the West

Muslim women in North America and Europe are free to pursue the education they choose. In some Muslim communities, women are given permission to lead prayers, teach classes, or present sermons.[9] North American and European Muslims often cite Qur'an 4:124 and Qur'an 9:71 when they talk about how their faith has liberated them, while often avoiding other problematic passages.

While many Muslim women in the "West" still may receive some guidance from their families about whom they marry, they are generally given much more latitude to make these choices than are Muslims in other countries. They often achieve higher levels of education and, on average, are more educated, have higher rates of participation within the labor force, and give birth to fewer children than their Middle Eastern peers. Muslim women in North America and Europe face problems of prejudice from non-Muslims and other unique challenges, but these problems are not based on women's civil and legal rights.

Women in Turkey

Kemalist Turkey has probably done more than any other Muslim-majority nation to encourage women to pursue education and enter into the workforce. These efforts have sometimes been misunderstood by Muslims in other nations. The Republic of Turkey, for example, has had laws in place since 1980 prohibiting women from wearing headscarves if they wish to enter a university or any state-appointed office. In spite of this, over half of Turkish women have chosen to forego education and work so that they can wear their head-coverings. The law was finally overturned on January 28, 2008, by Prime Minister Recep Tayyip Erdoğan (b. 1954). The ban was strongly supported by Ataturk's Republican People's Party, which felt that it helped undergird Turkey's secular traditions.

Many secular Muslims worry that the rights of women may be eroding in modern Turkey. The JDP (Justice and Development Party) has stated, for example, that women are vital to society primarily because they are responsible for raising the next generation of Turks. Scholar Gameze Cavdar notes that women are "reduced" simply to their role as nurturing mothers, who should bear several children. In fact, Prime Minister Erdoğan has promoted such views, while at the same time mandating that maternity leave should be reduced from six months to only one month.[10] Women, according to Cavdar, have become increasingly restricted in a "systematic exclusion from the decision-making mechanisms" of society in the name of a more purified Islam.[11] This relegation of women to the specific role of submissive mother and housewife leaves much to be desired in the task of bringing Turkish women to complete equality with their male compatriots.

There are also many bright spots along the horizon, instances in which women who love Islam have taken a proactive stand to change their society. One organization based in Ankara, the "Women's Solidarity Association", has worked tirelessly to confront domestic violence against women. Many other groups have also made impressive strides to heal wounds and to educate people about the problems that some women face in Turkey. At the same time, women's issues have become a contested "battleground" pitting two differing views of Islam against each other within Turkey's shifting political arena.

Women in Saudi Arabia

Saudi Arabia is a nation where religious and national identities seem to be synonymous. Among Muslim-majority nations, it (along with Afghanistan during the rule of the Taliban) is easily one of the most restricted social contexts for women. Women, for example, are not allowed to drive an automobile (although this mandate is not always strictly enforced throughout the country). A woman cannot take public transportation without being accompanied by a male, and a woman must always be veiled. Women are required to wear a *niqab* or, at least, a *hijab* in all public settings. In order to protect family legacies, women's choices in marriage (and in divorce) are limited.

At the same time, women in Saudi Arabia are becoming more educated than ever before; they are also becoming active in affecting social changes. In 2005, for example, two women were elected to the Jeddah Chamber of Commerce and Industry (JCCI). One company ("Kingdom Holdings"), which is owned by a prince of the royal family, has even allowed women to choose whether or not they will wear the *hijab* or Western dress. Youth in the nation, increasingly educated and aware of events and trends worldwide, are beginning to push for social changes. Tensions are arising as discontented factions feel more confident to express their frustrations. The King has taken note of calls for change and has often been at the forefront of working to improve the status of Saudi women and to respond more openly to their specific concerns.

Since 1960, Saudi Arabian women have had access to formal public education but all schools remain segregated along lines of gender. Some Saudi women are training to become doctors, teachers, or other types of professionals. These social changes have raised questions about child care and domestic demands on Saudi men. Smith observes: "On the one hand women in Saudi Arabia appear by Western standards to remain under what many would call very repressive conditions. On the other hand, they are key players in what clearly is a changing social situation."[12] Saudi Arabia is a society in flux, and women are becoming increasingly vital in charting the future of that nation.

An unspeakably tragic incident took place that illustrates some of the daunting obstacles that women in Saudi Arabia are sometimes forced to experience. On March 11, 2002, a fire broke out in a teenage girl's school in Mecca. When the firemen and paramedics arrived at the scene of the fire, they were refused entry to the school by the religious police, who said that it was forbidden for men to enter the burning building because there were only women at the school. When the girls tried to frantically flee the burning building (their clothing was on fire) their exit from the facility was blocked by the religious police. Fifteen girls were burned alive for no justifiable reason. An outcry swept across the entire world, forcing King Fahd (1923–2005) to make policy changes so that such an atrocity would never happen again within the Saudi Kingdom.

Women in Iran

The story of women's rights in Iran is one marked by many twists and turns within the last century. The end of the Qajar Dynasty gave rise to the emergence of a women's movement where the rights of women in Iran were directly related to the very future of the nation in terms of its need to progress and modernize. Women demanded to be treated as equals and be able to participate more meaningfully in both the political and economic life of the nation. These calls demanded a response and clear progress for women in Iran was realized; especially in the nation's cities. Attempts to advance the rights of women in rural areas and among religious conservatives, not surprisingly were met with great resistance. The two regimes of the Shahs, following the 1906 Revolution, were very much a "mixed-bag" for the attainment of women's rights. Any progress that had been made under the Pahlavi Era, however, was greatly compromised by the cultural revolution that came with the 1979 Islamic Republic which connected "women's rights" with "Western innovation". The ruling Imams rejected many of the modest reforms for women that had been advanced by the Shah and replaced these steps forward with strict rules that unambiguously limited and defined the lives of women in Iran. At the same time, women have flourished in Iran's contexts of higher education, where they find a welcome, if temporary, sphere of independence and relative autonomy.

In Iran, women have had to fight to protect their right to study wherever they choose.[13] Many women in Iran passionately supported the revolution of 1979. This surprises some Westerners, who often present the Shah of Iran in a favorable light because of the many reforms that he initiated, which greatly unbridled Iranian women.[14] When the Ayatollah Khomeini (1902–1989) assumed power, he immediately mandated that all women wear the *chador*. This led to a number of protests such as one on Women's Day, 1979. Women who refused to comply with these laws, established in 1980, often lost their jobs. Women in Iran are no longer allowed to practice law, and education has become segregated. The minimum age for marriage has been lowered to 13, polygamy has returned, and laws are now in place that make it almost impossible for a woman to initiate a divorce. Economically, women have been forced to return to a more subjugated status. This is because fundamentalist Iranian clerics feel that women who work bring shame to their husbands and that work takes them away from their primary duties in the home.[15]

Women in Pakistan

In 2009, Muhammad Ramzan cut out the tongue of his wife (Fayyaz Mai) after she complained to him about his parents. Also in 2009, a pregnant Samreen Ali (aged 14) fled Pakistan after having been sold into marriage the year before and having been repeatedly raped by her new husband and physically abused by his family. In the same year, another man killed his wife "by cutting her lips off and hanging her from a tree" after a domestic quarrel.[16] These kinds of reprehensible atrocities by husbands against their wives and daughters have happened in many countries throughout the world, but they are often highlighted when they happen among the Muslim villages of Pakistan.

Pakistan, created in 1947, is a Muslim-majority nation that has undergone frequent cultural adaptations and transitions. In spite of decades of dictatorships and repressive laws aimed at women, the nation had a female Prime Minister, Benazir Bhutto (1953–2007), who came to power in 1988. Although Prime Minister Bhutto believed that the deplorable economic and social state of the country was tied to the oppression of women, her attempts to initiate major reforms to empower women were thwarted by those senators in the government who had taken their seats while the previous dictator, Zia al-Haqq, had been in power. Others who had supported Bhutto before her assassination, did so because of her promise that she would not dramatically alter the civic *status quo*.

Today, women in Pakistan are expected to wear a *burqah* to guard their modesty or, at least, a *chador*, which is a scarf or shawl worn over the head and shoulders. The Taliban instituted the same policy in Afghanistan. Women are segregated when using public transportation, in the workplace, and in schools. Smith writes that "The heritage of strong Muslim women's movements, traditions of sexual segregation, the restrictions of an often conservative religious establishment and the political maneuvers of Pakistan's leaders have combined to create a fluctuating and often frustrating climate for the women of the country."[17]

Pakistani women have faced stiff opposition from strident militant clerics who have tried to freeze women from working outside the home. Progressive Pakistani women have been castigated as "prostitutes" and "evil-handed maidens". Zealous extremists have been particularly upset at women who have worked in international companies, because they claim that these international organizations and businesses promote obscenity, vulgarity, and Christianity.[18] At present, a form of *purdah* is in effect under which women are required to segregate themselves from many areas of Pakistani life. Pakistan continues to be a nation in a state of constant transition; many of the social issues in the country increasingly revolve around the role of women in society.

The Intermingling of the Sexes

In February of 2007 a Saudi court convicted 20 foreigners, sentencing them to receive lashes and spend several months in prison. What was their crime? They were attending a party where alcoholic drinks were served and men and women were seen dancing together.[19] Muhammad Siddiqi warns that "the free intermingling of both the sexes has led to countless illegal acts, illegitimate babies, abortions and vast venereal infections in the European countries and in America."[20] The segregation of women is widespread in the public domain of many Muslim-majority contexts. Segregation is enforced to "protect" women and to keep them from "unconsciously submitting to the flatteries and advances of men".[21]

Segregation of the sexes is often pronounced at masjids, where women are not always permitted to enter for public prayer or, if they are allowed to enter, are segregated into a separate area. Most women pray at home: those women who come to masjids are often out of sight and are forbidden from wearing perfume. Restrictions are also made about women attending funerals or visiting graves in mixed company. The *hajj* to Mecca should be a context in which women and men try to avoid mixing as much as possible. In many countries it is rare to see women walking on the streets after a certain hour and a number of businesses or recreational activities will be almost entirely patronized by men.

The Veil

The widespread Muslim practice of wearing a veil or head-covering is a subject of spirited controversy; some non-Muslims assume that the practice is oppressive instead of uplifting and respectable. The veil has often become a symbolic and metaphoric cliché with "multiple meanings", which frequently have come to symbolize all that is "heavy-handed, oppressive, and discriminatory" among Muslim communities.[22] Muslim women choose to wear the veil for many different reasons. In contrast, many non-Muslims assume that the wearing of the *hijab* (veiling or covering) is a "mask" or a form of social confinement and an implicit rejection of civic norms. This pejorative perspective is widely held in France, where the view has been promulgated, and common in other European countries. Most importantly, it should be stressed that guidelines about the clothing that Muslim women should wear are primarily cultural and not religious, varying widely in every imaginable diverse Muslim context.

The Qur'an states that women should hide their physical beauty (Q. 24:30–31; see also 33:53–59). This passage can be interpreted (and translated) in a number of different ways:

> And say to believing women that they cast down their looks and guard their private parts and do not display their ornaments except what appears thereof, and let them wear head-coverings over their bosoms, and do not display their ornaments except to their husbands or their fathers, or the fathers of their husbands, or their sons, or the sons of their husbands, or their brothers, or their brother's sons, or their sister's sons, or their women, or those whom their right hand possesses (slaves) or the eunuchs, or the children who have not attained knowledge of what is hidden of women.

Modesty and obedience to God's will are the primary objectives being preached by this revelation. God commanded Muhammad that his women "lengthen their garments" (Q. 33:59). The belief is that women are called to be the epitome of humility and modesty, and their dress and demeanor should protect them from the crafty wiles of lustful men. Muslims in North America and Europe face far fewer social expectations about their personal wardrobe choices, but some Muslim cultures are extremely strict about these issues. In 2006, a woman was murdered in cold blood in Pakistan because her gauzy head-covering was not deemed "Islamic enough".[23] Women in other nations, such as Iran and Saudi Arabia, "play around with the rules by sporting colorful scarves and wearing fashionable slacks, even shorts, beneath their enveloping robes which are a significant expression of female independence in the face of rules that seek to keep women submissive."[24]

Rational-choice sociologists would remind us that the various "meanings" in the wearing of the veil will vary from country to country. In Egypt, for example, a host of economic and social factors affect the way that some women choose to identify themselves by wearing *hijab*. The majority of women who have recently chosen to wear *hijab* in Egypt are highly educated and wealthy women; this is no coincidence. In contrast to Egypt, the women of Saudi Arabia are obligated by law to wear *hijab*; this lack of choice explains why the veil is seen by many as a form of oppression. More importantly, Saudi women are restricted in a number of other ways, with the claim being that such restrictions are extended for their protection. In Kuwait, two women elected to

the National Assembly in 2009 — Aseel al-Awadi and Rola Dashti —
decided not to wear a veil to their posts. Their decision outraged some
conservatives, who petitioned the national courts to ban these two
women from the parliament.[25] Muslim women in North America or
Europe often take pride in wearing the veil as an "empowering tool
of resistance" in the face of post 9/11 Islamophobia.[26] Other Muslim
women feel it is too much of an unwanted burden to constantly serve as
some kind of "representative" for over one billion people among those
who are often quite ignorant about Muslims and Islam.

Sexism and Gender Roles

The Qur'an is clear that men and women have different roles, which
many Muslims argue is not inherently oppressive but fundamentally
synergistic. At the same time, Islam says many different things about
women that should keep both foes and friends from making blanket
assertions about how women are either enslaved or liberated by its
divine message. Ghulan notes that "statements regarding the equal
status of women as individuals, worshippers, and pupils and a
woman's right to conduct business without her husband's consent can
be compared with those that allow for polygamy, give women lower
inheritance shares than men, or value women's testimony in court half
as much as men."[27] In a world where men were responsible for the
"social security" of a given family it was logical to mandate that the
inheritance of a son be twice the amount of the money designated for a
woman (Q. 4:2). Some Muslims have argued that the Qur'an has been
misrepresented or misunderstood in its calls for gender compatibility.
They have asserted that Western notions of the equality of women
have actually fostered a sense of competition between men and women
and have actually led to greater gender injustice. From a Western
perspective, however, such arguments only underscore a foundational
difference of opinion between those who see women as fully equal and
those who claim that women are inherently "limited" (by God) in how
they can live their lives and in what ways they can function within
civic society.

Progressives calling for a renewed *jihad* against sexism can draw on a
number of compelling resources in their struggle. One is the example of
Muhammad, who, the Hadith recounts, was an individual who washed
and stitched his own clothes as well as sharing cooking chores with
his wife.[28] There were women at the dawn of Islam who were given
significant business positions. Aisha, the Prophet's wife for example,
was a teacher of religion. One Hadith says that Islam "owes half of
all its religious teaching" to the sagacity of Aisha.[29] Khadija, known
in Islam as Tahira (the Pure) and Kubra (the Great), supported the

Prophet in every way and was the first person to accept the validity of Muhammad's revelation. Fatima, the youngest and only surviving child of the Prophet, is also greatly revered among Muslims. Islam honors many other women in history who were leaders of the *ummah* in both faith and devotion.

Sally Armstrong feels that, on the whole, the Qur'anic texts empower and honor women, but the actual socio-cultural realities of Muslim communities are often quite different: "The worldly observance of that doctrine is another matter entirely."[30] Like most faith traditions, Islamic history is mostly the story of men and male domination. Most of what many holy books, including the Qur'an, say about women focuses on the importance of marriage (Q. 25:54; 7:189; 30:21; 42:11; 24:32) and childbirth. Ali summarizes that "marriage is a contract which has for its object the procreation of children."[31] The Qur'an ensures a dowry for a woman and speaks against women being forced to marry against their will, but it is also true that a woman's worth lies in whether or not she is married. This view gave rise to the proverb that "it is better to have a husband of wood than to remain an old maid."[32]

These views explain why, in some Muslim-majority countries, it is frowned upon when a woman seeks to advance her education before her domestic duties. Muslim women throughout history, such as in the Ottoman Empire, were often encouraged to gain a rudimentary level of education, but were rarely allowed to extend their education to the same degree that was available to men. Those militant extremists in places like Afghanistan who throw acid on the faces of little girls and young women who are attending schools do so because they believe that "a girl once educated will become more difficult to control."[33] Few stories of courage are more inspiring than that of Malala Yousafzai who, as a 14-year-old girl, on October 9, 2012 was shot three times in the head by a would-be assassin for the "crime" of insisting that girls should also be entitled to an education in Pakistan. A nominee for the Nobel Prize in 2013, Malala has continued her efforts to work for peace. In March, 2014 she travelled to Pakistan to encourage those who had tried to kill her to reconsider their understanding of Islam: "If Taliban wants to implement an Islamic system, they should lay down their weapons, adopt a path of democracy, ask for the forgiveness of those families who have become victims of terrorism and take part in elections. You cannot end a war through war, nor is peace possible through bloodshed."[34]

Women traditionally marry at a young age in Muslim-majority contexts and are expected to bear as many children as possible. This fact explains why very few women in many Muslim contexts have traditionally worked outside the home. One exception to this trend has been the fact that, in many countries, women are seen as ideal teachers.

More recently women have also been admitted into some secretarial and nursing positions. The "facts on the ground" about such issues are much more indicative of local cultural expectations than they are about any religious issues relating to women in the workforce.

The very process of childbirth is often traumatic to a woman's health; this is especially true when the rigors of childbirth take place in medical conditions, which are anything but ideal. Women in many countries have a shorter life span than men because of complications they experience related to childbirth. In many cultural contexts, the worth of a woman is not only based on her being able to have children, but also with the *proviso* of her offspring being male.[35] The Qur'an seems to confront this favoritism because it can lead to infanticide: "When news is brought to them of the birth of a female child, his face darkens and he is filled with inward grief! With shame does he hide himself from his people because of the bad news he has had? Shall he retain it on sufferance and contempt or bury it in the dust? Ah! What an evil choice they decide on" (Q.6:151). Sadly, the practice of infanticide continues into the present. Jan Goodwin notes: "more than 500 of these babies are found every year in Karachi, in the gutters, the trash-bins on the sidewalks. The police bring them to us. Ninety-five percent of them are girls — considered a burden in this society."[36] Another horrible abuse often visited on women in some Muslim communities relates to the practice of clitoridectomies. The practice of female genital mutilation has no foundations in the revelations of the Qur'an or the legacies of Hadith. This practice is also unheard of within Muslim contexts in Asia and in most of Northern Africa. Due to the abusive nature of these practices, they will be discussed in greater detail in the section of this chapter entitled *Rape and Physical Abuse*.

Gender *Jihad*

Islam, like Christianity and Judaism, springs from a world where women have long been subjugated to men in clearly limiting social roles. In Judaism and Christianity, one account of creation begins with women originating from the borrowed rib of Adam, the first human. Within Islam, however, the creation story states that man and woman were created at the same time from black mud. Modern Muslims (along with Christians and Jews) try to blur these facts by emphasizing the many ways in which their religion shows respect to women. Many of these efforts, however, fail to dramatically confront the basic sexism inherent in a vast number of these religious cultures.

Christians and Jews interacting with Muslims can also readily admit to a long history of sexism. Some theologians have asked Christians to explore the use of the term "Father" to describe God or have asked

Jewish and Christian scholars to revisit the ways that the story of Eve's creation — and her sin in the Genesis account — has been used to sustain negative views of women. Our world demands that individuals of all faiths revisit our traditions' initial statements about women and try to reconnect them to our present situation. Instead of only defending the ways that our traditions have encouraged expressions of respect for women, Muslims, Jews, and Christians should also confront the many ways that our faith traditions have restricted women within our communities. Women throughout history have often been marginalized in the name of religion. These facts must be confronted and not brushed aside with defensive rhetoric. As the Qur'an says, we should become "Witness-bearers for Allah in the matter of justice — even though this may be against you" (Q. 4:135).

Gender roles were not always static in early Islamic societies. The Prophet insisted on the birth of baby girls being celebrated in the same way that the birth of a baby boy was celebrated. All Muslims — including all women — must do *salat* and make the pilgrimage and fast during Ramadan. The only exceptions for women are for those who are menstruating and those who are in childbirth. References to menstruation do not carry with them any linguistic connotation of being impure (Q. 2:222), although this has been contested by some non-Muslims. Muslims often cite these as examples of differentiation of biological roles, which does not imply a different worth or value for either gender.

Critics of Islam parade a host of passages from the Qur'an and Hadith that have been used to support sexism among Muslims. One oft-cited passage, for example, mandates that men should avoid harboring impure thoughts toward women and that women should dress modestly (Q. 24:30–31). These passages, however, should be examined in their specific socio-historical context. They should be read in the larger spirit of the Qur'an, which calls both women and men equally to strive toward godliness. As one Hadith reminds us, we should "address people at the level of their understanding", trying to work patiently toward effecting meaningful social change.[37]

The phrase, "men are guardians (*qawwamun*) over women" is found in Qur'an 4:34. This passage can also be translated to say that men shall "take full care of women", which may imply a high degree of respect and care as opposed to control. Some suggest that this oversight is limited to economic guardianship for women and their children. One reliable Hadith seems to continue with a patronizing view of women's roles in their relation to men. Bukhari attributes to the Prophet the saying: "Why didn't you marry a young girl so that you might play with her and her with you?" (Bukhari 7:62:16). One could not possibly find a sentiment more condescending to women than the one cited in a weak Hadith, which states "women are toys, so choose" (Kanz-el-Ummal, 21:919).

Answers to questions about the social role of women are best provided by Islamic female scholars, who challenge us to think about these passages and sayings with a fresh perspective. One assumption that should be recognized is that the Qur'an maintains that men and women both have equal responsibility before Allah to be faithful within Islam (Q. 33:35; 4:135). Qur'an 4:32 claims, "And in no wise covet the things in which Allah has bestowed His gifts more freely on some than on others: To men is allotted what they earn and to women what they earn." Both men and women stand equally before God on the Day of Judgment (Q. 3:195). Qur'an 4:32 and 48:5 repeat the phrase "men and women" to underscore that both stand on the same level in terms of their spiritual responsibilities.

While the Qur'an teaches that men and women are equal before God and will find themselves on equal footing in heaven, it is not the case that men and women are to be treated equally on earth. Qur'an 4:15–17 explains that God gives differing punishments for men and women: "If any of your women are guilty of lewdness, take evidence of four reliable witnesses from amongst you against them and if they testify confine them to houses until death do claim them, or Allah ordain for them some other way [honor killings presumably]. If two men among you are guilty of lewdness punish them both. If they repent and amend, leave them alone; for Allah is oft-returning, most Merciful" (Q. 4:15–16).

In this verse, the female consequence is highly specific and includes an exact nature and length of punishment. The situation for men is ambiguous because, it would seem, men have the option of repenting and, thus, not experiencing any punishment. Women might always have access to repentance on a vertical level with God, but that may not extend to their horizontal relationships with their communities. Nimat Hafez Barazangi states: "while the limited biological differences in procreation do not make all natural dispositions different, they can dictate social differences."[38]

There are differing views about the status of women in pre-Islamic Arabia. A common refrain is that, before Islam, women were treated as cattle and were not allowed to marry whom they chose or to own property. In contrast, Masoud Kazemzadeh notes that "women actively participated in battles and had the right and the effective power to divorce."[39] He notes that Muhammad's first wife Khadija "was one of the richest women in Mecca" and had the power to ask for his hand in marriage.[40] Khadija (565–623) clearly inherited the vast wealth and business acumen of her father and was known as *Ameerat-Quraysh* (Princess of the Quraysh) and *al-Tahira* (the Pure One). She was known as a savvy trader, who was generous in helping the poor as well as her needy relatives. In spite of her social role, she was not able to travel with her caravans and had no choice but to rely on the intermediation of male employees. It was a trusted relative Abu Talib who suggested that Khadija employ her distant cousin Muhammad ibn Abdullah, who was already known at that time for his virtue and honesty. Finally, after receiving the thorough recommendation of her trusted book-keeper Maysarah, she asked Muhammad to marry her. Observations about Khadija (such as her independent economic status and her ability to choose her own spouse) are often used by progressives to support their claim that women in pre-Islamic Arabia had unique benefits that many other women in other parts of the world did not as readily enjoy.

Marriage and Divorce

Fatima Mernissi (b. 1940) agrees with those who claim that, before Muhammad, the status of women in the Middle East was atrocious. Unwanted baby girls were buried alive, and many legal restrictions made their lives oppressive. The Qur'an emphatically attacks the Arab practice of female infanticide (Q. 6:151). When a woman's husband died in those "days of darkness" (*jahiliyya*), she was automatically re-assigned as the wife of one of her husband's relatives — a practice forbidden by the Qur'an (Q. 4:19).Working within that given social context, the Prophet effected a host of substantial changes for the women of his time. The allowance of polygamy came from a dire societal context in which many women were neglected without husbands, who had been lost in wars (Q. 4:3), but it was always stressed that multiple marriage partners must be treated with absolute equality and without any trace of favoritism (Q. 4:129).

Marriage and divorce are issues to be discussed in the context of Islamic family laws and the ways in which they can either empower or enslave women. According to the Qur'an (Q. 2:228), men can remarry immediately after they divorce, but women have to wait for a period of three months (called *'iddat*). Hassan explains: "women are subjected to this restriction because, at the time of divorce, a woman may be pregnant and this fact may not become known for some time."[41]

The Islamic tradition sees marriage as a holy institution given by God to humanity. In pre-Islamic Arabia, there were at least ten types of marriages; many of these were eliminated by the Qur'anic revelation.[42] Men still had the right to marry their slaves or women who were taken in battle. Qur'an 30:21 provides a noble list of criteria for those seeking to marry: "And among Allah's signs are this — He created you for mates from among yourselves, that you may dwell in tranquility with them and he has put love and mercy between your hearts." Some have used this passage to suggest that *muta*, or "temporary marriages", with prostitutes (or other women not their wives) for a set period of time are still permissible. Speaking of this verse, one Shi'a jurist wrote, "It is declared to be abominable, though not actually prohibited to marry in the *muta* form."[43]

The Qur'an stridently discourages Muslim men from marrying non-Muslims, but does allow men to marry "People of the Book" (Q. 2:221). Muslim women, however, are forbidden to marry a non-Muslim. The Qur'an does not eliminate, but does limit, polygamy among believers because each wife must be treated equally, which some have argued is impossible. Issues surrounding polygamy are still hotly contested throughout Muslim communities. It is generally assumed that any man who is about to undertake a second, third, or fourth wife will first get permission from the first wife, although this does not always occur in actual fact.

Arranged marriages are widespread in Islamic societies, although the roots of this practice are based more in culture than they are in religion. The Qur'an is clear that individuals should be free to marry whomever they desire (Q. 35:34). This passage, while confirming that the desires of men and women are equal in God's sight, also seems to speak against any notion that any person should be forced to marry someone whom they do not love. Muslim men are forbidden from to force the wife of a dead relative to marry them; to marry any woman who is a blood relative; to marry any woman that his father had previously married; to marry the daughter of any woman that he had sex with; to marry the wife of one of his sons; to marry two sisters; to marry a woman who is already married; or to marry or remarry any woman that he had had sex with and then took back a dowry or a portion of the bride price. What is vital to notice about these prohibitions is that all of them are directed toward men and without equal directives towards women, who are assumed to play a more passive role in the decision-making process, which may have been based upon an economic context, rather than a sexual context.

Divorce is permissible in all Muslim-majority countries. The Qur'an devotes an entire chapter (Surah 65, *at-Talaq*) to the topic. There are a number of discrepancies in laws about divorce that clearly seem to favor men. Allah allows the practice of divorce as long as clear guidelines are followed. Women can have their request for a divorce granted only if the man feels he must grant her wish in order to achieve self-preservation. Even women in an abusive relationship should understand that they can only divorce as the Qur'an prescribes and, after a divorce, must return to her family of origin and live under the roof of her father or brother.

Inevitably, tensions have arisen around this issue among Muslims. It will not be helpful for non-Muslims to stand on the sidelines and criticize Muslims for perceived failures in this regard. Many within other faith communities have a long way to go in the area of confronting sexism. At present, Muslims have little inclination to turn to others to learn from them ways to confront sexism for a number of reasons. It would be better for non-Muslims to affirm that which is positive within Islam and encourage Muslims in a collegial and non-threatening manner to carefully grapple with Qur'anic (and Hadith) passages that might be interpreted as inhibiting the empowerment of women.

Celibacy and Sexuality

The Islamic *ummah* expressly forbade celibacy and stressed that human sexuality was positive within marriage. In a significant passage, the Qur'an talks about the relationship between desire and sexuality without mentioning procreation (Q. 2:223). Islam, unlike the Judeo-Christian tradition, does not claim that Eve deceptively led Adam into temptation (Q. 2:35–36; see also Q. 20:120–122). Hassan notes, "it is extremely important to stress that the Qur'an provides no basis whatsoever for asserting, suggesting, or implying that *Hawwa* (Eve), having been deceived by *Shaytan* (Satan), in turn tempted Adam and led to his expulsion from *al-jannah* (paradise)."[44]

In spite of some weak Hadith that echo the Biblical story (and may have come directly from early Muslim interaction with Christians), the Qur'an itself does not say that Hawwa was created from "Adam's rib". This omission is frequently noted by Muslim feminists, while Islamist traditionalists tend to cite the Hadith that Eve was, in fact, created from Adam's rib. Stowasser writes: "Of the five Qur'anic accounts relating to Adam, the woman appears in three; in all three, the emphasis of the narrative lies within the disobedience of the human toward God."[45] A clear equality is evidenced in Qur'anic creation passages such as 30:21 and 4:1. Hassan again cites the difference between the Qur'anic omission and the aforementioned Hadith by asking: "If the Qur'an makes no distinction between the creation of man and woman — as clearly it does not — why do Muslims believe that Hawwa was created from the rib of Adam?[46]

Contraception and Abortion

There are a wide range of views among Muslim communities about contraception issues. Most Islamists have extremely conservative views, which consider "male semen to be sacred and its emission are never to take place outside the vagina."[47] Historically, however, most Muslims, have held much more progressive views on issues of sexual practice. Although barrier methods of contraception ('*azl*) were known to exist before the Qur'an, there is nothing within Islam (in contrast to Christian history), which explicitly opposes the use of contraception.[48] Further, Islamic scholars (such as al-Ghazali) never linked the use of contraception to abortion.[49] Al-Ghazali claimed that '*azl* was acceptable in order to "lead to a higher spiritual realization", "to preserve the beauty and health of one's wife", as well as "to prevent the birth of too many children".[50] One authenticated Hadith states: "We used to have recourse to '*azl* in the Prophet's age. He came to know of it but did not prevent us from doing so. If it were something to be prevented, the Qur'an would have prohibited it."[51]

Islamic communities have generally viewed abortion as a form of infanticide and usually discuss the practice in the context of forbidding the taking of human life. The Qur'an specifically states that life only begins when "semen enters the vagina and is mixed with the female egg."[52] The question for the Muslim is when the zygote assumes the attributes of a human being to the extent that an abortion would take an identifiable human life. Once a spirit (*ruh*) or soul (*nafs*)[53] is given to a human body, then one becomes a viable life. The Qur'an provides a careful description of the beginnings of life in Q. 23:12–14 and refers to the same process again in Q. 96:1–5.

Rape and Physical Abuse

The Prophet declared that those who beat or abuse women cannot be considered as Muslims. Islam does not permit any sort of abuse against women — sexual, physical, verbal, or otherwise. Rape or any form of assault is considered one of the most serious crimes imaginable. In spite of this, rape has been prevalent among Muslims in North America and Europe with devastating consequences, such as the spread of HIV/AIDS: a number of organizations have been formed to help raise awareness of these problems among the Muslims of these areas.[54] Culturally appropriate health services have been launched to help Muslims deal with these issues in a sensitive way. Because of a cultural reticence to participate in HIV pre- and post-test counseling and prevention programs, many problems related to AIDS among Muslims have been ignored.

Rape is unquestionably one of the most widespread and violent forms of sexual injustice. It is an ancient problem mentioned repeatedly in the Bible (2 Sam. 13:10–14; Jdg 19:1–30). Rape is a crime committed against unwilling women and men that is often hidden or not reported. One source noted that ten percent of all boys will be sexually molested in the United States before they reach their eighteenth birthday.[55] Islam obviously forbids any form of rape or pedophilia. Those who carry out such sins cannot be considered part of the Muslim *ummah*. Although physically violent rape is most pronounced, there are many forms of rape. Many women feel they have no choice but to provide "sexual favors" to someone in exchange for keeping their job. As it becomes internalized, sexism fosters social and cultural forms of "rape", in which women come to see themselves as inferior to men and thus allow themselves to be subjected to sexual control. Verbal abuse against victims underscores feelings of self-blame and low self-esteem. Poverty directly contributes to prostitution and other forms of sexual injustice. Esack writes, "The suffering of women, like that of any injustice, is part of our existence, of what we live for and, for far too many, die for."[56]

Another compelling social justice issue is how women are often mistreated when working as prostitutes. While in some cases and in some socio-economic contexts some women chose to work as prostitutes this is not usually a choice, but a forced necessity for many women in many poorer nations. Pakistan (and many other places) is a context where many women who are prostitutes cannot be described as individuals who have freely "chosen" this pathway towards daily survival. Is there any genuine "choice" to be had for many trapped in abysmal situations? Is it not the case that all forms of prostitution are forms of sexual slavery to varying degrees? One thing is certain: sex-workers, driven by economic hardship and social stigmatization, are often those who are the most vulnerable to violent rape and unchecked physical abuse. The lives of the vast majority of sex-workers in Muslim societies are filled with violation, stigmatization, marginalization, coercion, and oppression on a host of levels. Humane efforts to unionize and empower sex-workers (and their families), such as those led by University of Pennsylvania scholar Toorjo Ghose, should not be hindered by so-called moralists who ignore the challenges and difficulties that these women face without a shred of empathy or concern.

Physical violence against Muslim women is widespread — as it is among women throughout the world. Some sexual and physical abuse originates from the families and close friends of those who are abused, and such abuses are often unreported and unchallenged. It is salient to note, however, that in many Muslim-majority countries, rape can be punishable by lengthy prison terms, life imprisonment, or even death. This "zero-tolerance" approach in the legal realm, as well as the complex challenges related to the inevitable under-reporting of sexual violence, explain why rape is consistently cited as a problem in the single digit percentiles in almost all Muslim nations. Violence against women fundamentally challenges and erodes social cohesion.[57]

Does the Qur'an, however, allow for men to beat their wives? Many Muslim women report having been beaten by their husbands, who claimed that God had given them that right. Surah 4:34 is translated by Yusuf Ali as explaining, "As to those women on whose part you fear disloyalty and ill-conduct, admonish them (firstly), (next) refuse to share their beds, (and last) beat them (lightly)." Some Muslims have tried to moderate the intent of this divine command to beat women by noting that the beating should only be lightly and after first admonishing them and withholding sexual privileges. Ali's commentary clarifies: "if this is not sufficient some slight physical correction may be administered, but Imam Shafi'i considers this inadvisable, though permissible and all authorities are unanimous in deprecating any sort of cruelty."[58]

One Hadith tells of a friend of the Prophet (Umar) who requested permission from the Prophet to beat his wife, which was granted (Abu Dawud 2:2141). Another Hadith reassures women, "A wife has a right not to be struck on her face."[59] There is also a reliable Hadith cited by Muslim (4:2127), which relates an experience of Aisha, the wife of the Prophet: 'He (Muhammad) struck me (Aisha) on the chest which caused me pain." Another reliable Hadith (Bukhari 7:72:715) tells of a woman who came to Aisha because her husband had beaten her so extensively that her skin was blotched, which caused Aisha to say "I have not seen any women suffering as much as the believing women. Look! Her skin is greener than her clothes." El-Fadl wisely rejects giving any credence to any Hadith, reliable or otherwise, which condones any form of beating women. He writes: "If a Hadith with serious theological and social implications is suspect for any reason, then it should not be relied upon unless its authenticity can be conclusively established."[60]

Female Genital Mutilation (FGM)

One particularly widespread ritual of physical abuse in many Muslim-majority countries is the practice of clitoridectomies or "Female Genital Mutilation" (FGM). Why is this done? It is a traditional practice that has existed for centuries, justified by the thin varnish of religious significance. In some cultures, a woman cannot be married unless she has been "circumcised". Women are seen in these contexts to be inherently "over-sexed" and FGM is seen as a necessary practice to ensure a woman's virginity until marriage, as it is done with the intent of curbing the sexual desire of women. Women are "freed from sexual bondage" so that they can fulfill their duties as mothers. FGM is glowingly described as being "hygienic" and "purifying" by its religious and cultural supporters, who also claim that it promotes fertility and general bodily health.

These dubious arguments are not unique to the Muslim world: FGM predates Islam and has been practiced throughout the world. Rituals surrounding FGM originate from sexist fears of the power of female sexuality; such anxieties have been expressed in a number of different ways throughout history. In ancient Egypt, the widows of deceased Pharaohs were ritually buried alive in order to insure that they would not have sex with another man after the death of their husband.[61] Female genital mutilations were prescribed as a medical solution in nineteenth-century Europe and North America as a way to "correct" female masturbation practices.[62]

In many Muslim-majority countries, FGM is banned as being un-Islamic (based on Q. 4:1). However, FGM is common in some Muslim societies, particularly in North and Sub-Saharan Africa. Some of the major sites for this practice are Ethiopia, Kenya, the Sudan, Somalia, Mali, Yemen, Oman, Bahrain, and, until recently, Egypt. FGM is also practiced secretly among some communities living in Europe and North America.[63]

FGM is practiced in a number of different ways. Dorkenoo reports that traditionally "mutilations are performed with special knives, with razor blades, with pieces of glass or scissors."[64] Saw-toothed knives are used in Mali, while blunt razors are utilized in the Sudan. This practice may have a cultural rationale, but they must be opposed because of their barbarity. FGM is not exclusive to Muslims; it is also practiced by Christians and adherents of traditional religions throughout Africa.

Among Muslims, FGM is supported by both men and women who feel it is a God-given religious obligation. It is often described as virtuous but not obligatory. One among many Hadith states that the Prophet commanded this ritual: "The Prophet, having seen Umm Atiyyah, the circumciser, instructed her to cut slightly and do not overdo it because it is more pleasant for the woman and better for the husband. . . . Female circumcision is a *makrumah* (an honorable act) and is there anything better than a *makrumah*?"[65] The idea is that a woman who has been circumcised will find sexual intercourse less pleasurable and, thus, will be more likely to remain faithful to her husband. Opponents of FGM refute these Hadith, saying that they are weak and unreliable. Imam Shaltut writes that these Hadith "are neither clear nor authentic".[66]

Inarguably, FGM leads women into a host of infections and diseases. Jawad claims, "The most immediate complications are pain because the operations are often done without the use of anesthesia, hemorrhaging to blood vessels such as the dorsal artery of the clitoris, panic and shock due to a sudden loss of blood, urinary retention and infection due to the use of unsterilized instruments, fever, tetanus, and blood poisoning due to the unhygienic conditions during the performance of the operations."[67] When FGM is performed, there are usually few medicines to administer pain control, although sometimes a Vaseline-like product or herbal remedy is applied. Most of all FGM leads to an increased risk of hemorrhaging, septicemia, tetanus infections, and dyspareunia (painful sexual intercourse). FGM can also lead to women contracting HIV/AIDS.[68] Countless women have died because of infections related to this practice.

FGM cannot be tolerated, much less condoned. It should, however, be understood through the lens of traditional cultures. Only education that makes medical practitioners, religious leaders, midwives, and members of communities aware of these dangers will end this barbarous ritual. Religious leaders should accept a central role in bringing this cruel practice to an end. Individuals need to be confronted with the inarguable medical facts in order to dispel historic myths about its supposed benefits. Studies have shown that increased education correlates with the decreased practice of FGM. In the meantime, people of faith must work to create culturally acceptable alternatives to FGM rituals.

"Honor Killings"

Islamic legal codes impose severe punishments on women who have committed acts of sexual misconduct, including burying them up to their armpits before ritually stoning them to death. Sometimes family members take the law into their own hands in order to be "merciful" and to spare those condemned a more public and brutal death. This has sometimes been called "honor killing" because some women have been killed, it is claimed, in order to protect a family's "honor". The United Nations Population Fund (UNFPA) "estimates the annual worldwide total of honor-killing victims at 5,000 (although it is probably much, much higher)".[69] The killings occur because many traditional social patterns, which assert that a woman's purity defines the honor of her family, run into contact with children reared in a completely different social ethos. Women who are perceived to be immodest, who seek divorce, who break off an arranged marriage, or any number of other random offenses are often the victim of these murderous attacks by their own families. The situation is as complex as it is tragic: Harik and Marston are correct in saying that "women are both supported and suppressed by the family system" within many Muslim societies.[70] All too often, women are stoned to death for "honor"; no legal proceedings are brought against those — often family members themselves — who carry out these crimes against young women.

Honor killings happen amongst many Muslim communities throughout the world. Charles Kimball recalls an honor killing he observed in Iraq: he was drinking coffee when "a young woman screaming came running down the street." He looked up and saw a 19 or 20-year-old girl being chased by a man who turned out to be her father. Her father caught her by the hair and cut her throat. When Kimball asked what happened to the killer he was told: "Nothing. It was an honor killing."[71] In North America, 2009, a girl was killed in Canada when she began dating a non-Muslim. In 2007, an Egyptian man in Arlington, Texas cut the throats of his two teenage daughters when they began to wear lipstick, listen to popular music, and express questions about Islam.

Homosexuality and Homophobia

Islamic law has consistently offered two definitions of homosexuals —
those men (and not women) who are sexually attracted to their own sex,
and those men who have anal intercourse with other men. Homophobia,
for the purposes of this book, is defined as the irrational fear of,
aversion to, or discrimination against homosexuality or homosexuals.
Of the (more than) 80 countries in the world in which homosexuality is
explicitly condemned in the criminal code, more than 25 are countries
in which Muslims are in the majority.[72] In 2014, both Nigeria and
Uganda passed new laws that criminalize both the real or perceived
sexual orientation of homosexuals. Amnesty International reported that
ten people in Nigeria were immediately arrested when the law went
into effect[73] while President Youweri Museveni of Uganda signed a law
which allowed for homosexuals being able to be imprisoned for life.
Supporters, such as Ugandan MP David Bahati were euphoric at the
passage of the new law exclaiming: "This is a victory for the families
of Uganda, a victory for the future of our children."[74] All 7 countries in
which the death penalty can be extended to homosexuals are Muslim-
majority nations, which make the status of homosexuals in these
nations extremely vulnerable. Public, almost celebratory, executions of
homosexuals in Iran, such as an incident that took place in July of 2005,
have been particularly brutal.[75] In contrast, Muslim-majority nations
such as Indonesia have not yet made homosexuality an illegal act.

For many conservative Muslims, the growing social acceptance of
homosexuality is a "virus" from the contagious West that symbolizes
all that is inherently wrong with the modern and overly-tolerant,
liberal world. Homosexuals destroy culture and religion at the same
time and must be opposed without compromise. With the assertions
of the Qur'an as their primary weapon, the issue has become an easy
way for politicians or religious authorities to enrage local communities
and, in the process, gain increased political power. Homosexuals are
often seen as a much easier target (scape-goat) to attack than other,
more complicated, injustices. For example, militant fundamentalists
on the Philippine island of Mindanao made their anti-gay crusade
the centerpiece of their political agenda and called for the castration
and exile of all homosexuals.[76] Homosexuality is sometimes described
as a virulent "Western disease" and is seen as an evil moral disorder
embedded in the decadent corruption of the soul and spirit of a person
caught in the tentacled grip of satanic delusion.

Islamic views about homophobia and homosexuality often parallel
those of other religious traditions: Christians and Jews have long
looked to the story of the rain of fire on Sodom and Gomorrah as an
argument against the practice of sodomy (Gen. 19:1–5) although the

story is arguably about the violent rape of male visitors to their town.[77] The Sodom story is retold in Qur'an 7:81, 26:165–166, and 27:55. The Torah also talks about "sodomy" in a number of passages (Lev. 18:22–30; 20:13; Deut. 23:17, see also Jdg 19:15–30, 1 Kings 15:11–12, and Isa. 3:8–9). Fundamentalists argue that the practice of homosexuality is also mentioned in the New Testament (Rom. 1:24–25; 1 Tim. 1:9–10; 1 Cor. 6:9–10; Jude 1:7–8, 17–19). This specific interpretative legacy has had clear social consequences: today, many individuals beyond faith have caricatured the majority of Christians worldwide as being intolerant of gay and lesbian lifestyles.[78]

Because of the Sodom narratives (Q. 4:16; 7:81 and 27:55), many Muslims have concluded that the Qur'an condemns those men who willingly assume the passive-receptive role in anal sex (*ityan al-dhukur fi al-dubur*). At the same time, throughout history and across the world, many Muslim communities have tolerated a significant amount of homoerotic sentiment and homosexual behavior. In many countries, men look for young boys as "entertainment", and there are instances of fathers trading their sons with other men for casual sexual use. In some cultures, boys between the ages of 10 and 15 have been trained as dancers for the pleasure of homosexual audiences. Many of these boys, abused as children, will more than likely grow up and repeat the same practices of either abuse or homosexuality. In some Muslim contexts, homosexuals often identify themselves to others by the types of clothes or hair styles that they wear.[79]

Islamic law requires that a conviction for homosexuality only occur when four "trustworthy" men testify, and there is at least one first-hand witness of the penetration. In some instances, the accused must also make a full confession before a criminal conviction can be given. In fact, "traditional and modern Arab states (and non-Arab Islamic ones, with the exception of contemporary Iran) have not attempted to remove homosexual behavior or its recurrent practitioners from society."[80] Saudi Arabia, for all of its efforts, has only convicted a few people. Those convicted have been given prison sentences (five or six years) and whipped (usually with 2,000 lashes). Convicted homosexuals under the Taliban rule in Afghanistan were buried alive in large pits during public executions.

The fact that the subject is briefly raised in the Qur'an is proof that homosexual acts were being widely performed without too much alarm in many Arabian societies. Many men in Muslim-majority countries (such as Bangladesh) have been active in same-sex activities from time to time in their lives without identifying themselves as homosexuals. They are probably "even unfamiliar with such Western terminology".[81] Khaled El-Rouayheb argues that the actual term "homosexual" was not used among Muslims until the nineteenth century.[82] Before then what was consistently condemned was not homoerotic love — "expressed in countless pedarastic poems of love and affection" — but all forms of anal intercourse.[83] Love poems written by men to each other were openly expressed without fear of censure because they had nothing to do with what was prohibited, namely anal sex.[84] Tolerance and intolerance were not issues because the widely held assumption was that there have always been stories of men who loved other men. In fact, some have argued that "consistent patterns of Islamic homosexualities can be traced over centuries."[85] While homosexuality has always existed in Muslim-majority cultures, homophobia among Muslims is a relatively recent phenomenon.

As mentioned earlier, the few verses on this topic include Qur'an 4:16; 7:80–84 and 27:54–58. Qur'an 4:16 is a verse that deals with the issue of how to punish those who are caught in homosexual activities. It says that if "two men are guilty of lewdness they should both be punished", but they can also be "left alone if they repent and amend their ways." Homosexual Muslims interpret "lewdness" in this text to refer to a public display of affection, which can be violent or even rape. Qur'an 7:81 says that men who "practice their lusts on men in preference to women" are guilty of "transgressing beyond bounds".

Some Muslims also see Qur'an 26:165–166 as an indictment against homosexuality: "Of all the creatures in the world, will you approach males, and leave those whom Allah has created for you to be your mates? Nay, you are a people transgressing all limits" (see also Q. 29:28). Two frequently referenced Hadith declare: "If a man who is not married is seized committing sodomy he will be stoned to death" and "kill one who commits sodomy, and the one who lets it be done."[86] In addition to these passages and various Hadith, Islamic law condemns anal intercourse between males — not homosexual sentiment or preference.[87] Sabine Schmidtke argues that homoerotic desire is not seen as a mortal sin and that the Qur'an is vague about the exact legal punishment: "Mutual attraction between males was unanimously viewed to be perfectly normal and natural."[88]

Muslims in Europe and North America (and even a few Muslim-majority countries) have begun to openly participate in gay rights and recognition movements. A number of Muslim homosexuals have formed organizations (such as the Al-Fatiha Foundation, which began in 1997 in the United States, and Queer Jihad) to reconcile Islam with homosexual practice.[89] In 2006, Al-Fatiha claimed over 700 members in several chapters and in four countries on three continents.[90] By the beginning of 2013, Al-Fatiha claims to have doubled in their membership since that time. Another group called GLAS (Gay and Lesbian Arabic Society) is based in New York and focuses on fighting for the rights of gay Muslims worldwide. There is also a section of a noted gay-Muslim mailing list called "Queernet", which mails out information about different meetings and initiatives that are specific to gay Muslims. A major focus of these advocacy groups has been to look at the ways that laws in Muslim-majority countries promote homophobia and marginalize homosexuals. In 2001, al-Muhajiroun, an extremist group based in the United Kingdom, issued a *fatwa* that called for the deaths of those involved in the organization.[91] If the Qur'an and Hadith unambiguously condemn homosexual acts, these extremists reasoned, how then can these groups continue to exist and claim Islam as their faith? Some men have "appeared to resolve their Muslim-gay identity conflicts by reinterpreting doctrine and emphasizing aspects of Islam that promote peace, tolerance, and justice."[92]

Confronting Injustice

Fatma Sahin (b. 1966), the leader of the women's division of Turkey's JDP reminds us that "when you change the status of women, you change the entire society."[93] Sexism and homophobia are widespread throughout the world including all Muslim-majority countries. While a dictionary definition of sexism might be "discrimination against a person based on his or her gender", it can also include attitudes, conditions, or behaviors that promote many stereotypical characterizations. Homophobia, the fear or contempt of homosexuals, is one such expression of a desire of the majority and the powerful to denigrate minorities and the less-powerful. Both sexism and homophobia stem from a lack of respect for others and seek to limit any aspect of interaction that one person can have with another, solely on issues of gender or homosexual practice. Of course, sensitive teaching strategies will eventually have to emerge within conservative communities in order to educate young people by providing information about different values without seeming to force those values on anyone.[94] Whether someone is male or female, heterosexual, bisexual, or homosexual, the Qur'an does not discriminate when it says "O Mankind! Reverence your Guardian Lord, who created all of you from a single person" (Q. 4:1).

Non-Muslims should be slow to offer their judgments about the roles and status of women within the Muslim world because many Muslim women assert confidently that it is their Western sisters (and not those who are Muslims) who are being oppressed. It is also the case that attacks against Islamist sexism and homophobia can also serve as effective conduits for the further marginalization of Muslims worldwide and become tools to bolster Islamaphobic agendas. Focusing on "scatter-shot" anecdotes and random examples of injustice can become an ideal way to make one's enemy more barbaric and inhumane.

Sometimes Muslim women speak about their authoritative "wisdom" and extensive "influence" in civic society even while admitting that men often hold more visible and public roles of authority. Some Muslim women cite the advances of Muslim women, such as Benazir Bhutto, to illustrate that many Muslim-majority nations are actually, in ways, more progressive with respect to these issues than nations, like the United States, which have yet to elect a female President. Such arguments blur the obvious facts that oppression in any context is often dynamically dependent on those who are being oppressed willingly embracing the facts and "benefits" of their own oppression at the hands of those who are dominant.

Sonya Fernandez reminds us that the discourse about women's rights among Muslims invites unhelpful polarizing contrasts between "us and them, Islam and the West, the savage and the civilized, and the free and unfree which are together inaccurate and Islamaphobic."[95] Such conversations, bereft of the multiplicity of meanings, often present the West as a solution to what is interpreted as the inherently vile nature of Islam as Islam. Stereotypes replace nuanced and multivalent realities and demonize Muslims, who need to be saved from themselves by European and North American crusaders. Such views conjure up the colonial legacy of self-righteous missionaries intent on civilizing the barbarians. All these issues, Fernandez reminds, should be "located within their socio-cultural contexts" instead of being judged with the same attitudes of "racial and moral superiority that informed the imperialism that occurred."[96]

It must be emphasized again that instances of honor killings, FGM, rape and other crimes against women are not "Islamic" in any way and are not condoned by Islam's divine revelation. Muslims and non-Muslims should look carefully within their own traditions in order to confront the multivalent issues surrounding the many forms and expressions of sexism and homophobia. Should we oppose injustice, for example, when those who are oppressed wish to remain in their oppression? Rhetoric is best joined with concrete actions: platitudes fail to improve the plight of women where they are suffering a host of injustices related to sexist attitudes, some of which seem self-imposed. Goodwin summarizes this problem: "It is ironic that the most outstanding contradiction regarding the inequalities suffered by Muslim women is that Muhammad was among the world's greatest reformers on behalf of women. He abolished such sex-discriminating practices as female infanticide, slavery and levirate marriages. . . . Today's Islamic spokesmen frequently extol the Prophet's revolutionary innovations, but usually fail to note that they are rarely honored in reality."[97]

9. Islamic Stewardship and Responses to Environmental Degradation

You created the night, I made the lamp. You created the clay, I made the cup. You created the forest, the mountain, the desert; I made the walk, the garden, the orchard.

— Muhammad Iqbal

Allah is the one who created for you all things that are on the earth; then he turned to the heaven and made them into seven firmaments. And of all things he hath perfected knowledge.

— Surah 2:29

Science and Islam

The teachings and study of science need not be seen as contradicting the faith of Islam in any way. While some have claimed that religion is outside the scientific realm, within Islam science serves as an extension of faith and illuminates its truths. It can best be understood through the lens of Allah's creative power. Science that confirms Qur'anic revelation is seen as a helpful guide to the faithful that assists them in making ethical decisions about their daily lives.

It has been argued that the Islamic understanding of science does not coincide with what is meant by the term in the European intellectual tradition because, instead of beginning with independent exploration, the Muslim scientist begins with Qur'anic revelation. In spite of this unique conception of the term "science", Muslims, such as al-Hafiz, have claimed that Islam has always promoted the work of scientists and naturalists throughout history, asserting that no divide should be made between the physical and spiritual realms because they are inextricably linked together.[1] Muslims have been encouraged to use reason freely to explore the complications of the planet and its needs with the assurance that all questions that might arise are able to be answered by scientific insights and reason, which supports, and will never contradict, the truths of Islamic revelation. Science, in the historic Muslim context, has not been seen to "compete" with the natural world but to function in a "co-operative" sense (a term also used by the Russian scientist Peter Kropotkin, 1842–1921) with its inherently revelatory sacredness and givenness. Scientific interrogation is rooted in deep spiritual (or "metaphysical") values that are ever-aware of God's transcendence.

There are reportedly specific examples of Qur'anic references to scientific phenomena. For example, according to the Qur'an, plants enrich the soil and protect it from wind and water. Plants do not only provide food for animals but animals, by releasing carbon dioxide, also give back to plants. Plants are created in "diverse pairs each separated from the other" (Q. 20:53) and for the benefit of all members of the earth's *ummah* of life. God has provided plants and natural resources as "provision for you (humanity) and your cattle" (Q. 80:24–32). Trees are not to be cut down unless it is absolutely necessary. One Hadith quoted in Bukhari affirms, "Whoever plants a tree and looks after it with care until it matures and becomes productive will be rewarded in the hereafter."[2] It is also related that the first rightly guided Caliph, Abu-Bakr, gave his troops the command: "Do not cut down any trees and do not kill any animals except for food in enemy territory."[3]

Islamic Environmentalism

Environmental degradation has been a major concern in Europe and North America since the nineteenth century, when the factories of the Industrial Revolution spewed pollution and waste on an unprecedented scale. In many nations of our modern world, wanton disregard for environmental concerns continues unabated. In many places, air has become almost impossible to breathe, thick with smoke and soot. It is also common that water and soil have been contaminated beyond any hope of a quick recovery. Only recently, have Europeans and North Americans become aware of such notions as "global warming", "greenhouse gasses", "endangered species", "acid rain", "desertification", "climate change", and the preservation of the rain forests. Previously arcane discussions about ozone layers and the melting of ice-caps in distant climes now directly affect everyone.

Long before the institution of Arbor Day, Earth Day and the Kyoto or Copenhagen Protocols, the Qur'an called on the people of the earth to preserve the frail inter-relationship of clean air and clean water. The Qur'an revealed to humanity, "Don't you see that Allah makes the clouds move gently, then joins them together, then makes them into a heap?"(Q. 24:43). In the same way, when YHWH created the earth, the Hebrew Bible recounts the divine declaration that "all was very good" in the initial creation.

While it is true that many Muslims show little regard for the environment, others claim that Islam is the only major world religion that has consistently called for the preservation and protection of the environment. Fazlun M. Khalid connects modern environmental injustice with spiritual health: "We have lost the ability to distinguish between need and greed. We have lost the intuitive knowledge of relating to each other, to nature, and to the environment. And as a result we have lost a sense of proportion and balance. All these are symptoms of a disconnected people."[4] The solution to this quandary is found within the foundational texts of Islam that provide Muslims with a strong emphasis on environmental justice. It is a topic that is an ideal locus for Muslim, Christian and Jewish partnerships focused on promoting mutual understanding that lead to shared social justice initiatives. It is also relevant because few non-Muslims appreciate how consequential this theme is to Muslims.

Theological Foundations

As in all Islamic *kalam*, the idea of *tawhid* (the oneness of God) functions as the starting point for understanding God's relation to His creation. All creation affirms the oneness of God and is within the *tawhid* of God's oversight. There is nothing of the creation that is part of God or connected to the nature of God, but the creation exists as a complete affirmation in itself of God's oneness and the ways in which God's *tawhid* is expressed in mercy and power. It is the unity of Allah that determines the fundamental nature of all of creation, which is divine property and responsibility (Q. 30:26–30). One should enjoy creation but must never worship anything but the Creator (Q. 41:37).

Humanity is created to affirm God's oneness, as is all of the created order. God has entrusted humanity with the earth (Q. 33:72). Islam is a communal religion that includes the *ummah* of all living beings — plants and animals as well as human beings (Q. 6:38). *Tawhid* undergirds the ideas that Muslims have about the interconnectivity of life on earth: the physical and the spiritual worlds are inexorably linked together. The physical world is created by God to be a place of peace and security (Q. 15:45). When the *tawhid* of God is invoked, all society benefits from the harmonious worship of God throughout the created order. Dien explains: "The belief in the oneness of the Creator leads to the unification of all human energies to act under the command of the Creator. This unification extends itself to include all the cosmic forces which should be seen as one force acting in one direction, applying to the divine order. In this way, we can construct a holistic final shape for the whole of existence, as seen by Islam, with the natural environment as an integral part."[5]

Humanity began in Eden's well-watered garden and the paradise to come will also be a rich realm of verdant flowers, trees, and beautiful gardens. Creation is God-ordained to declare the praises and glory of God. The world was created from a perfect vision (Q. 60:61–62). Allah gave humanity a splendid creation, and, in its fundamental nature (*fitrah*), it is a "wonderful sign", an expression of the power of God and the glory of the divine will. One should study the created order so that they can appreciate God's ways and to better understand how to live within the world.

Unlike in the Jewish and Christian story of a denigrated natural world, the garden that Adam and Eve left was not directly punished and debased for any human failure. One Hadith of the Prophet explains that the world has never been profaned: "all the world is a masjid." All of nature is completely and totally submissive to God's will and is filled with signs (*ayat*) of divine glory. Nothing was created in vain or without purpose. Indeed, nature has no "meaning" apart from God's will and God's glory. There are over five hundred verses in the Qur'an that affirm the magnificence of Allah's artistry in creation. Allah provides the rain that falls on the barren deserts and brings them to life. A theme that extols God for revealing holy power in the creation of the winds and the mountains is a frequent refrain (e.g. Q. 2:164). Creation is a revelation of God so that humanity "may learn wisdom" (Q. 7:64; 67; 15:26, 28). The created order reveals God's continuing mercy (Q. 7:57–58). All of life derives from Allah (Q. 40:62) and humanity has a responsibility to be faithful stewards of creation and to express their right relation with God through proper care for the world.

Humans are higher beings (*ashraf ul-makluqat*) because they have been given reason. Our brain capacity is far greater than our ability to utilize it. This potential means that humans have a unique responsibility within the created order to serve as God's chosen trustees (*khalifa*) of the earth, although many resist accepting that responsibility (Q. 33:72–75). Malaysian Chandra Muzaffar (b. 1947) explains, "The human being, both in individual and in the collective sense, is the vice-regent of God and as such we must submit ourselves to doing what we know to be right."[6] Allah watches our actions and will weigh them in the balance (Q. 55:6–9) on the Final Day. Particular punishments will be meted out to those who are not faithful stewards but carelessly abuse the land (Q. 89:11–14). Christians might find resonance in this theme with the injunctions of Christ to His followers that they live as "good and faithful stewards" (Matt. 25:23) of all that God has given.

Allah fashioned humanity by "breathing into him" the spirit of life (as opposed to creating them in the divine image) and establishing that the angels should bow down before humanity (Q. 15:29–30). Humanity is called to serve God as "inheritors of the earth" (Q. 6:165). Humans must preserve the essentials of life, particularly water, the source of all life (Q. 21:30). Their relationship with the created order is unambiguous and does not leave room for practices that "dominate" creation through overconsumption and unchecked technological advance. Humans are called to be the stewards, but not the owners, of the earth, because everything belongs to God and God alone (Ps. 24:1).

Allah has blessed human beings with reason, and this gift teaches humanity to protect the environment by following a reasonable and logical middle path (*mizan*). Reason allows us to properly take care of all the resources that have been entrusted to our care and to use them appropriately in a way that ultimately blesses the entire community. Environmental degradation occurs because some within humanity fail to recognize God's mercy in the physical world (Q. 28:73; 55:5).

Contemporary Issues

The cyclical and harmonious patterns of the natural world are presently in crisis. Initial awareness of these problems have led the scientific and political communities to search for answers to environmental imbalances. Increasingly, however, it is becoming apparent that historic faith communities need to become more vocal in supporting faith-based solutions to these demanding environmental challenges because many people have failed to grasp the significance of our shared environmental problems. From a Biblical and Qur'anic point of view, Allah has created an amazing physical world and has called humanity to serve as co-regents within the created order. These facts have been ignored; yet they hold the potential to reframe the issues of environmental activism by challenging religious adherents to see that working for environmental causes is a spiritual responsibility, not merely an issue of economic self-interest or political concern.

Many Arab Muslim countries have oil-based economies and also burn huge amounts of relatively cheap (and more easily accessible) fossil fuels. These two factors might discourage some nations from embracing environmentalist policies that might encourage less dependence on oil. While some argue that Muslim-majority nations "blessed with the wealth of oil, should, in theory, be models of environmental concerns and control", this has not always been the case.[7] Fossil fuel resources have been exploited and consumed with reckless abandon. There have been a number of major incidents in which millions of gallons of oil have spilled into the sea.[8] Unfortunately, many Muslim communities have been slow to embrace environmental activism as a vital concern of practicing stewardship and expressing faith.[9] The short-sighted environmental destruction that usually results from such incidents have long-term ramifications, which tear to shreds already fragile ecosystems.

While some Muslim-majority nations are relatively impoverished and are continuing to develop, a number of other, more affluent, Gulf State Muslim-majority nations cannot hide behind the "excuse" of economic limitations. Of course, it should go without saying, that the vast majority of all nations, Muslim or non-Muslim have woeful records when it comes to preserving frail ecosystems and putting the needs of the environment above short-term economic considerations.

Environmental abuses directly contributed to the disastrous drought in the Sahel, the ecoclimatic region between the Sahara in the North and the Sudanese valleys of the South of Africa. In many Muslim-majority countries, neglect for the environment springs from the fact that the political realities are more authoritarian than they are Islamic in nature.[10] Short-term neglect and mismanagement of limited environmental resources in these nations have resulted in long-term problems. There are many other ways that environmental injustice has been the result of short-sightedness at the level of political and social policy-making. In many Muslim-majority countries, neglect for the environment has sprung from the fact that political realties have been more authoritarian than they have been "Islamic" in nature. Farid Esack illustrates this by recounting that, when he took his pilgrimage to Mecca, he found no official signs pointing toward holy sites (such as the Cave of Hira) but that these sites could be easily found by following the thousands of discarded Pepsi bottles and cans that littered the horizon.[11]

Islamic respect for nature (*khilqah*) is deeply rooted in the faith. The Qur'an speaks extensively about humanity's relationship with and responsibilities toward the natural realm. Chapters of the Qur'an are even named after animals and insects as a way of giving these creatures honor in divine revelation.[12] Husain Sadr notes that there are "accurate Qur'anic accounts and interpretations of several scientific principles and disciplines such as cosmogony and cosmology, astronomy, anatomy, geology, mineralogy and metallurgy, meteorology, agriculture, and horticulture."[13] Muslims are to reflect on God's signs of truth (*ayats*) embedded within the creation. Nature exists to be both ordered and known by humanity. The pursuit of scientific knowledge is invariably linked to a posture of worship and service to Allah.

For many Muslims, personal purity directly relates to care of the environment. When people are sinful, the environment will also suffer (Q. 2:19, 27–29). Environmental disasters do not occur as acts of God, but rather, they "have been invited by human follies as a warning and punishment."[14] Environmental degradation is a direct result of individuals failing to be grateful, not only for the actual gift of creation, but also for their own role within the larger created order of interdependency. That which harms the earth's ecosystem is sinful, and Islamic scholars cite with pride instances within their history in which "the development of technology under Islam was deliberately stifled when that technology became a threat to the natural environment."[15] The earth is sacred in that is invested with God's creative power. As Parvez Manzoor writes, there is, within Islam, "no such thing as a profane world" because, as one Hadith states, "this whole earth is a mosque."[16]

The gift of reason allows humanity to fulfill this task and to serve as faithful "inheritors of the earth" (Q. 6:165). Muslims are commanded to spread "perfect knowledge" (Q. 2:29) about the environment just as they are also enjoined to spread the truth of the Islamic faith. The high value given to reason is one of the reasons why Islam has always encouraged education, including environmental awareness. When reason is applied to environmental degradation, the community will encourage environmental education as a vital way to help individuals practice their faith in right relation with the created order. This life is a preparation for the afterlife (Q. 15:45); because of this, humanity should care for God's created order as an act of worship and stewardship. The world itself is created as an image or shadow that faintly mirrors the future paradise (Q. 40:61).

Managing Scarce Water Resources

Akutaruddin Ahmad, in *Islam and the Environmental Crisis* (1997), reminds his readers that "human beings are composed mostly of water" (71% of the human body).[17] Water management issues are of grave concern in our modern world. As much as 20 billion tons of unclean water — often poisoned by raw sewage — flows every year from rivers and lakes into the world's oceans. Over one million people in our world, mostly in rural communities, suffer from drinking unsafe water. These problems are much more readily apparent in the Southern hemisphere than they are in the North.

The word "water" appears over 50 times in the Qur'an, and water is, understandably, of vital importance in the relatively dry Arabian Peninsula, which enjoys only 0.09% of the world's fresh water supply. In spite of this scarcity, Middle-Eastern water has often been polluted or used inefficiently by a careless constituency. Worship is due to God because it is "He who sends down rain from the skies" (Q. 6:99), which sustains life and brings color to the world (Q. 35:27). Every Muslim should be thankful for this gift from Allah (Q. 56:68–70), and its significance is reinforced in the command that all prayers should begin with ablutions.[18]

Because water is essential to the process of preparing for prayer, when water is in short supply or contaminated, spiritual practice is also impacted.[19] The idea that being spiritually clean comes through interaction with a natural world that is physically clean is a compelling starting point for discussions about environmental concerns. Muhammad Saleh Farsy writes that "Muslims are to be clean and free from any blemishes" and are commanded to be clean on many levels (Q. 74:4–5). They should also maintain a clean physical domain in which to carry out their spiritual practice.[20] Because Muslims are required to keep away from filthy places, they must ensure that their immediate environment is clean. This can provide a foundation for speaking to communities about dealing with litter issues or other practical day-to-day dimensions of environmental cleanliness.

Water is that which brings the various distinct forms of life into existence (Q. 20:53), and it is a vital link in the world's amazing ecosystem. It must be shared by animals, vegetation, and among all members of a given society (Q. 54:28); that is why it should be protected by everyone from any type of impurity (*najasa*) that might contaminate the public supply. One Hadith states that the Prophet encouraged that water should never be wasted in excessive amounts when doing ablutions (*wudu*), even if one was beside "a flowing river".[21] Throughout history, Muslim empires such as those in India and the Ottomans spent tremendous resources on the construction of water reservoirs and aqueducts.[22]

Desert Reclamation

In Central Asia, and throughout Africa (particularly the Sahel) and the Middle East, desert reclamation remains the primary environmental challenge facing Muslim communities. A desert is not to be seen as a "dead land", but as a complex and delicate ecosystem that requires particular attention for wise management and the efficient protection of the scant available water resources in order to preserve the frail environmental balance between the basic needs of both wildlife and human communities.

Reclamation of the desert creates hospitable and arable land, which facilitates wildlife and vegetation to expand and to be wisely preserved for future generations. As one Hadith attributed to the Prophet states, "whoever brings dead land to life, for him is a reward in it, and whatever any creature seeking food eats of it shall be reckoned as a charity for him."[23] Desert land is reclaimed (*ihya*) when an individual purchases un-owned land or when land is granted (*iqta*) or leased (*ijarah*) by the state to cultivators. Land can also be given charitably (*waqf*) for the public good. An appointed officer (*hisbah*) of the state should oversee the proper (intended) uses of these protected zones (*haram*) and reserves of land (*hima*) designated for environmental reclamation and preservation.

Air Quality

Clean air is another treasure to be protected in order to sustain life. The air that we breathe belongs to Allah; the Qur'an explains: "Winds like the heralds of glad tidings go before His mercy" (Q. 7:57). Dr Abu-Bakr Ahmed Bageder of the International Union for World Conservation of Nature (IUCN) states that "any activity which pollutes it (air) and ruins or impairs its function is an attempt to thwart and obstruct God's wisdom toward His creation."[24] The Iranian government has waged a constant battle with this problem which worsens every winter and which also has been exacerbated by sub-standard quality fuel. The government has frequently closed schools, banks, and government offices when the problem became acute. According to one environmental government official, who likened going outside with "suicide," said that there were only "three days of clean air in the city [Teheran] in 2013."[25]

As much as 20 billion tons of carbon dioxide is released into the air every year, which has been a major factor in the world's ongoing global warming crisis. Sadly, some of the most polluted air in the world is to be found within the boundaries of certain Muslim countries. The oil fires lit by Saddam Hussein's armies as they retreated from Kuwait during the first Gulf War caused over 99 million tons of sulfur oxide, 68 million tons of nitrogen oxide, and 77 million tons of carbon monoxide to be released into the air.[26] The United States and the People's Republic of China are the greatest culprits, but many studies have also cited Indonesia as a major source of the world's air-pollution partly because of extensive deforestation projects.

Since the Iranian Islamic Revolution of 1979, Iran's carbon emissions have risen by over 240%. Teheran arguably has the worst air-pollution problem (along with Beijing) of any locale throughout the entire world. Further, Iran has little infrastructure in place to support the use of renewable energy sources. Part of this problem relates to both prevailing wind patterns and the topographic layout of the city — surrounded by hills — which tends to trap all carbon emissions. The major problem, however, is the preponderance of the city's industries and private homes — combined with heavy traffic — that expend pollution at exponentially staggering levels. Present attempts to deal with the situation by building nuclear power plants have been met with stiff opposition by Western nations who fear that such facilities will eventually be used to create lethal nuclear weapons.

The Care of Animals

Animals were "created from water" (Q. 21:30; 24:45) to live within distinct "communities" (Q. 6:38) and were intended to exist as the "possession of humanity" (Q. 16:10–11). The fact that many species are now endangered illustrates the point that humanity has not fulfilled its responsibility to God to protect the animal kingdom, which has been created for the benefit of humanity as food, assistance in work, and even for beauty (Q. 16:5–8). The biblical King Suleyman is presented as a role-model who shows tender care for all animals — even small ants and birds — whose languages he understands and with whom he lovingly interacts; promising to protect them from harm (Q. 27:16, 18-19).

Animals should never be mistreated and their lives must never be taken unnecessarily. For example, a Hadith relayed by abd-Allah ibn-Amr' warns that using animals for target-practice is expressly prohibited.[27] Hunting is permissible only when meat is needed as food, and hunting should never be pursued as a sport because it is unkind and unnecessary. When an animal absolutely must be killed, the killing should be quick and humane, following the mandates of *hallal*. The Qur'an asserts that even lowly ants should be protected. In one story, an ancient prophet destroyed an ant colony because the ants had stung him. Allah chided the prophet by saying: "because one ant stung you, you burned a whole community that glorified me?"[28] According to one Hadith, the Prophet Muhammad reminded the faithful that kindness to God's creatures is an act of worship and is a reflection of the kindness of God.[29]

Once while the Prophet was travelling, one of his companions removed a baby pigeon from its nest. A Hadith of this story relates that the mother of the bird came to the Prophet and asked him if he knew who had taken her chick. The Prophet looked into the matter and made sure that the birds were returned to their nest. Another Hadith warns that whoever kills a bird for amusement will be judged on the final day because the bird will ask Allah for recompense and it will be given to the bird at the expense of the hunter.[30]

One eighth century prose writer and scholar, al-Jahiz (776–868), wrote an intriguing study called the *Book of Animals*. While this treatise is not an exercise in modern zoology, it is a fascinating work of appreciation in which al-Jahiz discusses a host of humorous observations about animal behavior. It has even been suggested that this book flirts, one thousand years before Darwin, with the idea of evolution. Al-Jahiz writes about a theory he calls God's "planned disorder", in which changes in the environment are observed to bring about gradual transformations in an animal's characteristics.[31]

More recently, the criteria of *hallal* have put pressure on the practices of modern animal slaughter. Questions are raised, for instance, about how the need to prevent unnecessary animal suffering during sacrificial slaughter can be extended to account for whether or not such animals have suffered during life. The attention to specific *hallal* techniques of slaughter, therefore, should attend to the ways animals bear the suffering during life from modern injustices of overconsumption, factory-farming and inhumane treatment. In the words of Tariq Ramadan, "Respecting the lives of living animals is more important than the "techniques" used to slaughter them, because wasting food is unacceptable, because higher goals cannot be ignored in the name of means and productivity!"[32]

Islamic Environmental Organizations

There are numerous environmental organizations within the Muslim contexts worldwide that promote the conservation of resources and the conviction that all Muslims have a "social contract" with Allah and with each other to care for our God-given "divine environment" (*al-muhit*). These organizations include (among many too numerous to cite) the Arab Environmental Association, Eco-Friends Middle East, the Alliance of Religions and Conservation (ARC), and the IUCN (the latter two organizations are strongly supported by a number of Muslim-majority nations).[33]

Sri Lankan Fazlun Khalid (b. 1932), founder of the Islamic Foundation for Ecology and Environmental Sciences (IFEES), calls Muslims to a balanced middle-path (*mizan*) in dealing with the delicately fragile and interrelated world of environmental considerations. The IFEES, founded in the mid-1980s, is a non-governmental organization that is collaborating with a host of different organizations, including the United Nations, to raise environmental awareness among Muslim societies.[34]

One group of international Muslim scientists gathered in 1983 for an environmental sciences conference, which examined how Qur'anic principles relate to Western environmentalist concerns. This led to a document entitled *The Islamic Principles for the Conservation of the Natural Environment*. This paper analyzes the various ways in which Western and Muslim-majority nations participate in environmental preservation. Principle Seven of this document states, "States shall co-operate in a spirit of global partnership to conserve, protect and restore the health and integrity of the Earth's ecosystem. In light of widely divergent contributions to the many challenges of global environmental degradation, nation states have common but differentiated responsibilities."[35] This statement affirms that Muslims should partner with all individuals and communities of good-will in order to advance environmental protection.

The Natural Balance

Nature is in a faithful balance (Q. 15:16). The balance within nature teaches humans also to live with moderation (Q. 7:31). For Muslims, this will mean practicing their faith both in terms of personal practice and also in light of mandated "social functions in the service of mankind and other beings."[36] The natural balance is ordered to "preserve justice and equality and man with intelligence and volition should not disturb this balance."[37] The degradation of the natural order is a spiritual offense in that it corrupts the holy intentions of God, the Almighty Sustainer. Environmental abuses, indeed, often begin in issues relating to immorality, such as greed or a desire for power. Conservation preserves God's blessings and allows humanity to worship Allah with a greater understanding of the fact that all of creation is an expression of divine generosity. Environmental conservation and education about environmental challenges are simply two more ways in which Muslims can serve God and "actively promote virtue in every aspect of life".[38]

When a Muslim community in Central Texas contributed significant labor and time to restore lands in the government-sponsored Waco Wetlands Project, they were participating in acts of worship toward God as well as acts of connection with the larger community. The practice of worship (*ibadah*) mandates that Muslims work for all forms of justice (*'adl*), including environmental challenges. Worship is an obligation, and, therefore, using natural resources in a way of right stewardship that honors God is also an obligation. The entire earth is a masjid for worship, with Muslims being given the duty to serve as trustees over resources for the sake of the common interest (*istislah*). This call to stewardship means that environmental resources should not be unnecessarily squandered or wasted (*dhiya*). The earth is owned by Allah, and we are only users of its resources, never its masters. Nature is not to be dominated or exploited because a *khalifa* has no actual right to rule, nor any actual claim to ownership. The *khalifa* will be judged on the final day for the quality of their stewardship. In a real sense, the misuse and debasement of the natural world leads to human debasement.

Those actions within nature that are beneficial to the public interest are *hallal* (pure or positive), while those exploitative actions are *haram* (impure, to be criticized). God owns all land for humanity's mutual benefit, and, thus, lands should be allocated (*itqa'*) for everyone's benefit. The belief that Allah owns all land reminds Muslims that they are only borrowing or being allowed to manage a portion of someone else's property. This worldview calls for believers to show great respect for what has been entrusted to them and to live with a healthy fear of God in protecting what has been given as a trust. One Qur'anic passage emphasizes this point with force: "Those who break Allah's covenant after it is ratified, and who surrender what Allah has ordered to be joined, and do mischief on the earth; these cause loss only to themselves (Q. 2:27).

Promoting Care for the Land

Fertile land is not abundant throughout the Arabian Peninsula and human exploitation, inefficient farming techniques, and population pressures have further contributed to the reduction of the limits of the land's capacity to be fully productive. Because of this inevitable problem, the jurists of Islamic history have mandated that certain areas of land, such as riverbanks, shade-trees, wells, and springs, were to be set aside as "banned zones" (*haram*) and were not to be developed or abused.[39] Land is either cultivated (*'amir*) or it is considered dead-land (*mawat*). An imam has the right to give unproductive land to those who are willing to cultivate it; the new owners will be considered to be the caretakers of that land for the extent of their lifetime. No one's rights should be infringed upon in the question of "ownership" while one is living on and utilizing the land. On the other hand, unutilized land — according to one Hadith of the Prophet — is designated as land that cannot be privately owned by any one individual: "Pasture-land, woodland, wildlife and certain minerals, including water cannot be privately owned in their natural state since this will cause harm to others."[40] The concept of land ownership within Islam is not so much one of personal control or economic domination, but of what Dien calls the "guided utilization" of shared land resources across many generations.[41] Western countries, by comparison, often view private property as a reflection of one's own individual autonomy from both the state and other citizens. Proper utilization of land and proper tending to its environmental stability and well-being are not implicit to the meaning of ownership and thus, not subject to broader communal needs. It is easier for such a view to exploit land and resources for lucrative profit, which subjects the vitality of land to the advancement of market expansion.[42] One would hope that all nations would aspire to the just use of land for the benefit of future generations. Sadly, this noble ideal has often been ignored in the practices of modern Muslim-majority countries.

Not only are devout believers commanded not to degrade the environment; they are mandated to proactively nurture, protect, and even reconstruct the fecundity of the land and to shepherd the earth's limited resources. Reconstruction is done through community-guided acts of preservation. The idea of a wildlife (or environmental) reserve can be found in Islamic laws that mandate that certain land should be set aside as "guarded" or "protected" (*hima*) lands. Lands can be designated as *hima* if the community shares a distinct need to protect the land. This land cannot have any buildings or be cultivated in any way. Issues of land ownership and use should be seen within the framework of God's mandate that believers work for social justice. Allah has placed humanity within the *ummah* of nature and given nature to humanity as a trust (*amana*) and as a place to advance worship and wisdom. Living in right ethical relation with nature makes an individual aware of God's greatness and compassion toward creation. Sadly, the quick pace of economic development in some settings in Muslim-majority countries has also resulted in extensive environmental degradation. Only recently have Muslims begun to address these problems with the positive resources of their faith.

Conclusion

In this section, I have sought to help the reader appreciate how the Qur'an calls for care for the animal kingdom. Sadly, in many Muslim-majority contexts, Qur'anic ideals have been trampled underfoot and animals have been abused and mistreated. In spite of these failures, the very fact that there is such an emphasis provided within God's divine revelation to the House of Islam speaks volumes about how animals merit human respect and protection. God's call for peace and social justice among humanity also extends into human interactions with all forms of creation who share a fragile home.

While it is argued by some that Satan bears some responsibility for the world's environmental problems (see Q. 15:38), the obvious blame for the extent of contemporary environmental degradation should be given to unfaithful humanity. This is underscored by the fact that Satan is never to be understood to have power outside that which is allowed by the Almighty. The idea that Satan is a dutiful servant of Allah can best be understood by non-Muslims by seeing how similar this notion is to the description of Satan given in the ancient book of Job (as opposed to how his persona came to be understood by Medieval Christians).

Islam teaches that the misuse of the earth is a serious sin against God. Allah created the world in perfect order (Q. 15: 16–23); this balance (*tawazun*) is now under attack. When humanity does not obey Allah, natural disasters will ensue either directly or indirectly (Q. 2:27). When individuals harm their environment, they are actually bringing harm to themselves (*zulm al-nafs*). Allah alone can bring life, death, and resurrection (Q. 2:28; 15:23) to the land, because God alone actually has "power over all things" (Q. 41:39). A strict reading and interpretation of these passages led some Muslim clerics to explain that Hurricane Sandy, a devastating storm that struck New York and New Jersey in 2013 was a sign from God and a curse against America for its previous support of films that were seen to denigrate the honor of the Prophet Muhammad. Fortunately, such views when posted online led to a strong backlash from Muslim readers who were outraged at such sentiments. One respondent explained: "This hashtag doesn't represent Muslims but represents a terrorist. We ask God to help and save Americans." Further, in the aftermath of this hurricane, a number of organizations, including the Iranian Red Crescent Society, offered to send workers to New Jersey to aid in recovery efforts.[43]

The fact that oil has been found in the compact deserts and rocky landscapes of the Arab world has been the source of both economic benefit and many ecological nightmares. The discovery of vast amounts of fossil fuels has led to tremendous cultural and political tensions as various nations have vied to control oil reserves. Abu-Bakr Amhed Bagader has said the root cause of all environmental degradation is humanity's materialistic drive, selfish greed, and careless disrespect for God's creation.[44]

The Qur'an, in Surah 2:31–35 presents an account of creation that has only minor differences from the Judeo-Christian Genesis narrative. Unlike the Genesis account, though, in the Qur'anic version the original paradise was never made outside the limits of human habitation. Some Muslims have suggested that Islam is free from the Judeo-Christian idea that humanity must have dominion over the earth, and thus is superior to all other religions, as humanity is viewed as living in harmony with creation.

Historically, this theme in Genesis has emboldened countless Christians and Jews to justify the misuse of natural resources as an act of worship. During the Industrial Revolution, for example, technological progress went forward as humans conquered and defeated the natural world without much concern for being faithful stewards of the land. While humanity is distinguished as "the best of creation", this does not give humanity any occasion for arrogant pride in how their natural environment is viewed.[45] Present environmental problems in Muslim-majority nations have often originated from Muslims not following their own mandates to serve as guardians of God's creation. At the other end of the spectrum, Islam forbids the idolatry of worshipping that which is within the created, natural order. Islam, as in all things, seeks to strike an appropriate balance, with humanity placed firmly within the natural order as a *khalifa* responsible for its proper care and maintenance.

People of faith can agree on the many obvious benefits of supporting environmental partnerships that preserve resources and provide cleaner air and water. The relationship between nature and human ethics is an axial theme in the Qur'anic revelation. Each Muslim must work to enhance the public welfare (*istislah*), which includes the promotion of a comprehensive way of thinking about the environment. Ziauddin Sardar writes: "Combine the concepts of *tawhid*, *khalifa*, *amana*, *hallal*, and *haram* with words for justice (*'adl*) and moderation, temperance, balance, equilibrium, harmony, and the concept of public welfare (*istislah*), and one has the most sophisticated framework for an environmental ethic that one can possibly desire."[46] The relevance of Islamic moral and ethical ideas about humanity's proper relationship with the created order (*qasd*) cannot easily be overstated, and has often gone unappreciated.

The principle of stewardship militates against any form of wastefulness, whether corporate or individual. God does not love those who are excessive and are "wasters" (Q. 7:31; see also 6:141). In one Hadith, Jabbar, a friend of the Prophet, was said to have left some food on his plate following a meal. The Prophet noticed this and commanded his friend not only to finish the wasted food but even to lick his fingers because "the Devil stands next to one who eats and whatever is left on one's plate becomes food for the devil." The Qur'an warns that those who "squander and waste are the brothers of Satan" (17:27).[47] Taking these personal values to a wider context will mean that believers will practice moderation in the use of all resources and will eschew any wastefulness or the overuse or misuse of God-given resources. While this principle of moderation may backhandedly support the use of resources even beyond need in order to avoid potential waste, such interpretations depend on the false assumption that vital resources are limitless and can be consumed without discretion. The notion that resources should not be squandered, on the other hand, implies that such resources are limited and, when obtained, should work to their full potential to meet present needs. Even times of abundance, then, are not meant to be wasted on those who have plenty. Allah has blessed us with abundance but "every single thing is before His sight, in [due] proportion" (Q. 13:8), which reminds us to use these gifts from God in our natural world in ways that bring honor to the divine name.

The way a Muslim cares for the earth is a testament to his/her love for the Creator. God gave the earth to humanity as a precious gift (*amana*). When we debase the natural world we are also debasing our own selves, as well as making light of and misusing God's gifts to us. Akutaruddin Ahmad calls on Muslims to "be free from any desire but live only to please Allah. . . . [L]iving thus will not pollute and will not waste and we will be able to care for all things and beings as trustees of Allah."[48] As one Hadith explains: "Whoever is kind to the creatures of God is kind to himself." M.A.S. Abdel Haleem explains: "Man cannot save the natural environment except by rediscovering the nexus between the Supreme Artisan and nature, His creation, and becoming once again aware of the sacred quality of His works."[49] Because the ultimate goal of every Muslim is to do what is right and good with pure intent, action — and advocacy for action — are required to guard the earth as Allah commands. As we are gentle guardians over the rich resources of the earth we are also caring for the public welfare (*istislah*). All of us are called upon to carefully preserve God's most sacred and precious gift to all of us — life itself.

10. Creating Multifaith Social Justice Partnerships

The basic aim of interfaith dialogue should be to address common human issues, to take a stand together against things that create poverty and harm the dignity of humans. The Qur'an commands this: Help ye one another in righteousness and piety, but help ye not one another in sin and rancor. Fear Allah, for Allah is strict in punishment (Surah 5:2).

— Mustafa Koylu

Justice is truth in action.

— Benjamin Disraeli

A God of Justice

Edmund Burke (1729–1787) famously asserted that "all that is needed for the triumph of evil is that good men do nothing."[1] For Jews, Christians, and Muslims, God is a God of justice. Theological assertions and pious platitudes, however, are not enough to actually change the pressing problems of our world, so concrete steps and specific actions must be undertaken. Deuteronomy 1:18 declares that God "executes justice for the orphan and the widow and loves the strangers, providing them with food and clothing." Israel is instructed to worship through justice (Mic. 6:8). God established the "year of jubilee" as a way to demonstrate social justice (Ex. 23:11; Deut. 15:1–6). God forbids people from denying justice to others (Ex. 23:6) or to "pervert justice" (Lev. 19:15).

Jesus announced that his mission was to inaugurate the year of jubilee; promoting a concern for social justice throughout his ministry. Christ fed the multitudes and interacted with the "lowest" individuals in society. He taught that when charity is done to the destitute it is done unto God (Matt. 25:34–40). Paul the apostle told the early church to "share with all in need" (Rom. 8:13). James clarifies this intention when explaining that God wants believers to practice the pure religion of caring for "orphans and widows in distress" (James 1:27).

This book has shown that the drive for social justice is at the heart of the practice of Islam. Devout Muslims practice their faith by giving to their neighbors and by reaching out to the poorest of the poor. *Zakat* in aid of the poor is one of the five pillars of Islam; God mandates that these alms go to the "poor and needy . . . for those in bondage and in debt for the cause of Allah, and for the wayfarer" (Q. 9:60). Muslims, like people of many other faiths, are commanded to give to all who ask (Q. 2:177).

Globalizing Challenges

Martin Luther King believed: "As long as there is poverty in the world, I can never be rich; even if I have a billion dollars . . . I can never be what I ought to be until you are what you ought to be. This is the way our world has been made by God. No individual or nation can stand out boasting of being independent from the blessing and enabling power of God: we are interdependent."[2] All people of faith who see the world in this way are driven, in theory at least, to establish social justice partnerships in order to help both individuals and larger communities. A host of social injustices demand resolution as never before in world history.

Cross-currents of globalization and a host of technological advances have created a planet that seems smaller, increasingly interrelated, and interdependent. Sometimes interactions between faith communities raise new questions as well as providing for new opportunities. Before the "face to face" encounters of our modern age, the awareness of those in other traditions was often as if one was "seeing in a mirror dimly" (1 Cor. 13:11). Mutual learning through personal interactions offers the hope for eventual partnerships among friends for the cause of needed social change. Martin Forward explains that "unless we choose to live in geographical or mental ghettoes" it will become inevitable that we will "come into contact with people of quite different religions who strive after holiness" and also aspire to social justice.[3]

One of the first globalizing forces in world history has been religion. Clearly, Muslims and Christians (and many others), have been committed to the task of internationalizing their faith communities through their passionate belief in a transcendent reality and a transnational truth. Thomas Simons calls the religion of Islam "a globalizer" and he argues that, unlike the Vedic traditions, Islam has struggled with appreciating and respecting the various cultural identities that they have encountered in their historical advance, "even while trying to supersede" the significance of ethnic distinctiveness.[4] When other people of faith have met the globalizing forces of Islam and have begun to examine how their faith communities can exist in multifaith dialogue in this age of globalization, it becomes apparent that new paths forward need to be found for people of various faiths to become a "multireligious people".

Gandhi's Example

In thinking about how people of goodwill can partner for social justice, it is instructive to consider the legacy of Mahatma Gandhi (1869–1948). The forces of globalization do not diminish the verity taught by Mahatma Gandhi that all human rights issues are best addressed at a local level; in specific socio-cultural contexts. Although Gandhi lived in a time of significant multifaith tensions, he worked valiantly to foster a genuine appreciation for Islam within his own specific socio-cultural context. Gandhi extensively studied the Qur'an because, as he claimed, he genuinely wanted "to know from the inside the hearts of his Muslim fellow-workers."[5] This deep curiosity combined with genuine humility became the engine of his search to build stronger networks of trust between Hindu and Muslim communities throughout India. This path was consistently fraught with danger and offered no certain promise for a resolution to the complex multifaith challenges that Gandhi was facing in India. Ultimately, it was his positive and empathetic views of Islam — and his eager willingness and genuine openness to valorize peaceful social activists who were also Muslims — that led to his assassination at the hands of intolerant Hindu extremists in 1948.

Gandhi's quest to study Islam was motivated by what Sheila McDonough has called his "intense desire to communicate" across any and all necessary lines of cultural and social division.[6] Gandhi was not only a man of faith but also a seeker of truth; he was an unpretentious soul who sought to respond to the world in which he was living with courage in the face of great obstacles. Gandhi skillfully used religious terms and the shared language of faith to motivate others to join him in partnerships for social change. Everything that he said about Muslims seemed to be motivated toward a singular end, the promotion of "heart-unity". Gandhi chose to see Islam as a faith that proactively promoted peace and wrote that he felt that "non-violence had a predominant place in the Qur'an."[7] Fanatics, he believed, had twisted the authentic message of the Islamic faith, but Gandhi was confident that the *ummah* could withstand these obstacles: "I have not a shadow of doubt that Islam has sufficient resources within itself to become purged of illiberalism and intolerance."[8] In the name of God, Gandhi was able to motivate Muslims of goodwill, such as Maulana Abul Kalam Azad (1888–1958), Abdul Ghaffar Khan (1890–1988), and others, to join him in a mutual *jihad* against the social oppression of their time.

Constructing Multifaith Partnerships

Most faith traditions support the conviction that injustices must be opposed. These similar points of view form a strong base of agreement on which partnerships to confront social injustices can be built. Why is this even an issue? Many Christians, Jews, and Muslims have not worked to partner with each other for social justice for a number of reasons. Cultural differences and social priorities provide the most obvious barriers. Further, the long and tense histories of Muslim and Christian or Muslim and Jewish interactions has provided little ground for lasting mutual trust. Even today, many media depictions present Muslim jihadists and Christian crusaders at odds with each other, moving toward increasing hostility. Many European and North American media depictions of Muslims have presented their ways of life, values, and message as fundamentally opposed to traditional Judeo-Christian values and ideals.

Questions of synthesis and dialogue are not idle theoretical constructs. Issues of "worldview" surface at this point: should people from different faith communities focus more on their differences or more on their similarities, or, as often occurs, exclusively on either their differences or their similarities? Is it the case that there is something within our various European and North American cultures that seeks to universalize "Western" values? If so, how should that trend interact with the particulars of a Qur'anic worldview? Are forces of globalization particularly "Western" and do they compete with or challenge Islam? Do "Western" cultures and faith communities foster abstract, simplistic, and reductionistic pre-fabricated notions of Islam based on orientalist assumptions that make dialogue deeply problematic? These are increasingly central questions to contemporary Muslims and non-Muslims who are supportive of both multifaith understanding and the progress of social justice.

Because Islam is a practical and grounded tradition, which is given to working through the will of Allah in this earthly reality, and because Muslim intellectuals historically have not felt compelled to fabricate an idealistic, protective "hothouse" for its central ideas, it is an *ummah* that is largely committed to confronting social injustice and is also willing to join with any and all who are equally dedicated to this holy task of faithful people. Interfaith partnerships, then, are not only welcome; they are actively encouraged in Islamic literature and within the historic tradition.

All people of goodwill can forge partnerships rooted in tolerance that do not compromise the faith of any adherent from any given tradition. In fact, "tolerance is inseparable" from the ways in which we define our identities, yet does not exclude dimensions of conflict, without which "there is no identity".[9] Identity will invariably create differences, but these can be respected and appreciated. Ideally, tolerance will mean the complete recognition and respect for a differing point of view. Christians, Jews, and Muslims can have this level of toleration for each other because these traditions teach humility and compassion for others. Individuals of all faiths should easily be able to acknowledge the inherent limitations of our own finite points of reference.

Divine Intolerance and Godly Tolerance

Only the Divine is capable of encompassing all truth: some would say that this means that God Himself is intolerant; one expression of this would be the divine response to Sodom and Gomorrah (see Gen. 19:1–29). God did not tolerate the evil that existed in Sodom and proceeded to brutally destroy the city for its evil practices. One could argue, however, that even here, God's "intolerance" was against sin, rather than those who committed those acts. This is a possible rendering because there are a number of passages in the Hebrew Bible that call individuals to be accepting of others who do not share the same faith (Lev. 19:33–34).

Jesus, the Palestinian Jew, quoted Leviticus 19:18 when telling His followers to love one's neighbor as one loves one's self (Matt. 22:39). The New Testament commands Christians to "give no offense to Jews or to Greeks or to the Church of God, just as I try to please everyone in everything I do" (1 Cor. 10:32–33). Paul encouraged Christians to avoid offending Jews, pagans, and other Christians. It is probable, that had Muslims lived at the time that Paul wrote those words; their names would also have been added to this list. Many Christians, however, hide behind the non-biblical term "exclusivism" (coined by Alan Race along with the terms "inclusivist" and "pluralist" as a way to define paths to God) in order to practice an anachronistic form of exclusivist tribalism against the "other". Instead of citing this passage, they turn to Galatians 1:10, where Paul asks, "Am I now seeking human approval or God's approval?"

Instead of relying on the Bible and the Qur'an, some Muslims and Christians have chosen to limit their interaction with people of other faith communities by using the invented categories of "inclusivism" and "exclusivism" to define their worldview assumptions about the other. God is the final judge, and it is the duty of all believers of any faith to witness in humility to each other concerning the truths that they believe instead of excluding and judging others with arrogance. The Bible both speaks of God writing eternity in the hearts of all people and not being a respecter of any person (Acts 10:32) while also asserting that, for Christians, Christ is the only way to God (John 14:6) and that, for Christ's followers, Christ's name is the only way to salvation (Acts 4:12).

Some people struggle with the idea of partnering with individuals of other traditions who do not share the same cherished faith convictions. In a previous book, *No God but God: A Path to Muslim-Christian Dialogue on*

God's Nature (2003), I detail why Christians should not avoid discussing differing theological views about the nature of God and the uniqueness of Christ in their interaction with Muslims. Yet, such differences should not provide the only context in which people of various religious traditions interact with each other. In fact, these very distinctions provide a wonderful platform for prismatic discussions that hold the prospect for vital friendships, as well as for creative intercultural and interfaith insights.

Both the Bible and the Qur'an have been interpreted very differently at specific times and by various communities of believers. Some readers, for example, feel that the writers of the New Testament used highly metaphoric and emphatic language when affirmation of Christ's uniqueness in John 14:6; this influences the interpretation and is vital to remember when discussing the verse. What is undeniable about this particular passage, however, is that what was spoken in this message to believers comes immediately after Christ told them not to be arrogant. Such a mindset of self-assurance is often evident when certain Christians quote John 14:6 without any contextual regard to its original audience or the implicit call to assume a posture of humility that is described in John 14:1–5, or in light of the entire book's larger context and intended audience.

Christians or Muslims who believe that they alone have an exclusive claim on the truth should remember that other "Fathers of the Faith" (such as Paul or al-Ghazali) who also believed in this doctrine did not feel obliged to denigrate or exclude others as they held to these convictions. Paul, for example, refused to argue that God had abandoned the Jewish people (Rom. 9–11), and his posture toward Jupiter-worshippers in the book of Acts was consistently patient and respectful because his priorities were fundamentally missiological and not theologically vindictive. Wesley Arirajah writes about John 14:6 that, "What we should remember, however, is that these are all statements of faith about Jesus the Christ. They derive their meaning in the context of faith and have no meaning outside the community of faith. They hold enormous significance for Christian people today, as in the past." Believing in the truth of John 14:6, as I do, does not imply that I should assume God's job of determining who will or will not spend eternity in heaven. Such weighty, eternal decisions are, obviously, entirely up to God. Believers — Muslim or Christian — should not presume to sit on God's Great Throne of Judgment, announcing with dismissive assurance the eternal fate of others.

Relational Dynamics

The theological rigidity of some people of faith often expresses itself relationally. Christians, for example, sometimes forget Christ's claim that the Holy Spirit will manifest the divine presence in followers by making them as supple and as flexible as the wind (John 3:8). The "god" of religiously assertive sectarians seems small and strangely limited by the interpretations and assumptions of those who alone claim to be able to understand God's will and divine ways. The shrill arrogance of some voices demands that listeners either blindly accept their message without reason, moderation, hesitation, or compromise, or reject their message as a falsehood. Some exclusivists attack others as a way of reinforcing their own group identity as "truth-holders". They worship truth-claims instead of the God of all truth. In the words of Peter Gomes (1942–2011), "literalism is the hostage to the eighteenth-century illusion that truth and meaning is the same thing."[10] The Bible, or Qur'an, becomes a weapon and battering-ram instead of a healing balm in the hands of those who are certain that they alone have (and must guard) all truth. Symbolic language among such aggressive Christians replaces the living Christ of history. Some spread verses of scripture along the road like so many tacks waiting to deflate the unsuspecting. As Tertullian (160–220) warned when the Christian Bible was first canonized, "I fear they will bury the Holy Spirit in their book."[11]

What is needed, according to Pope Paul VI (1897–1978), is a "fresh approach to non-Christians." Writing specifically of Muslims, the Pope wrote (in *Nostra Aetate*) that "The Church has high regard for Muslims. They worship God who is one, living and subsistent, merciful and almighty. They strive to submit themselves without reserve to the hidden decrees of God, just as Abraham submitted himself to God's plan; they await the Day of Judgment and the reward of God following the resurrection of the dead. For this reason, they highly esteem an upright life of worship to God, especially by way of prayer, alms-giving, and fasting."[12] Pope Benedict XVI (b. 1926) in *Charity in Truth* reasserts this message that any proclamation of belief should be presented with a spirit of humility and love. Pope Francis has continued forward a deep commitment to relational and incarnational engagement as expressed in comments (during his first year as the Bishop of Rome) regarding homosexuals, atheists, and those who are outside the faith.

The guiding text of *Nostra Aetete* pleads with Christians to avoid quarrelling with Muslims in order to "promote peace, liberty, social justice, and moral values."[13] In another letter (*Lumen Gentium*), the Vicar of the Roman Catholic Church declares, "Those who, through no fault of their own, do not know Christ or His Church, but who nevertheless seek God with a sincere heart, and moved by grace, try in their actions to do the divine will as they know it through the dictates of their conscience — those too may achieve eternal salvation."[14]

Islam has also had its share of fundamentalist and strident voices that are more interested in assertion than mutual respect and understanding. Extremists refute the idea that multifaith dialogue with Christians is beneficial, because, they argue, Christians are polytheists (*mushrikin*) who hold to heretical (*shirk*) doctrines. Islam is the only way: what is there to talk about since Islam is the absolute and final truth given by God to humanity? In one of the clearest acts imaginable of religious exclusion, non-Muslims are not invited to participate in, or even to observe, the holiest shrines of the faith in Mecca and Medina. Only the insider merits entry into these holy and segregated cities. Humanity, progressive Muslims assert, is one family that will ultimately be united within Islam and will one day be able to enjoy the same blessings of *hajj*.

Progressives reaffirm a major conviction of Islamic religious and intellectual history — that only God knows those who will be saved and who will fall into the eternal fire. El-Fadl explains: "Although the Qur'an clearly claims that Islam is the divine truth, and demands belief in Muhammad as the final messenger in a long line of Abrahamic prophets, it does not completely exclude the possibility that there might be other paths to salvation."[15] The message of the Qur'an clearly tells Muslims, "Surely, those who believe, those who are Jewish, the converts, and the Christians; any of them who believe in God and believe in the Last Day and lead a righteous life, have nothing to fear, nor will they grieve" (Q. 5:69). This passage seems to accept the paths of other religions to God because of the great mercy and deep compassion of the Almighty.

Historically, Muslim communities have usually been tolerant — once taxes have been paid and other forms of obsequiousness have been observed. In the context of an intolerant Europe, however, such indignities were relatively minor compared to a myriad of frequent inquisitions, expulsions, persecutions, and burnings at the stake that many Jews, Muslims, or "heretical" Christians experienced. Islamist revisionists in recent decades have marred this legacy; they should not be allowed to cause Islam to be widely perceived wrongly in Europe and North America. Those who argue that Islam is intolerant cite Qur'an 9:5 and Q. 9:29, while those who claim that Islam is tolerant point to Qur'an 109:6 and Q. 5:48. The Ayatollah Seyyed Mohammad Mousavi Boujnourdi speaks for all progressive and moderate Muslims when he explains that throughout Islam's intellectual history, "tolerance has always been a basic principle of Islam and a religious moral duty."[16]

Combating Drugs: A Model

People of goodwill can begin almost anywhere in the work of forging meaningful social justice partnerships. Many of the deep social problems that affect one community are common to other communities. One example of a possible partnership, to illustrate this fact, is in the area of addressing the manufacture, sale and use of drugs.

The Qur'anic basis for abstaining from drugs is Q. 5:90–91 and Q. 2:219, which command against believers taking any "intoxicants" (as well as playing games of chance). Of course, there are many ways to define such a term; some have even concluded that Muslims cannot use many cough syrups, pain medications, anti-depressants, and even vanilla extract and marshmallows (as they sometimes contain alcohol in their ingredients). When it comes to clearly narcotic substances, many Muslim-majority nations impose harsh laws (including capital punishment) for the use and transport of drugs. In Iran, four men were hanged in June 2007 for trafficking several pounds of heroin and opium. In 2006, 20 individuals were publicly beheaded in Saudi Arabia for distributing drugs. It is well-known that Afghanistan is responsible for the harvest of 95% of the world's opium crop and is the largest supplier of heroin — although opium is also being grown widely in Iran, Pakistan, Turkey, and Turkmenistan. There also seem to be close links between terrorists and those within the drug trafficking trade. Drug consumption is on the rise among the youth of Iraq and drugs often easily cross the nation's weak borders. Young people in Yemen and East Africa have frequently become psychologically dependent on *khat* (or *qat*), a leafy-green substance that is widely accepted among members of the culture. Prescription medication abuses and the inhalation of glue and other substances are also on the rise. Turkey, Morocco, Syria, Jordan, and Lebanon are other Muslim-majority countries with increasing concerns about rampant drug abuse and the criminality related to the widespread transport of drugs *en route* to Europe and the Americas.

Because this problem has gone on for centuries around the globe, it is one example of a social problem on which individuals of goodwill can partner together in order to bring substantive change. Many countries have a host of educational resources as well as extensive experience in dealing with these problems. Faith-based programs, which deal with rehabilitation and care for drug-users, can be embraced by people of various faith traditions as a way to build bridges of mutual respect and shared social assistance.

West African Interfaith Partnerships

Another challenging context for multifaith partnerships is West Africa. The nation of Ghana is a place in which Muslims and Christians are working together for social justice. While such statistics are often contested, about 70% of Ghana's 22 million people (as of the year 2000) are Christians, about 15% are Muslims (mostly in the North), and the remainder are adherents of traditional African religions.[17] The Ghanaian government works to ensure religious freedom and multifaith toleration and provides religious education in the public schools for people of all faiths. When tensions between Muslims and Christians arise they often relate to Evangelical/Pentecostal or extravert Islamist missionary activity; often insensitive and aggressive in nature.

Multifaith social justice partnerships can build trust and inclusion in countries such as Ghana or Nigeria, in which religious tensions are increasing among the various faith communities. Shared projects not only can result in tangible outcomes, but can also provide a social context where people can respectfully support and affirm each other. These partnerships against social injustice should never become evangelistic subterfuges masquerading as meaningful multifaith discussions. Sometimes they may result in confrontations of difference as individuals and communities work together in ways that they have never worked together previously. People of confident faith, however, need not fear disagreement or variant interpretations, knowing that all difference finally is left to God's unerring judgment. There are plenty of questions to occupy our mutual attention, while we also recognize that there are a host of assertions and faith claims that are anything but negotiable. We should remain open to all creative and constructive relational possibilities in a posture of humility while also remaining faithful to that which we have received and have come to know as truth within our cherished communities of faith.

Changing Realities

Globalizing patterns are increasing, and people of different faiths are interacting with each other in a host of contexts and cultures as never before. Among the many lessons of the tragic events of September 11, 2001, one is that there are labyrinthine dangers that may befall people whenever others feel marginalized and ignored by those with secure power and entrenched privilege.

Most multifaith and multicultural interactions are not particularly rooted in any conscious reflection. Individuals from various faith traditions should take time to consider what their scriptures say about these interactions and about God's possible intentions for interfaith interactions. How is appropriate respect to be communicated to people of other religions? Until such questions are resolved, can Muslims, Jews, and Christians proceed together in social justice partnerships even though not every "t" has been crossed or every "i" dotted in the process of careful theological investigation?

Truth matters and differences are undeniable. This, however, cannot be the final word in matters of multifaith engagement. While theological categories might be exclusive, relational or missiological priorities should always be inclusive in a way that mirrors God's vast heart embracing love for all creation. Christians, Jews, and Muslims have ample theological grounds for seeking to cherish people of other traditions dynamically: God embraces all of humanity and His infinite love is inclusive. Miraslov Volf (b. 1956) expounds: "A simple willingness to embrace the other does not suffice. The further step of actually embracing them is needed. As we argue with others about issues of truth and justice, we are making sure that embrace, if it takes place, will not be a sham, a denial of the truth, or a trampling of justice."[18] Faith is required: all people of faith can confidently proceed with the assurance that God will guide them in appropriate and faithful interactions. Those who feel that God has told them not to interact with others should be asked to explain how such a polarizing and insular position gives glory to the God of all the earth.

Those who reject social justice partnerships on theological grounds (or because of theoretical abstractions) have failed to root their faith in the concrete facts of relationships. What is probably happening is that such individuals are afraid of others who are different, hold differing views, and look at the world in a dramatically different way. These three traditions specifically call for active engagement in love for all humanity as an act of worship to the Creator of all creation. All of us claim to spring from Eve and Adam and face common temptations from Satan to keep us from our divine destinies as servants of God. Furthermore, the Books of Moses show that God has placed His creation under a series of covenants (such as the Noahic covenant for all humanity) and that these divine promises are irrevocable.

Much has been made of the fact that these three traditions are rooted in the story of Abraham. Christians and Jews often call themselves the "Children of Abraham". Some Arabs have widely claimed that their culture descended from Abraham's firstborn son, the Prophet Ishmael.[19] In the context of building multifaith partnerships for social justice, the story in Genesis of God's provision for Hagar and Ishmael (Gen. 16:7–13) shows the mercy of God for individuals who are experiencing oppression and injustice. God gives Hagar hope in the middle of her myriad troubles that her situation will eventually change for the better. The name Ishmael (*Yishmae'el*) means either "God hears" or "God will hear", and Culver observes: "The fact that God's hearing relates to Hagar's affliction is a key component in the promissory aspect of Ishmael's name."[20] For centuries, at least five times a day, the children of Ishmael have been crying out to God in prayers; it is amazing that some narrow-minded Christians deny that God hears these prayers. What is actually the case is that some Christians are unwilling to hear the prayers of Muslims because of static, insular preconceptions and misdirected pride.

Benefits of Multifaith Partnerships

Partnerships for social justice make concrete one's devotion and are an expression of one's quest for faithful living for God's honor. Random acts of kindness are not initiated to "appease" God but serve as expressions of devotion (see Q. 22:37). God commands Muslims to accept others who have received divine revelation: Qur'an 29:46 enjoins that Muslims should say to Jews and Christians, "We believe in the revelation that has come down to us and in that which came down to you: our God and your God is One; and it is to Him that we bow." Allah created people of all faiths to be unique and gave unique revelations to different prophets throughout time. Islam does not affirm the unity of religions; it does, however, affirm the unity of all humanity. This is the ultimate foundation for meaningful Muslim, Jewish, and Christian partnerships for peace and social justice. Aalia Sohail Khan states that Islam "deplores the divisions among Christians and Jews and calls on them to be at one with the Muslims in worshipping one God."[21]

Examples of Interfaith Social Justice Partnerships

In varying contexts, Muslims, Jews, and Christians have already worked together to promote issues of social justice. Most of these partnerships happen at the grassroots level, but there are also a number of initiatives that are going on at the denominational and international level. Among Christian organizations, the Roman Catholic Pontifical Council for Inter-religious Dialogue, the Columban Center for Christian-Muslim Relations, the Center for Muslim–Christian Understanding, and the World Council of Churches have all created structures for interaction that have stressed the need for creative and effective social justice partnerships.

In the United Kingdom, Christian Aid, the Citizenship Foundation, OXFAM, JCORE, World Jewish Relief, and Save the Children (among other organizations) have formed a network of non-profit organizations in 2002 called "Diversity and Dialogue". The purpose of the "Diversity and Dialogue" program is to build friendships (among students in particular) that will ultimately result in partnerships that address social justice issues. These groups are joining together because they are ambitiously determined to "make poverty history", basing their actions on the Millennium Development Goals established by the United Nations in 2000. In the United States, Co-operative Metropolitan Ministries (CMM) is one instance of many different interfaith coalitions that are made up of Christian, Jewish, and Muslim congregations. These groups are working together in specific ways both to combat injustice and to build bridges of mutual respect between adherents of differing religions.

In Palestine, there are a number of multifaith projects in which Jews, Christians, and Muslims are joining together to address the tensions between the Israelis and the Palestinians. I will only cite the "Oasis of Peace Village" (*Neve Shalom/Wahat al-Salaam*), which was founded in 1979 by Father Bruno Hussar. The biblical inspiration for the village is Isaiah 18:32, which states that "my people shall dwell in an oasis of peace". Individuals are working together in a shared community, and children in this village receive bilingual and bicultural education that honors both Israeli and Palestinian cultural and historic values. The community also opened a "School for Peace" to which visitors can come and support the ministry and where students can learn how to find concrete ways to advance peacemaking efforts in their war-torn region. Similar programs are in existence in other parts of the world: in St Paul, Minnesota, Muslims, Jews, and Christians live and work together in joint social projects through their places of worship in a program called "Congregations in Community" (funded by the McKnight Foundation). The Federal Housing and Urban Development office even has a program called the "Center for Community and Interfaith Partnerships" to promote these kinds of programs, which seem to be preset in dozens of cities in the USA.[22]

Lebanon's July War of 2006

The "July War" (July 12–August 14) of 2006 that devastated so much of the country of Lebanon was a war between the Shi'a Muslim group Hezbollah and the State of Israel. This war resulted in the deaths of almost 2,000 people and the displacement of about 900,000 Lebanese citizens — many of them in the Bekaa Valley and in Beirut's southern suburbs. The long-term effects of this war in terms of economic development — as well as environmental and housing issues — are dramatic and are still not fully understood.

From this tragic crisis, however, came a host of constructive and effective social justice partnerships among Muslims, Jews, and Christians. The "Islamic Relief Organization" served more than 200,000 people and worked closely with the Church of Jesus Christ of Latter Day Saints (Mormons), who sent more than 2.5 million dollars of aid, food, and relief supplies to Lebanon.[23] Habitat for Humanity in Lebanon worked closely with both churches and masjids in building homes and trying to re-unify devastated communities. In addition to these organized efforts, countless individual Muslims, Jews, and Christians worked together at the ground level. Suad Hajj Nassif, the head of the Middle East Council of Churches, noted that countless Christian families and Muslim families found themselves living in each other's homes during times of crisis.

Prismatic Revelations

Differences are inherent in humanity and this seems to be a reflection of Allah's wisdom and will for the world (see Q. 5:48, also Q. 21:7). Differences should be accepted and embraced as opportunities to learn instead of being ignored or simplistically caricaturized so that they become barriers to meaningful interaction. People from various religious backgrounds, while recognizing their real differences, should also look for common ground in social justice work that will also promote mutual respect and increased interfaith understanding. Theological debate may be inspiring to some individuals, but it does not usually advance far enough to change the fundamental injustices in our broken world.

What does God require of us? One prophet announced that humanity was required to "do justice, love mercy, and walk humbly before our God" (Micah 6:8). The forging of meaningful multifaith partnerships for social justice will be demanding both theologically and relationally. Islam agrees with the Christian revelation that, on the Final Day of Judgment, many individuals will be surprised by God's judgments. Jesus will separate individuals in the same way that a shepherd separates sheep from goats, and those who will enjoy God's presence are not those who glibly mouthed right beliefs, but those who dynamically worshipped God and practiced their faith by feeding the hungry, welcoming strangers, clothing the naked, taking care of the sick, and visiting those languishing in prison (Matt. 25:31–46). The Qur'an is clear that "those who were not careful to feed the poor . . . will have no advocate on that Day" (Q. 69:13, 35). Sincere people of all faiths (or of none) can find a shared way of relating to each other; working together for social justice. Because this work is divinely-mandated, believers are promised that God will empower us with the direction that we need: "Those who struggle in our path, unto them We shall show them Our ways" (Q. 29:69).

Conclusion

The White Rabbit put on his spectacles: "Where shall I begin, please your Majesty?" he asked. "Begin at the beginning", the King said very gravely, "and then go on until you come to the end: then stop".
— Lewis Carroll

Judaism advocates for the work of *tikkun olam* — healing a shattered world for God's glory. Christians speak of God the Father sending and sacrificing His only Son, instead of sending a book or words in response to human weakness. Christ comes to transform and reconcile humanity's imperfect and fallen order and to present humanity to God as a gift, which is healed and restored to God's original intention. Islam also teaches that healing and restoration are at the center of God's overarching activity in the pages of human history. God is transcendent and above creation, but is also fully committed to humanity being restored in eternal mercy and love (see Q. 23:109). God gives us all that we need for our lives (Q. 16:10–11) and asks us to be just and merciful to others in return for the gifts that we are given. The righteous respond to Allah's blessings by giving themselves sacrificially and willingly to the work of social justice among all of humanity (Q. 2:177).

It is high-time for Muslims, Jews, and Christians to begin to listen to each other's views on social justice issues with an increasingly transparent posture of engagement. Jesus said, "If you have seen me, you have seen the Father." All too often, those who observe Christian, Jewish, and Muslim relations do not see this same level of authentic genuine honesty. Instead, some Christians, Jews, and Muslims promote hidden agendas to proselytize, to assert their superiority, or to underscore differences with each other.

Each individual person of faith should consider making a commitment to work for the promotion of social justice partnerships. It is a tremendous challenge that is often set aside: the Islamic term for "hypocrite" is *munafiq*, which literally means a "heavy one", because they are burdened both with knowledge of what they should be doing and what they are actually doing. The task of living is to apply faith to the vagaries of life and to act on those convictions in a demanding and diverse world. The challenge for Muslims — and indeed for all of us — is to "be consistent as you have been instructed" (Q. 11:113). Islam, by definition, is livable and realistically attainable as well as demanding and consistently bold in confronting social injustices.

The Islamic concept of personal "revival" or "recommitment" (*islah*) brings hope to individuals willing to change. It is realistic and achievable, seemingly in contrast to the more demanding Jewish and Christian ideal of complete moral perfection. Beyond this ethical challenge, all of us can agree that God has gifted each of us with the freedom either to live for ourselves or in service of others. These three faith traditions affirm that each individual must decide either to accept social and structural injustices fatalistically or to work diligently toward meaningful social change. We should follow our conscience proactively and not become passive slaves to mere moral expediency and comfortable convenience. Our God-given conscience will probably lead us to the higher moral path of social engagement: as one Hadith of the Prophet teaches: "Seek a *fatwa* [legal opinion] from your own heart."[1]

The work of creating a better world for future generations calls for tremendous struggle, both individually and corporately. In this task, we will need to rely on each other as we work to be faithful to "One God, maker of Heaven and Earth". When a Muslim is called to "bear witness" to the creed of Islam, this means more than simply giving casual assent to inspiring words and remote, lofty ideals. It requires a life that "incarnates" the beliefs concerning social justice that are being espoused. The Qur'an says the Prophet was a "beautiful model" (Q. 33:21) who practiced what he preached in the actions of his life. Esack relates a beautiful Hadith of inclusion and acceptance reflective of that which is best within the Islamic tradition: "Wisdom is the lost property of the believer, we retrieve it from wherever it comes" even if that is from the *mustad 'afun fi'l-ard* — the downtrodden of the earth.[2] Muslims and non-Muslims of devout faith are called to remain as faithful co-strugglers in the righteous path of God.

Without apology, both Christianity and Islam are religions that promote mission. Members of both faiths are commanded to be witnesses to the truths that they have received and to give themselves to the work of faithful witness among those beyond the bounds of their faith communities. This proclamation, however, should be rooted in the Christian doctrine of the Incarnation and the Muslim doctrine of tolerance based on God's overarching sovereignty. One of the implications of these doctrines is that "some things must be lived before they can be understood."[3] The ways in which Mahatma Gandhi experienced Christianity as a young man — both in England and, especially, in South Africa — painfully speaks to the importance of rooting faith in concrete ethical concern and not only in pristine ideals and distant theological abstractions. Gandhi fell in love with the melodic teachings of Jesus but was deeply disturbed by the vile racism that he encountered from those who self-righteously asserted that they were Christians. Countless Muslims, Jews, and Christians tell the same story: actions of love speak much louder than pious words.

There can be extensive multifaith theological and philosophical discussions through which people of various faiths can listen and learn from each other. One cannot avoid the fact that God's revelation in the Qur'an emphatically states that the core, foundational doctrines of Christianity — the Incarnation, Salvation through the death and resurrection of the Son of God and the Triune nature of God — are presented in error by their Christian neighbors. The weight of Islamic teaching has consistently worked to discredit these foundational Christian claims. Certain passages in the Bible seem equally immovable when it comes to creating a shared space for interfaith mutuality at the theological level. Theologically, it may be the case that, in this life and on this side of eternity, Muslims, Jews, and Christians cannot find harmony on certain fundamental questions about the nature of God and God's divine action and intent toward humanity. Such facts, however, are not so overwhelming as to prevent the discovery of some relational ground for common intellectual and theological engagement. Discussions, for example, about whether or not Christians, Jews, and Muslims serve the same God are actually framed as nothing more than either frail attempts at meaningful relational respect or an opportunity to exert an exclusionist view while at the same time such a debate is probably not even a constructive theological discussion — and certainly not a very helpful or comprehensive debate. The question that is far more significant is: how is God revealed in Christianity, Judaism, and Islam? Interfaith dynamics rooted in theological assertion quickly confront the fact that one cannot proceed very far in the annals of Christian theology, or historic Islamic and Jewish philosophical responses to Christianity, before realizing that the God revealed as incarnate in Christ — worshipped as God by Christians — is not conceivable according to the basic assumptions of Jewish and Muslim revelations.

Doctrinal differences, however, need not be a hindrance to multifaith interaction. On the contrary, once people of goodwill are clear about what our various faith traditions believe, both in both commonality and difference, we can we move on to more substantial grounds for meaningful, mutual dialogue. This level of honesty and transparency might actually be a welcome surprise in multifaith interaction and might create new avenues for interaction and partnerships. This view is at the heart of David W. Shenk's seminal discussion of how Muslims, Jews, and Christians can find great positive benefit in mutually "evangelizing" each other. Shenk writes: "In times like this, when nations are in turmoil, it is vitally necessary for communities of faith to be present everywhere to give witness to the conviction that God's kingdom is not established with the clenched fist or the indifference of folded arms, but rather in a man crucified on a hill called Golgotha. . . . This kind of witness is a surprise and is most effectively expressed in communities who actually demonstrate that suffering love does triumph over evil."[4]

This position offers a starting point and not an ending point: once we can accept the obvious fact that these faiths are distinct and hold divergent religious-claims, we can then work as communities of faith to build relationships that are meaningful and productive. These will not be based on theological arguments (or even compartmentalized, simplistic agreements), but on shared ethical and moral convictions about pressing social justice issues that we all can agree should be addressed with pragmatism and urgency.

Perhaps the single most significant task for these believers in their mutual interaction aimed at establishing God's kingdom of peace and justice on the earth is a long term commitment to the task of building multifaith social justice partnerships. Other individuals or communities may oppose — or at least not understand — such a faith-based commitment. In 1633, church officials found Galileo guilty of heresy for supporting Copernicus's scientific conclusion that the sun — not the earth — is at the center of our universe. After seven years of house arrest, Galileo finally recanted his views. Likewise, some people of faith have also given up on their convictions instead of pursuing other shared convictions about the need to build stronger multifaith and multicultural relationships.

People of faith should continue to be questioned about their willingness or unwillingness to engage in extensive multifaith interactions. The idea of toleration is recast by some critics to mean simply a mindset of non-interference with others. Lebowitz warns that, "tolerance, understood this way, is a virtue for people who are suspicious of each other."[5] It is not enough simply to avoid confrontation and take the easy path of relational blindness toward difference. Deeply ingrained social injustices will not change into interfaith social justice partnerships until a sturdy group of patient and dedicated believers is willing to be relationally persistent and morally proactive. Pilate found "nothing wrong" with Jesus and yet allowed for the Nazarene's execution because it was the easy and popular path of least resistance. Eventually, however, determination to advance multifaith partnerships able to bring about social justice changes will overcome the inflexible resistance of those self-assured zealots who would put their own assertive religious ideals at the center of everyone else's universe.

Advancement in multifaith interactions should proceed in ways that honor God: true adherents of faith will also be individuals who fight for justice and peacemaking even when such causes are extremely difficult. Change will not come from groups of individuals ceremoniously lighting candles or casually singing schmaltzy songs that promote an ideal but artificial unity. The world has had enough of empty platitudes and impotent words bandied about as unchallenged maxims. History shows us that substantial social justice changes will only come through persistent dedication and undeterred effort. Martin Luther King, for example, not only wove the lofty theme of brotherly love through his eloquent sermons, but also pursued an unending march of gritty and intentional actions that he almost certainly realized would eventually lead to his own murder. King, however, had far more than an amorphous cloud of vapid dedication to rely upon. He had a solid and tested faith, a sharp and reason-seeking intellect, and a vivid grasp of the specific situation and individuals he sought to change.

Albert Einstein (1879–1955) opined: "The significant problems that we face today cannot be solved by the same level of thinking we were at when we created them."[6] Contemporary multifaith engagements are often marked by a host of misconceptions, misunderstandings, inaccuracies, and unsympathetic renderings. The recognition of such flawed starting points need not derail our mutual efforts for social justice. In this struggle, we should refuse the temptation to allow past failures to deter future interactions. While we need to come to terms with our own limitations, we also should not underestimate the power of a loving God to work within the hearts of those who seek a more righteous path forward. It would be amazing what would happen if Christians sought to imitate the humility of Christ, Jews sought to imitate the humility of a young King David, and Muslims sought to imitate the humility of the Prophet Muhammad. The degree to which communities of Muslims, Jewish, and Christians can be humble enough to learn and listen to each other is the degree to which progress can be made in the promotion of greater mutuality between our communities of faith.

Said Nursi (1876–1960), a Turk wounded in World War I, spent two years languishing in a Siberian concentration camp. He returned from this harrowing experience with a new vision for "evangelism" among his fellow Muslims. He wrote: "Dear Brothers, our duty is to do positive action and not negative action . . . our action towards non-Muslims is based on convincing. That is because we know them as a civilized people. It is our duty to show them that Islam is lofty and beautiful . . . one cannot achieve a noble goal with evil means. Therefore, the path of non-violence was the path of Islam."[7] Nursi noted that, even though the Prophet faced many obstacles and enemies, he consistently maintained his hope on his steady pilgrimage from

Mecca to Medina. It is this same determined journey that Muslims should undertake again, with the same solid hope and faith in God. Nursi and others have worked to build social justice partnerships with Jews and Christians while also giving the strength of their lives in the path of peacemaking.[8]

There is an Arabic proverb that reminds us, "consistency is greater than greatness" and a Qur'anic passage that relates, "Be consistent as you have been instructed."[9] What is required is a consistent track record of communication that will build trust and strengthen an embrace of the shared heritage that begins with Father Abraham. Dramatic changes, as welcome as they might be, are far less plausible than measured, consistent steps forward toward mutual respect and sustainable change.

Hope is the soil which nurtures multifaith interaction. It is much easier to become cynical and aloof. Near the end of the illustrious career of Dr Wilfred Cantwell Smith (1916–2000), I had the privilege, as a young man, of spending a number of hours visiting Harvard University in the book-crammed office of this sage scholar. This was an experience that left a lasting impression because of Smith's warm kindness toward someone whom he had never before met. He was a man of hope; a believer in the Christ of infinite resurrection possibilities. Smith gave his professional life to the conviction that the comparative study of religion could foster a greater degree of interconnectedness among people as they learned more about each other's similarities as well as recognizing each other's differences. Smith's words on multifaith partnerships summarize a process that all of us will benefit from as we commit ourselves to social justice as people of faith:

> The traditional form of Western scholarship in the study of other religious traditions was that of an impersonal presentation of an *it*. The first great innovation in recent times has been the personalization of the faiths observed, so that one finds a discussion of a *they*. Presently, the observer becomes personally involved, so that the situation is one of a *we* talking about a *they*. The next step is a dialogue where *we* talk to *you*. If there is listening and mutuality, this may become that *we* talk with *you*. The culmination of the process is when *we all* are talking *with* each other about *us*.[10]

This book has been written with the hope of finding some steady and sure ground to share together as Muslims, Jews, and Christians for our mutual benefit. May God in His infinite mercy help each of us to walk together toward a shared *ummah* of peace and justice. May we keep our hearts open to each other and abrim with the hopeful warmth of divine love and the humane gift of mutual respect.

Notes

Introduction

1. Timothy C. Tennent, *Christianity at the Religious Roundtable: Evangelicalism in Conversation with Hinduism, Buddhism, and Islam* (Grand Rapids, MI: Baker Academic Books, 2002), 152.
2. The Qur'an, for example, forbids Muslims from "serving other Gods" (Q. 24:55), and making idols (Q. 4:116). The Qur'an also forbids covetousness (Q. 4:320), and murder (Q. 6:151), and commands individuals to honor their mother and father (Q.6:151).
3. Nathan Lean, *The Islamophobia Industry: How the Right Manufactures Fear of Muslims* (London: Pluto Press, 2012), 81.
4. Asaf Hussain, *Beyond Islamic Fundamentalism: The Sociology of Faith and Action* (Leicester, UK: Volcano Press, 1992), 22. A claim of some Christians was that the Prophet was a pedophile who suffered from epileptic fits which he construed as encounters with God.
5. The terms "British" and "European" are sometimes used interchangeably in this book. The sometimes-contested relationship between Britain and Europe are far beyond the focus of this research.
6. Michael Novak uses this phrase but its origin is uncertain.
7. David W. Shenk, *God's Call to Mission* (Scottdale, PA: Herald Press, 1994), 81.
8. Shabbir Akthar, *The Final Imperative: An Islamic Theology of Liberation* (London: Bellew Publishing, 1991), 102. In contrast, Akthar claims: "Islam, however, judged by standards intrinsic to the faith has always had a strikingly good record. Indeed, in general, Islam's record is, even when judged by exterior, allegedly higher Christian standards, honorably distinguished by its relative tolerance of alien convictions."
9. Only about 12% of all Muslims around the world are Arabs. Jonathan Curiel in *Al-America: Travels Through America's Arab and Islamic Roots* (New York: New Press, 2008) argues that one way to counter Arabo-phobia is to help people appreciate how many terms in the English language actually have their origin in Arabic (the sixth largest linguistic contributor to the language) including such terms as average, amber, cipher, coffee, chess, check, fanfare, giraffe, lemon, orange, endive, apricot, artichoke, sugar, spinach, jasmine, magazine, monsoon, mummy, racket, sequin, sherbet, sofa, syrup, tariff, traffic, tuba, zenith, and most "al-terms" (e.g. alcohol, alcove, algebra), along with English words that relate to place names such as Mocha (Mecca) or tangerine (Tangiers). Curiel also notes (72) that the exclamation "check-mate!" comes from the Persian "Shah-mat!" ("The King is dead!").

10. Lawrence Davidson, *Islamic Fundamentalism: An Introduction* (Westport, CT: Greenwood Press, 2003), 73.

11. Deepa Kumar, *Islamophobia and the Politics of Empire* (Chicago: Haymarket Press, 2012), 43.

12. Lean, 67.

13. Andrew Shyrock, ed. *Islamophilia: Beyond the Politics of Enemy and Friend.* (Bloomington: Indiana University Press, 2010), 5.

14. Lean, 70.

15. Fred Halliday, "Anti-Arab Prejudice in the UK: the 'Kilroy-Silk Affair' and the BBC Response", in *Muslims and the News Media*, ed. Elizabeth Poole (London: I.B. Tauris, 2006), 24. Robert Kilroy-Silk was a daytime talk-show host employed by the BBC. His letter was dated January 11, 2004.

16. Davidson, 73.

17. Davidson, 73.

18. Karim H. Karim, "American Media Coverage of Muslims: The Historical Roots of Contemporary Portrayals", in *Muslims and the News Media*, ed. Elizabeth Poole (London: I.B. Tauris, 2006), 120–121.

19. Karim, 121.

20. See Edward Said, *Covering Islam: How the Media and Experts Determine How We See the Rest of the World* (New York: Vintage Books, 1997 [1981]). Said argues that media coverage "has served purposes only tangentially related to actual knowledge of Islam. The result has been the triumph not just of a particular knowledge of Islam but rather of a particular interpretation which, however, has neither been unchallenged nor *impervious* to the kinds of questions asked by unorthodox, inquiring minds" (169).

21. In transliterations of names, places, book titles, and terms I have followed the Library of Congress system of transliteration which excludes diacritical remarks. Exceptions have been made when citations have come directly from other sources as well as when using terms already familiar to a wide audience.

22. Lawrence Rosen, *Varieties of Muslim Experience: Encounters with Arab Political and Cultural Life* (Chicago: University of Chicago Press, 2011), 67.

23. Charles Kimball, *When Religion Becomes Violent: Five Warning Signs* (New York: Harper Books, 2002), 25.

24. Karen Lebacqz, *Justice in an Unjust World: Foundations for a Christian Approach to Justice* (Minneapolis: Augsburg Press, 1987), 11.

25. John Esposito, *The Islamic Threat: Myth or Reality?* (New York: Oxford University Press, 1999), 3.

26. Pierre Bourdieu, *Sociology as a Martial Art: Political Writings*, ed. and trans. Gisele Sapiro (New York: The New Press, 2010), 19.

27. Bourdieu (2010), 159.

28. Hussain, 36.

29. Rosen, 28.

30. Hussain, 155.

31. Rosen, 30–31. Rosen mentions that a frequent Hadith states, "He who believes, believes, he who does not believe, disbelieves" (30).

32. Bourdieu (2010), 173.

33. Some Muslims, such as Ashgar Ali Engineer, argue that the Qur'an promotes

democratic responses to external forces. In contrast, extremists suggest the exact opposite. Reza Davari Ardakani, an Iranian neo-conservative, has written dozens of books against concepts such as democracy and pluralism. Moderate views on these issues are also espoused in Iran, such as in the writings of Seyyed Mohammad Khatami, the former President of Iran.

34. Surveys have shown that between 65% and 75% of all American Muslims register to vote, which puts American Muslim political participation well above the national average. The percentages come from Asman Gull Hasan, *American Muslims: The New Generation* (New York: Continuum International Publishers, 2002). Hasan makes the following observations about Islamic political activity relating to Bush and Clinton: In the 1992 and 1996 elections, Muslims voted overwhelmingly for Democratic candidates. Under the Clinton Administration, Muslim chaplains were appointed for the first time to the United States Military and the first Muslim was chosen to serve as an Ambassador, Osman Siddiqi (Fiji). Clinton invited several leading Palestinians to the White House and was accused of being overly friendly to Hamas (Steve Emerson, "Friends of Hamas in the White House", *The Wall Street Journal*, March 13, 1996). However, the Muslim community gave 72% of their vote to George Bush in the 2000 election. Perhaps the fact that Clinton had been caught in a sex scandal had something to do with this result. Perhaps another factor was Clinton's support of the 1996 Anti-Terrorism Act, which allowed for secret investigations that many Muslims perceived as anti-Islamic (see Leon Howell, "Muslim Leaders Urge Ban on Secret Evidence", *The Christian Century* 117 (2001), 749). Finally, Gore's choice of a Jewish running mate and his perceived strong support of Israel may also have been factors. The Muslim community, that had so strongly supported Bush in 2000 turned against him in the 2004 elections and 93% of American Muslims voted in favor of the Democratic nominee. Initially, Bush garnered strong support among Muslims. After 9/11, Bush was the only sitting President ever to visit a masjid and, when attending, he respected the tradition of removing his shoes and kissing the Imam. After 9/11, Bush also hired a Muslim-outreach staffer (see *Journal of Church and State*, December 2001). In his speeches, Bush spoke of the Islam with high regard. Most of this goodwill, however, waned with the "Patriot Act" and the Iraq War. In 2004, Keith Ellison was elected as the first Muslim Senator (Minnesota). Muslims have also won various electoral campaigns in North Carolina, Alabama, Tennessee, Missouri, New Hampshire, and New Jersey.

35. Zeki Saritoprak, "An Islamic Approach to Peace and Non-violence: A Turkish Experience", *The Muslim World* 95 (2005): 415.

36. Farid Esack, *On Being a Muslim: Finding a Religious Path in the World Today* (New York: One World Publications, 2000), 27.

37. Esack (2000), 2.

38. Esack (2000), 2.

39. Aaron Hughes, *Theorizing Islam: Disciplinary Deconstruction and Reconstruction* (Sheffield, UK: Equinox Publishing, 2012), 115. Hughes claims that "the academic study of Islam has become more, not less insular and apologetic. It is within this latter context that scholars of Islam have presented themselves to their colleagues, to the media, and to the general

public as *de facto* interpreters of Islam. They have largely invoked their authority to elevate their particular and idiosyncratic interpretation of Islam (e.g. liberal and egalitarian) over others, and in the process, deemed their version to be somehow more authentic and normative" (2). Hughes hopes to establish "what I hope will become the New Islamic Studies", which he claims "must be part of the new conceptual modeling that is currently going on in religious studies. Scholars of Islam, students . . . and general audiences must be exposed to a more nuanced version of the manifold traditions, practices, rites, and ideologies that we often conveniently label Islam" (131–132).

1. Islam's Divine Mandate for Ethical Action against Social Injustice

1. Akthar, 107. Akthar continues: "But once the season of education is over, God wants the lesson learnt. The Lord of Muhammad is compassionate yet vigilant, watching over His servants from the 'watchtower' (mirsad). God in the Islamic conception is neither a tragedarian nor a sentimentalist. From cover to cover of the Qur'an, one discerns a total understanding, without illusions, of human nature as it is and of the related need for the firm yoke of the Law. For men do not easily change for the better. The aim for revelation, however, is not to impose from the outside, unrecognizable duties, but rather to extract from within man an awareness of duties implicitly recognized to be binding. It is in this context that the scripture calls upon its readers time and time again to think reverently, to bring their eyes close to the texture of their morality" (107–108).
2. Esack (2000), 25.
3. This was not my argument in my first book, No God But God: A Path to Muslim–Christian Dialogue on God's Nature (Maryknoll, NY: Orbis Books, 2003), although some readers reached that conclusion.
4. Daud Rahbar, God of Justice: A Study of the Ethical Doctrine of the Qur'an (Leiden, the Netherlands: E.J. Brill, 1960), 25.
5. Jon Hoover's scholarship is of particular note on this topic: Ibn Taymiyyah's Theodicy of Perpetual Optimism (Leiden, the Netherlands: E.J. Brill, 2007). He has also written extensively on Islamic Universalism.
6. David Waines, Introduction to Islam (Cambridge: Cambridge University Press, 2003), 130–131.
7. I have not been able to verify this citation but include it in hopes of further assistance. Omar Malomari claims this ratio according to a conversation with Denise Hearn, Baylor University student, Autumn, 2007.
8. Rahbar, 5.
9. Sayyid Qutb, Social Justice in Islam, trans. John Hardie (New York: Islamic Publishers International, 1953, 10.
10. Qutb (1953), 10.
11. Yaacov Lev, Charity, Endowments, and Charitable Institutions in Medieval Islam (Gainesville: University Press of Florida, 2005), 116.

2. Islamic *Jihad* and the Path of Peace

1. Remarks by President G.W. Bush at the Islamic Center of Washington, DC, on September 17, 2001.
2. J. Howard Ellens, "Jihad in the Qur'an, Then and Now", in *The Destructive Power of Religion: Violence in Judaism, Christianity, and Islam Volume 3*, ed. J. Harold Ellens (Westport, CT: Praeger Publishers, 2004), 40.
3. James A. Beverley, "Islam — A Religion of Peace?", *Christianity Today*, 46 (2002), 42.
4. Majid Khadduri, *War and Peace in the Law of Islam* (Baltimore: Johns Hopkins Press, 1955), 141.
5. Hazrat Mirza Tahir Ahmad, *Murder in the Name of Allah*, trans. Syed Barakat Ahmed (London: The Lutterworth Press, 1990), 104.
6. Clinton Bennett and Geros Kunkel, "The Concept of Violence, War, and Jihad in Islam", *Dialogue and Alliance*, 18 (2004), 31.
7. Ellens, 41.
8. Michael Slackman, "Scholarly Cleric Wields Religion to Pierce the Foundation of Iran's Theocracy", *New York Times*, November 25, 2009, A8.
9. Esposito (1999), 30.
10. S.M. Farid Mirbagheri, *War and Peace in Islam: A Critique of Islamic/ist Political Discourses* (New York: Palgrave Macmillan, 2012), 8.
11. William of Tyre (ca. 1130–1186) observed: "It was impossible to look on the vast numbers of the slain without horror. Everywhere lay fragments of human bodies, and the very ground was hidden by the blood of the slain. Still more dreadful was to gaze upon the victors themselves, dripping with blood from head to foot." Jonathan Philips, *The Crusades, 1095–1197* (New York: Longman Publishers, 2002), 25.
12. Ellens, 39.
13. Sohail H. Hashmi, "Saving and Taking Life in War: Three Modern Muslim Views", *Muslim World* 89 (1999), 158.
14. A.G. Noorani, *Islam and Jihad: Prejudice versus Reality* (London: ZED Books, 2002), 45.
15. Ella Landau-Tasseron, "Jihad" in *The Encyclopedia of the Qur'an: Volume Three (J–O)*, ed. Jane Dammen McAuliffe (Leiden, the Netherlands: E.J. Brill, 2003), 36.
16. Nathaniel C. Funk and Abdul Aziz Said, *Islam and Peacemaking in the Middle East* (Boulder, CO: Lynne Rienner Publishers, 2009), 182.
17. David Dakake, "The Myth of Militant Islam" in *Islam, Fundamentalism, and the Betrayal of Tradition: Essays by Western Muslim Scholars*, ed. Joseph E.B. Lumbard (Indianapolis: World Wisdom Press, 2004), 3.
18. Bennet and Kunkel, 40.
19. Farid Esack, "In Search of Progressive Islam Beyond 9/11", in *Progressive Muslims on Justice, Gender, and Pluralism*, ed. Omid Safi (Oxford: One World Publications, 2003), 83.
20. M.R. Bawa Muhaiyadden, *Islam and World Peace* (Philadelphia: Fellowship Press, 1999), 81.
21. Youssef H. Aboul-Enin and Sherifa Zuhur, *Islamic Rulings on Warfare* (Carlisle, PA: Strategic Studies Institute Publishing, 2004), v.
22. A. Rasheed Omar, "Islam and Violence", *Ecumenical Review* 55 (2003), 162.

23. Esposito (1999) 30.
24. David C. Cook, *Understanding Jihad* (Berkeley: University of California Press, 2005), 2, 35.
25. According to Cook, only four of the 150 references refer to physical warfare (Cook, 43). The number of 150 references is also cited in Ellens, "Jihad in the Qur'an", 43.
26. Esposito (1999), 31.
27. Khadduri 68.
28. Peter Partner, *God of Battles: Holy Wars of Christianity and Islam* (London: Harper Collins Publishers, 1998), 35 cite the number of battles as 27, while the reference to the 59 military campaigns that the Prophet organized comes from Cook, 6.
29. Ellens, 48.
30. Omar, 159.
31. Mohammed Abu-Nimer, *Nonviolence and Peace Building in Islam: Theory and Practice*. (Gainesville: University of Florida Press, 2003), 32.
32. Karen Armstrong, *Muhammad: A Biography of the Prophet* (San Francisco: Harper Books, 1992), 168.
33. Aboul-Enin, 5.
34. Ellens, 48.
35. Bennet and Kunkel, 37.
36. Landau-Tasseron, 42.
37. Munawar A. Anees, "Salvation and Suicide: What Does Islamic Theology Say?", *Dialog: A Journal of Theology*, 45 (2006), 275.
38. Carl Raschke, *Postmodernism and the Revolution in Religious Theory: Toward a Semiotics of the Event* (Charlotte: University of Virginia Press, 2012), 79.
39. Rosen, 46.
40. Suheil Laher, "Indiscriminate Killing in Light of Islamic Sacred Texts", in *The State We Are In: Identity, Terror, and the Law of Jihad*, ed. Aftab Ahmad Malik and Tahir Abbas (Bristol, UK: Amal Press, 2006), 44–45. The citation against killing women and children is narrated by Abu Dawud, Nasa'i, and Ibn Hibban. The injunction against killing "people in cloisters" is a Hadith of Tirmidhi, and the citation relating to the elderly is a Hadith collection of Abu Dawud.
41. Hadith of Abu Dawud 14: 2667. See also Mbaye Lo, "Seeking the Roots of Terrorism: An Islamic Traditional Perspective", *Journal of Religion and Popular Culture*, 10 (2005), 3.
42. Khadduri, 127–128.
43. Muhammad Hamidullah, *The Muslim Conduct of State*, seventh edition (Lahore, Pakistan: Islamic Foundation, 2004), 441.
44. Khadduri, 103–104.
45. In 630 CE, the Prophet authorized the use of a *mangonel* (a catapult-like weapon) during the siege of Taif. This was allowed even though there was a high chance that innocent bystanders would perish. The use of this weapon was deemed necessary to end the siege even if non-combatants are killed unintentionally. Khadduri cites several jurists (such as al-Zuhayli) who accept that non-combatants will often become victims in warfare. Their deaths might even aid in an army's ultimate success. If the larger community will benefit from such "collateral damage", then such deaths can be seen as justifiable (Khadduri, *War and Peace*, 141).

46. David Oualaalou is quoting a Hadith cited by Ahmed (23804), Abu Dawoud (3111), and al-Nasa'i (1846), and attributed to Jabbar ibn-Ateek. Personal correspondence with the author, unpublished, July 27, 2013.

47. Majid Khadduri, *The Islamic Conception of Justice* (Baltimore: Johns Hopkins Press, 1984), 165. Khadduri taught at Johns Hopkins. Before immigrating to the United States in 1947, Khadduri worked with the Iraqi government and was a member of the Iraqi delegation to the signing of the UN Charter. Khadduri also wrote *The Islamic Law of Nations*, which likewise deals with this theme.

48. Khadduri, 141.

49. Bat Ye'or, *The Dhimmi: Jews and Christians Under Islam*, trans. Paul Fenton, David Littman, and David Maisel (Philadelphia: Fairleigh Dickinson University Press, 1985), 45.

50. *Al-Ansar* 15, August 10, 2002. This is an al-Qaeda affiliated online magazine. It has a series of articles with titles such as "Allah Will Torment Them by Your Hands" and "A Treatise on the Ruling Regarding Weapons of Mass Destruction against the Infidels".

51. Reported in *The Daily Mirror*, [http://www.mirror.co.uk/news/uk-news/lee-rigby-murderer-michael-adebowales-3184485] (accessed March 17, 2014).

52. See Basheer M. Ali, "Fatwa and War: On the Allegiance of the American Muslim Soldiers in the Aftermath of September 11th", *Islamic Law and Society*, 11 (2004), 78–116.

53. Khadduri, 267.

54. [http://www.memri.org/bin/articles.cgi?Page=subjects&Area=jihad&ID =SR2504] A special report of the Middle East Media Research Institute, number 25, dated January 27, 2004 (accessed January 3, 2013).

55. I have been unable to find any textual or linguistic justification for this interpretation.

56. Abdul al-Mawdudi, "Human Rights in Islam: Enemies Rights in War", *Al-Tawhid Journal*, 4 (1987), 3.

57. Mawdudi defines non-combatants as "those who lack the mental and physical capacity to fight, or those who do not ordinarily fight" which would include women, children, the sick, the elderly, the blind, the insane, travelers, hermits and religious figures (Hashmi, "Saving and Taking Life", 170).

58. Sheila McDonough, *Muslim Ethics and Modernity: A Comparative Study of the Ethical Thought of Sayyid Ahmad Khan and Mawlana Madudi* (Waterloo, ON: Wilfred Laurier Press, 1984), 58.

59. Bennett and Kunkel, 44.

60. Sayyid Qutb, *Milestones* (Delhi, India: Markazi Maktaba Islami, 1988), 58.

61. John Esposito, *Islam: The Straight Path* (New York: Oxford University Press, 1988), 171.

62. Karen Armstrong, *The Battle for God: Fundamentalism in Judaism, Christianity and Islam* (London: Harper Collins, 2000), 243.

63. Tarel Heggy, *The Arab Mind Bound* (London: Valentine Mitchell, 2011), 50.

64. I heard this motto while visiting Beirut, Lebanon in October, 2009.

65. For example, [http://www.youtube.com/watch?v=IFttV5TnAZM] (accessed January 2, 2013).

66. Abdul Aziz Said, ed., *Peace and Conflict Resolution in Islam: Precept and Practice* (New York: University Press of America, 2001), 171.

67. Mahmoud Mohamed Taha, *The Second Message of Islam* (Syracuse, NY: Syracuse University Press, 1987), 147.
68. Taha, 161.
69. Farid Esack, "To Whom Shall We Give Access to our Water Holes?" *Cross Currents*, 51 (2002): 503–504.
70. Esack (2002), 517.
71. Esack (2002), 505.
72. Kumar, 54.
73. John Ferguson, *War and Peace in the World's Religions* (New York: Oxford University Press, 1983), 103.
74. Charles Kimball, *Striving Together: A Way Forward in Christian-Muslim Relations* (Maryknoll, NY: Orbis Books, 1991), 160.
75. Jenkins, Philip. *Laying Down the Sword: Why We Can't Ignore the Bible's Violent Verses* (New York: Harper Collins Publishers, 2011), 125.
76. Jenkins (2011), 163.
77. Jenkins (2011), 163.
78. Aalia Sohail Khan, "Islam: A Religion of Peace and Tolerance", *Hamdard Islamicus*, 20 (1997), 87.
79. Aboul-Enin, 47.
80. Noorani, 46.
81. Noorani, 47.
82. Hadith attributed to Muslim (4313) quoted in Rudolph Peters, *Jihad in Classical and Modern Islam* (Princeton, NJ: Markus Weiner Publishers, 1996), 81.
83. [http://www.muslimnews.co.uk/news.php?article=5270] (accessed January 4, 2013).
84. Ahmad, 120.
85. Melody Moezzi, *War on Error: Real Stories of American Muslims* (Fayetteville: University of Arkansas Press, 2007), 155.

3. Islamic Responses to Poverty and Economic Oppression

1. Al-Tayib Zein al-Abdin, "Zakat and the Alleviation of Poverty in the Muslim World", *Hamdard Islamicus*, 20 (1997), 66.
2. These standards change but the standard of $1 (US) a day was established by the UNDP in 1983.
3. Al-Abdin, 66–67.
4. Lebacqz, 13.
5. Esack (2000), 104.
6. Rodney Wilson, *Economics, Ethics and Religion: Jewish, Christian, and Muslim Economic Thought* (New York: New York University Press, 1997), 115.
7. Wilson, 117.
8. Sule Ahmad Gusau, "The Prophet Muhammad and the Problem of Poverty and Distress", *Hamdard Islamicus*, 6 (1993), 19.
9. Al-Abdin, 71.
10. Noorani, *Islam and Jihad*, 138. The Universal Islamic Declaration of Human Rights was crafted in Cairo (1980) by a group of scholars unhappy with some of the un-Islamic qualities of the UN Universal Declaration on Human Rights (UDHC, 1948).

11. Esack (2000), 105.
12. Gusau, 19.
13. Gusau, 21–22.
14. The term *sufrah* actually means a "table" or a "place of eating", or a "dining area", but specifically refers to a place with all of the plates, bowls, and all utensils already prepared. The term sometimes also appears in transliterations as *sufrah* which is an archaic term describing a bench or shelf. This version implies that there was a bench in the Prophet's masjid where people could meet him. Some have even conjectured that the word "Sufi" comes from this rendering of *suffah*; although the general consensus is that the word "Sufi" comes from the Arabic term *suf* in reference to wool and the woolen garments that the devout wore.
15. Adam Sabra, *Poverty and Charity in Medieval Islam* (New York: Cambridge University Press, 2000), 17.
16. Omer Faruk Senturk, *Charity in Islam: A Comprehensive Guide to Zakat* (Somerset, NJ: Light Publications, 2007), 42.
17. Gusau, 19.
18. Amy Singer, *Charity in Islamic Societies* (Cambridge: Cambridge University Press, 2008), 34.
19. Safiya Aftab, Naved Hamid, and Safdar Parvez, *Poverty in Pakistan: Issues, Courses, and Institutional Responses* (Islamabad: Asian Development Bank, 2002), 54.
20. Funds are distributed "privately" in that they do not first pass through any government organization or a public body such as a masjid committee. A masjid committee is the way that alms are distributed among the Muslims in Nigeria and Ghana. Emirs, notable wealthy Muslims, and others, give their funds to these committees and they are distributed by imams. The result of this "official" system, in which there is no accountability, is quite a bit of corruption and only a small amount of money going to aid the poor. The money that does reach the poor is usually given to men, and so there is almost no benefit to poor women.
21. Senturk, 46.
22. Singer, 67.
23. Gusau, 27.
24. This Arabic word *sadaqah* is also related to the Arabic words for "truthfulness" and even the word for "belief" according to [http://www.viewislam.com/pillars/pillar4.htm] (accessed May 13, 2012).
25. Aid in Kashmir was directed both to short and long-term projects. Islamic Relief Worldwide, "Pakistan Projects, 2000–2012", [http://www/islamic-relief.com/projects/pakistan/index.htm] (accessed May 2, 2012).
26. Shortly after the Hijrah to Medina, Zayd married Zaynab. However, God revealed to the Prophet that he should marry Zaynab after she divorced her husband (Q. 33:37). After this, Muhammad repudiated Zayd as his adoptive son whereupon he assumed his original name Zayd ibn Haritha (Q. 33:4–5). Some scholars see in this repudiation a larger rejection of all forms of adoption and go so far as to claim that adoption is sinful because it is based on fictional relationships. Most importantly, the negation of Zayd as an adopted son nullified any possible claim that he might have had as the Prophet's legal or spiritual heir. This event does not nullify the commitment to care for all who are orphaned.

27. Eric Chaumont and Ron Shaham, "Yatim", in *Encyclopedia of Islam*, ed. P. J. Barman, *et al.* (12 vols. Leiden, the Netherlands: E.J. Brill, 1960–2005), 11:299. An orphan's status in pre-Islamic Arabia was originally determined by whether or not he/she had a father. Over time Islamic orthopraxy has evolved given differing cultural contexts and preconceptions about the status of orphans whether they are fatherless or parentless.

28. A biological relationship, it was deemed by legal scholars, was based on the practice of suckling (*rada'a*). If two children had been suckled by the same mother then they are prohibited (*tahrimat*) from marrying each other. Although suckling does establish a biological relationship it does not automatically establish maintenance and inheritance rights. There are other issues about orphaned girls in terms of who they can marry and their claims on inheritance. If an orphaned girl lives with men in her guardian's family she would have to cover her head and could not be isolated in a room with any of them because they could potentially marry her. In spite of the specificity of such rulings, there is room for cultural adaptations. Differing geographical locations have resulted in differing variations on laws pertaining to orphan care.

29. For some Jews, the idea of a father and his adoptive son was seen as analogous to the adoptive relationship that God had with the nation of Israel. Christians noted that, in a theologically metaphorical sense, God sent His son to be "adopted" by Mary and Joseph. Early Christians in the Roman Empire often rescued children who had been abandoned at birth and raised them as their own because of their conviction that those children were deserving of a chance to live their lives for the greater glory of God.

30. According to Dr Hatoon al-Fasi from the King Saud University, approximately 30% (2008) of all Saudi citizens are considered by the government to be in a state of poverty. [http://gulfnews.com/news/gulf-saudi-arabia/education-key-to-tackling-problem-of-saudi-poverty-1.136399] (accessed April 13, 2013).

31. Esack (2000), 105.

32. Esack (2000), 81.

33. Esack (2000), 2.

34. Esack (2000), 79.

35. The two major government-sponsored micro-finance projects are the Pakistan Poverty Alleviation Fund (PPAF) and the Khushi Bank. The PPAF is designed to aid the poor who have never received funds before due to a low amount of collateral. The Khushi Bank has the same approach. The government also gives pensions and social security to the elderly and to those who are unemployed.

36. Aftab and Parvez, 54.

37. Hilal Khashan, "Collective Palestinian Frustration and Suicide Bombings", *Third World Quarterly* 24 (2003): 1055.

38. Noorani, 80. This is also the argument of Daniel Pipes, *Militant Islam Reaches America* (New York: W.W. Norton and Company, 2003), 53ff.

39. Noorani, 47.

40. Pipes, 53. Regarding the State of Israel, Pipes can be counted on to provide a sympathetic view of their actions. For example, Pipes quotes Sharon Peres as saying: "Fundamentalism's basis is poverty and it is a way of protesting against

poverty, ignorance and discrimination" (54). In contrast to this argument, almost all of the World Trade Center bombers, Osama bin Laden himself, and many other militant leaders, were often wealthy before they began their jihadist quest. Pipes claimed that "the Canadian Security Intelligence Service found that the leadership of the militant Islamic group Al-Jihad is largely university educated with middle-class backgrounds" (55). Islamist seminars are held over banquets in "some of Cairo's most luxurious homes, and in Egypt's seaside resorts that appeal to the wealthy's sense of style and comfort" (56). Pipes notes that many suicide bombers came from wealthy families and claims, "It could quite be, quite contrarily, that militant Islam results from wealth rather than poverty. . . . [T]here is the universal phenomenon that people become more engaged ideologically and active politically only when they have reached a fairly high standard of living" (61). In spite of this, the causes of poverty do lead to a sense of anger which may explain why many of the foot-soldiers of extremist causes are often recruited from among the poor.

41. Pipes, 53.
42. Noorani, 80.
43. Muhammad Nejatullah Siddiqi, *Muslim Economic Thinking: A Survey of Contemporary Literature* (Leicester, UK: Islamic Foundation, 1981), 12.
44. Sabra, *Poverty and* Charity, 20. Sabra also cited al-Ghazali (20) in the recognition of five distinct levels of poverty: 1. *Zahid*: a beggar who hates wealth so much that he/she flees from it; 2. *Radin*: a deprived person who neither desires nor flees from wealth; 3. *Qani*: a contented person who does not seek wealth even though he/she does not have it; 4. *Haris*: a wretched person who abandons seeking wealth due to the inability to attain it and 5. *Mudtrr*: a miserable person who lacks even the most basic provisions (such as a piece of bread to survive). Al-Ghazali, perhaps influenced by Christian monks, also wrote that there were some who sought poverty as a way to express their piety to God; some chose poverty as a way to glorify God in this life.
45. Engineer, Ashgar Ali, "On Developing Liberation Theology in Islam" in *Voices from the Margin: Interpreting the Bible in the Third World*, R.S. Sugirtharajah, ed. (Maryknoll, NY: Orbis Books, 1995), 397.
46. Liberation theology has a long and diverse history. Many cite Gustavo Gutierrez and Leonardo Boff as some of the first Liberation Theologians. They were probably influenced by the writings of the great Brazilian pedagogist Paulo Freire.

4. Islamic Responses to Political Oppression

1. Based on "Oppression", in the *American Heritage Dictionary of the English Language*, ed. Peter Davies (New York: Dell Publishing, 1973), 499.
2. Daniel Pipes, *In the Path of God: Islam and Political Power* (New York: Basic Books, 1983), 43.
3. There are hosts of Hadith that support this view that God will resolve all injustices on the Final Day. I will cite only one here: "There was none amongst the bondsmen who was entrusted with the affairs of his subjects that he was dishonest in his dealings with those over who he ruled that the

paradise is not forbidden to him." From Abdul Hamid Siddiqi, ed., *Sahih Muslim* (Lahore, Pakistan: Hafez Press, 1976), 81–82. See similar Hadith from this collection on pages 1016–1017 and 1025.

4. Khadduri, 23.

5. Bernard Lewis, *Islam: From the Prophet Muhammad to the Capture of Constantinople, Volume 1: Politics and War* (Oxford: Oxford University Press, 1974), 170–171. The same views are expressed by Al-Rabi, who emphasized the community's duty to be obedient. Al-Farabi (870–950) was another scholar who thought that it was solely God's duty to deal with an unjust ruler.

6. "If he reverts to atheism or stops praying and encourages others to do the same; for tyranny and corruption, insanity, deafness, muteness, senility, if he becomes a prisoner of war for a long period, or it is believed that this will endanger the interests of the nation." Abu Al-Hassan Al-Mawardi (974–1058) took a more cautious position stating that there are only two reasons for a leader to be deposed: First, *hajr*: If a leader comes under the influence of an advisor to such an extent that his actions are un-Islamic; Second, *qahr*: if the leader becomes a prisoner of a strong enemy and his release is impossible to accomplish." Both are cited in Tariq Ismael and Jacqueline S. Ismael, *Government and Politics in Islam* (New York: St Martin's Press, 1985), 13, 17.

7. Siddiqi, 1022.

8. Murata Sachiko and William C. Chittick, *The Vision of Islam* (St Paul, MN: Paragon House, 1994), 33.

9. See Joseph R. Gusfield, "Tradition and Modernity: Misplaced Polarities in the Study of Social Change", *American Journal of Sociology*, 72 (1967), 351–362.

10. Kumar, 59.

11. Larbi Sadiki, *The Search for Arab Democracy: Discourses and Counter Discourses* (New York: Columbia University Press, 2004), 169.

12. [http://www.almaqdese.com/c?c=1.1] (accessed January 3, 2013).

13. Pramano U. Tanthhowi, *Muslims and Tolerance: Non-Muslim Minorities under Shariah in Indonesia* (Chang Mai, Thailand: Silkworm Books, 2008), 44.

14. Pipes, 37.

15. Karen Armstrong, *The Battle for God: Fundamentalism in Judaism, Christianity and Islam* (London: Harper Collins, 2000), 237.

16. Souad Ali, *A Religion, Not a State: Ali Abd Al-Raziq's Islamic Justification of Political Secularism* (Salt Lake City: University of Utah Press, 2009), 1.

17. "Our Testimony: The Muslim Brotherhood Online", May 30, 2006, [http://www.ikhwanweb.com/Home.asp?zPage=Systems&System=PressR&Press=Show&Lang=E&ID=4541] (accessed January 3, 2013).

18. Critics point to Saudi Arabia and other nations where Islamic law is in place but has not produced uniform justice. One response would be that the complete enactment of Islamic law might take some time, as judges (and other actors) in these courts progressively become more Islamic in their ideas and actions.

19. Some historians have countered that the Spanish Empire in South America is a good example of a region in the world in which violence did indeed create national unity. Centuries of South American riots, instability, dictatorships, and social disequilibrium, however, seem to dramatically weaken that argument.

20. Desmond Tutu, "Freedom Fighters or Terrorists?" in *Theology and Violence: The South African Debate*, ed. Charles Villa-Vicencio (Grand Rapids, MI: Eerdmans Press, 1987), 75.
21. This is a term that El-Fadl uses in "Islamic Law and Muslim Minorities: The Juristic Discourse on Muslim Minorities from the Second/Eighth to the Eleventh/Seventeenth Centuries", *Islamic Law and Society*, 22 (1994), 141–87.

5. Islamic Civil Rights and Individual Human Rights

1. Rosen, 37.
2. Roger Garaudy, "Human Rights and Islam: Foundation, Tradition, Violation", in *The Ethics of World Religions and Human Rights*, ed. Hans Küng and Jürgen Moltmann (London: SCM Press, 1990), 49.
3. Bernard Lewis, "On Revolutions in Early Islam", *Studia Islamica* 32 (1970): 215.
4. Fatima Mernissi, *Islam and Democracy* (Cambridge: Perseus Press, 2002), 87.
5. Ali Mohammadi, "The Culture and Politics of Human Rights in the Context of Islam," in *Islam Encountering Globalization*, ed. Ali Mohammadi (London: Routledge Curzon Press, 2002), 115.
6. Mohammadi, 115.
7. Abdul Aziz Said, "Precept and Practice of Human Rights in Islam", *Universal Human Rights*, 1 (1979): 73.
8. Esposito cites the 2006 Gallup Poll in a series of Muslim nations in reference to the United States: "When asked if they would include provisions for freedom of speech, defined as allowing all citizens to express their opinions on political, social, and economic issues of the day if they were drafting a constitution for a new country, overwhelming majorities (94% in Egypt, 97% in Bangladesh, 99% in Lebanon, etc.) in every country responded yes, they would." John Esposito, *Muslims in the West — A Culture War?* [http://www.freemuslims.org/news/article.php?article=1309] (accessed January 4, 2013).
9. Meryl Wynn Davies and Ziauddin Sardar, *Distorted Imagination: Lessons from the Rushdie Affair* (London: Grey Seal Books, 1990), 233.
10. Rosen, 37.
11. Rudolph Peters and Gert J.J. DeVries, "Apostasy in Islam", *Die Welt des Islams*, 17 (1976–1977), 2.
12. Abdullah Saaed and Hassan Saaed, *Freedom of Religion, Apostasy, and Islam* (Aldershot, UK: Ashgate Publishing, 2004), 36.
13. Saaed and Saaed, 15–16. There are many Christians that also regard religious diversity as a 'problem' see Joseph Kim, *Reformed Epistemology and the Problem of Religious Diversity* (Cambridge, UK: James Clarke & Co., 2012).
14. Forough Jahanbakhsh, *Islam, Democracy, and Religious Modernism in Iran (1953–2000)* (Leiden, the Netherlands: E.J. Brill, 2001), 30.
15. Saaed and Saaed, 59.
16. Jahanbakhsh, 31.
17. Jahanbakhsh, 31.
18. [http://www.masud.co.uk/ISLAM/nuh/bida.htm] (accessed January 5, 2013).
19. Charles Selengut, *Sacred Fury: Understanding Religious Violence* (Walnut Creek, CA: Altamira Press, 2003), 161.

20. See Ziauddin Sardar, *Desperately Seeking Paradise: Journeys of a Skeptical Muslim* (London: Granta Books, 2004) on this topic. Sardar discusses the issue at length in Chapter 13 of this book (278–293).

21. Reported in the *Daily Mail* newspaper [http://www.dailymail.com.uk/news/article2560683/Iranian-mullah-revives-death-fatwa] (accessed March 17, 2014). It is not unusual that a *fatwa* would address a literary text or artistic creation. *The New York Times* reported that *fatwas* have even been issued by Saudi Arabian clerics against the watching of soap operas and the evils of cartoons; Micky Mouse was declared a "Soldier of Satan" (NYT, April 4, 2014, A5). See [http://www.nytimes.com/2014/04/05/world/middleeast/conservative-saudi-cleric-salman-al-awda.html?_r=1#story-continues-4] (accessed April 10, 2014).

22. John L. Esposito, "It's the Policy, Stupid! Political Islam and the United States Foreign Policy" [http://hir.harvard.edu/articles/1453/2/] (accessed January 17, 2013).

23. Abdulaziz Sachedina, *The Islamic Roots of Democratic Pluralism* (Oxford: Oxford University Press, 2001), 138–139.

24. Mohammed Abu-Nimer, *Nonviolence and Peace Building in Islam: Theory and Practice* (Gainesville: University of Florida Press, 2003), 79.

25. Khaled Abou El-Fadl, *The Place of Tolerance in Islam* (Boston: Beacon Press, 2002), 95–96.

26. Ziauddin Sardar, *Islam, Postmodernism and Other Futures: A Ziauddin Sardar Reader*, ed. Sohail Inayatullah and Gail Boxwell (London: Pluto Press, 2003), 243.

27. Ahmed S. Moussalli, *The Islamic Quest for Democracy, Pluralism and Human Rights* (Gainesville: University Press of Florida, 2001), 85.

28. [http://www.jamaat.org/islam/HumanRightsCitizens.html] (accessed April 13, 2013).

29. Pipes, *In the Path of God*, 45. See also Ihsan Yilmaz, "State, Law, Civil Society and Islam in Contemporary Turkey", *Muslim World*, 95 (2005): 388ff. Another article on Turkish Islam is Bulent Aras, "Turkish Islam's Moderate Face", *Middle East Quarterly*, 5 (1998): 23–30.

30. Moussalli, 149.

31. The Islamic Stated Document (PAS) of Malaysia written by the *Party Islam of Se Malaysia* is similar to the United States "Bill of Rights". It also cites Qur'an 2:256 and 8:29 as rationale for this toleration.

32. "Exodus from North Signals Iraqi Christian Decline", New York Times, March 10, 2012, [http://www.nytimes.com/exodus-from-north-signals-iraqi-christian-decline.html] (accessed July 27, 2013). The article cites the "International Organization for Migration" in discussing the massive decline of Christians.

33. Betty Jane Bailey and J. Martin Bailey, *Who Are the Christians in the Middle East?* (Grand Rapids, MI: Eerdmans Publishing, 2003), 193.

34. The United States government has allocated 1.3 billion dollars in military aid and 250 million dollars in "economic support" including funds designated for education for the fiscal year 2014 [http://www.dailynewsegypt.com/2014/01/14/us-congress-makes-1-3-billion-in-military-aid-available] (accessed March 18, 2014).

35. Moussalli, 87.

36. Elizabeth More, "The Universal Declaration of Human Rights in Today's World", *Journal of International Communications* 11 (2007), 2.
37. The United Nations Declaration of Universal Human Rights, 1948, Article 1. Human rights, as defined by the UDHR, are inclusive of all human beings irrespective of membership in a particular social or religious group. Even among non-Muslim nations there is no uniform consensus on this definition.
38. David Little, John Kelsay, and Abdulaziz A. Sachedina, *Human Rights and the Conflict of Cultures: Western and Islamic Perspectives on Religious Liberty* (Columbia: University of South Carolina Press, 1988), 33.
39. Khaled Abou El-Fadl, "The Human Rights Commitment in Modern Islam", in *Human Rights and Responsibilities in the World Religions*, ed. Joseph Runzo, Nancy M. Martin, and Arvind Sharma (Oxford: OneWorld Publications, 2003), 302.
40. Seyyed Hussein Serajzadeh, *Islam and Crime: The Moral Community of Muslims* (Teheran, Iran: Teheran Teacher Training University Publications, 2006), 1.
41. Virginia Mackey, "Punishment in the Scripture and Tradition of Judaism, Christianity and Islam" in *Crime, Values, and Religion*, ed. James Day and William Laufer (New York: Ablex Publishing Company, 1987), 53–54.
42. Davies and Sardar, 233.
43. Timothy D. Sisk, *Islam and Democracy: Religion, Politics and Power in the Middle East* (Washington, DC: United States Institute of Peace, 1992), 27.
44. Esack (2000), 6.
45. Esack (2000), 49.
46. Muhammad Iqbal *The Reconstruction of Religious Thought in Islam* (Lahore, Pakistan: Ashraf Publications, 1960), 2.
47. Iqbal, 4.
48. The term "conservative" comes from the Latin word "to save" or "to preserve". Conservatives generally see themselves as preserving a certain tradition. My argument is that extremists are endorsing something radical and new in Islamic history. Therefore, extremists are not truly "conservatives".
49. Elizabeth M. Bucar and Barbara Barnett, eds *Does Human Rights Need God?* (Grand Rapids, MI: Eerdmans Publishing, 2005), 293.
50. See [http://worldjusticeproject.org/what-rule-law] (accessed March 18, 2014).
51. Lynn Hunt, *Inventing Human Rights: A History* (New York: Norton and Norton Company, 2007), 214.
52. Mary O' Donnell, "Lament for Babi Yar", in *Human Rights Have No Borders: Voices of Irish Poets*, ed. Kenneth Morgan and Almut Scheppler (Dublin: Marino Books, 1998), 127–128.

6. Genocide and Atrocity among Muslims

1. Selengut, 17.
2. Selengut, 3.
3. The United Nations identifies genocide as "acts committed with the intent to destroy, in whole or in part, a national, ethnical, racial, or religious

group such as: (a) killing members of the group; (b) causing serious bodily or mental harm to members of the group; (c) deliberately inflicting on the group conditions of life calculated to bring about its physical destruction in whole or in part; (d) imposing measures intended to prevent births within the group; (e) forcibly transferring children of the group to another group." The United Nations ratified this in the Universal Declaration of Human Rights on December 10, 1948.

4. Lawrence M. Wills, *Not God's People: Insiders and Outsiders in the Biblical World* (Lanham, MD: Rowman and Littlefield, 2008), 14.

5. Jenkins, 7.

6. Leo B. Lefebure, *Revelation, the Religions, and Violence* (Maryknoll, NY: Orbis Books, 2000), 57.

7. Jenkins, 7. Referring to these many violent biblical texts, Jenkins calls them "Canons of Hate" (8).

8. See mentions of hell and punishment in Qur'an 2:39; 2:89–90; 31:37; 33:7–12; 44:40–49; 52:1–15; 56:52–56; 69:30–37; 70:15–16.

9. Even Nazism and Stalinism functioned in some ways as religions because of the ideological worldviews they fostered in their devotees.

10. A Jewish tribe in Qaynuqa (624) and a Jewish tribe from Nadir (625) had been expelled before this incident because of their complicities in assassination attempts against the Muslim community. The Jewish tribe of Qarayzah had lived in Medina and initially seemed to remain neutral. It was then reported that Jews were involved in stirring up animosity amongst the Meccans toward the Muslims of Medina. The greatly outnumbered Muslims built trenches north of Medina as the Meccans began their attack. This strategy of using trenches in defensive warfare was new to Arabia and may have originated from Persia. In any event, the Meccans were unprepared, and, according to the Qur'an, no actual battle had to be fought (Q. 33:25). God also sent violent winds to protect the Muslims (Q. 33: 9). The Meccans were forced to retreat because they had been weakened and their animals were dying. Once the Meccans had retreated, tradition affirms that the Angel Gabriel told the Prophet that the battle was not over because the Bani (tribe) Quraiza, the Jews, had yet to be confronted. The first stage of a 25 day siege against the Jews included the Prophet employing a poet (Hassan bin Thabit) to abuse them in verse. The Jews did not mount a strong resistance in the face of 3,000 Muslim troops. Negotiations for surrender began and were soon moderated by Sad bin Muadh who was a non-Muslim leader of a large Medinan tribe known as the Aws (or Aus). Bukhari notes that the judgment was that the women and children should be spared but that all others should be killed. Between 300 and 600 men and boys were decapitated but Ibn Ishaq (d. 767) quotes a higher number of 800–900. Ibn Ishaq also says that the Prophet took one woman for himself, the Jewess, Rayhana bint Amr: "The apostle had proposed to marry and put a veil on her but she said: 'Nay, leave me in your power, for that will be easier for me and for you.' So he left her." She had shown repugnance towards Islam when she was captured and clung to Judaism (Ibn Ishaq, 466). The wealth of the Jewish community was distributed amongst the troops, and the Prophet took a fifth of all of the spoils for himself (see also Q. 8:1, 41). The events are also alluded to in Q. 33:25–27.

11. This story is retold by Ibn Ishaq, *Sirat Rasul Allah*, trans. Alexandre Guillaume (Karachi, Pakistan: Oxford University Press, 1998), 515: "The Apostle gave orders to Al-Zubayr bin Al-Awwan, 'Torture him until you extract what he has', so he kindled a fire with flint and steel on his chest until he was nearly dead. Then the Apostle delivered him to Muhammad bin Maslama and he struck off his head in revenge for his brother Mahmud."

12. This has been reported by *The Independent*, among others [http://www.independent.co.uk/news/uk/politics/exclusive-devastating-dossier-on-abuse-by-uk-forces-in-iraq-goes-to-international-criminal-court-9053735.html] [http://search.proquest.com/docview/231681816] (both accessed March 13, 2014).

13. Esack (2000), 20.

14. See [http://www.washingtontimes.com/news/2013/nov/25/obama-wont-acknowledge-armenian-genocide-turkey/] (accessed March 13, 2014).

15. See [http://www.huriyetdailynews.com/armenian-church-in-eastern-turkey-becomes-hayloft-after-service-as-school.aspx?pageID=238&nID=63392&NewsCatID=375] (accessed March 18, 2014).

16. Vahakn Dadrian, quoted by Andrew Bostom, "The Jihad Genocide of the Armenians", *American Thinker*, April 22, 2005, 1.

17. Carolyn Forche, ed., *Against Forgetting: Twentieth Century Poetry of Witness* (New York: W.W. Norton and Company, 1993), 57–59.

18. The TARC was formed on July 9, 2001 and is made up of Turkish and Armenian participants. On February 4, 2003, the ICTJ provided TARC with a document of its legal findings. This document was released to the public on February 10, 2003, and can be seen in its entirety at the website of the ICTJ.

19. Bostom, 2.

20. For the most part, Arabs played a supporting role in helping the Nazis and Vichy French to persecute Jews in Arab lands. Many Arabs did more than just collaborate but played an active role. Most Arabs, however, were indifferent and allowed these atrocities to take place.

21. Robert Satloff, *Among the Righteous: Lost Stories from the Holocaust's Long Reach into Arab Lands* (New York: Public Affairs, 2006), 162.

22. Satloff, 163.

23. Peter Balakian, *Black Dog of Fate: An American Son Discovers His Armenian Past* (New York: Doubleday Books, 1998), 278.

24. Francois Gautier, *Rewriting Indian History* (Delhi, India: Vikas Publishers, 1996) claims that they sought to kill 100,000 Hindus every year. He also claims that in 1399, Timur killed 100,000 Hindus in a single day. Gautier claims that between 1000 and 1525 (the advent of the Mughal Era) the Hindu population decreased by 80 million: "Indeed, probably the biggest Holocaust in the whole history of the world (89)."

25. While some British historians were more objective in their treatment of Indian history many supported the "party line" (so-called Macaulayists) in the interest of promoting British power in India. Some historians felt an affinity with Muslim rulers and saw themselves as a modern-day version of those brilliant outsiders who had a divine-right to rule. Muslim historians, predictably, tell a different story than do Hindu historians. The last Hindu Kings (Prithviraj Chauhan and Jaichandra Gahadawal) were defeated in North India between 1192–1194 which opened the way for the Afghani

warlord Mahmud Shahabuddin Ghori (Ghauri) to destroy monasteries, slaughter monks, and burn villages. Ghori paid particular attention to burning manuscripts in monasteries such as the university at Nalanda which reputedly housed millions of manuscripts in many languages (according to *Rewriting Indian History* by Francois Gautier).

26. Faiz Ahmad Faiz, "Once Again the Mind", in Forche, 524.
27. Jamal Hasan, "Pakistani-Islam's Global Ploy and Suppression of the Bengali Genocide Tragedy", 1 [http://www.faithfreedom.org/oped/JamalHasan50126. htm] (accessed May 9, 2012). See also Abul Kasem, "Mindset of Pakistanis favoring the 1971 Genocide", *News from Bangladesh*, November 22, 2000. Recent nationwide trials in Bangladesh (2012–2013) have focused on this era.
28. Samuel Totten and William S. Parsons, eds, *Century of Genocide: Critical Essays and Eyewitness Accounts* (New York: Routledge Press, 2009 [1997]), 297.
29. Hasan, 4.
30. Hasan, 4.
31. Totten and Parsons, 297. As of this writing, Jahan was affiliated with the Southern Asian Institute at Columbia University as a senior research scholar. After she finished her doctorate from Harvard in 1970, she returned to teach political science at Dhaka University (1970–1993) and was eyewitness to the horrific atrocities of this civil war.
32. Along with the BJP, other groups involved were the Rashtriya Swayamsewak Singh (RSS), the Bajrang Dal, and the Vishwa Hindu Parishad. Sadly, major international Muslim organizations, such as the OIC, did not issue any statements of condemnation due to sensitive political considerations.
33. See the section on Cambodia online: [http://www.mediamonitors.net/soharwardy1.html] (accessed March 13, 2014).
34. Lawrence Davidson, *Islamic Fundamentalism: An Introduction* (Westport, CT: Greenwood Press, 2003), 80.
35. Reported by *The Huffington Post* [http://www.huffingtonpost.com/2014/03/15/syria-war-children-4967063] (accessed March 17, 2014).
36. Robert Spencer, "Affluent Genocide", *Front Page Magazine*, October 14, 2003, 1. Spencer quotes Maulana Inyadullah of al-Qaeda as saying after 9/11 that: "The Americans love Pepsi and we love death."
37. See Noam Chomsky [http://www.alternet.org/world/noam-chomsky-what-american-media-wont-tell-you-about-israel] (accessed March 18, 2014).
38. The New York Times reported this [http://www.nytimes.com/2014/03/17/world/middleeast/palestinians-split-in-gaza-as-hamas-blocks-fatah-rally] (accessed March 17, 2014).
39. On Baluchistan, see Ali Banuazizi and Myron Weiner, *The State, Religion, and Ethnic Politics: Afghanistan, Iran, and Pakistan* (Syracuse, NY: Syracuse University Press, 1986).
40. The Baha'i are Universalists who believe in the messages of all of the prophets who are sent to specific cultures to give the same message. Since, this includes prophets outside of Islam they are viewed by Muslims as heretical.
41. Samantha Power, *A Problem from Hell: America and the Age of Genocide* (New York: Basic Books, 2002), 187.
42. Jeffrey Kluger, "How Haditha Came to Light", *Time Magazine*, July 12, 2006, 22.

43. Antenor DeWolf, "Modern Condottieri in Iraq: Privatizing War from the Perspective of International and Human Rights Law", *Indiana Journal of Global Legal Studies*, 13, (2006): 315–356, reports that some PMSC's at Abu Ghraib conducted interrogations that included: "Punching, slapping, and kicking detainees; videotaping nude male and female detainees; forcibly arranging detainees in various sexually explicit positions for photographing; forcing nude male detainees to wear women's underwear; forcing groups of male detainees to masturbate while being photographed and videotaped; arranging nude male detainees in a pile and then jumping on them; and positioning a nude detainee on a box, with a sandbag on his head, and attaching wires to his fingers, toes, and penis, to stimulate electric torture" (350).

44. *Private military/security companies: Rules should be implemented*, Keynote address by Christine Beerli, vice-president of the ICRC, Montreux +5 Conference, Montreux, Switzerland, 11-13 December 2013.

45. Jonathan Glover, *Humanity: A Moral History of the 20ʰ Century* (New Haven, CT: Yale University Press, 2001), 137.

46. Bosnian Serbs used the term *etnicko ciscenje* or "ethnic cleansing", a phrase reminiscent of the Nazis' *sauberung* or "cleansing" of Jews. Power, *A Problem from Hell*, 249).

47. Incidents such as these inspired thousands of believers throughout the Muslim world to travel to Bosnia in order to provide assistance to their suffering Muslim sisters and brothers.

48. Enes Zunic writes: "We were living with Serbians and Croatians peacefully, but all of a sudden we saw that our neighbors, playmates, classmates, colleagues, and business partners had turned their guns on us in the same streets in the same towns where we had lived together for ages. Looking back, I cannot see any real reason why they had started genocide. We have never threatened any of them; we had never harmed any of those people. Yet, I now realize that we were different from Serbs and Croatians. We had Muslim names such as Muhammad, Esad, Khatice, and Amina, and that was enough reason for them to pull the trigger. I now see that our Muslim identity must have been the reason behind all the grievances inflicted upon us" (Talip Kucukcan, "Encountering the Victims of Genocide: Observations of a Traveler", *Journal of Muslim Minority Affairs* 16 [1996], 318).

49. Michael Sells, *The Bridge Betrayed: Religion and Genocide in Bosnia* (Berkeley: University of California Press, 1996) writes: "Serb army officials used alcohol to break down the normal inhibitions of the young men in their commands. Serb soldiers were kept drunk night after night, weeks at a time; military convoys were accompanied by truckloads of plum brandy (*sljuvovica*). In Sarajevo, there was an evening *slijvovica* hour during which Serb soldiers would get drunk and broadcast over loudspeakers, in grisly detail, what they were going to do to Bosnian civilians when they got hold of them. Survivors of mass-killings reported that once the soldiers began drinking atrocities followed" (74).

50. Sells, 19.

51. Sells reports of one chant that stated "The high mountains reek with the smell of non-Christians" (41). Terms and images are frequently used to note that the land is defiled with this presence. After slaughtering, Serbs

would go straight to communion without going to confession, which was mandatory after other acts of bloody violence in war-time. Sells writes that, "Christo-Slavism — the premise that Slavs are by essence Christian and conversion to another religion is a betrayal of the people or race" is another factor in this toxic mix of religion and violence (Sells, 51).

52. Sells, 82. Radovan Karadzic, a war criminal, was also declared "one of the most prominent sons of our Lord Jesus Christ working for peace" by the Greek Orthodox Church (Sells, 85).

53. Branimir Anzulovic, *Heavenly Serbia: From Myth to Genocide* (New York: New York University Press, 1999), 178.

54. Sells, 21–22.

55. Sells writes: "In the summer of 1992, UN Peacekeepers under the command of the Canadian General Lewis McKenzie frequented the rape camp known as Sonja's Kon Tiki in the town of Vogosca near Sarajevo. Even after they learned that the women at Kon Tiki were Muslim captives held against their will, abused, and sometimes killed, UN Peacekeepers continued to take advantage of the women and to fraternize with their Serb nationalist captors. Only 150 yards away from Sonja's, scores of Muslim men were being held in inhumane conditions but the peacekeepers took no notice" (Ibid., 132–133).

56. The acronym 'UNPROFOR' stands for the United Nations Protection Force (Bosnia). UNPROFOR worked in conjunction with forces from the North Atlantic Treaty Organization (NATO) which were also in the region. Srebrenica was declared a "safe-area" by UNPROFOR on April 16, 1993. When this safe-area was overrun, the Serb General Ratko Mladic drank a toast with the Dutch commander of Srebrenica at "the same time that Mladic's men were selecting thousands of boys as young as 12 years of age, men, and some women for torture, rape, and mass killings, but Bosnian Serb nationalist authorities have refused war crimes investigators access to the graves. An estimated 8,000 people are missing; but after severe grave-tampering, it is impossible to determine how many were killed" (Sells, 27). The French General Bernard Janvier was the Senior UN official who had repeatedly recommended that the UN forces should abandon the Srebrenica safe-area. Janvier's standing orders from the United Nations Security Council (Resolution 536) were to "use the necessary measures, including the use of force, to defend the safe-areas."

57. Numbers vary between 7,000 and 9,000. There are 8,400 people buried at the Srebrenica cemetery and more are being found so that number may not be the real amount but may include some Bosnians killed in places other than the battery factory.

58. Seki Radoncic, *A Fatal Freedom* (The Hague, the Netherlands: Humanitarian Law Center, 2005) covers these forcible repatriations of Bosnian Muslims by the Montenegrin government.

59. See [http://www.allafrica.com/view/group/main/main/id/00025747.html] (accessed July 30, 2013).

60. Gray Phombeah, "Children Rescued from Muslim Torture in Kenya", BBC News, January 31, 2003 [http://www.hvk.org/articles/o203/19.html] (accessed January 10, 2013).

61. Emily Wax, "Islam Attracting Many Survivors of Rwanda Genocide: Jihad is Taught as a 'Struggle to Heal,'" *The Washington Post*, September 23, 2002, A10.

62. Teofilo Cabestrero, *Blood of the Innocent* (Maryknoll, NY: Orbis Books, 1985), 79.

63. Keith Morgan and Almut Scheppler, eds, *Human Rights Have No Borders: Voices of Irish Prophets* (Dublin: Marino Books, 1998), 83ff.

7. Islamic Social Equality in Response to Racism and Slavery

1. Lebacqz, 19.

2. Edward Blyden, *Christianity, Islam, and the Negro Race* (Edinburgh: Edinburgh University Press, 1887).

3. Holly J. Lebowitz, and Gary Orfield, eds, *Religion, Race and Justice in a Changing America* (New York: Century Foundation Press, 1999), 153.

4. Sanford Harper, unpublished graduate paper, University of South Florida, April 30, 2011, 2.

5. John Ralph Willis, *Slaves and Slavery in Muslim Africa* (Totawata, NJ: Frank Cass and Company, 1986 [1885]), 49.

6. Esack (2000), 56.

7. Azzedine Layachi, "The Berbers in Algeria: Politicization of Ethnicity and Ethnicization of Politics", in *Nationalism and Minority Identities in Islamic Societies*, ed. Maya Shatzmiller (Montreal: McGill-Queen's University Press, 2005), 196–197.

8. Liz Fekete. *A Suitable Enemy: Racism, Migration, and Islamophobia in Europe* (New York: Pluto Press, 2009), 27.

9. Timothy Savage, "Europe and Islam: Crescent Waxing, Cultures Clashing", *Washington Quarterly*, 27 (2004): 25–50 also talks about these changes. The statistics cited are from Ron Geaves, *Aspects of Islam* (Washington, DC: Georgetown University Press, 2004), 82–83.

10. Both CNN and the *Daily Mail* reported this [http://www.cnn.com/2010/WORLD/europe/10/28/uk.mohammed/] (accessed March 13, 2014) [http://www.dailymail.co.uk/news/article-2390945/Muhammad-Londons-favourite-boys-Harry-comes-overall.html#comments] (accessed March 13, 2014).

11. For examples see my article "Bubba's Islam: Perceptions of Muslims and Islam from a Waco, Texas Trailer-Park", in *Keeping it Holy: Southerners and the South and the Idea of Justice*, ed. Teresa Booker, forthcoming, 2014.

12. Moustafa Bayoumi, *How Does it Feel to be a Problem? Being Young and Arab in America* (New York: Penguin Books, 2008), 3.

13. Timothy Savage, "World Population Prospects: The 2002 Revisions-Highlights", published by the Population Division of the Department of Economic and Social Affairs, The United Nations Secretariat, February 26, 2003, 1.

14. Jenkins, 9–10: "Modern American racists love the story of Phinehas. In 1990, Richard Kelly Hoskins used the story as the basis for his manifesto *Vigilantes of Christendom*. Hopkins advocated the creation of a new order of militant white supremists, the Phineas [sic.] Priesthood, and since then a

number of sects have assumed this name claiming Old Testament precedent for terrorist attacks on mixed-race couples and abortion clinics. Opinions vary as to whether Oklahoma City bomber Timothy McVeigh himself was a Phineas Priest, but he was close to the movement."

15. Jenkins, 9.

16. Noteworthy pro-slavery apologetics included two books by Richard Furman, founder of Furman University. These are *The Peculiar Institution* and *Exposition of the Views of Baptists Relative to the Coloured Population in the United States in a Communication to the Governor of South Carolina.* These tracts are available at [http://alpha.furman.edu/~benson/docs/rcd-fmn1.htm] (accessed January 12, 2013).

17. Howard Thurman, academic mentor of Martin Luther King and author of *Jesus and the Disinherited,* did not think that St Paul's writings on slavery could be considered to be divine, which is why Thurman did not preach from Paul's letters.

18. William Gervase Clarence-Smith, *Islam and the Abolition of Slavery* (New York: Oxford University Press, 2006), 19.

19. The definition I am using for "slave" comes from the *Encyclopedia of the Modern Middle East and North Africa,* ed. Philip Mattar (Detroit: Thomson-Gale, 2004), 2073: "One whose labor is controlled and whose freedom is withheld, a person in a state of legal and actual servility or who is of slave origins, or a naturally alienated and generally dishonored person under permanent violent domination." In effect, Islamic law defined slavery as giving one person ownership over another person, meaning that the master had rights to the slave's labor, property, and sexuality and that the freedoms that slaves enjoyed were severely restricted (but not eliminated). In the Middle East, some people would sell themselves, or more often their children, into slavery. Individuals could also be enslaved for insolvency. People who were abandoned or kidnapped might also become slaves. Initially, most slaves were captives in war. Race (skin-color), unlike in the Atlantic/European slave trade, was not a significant factor in Middle Eastern slavery.

20. Senturk, 121.

21. Robert Davis, *Christian Slaves, Muslim Masters: White Slavery in the Mediterranean, the Barbary Coast, and Italy, 1500–1800* (New York: Palgrave MacMillan, 2003), 10. Davis states: "It would not be stretching the truth to say that the Muslims have put a million Christians in chains" (5).

22. The seventh-century conquest of North Africa was not ideal for the Muslim slave-traders since so many North Africans were Christians. This invasion did, however, provide access to already existing Roman slave routes which went through the Sahara and into the African Savannah, where non-*dhimmi* (potential slaves) lived. A second front for the Muslim slave-trade, closer to Arabia, opened along the coasts of Somalia, Kenya, and Madagascar. Some Africans, however, converted to Islam, which made their enslavability (at least in theory) unacceptable. Millions of slaves were extracted from Africa, and the trade in African slaves continued until the 1930s. Slavery was still legal in Saudi Arabia until the 1960s.

23. Robert Segal, *Islam's Black Slaves: The Other Black Diaspora* (New York: Farrar,

Strauss and Giroux, 2001), 50. For a discussion of this topic as it relates to the Muslim attitudes toward women during the era of the West African slave trade, consult chapter two of my book *Violence in God's Name: Muslim and Christian Relations in Nigeria* (Baltimore: African Diaspora Press, 2012).

24. In the Ottoman Empire, it was customary to release African slaves after seven years but to release European slaves after nine years because the Europeans were more expensive and less available in the slave markets and because of the perception at the time was that they worked better in colder weather (Clarence-Smith, *Islam and the Abolition of Slavery*, 67). Such negative stereotypes did exist within Muslim lands as it related to Africans. Bernard Lewis cites the twelfth century Egyptian writer al-Abshihi: "Is there anything viler than black slaves, of less good and more evil than they? The better you treat him, the more insolent he will be; the worse you treat him, the more humble and subservient he will be. I tried this many times" (Bernard Lewis, *Race and Slavery in the Middle East: An Historical Enquiry* [New York: Oxford University Press, 1990], 75).

25. Segal, 48–49. These citations come from Sayed Al-Andalusi, a Moorish judge from Toledo (ca. 1100). Segal quotes an Arab jurist living in the Malian university city of Timbuctu who observed that Africans were "inherently servile, ready to obey, and long-suffering in the face of all inconveniences" (59).

26. Willis, 35.

27. Hadith Muslim, 15: 4086: "Abu Mas'ud al-Badri reported: I was beating my slave with a whip when I heard a voice behind me saying: Understand, Abu Masoud — but I did not recognize the voice because of my intense anger. Abu Mas'ud reported: as he came near me I found that he was the Messenger of Allah (PBUH) and he was saying, Bear in mind, Abu Mas'ud, bear in mind. The Prophet then threw the whip from my hand and said to me: Verily, Allah has more dominance over you than you have over your slave. I then said that I would never beat my servant in the future." See also number 4094: "Your slaves are brothers of yours. Allah has placed them in your hands and they should eat what you eat and wear what you wear, and do not burden them beyond their capacities, and help them."

28. Arlene Swidler, ed. *Human Rights in the Religious Traditions* (New York: Pilgrim Press, 1982), 59.

29. Willis, 52.

30. Henry Bayman, *The Secret of Islam: Love and Law in the Religion of Ethics* (Berkeley, CA: North Atlantic Books, 2003), 134.

31. "People-Trafficking in Odessa: Sea of Tears" (no author cited), *The Economist*, September 23, 2006, 63.

32. John Eibner, "My Career Redeeming Slaves", *Middle East Quarterly*, 6 (1999), 12.

33. Segal, 221.

34. [http://freethoughtnation.com/contributing-writers/63-acharya-s/498-islam-disturbing-legacy-of-slavery] (accessed January 14, 2013).

35. Numerous human rights organizations can be contacted to learn what one can do to confront modern slavery. Abolitionist movements, chartered in the United Kingdom centuries ago, are still in operation.

36. Martin Luther King, Jr., *Why We Can't Wait* (New York: New American Library, 1964), 81.

8. Sexual Injustice, Sexism, and Homophobia among Muslims

1. Dunya Maumoun, "Islamism and Gender Activism: Muslim Women's Quest for Autonomy", *Journal of Muslim Minority Affairs* 30 (2010): 280.
2. Kumar, 44.
3. Geaves, 239. Geaves cites Ghada Karmi, who states that women were turned into "non-adults" by the revelation of the Qur'an which served to justify continued oppression of women and the suppression of any notion of gender-equality (240).
4. Ramsay M. Harik and Elsa Marston, *Women in the Middle East: Tradition and Change* (New York: Franklin Watts, 1996), 56.
5. Ayaan Hirsi Ali, *The Caged Virgin: An Emancipation Proclamation for Women and Islam* (New York: Free Press, 2006), 36.
6. Harik and Marston, 56.
7. Rosen, 64. The entire quote from the play *Les Co-Epouses* ("The House of Wives") reads: "We come into this world with a flower between our legs. It is the source of fear for as long as we have it and the source of unhappiness when we lose it. This cannot happen to a man because he is born with a gun between his legs. With that primary weapon, he wins all battles against flowers. Is that what one calls justice? Is it that? That's justice? Is it my fault that I was born a flower? Is it my fault that I am not a gun?" (64).
8. The Muslim organization *Muhammadiyah* was originally formed in 1912 to confront the expanding social influences of the Dutch colonial (and Christian) rulers. One of the initial goals of this movement was also to rid Islam of indigenous practices from Indonesian folk cultures which were not commensurate with Muslim practices. The founder, Ahmad Dahlan, hoped to create an off-shoot of the movement, which would address the specific needs of Indonesian Muslim women. In 1917, a few followers of Dahlan formed the organization *Ayesha* which initially focused on educating women to study the Qur'an. Over time it became more active in addressing a wide range of social issues affecting Muslim women. A counter movement called *Nahdlatul Ulama* was formed in 1926, which sought to preserve traditional Indonesian Muslim practices (such as the chanting of the Qur'an). They also eventually set up teaching centers aimed exclusively for women. It was not until 1946, however, that a woman's branch of *Nahdlatul Ulama* was formed (*Muslimant Nu*). Unlike *Ayesha* this group did not propose that women venture out from the traditional social roles that had historically been assigned to them. It was this more restricted role that came to ascendancy with General Suharto's 1966 uprising, which called for the "housewifization" of Indonesian Muslim women. When Suharto's reign ended in 1998, women's movements were able to function with more freedom as women became more educated (and active) in political and economic life.
9. Ilyas Ba-Yunus and Kassim Kone, *Muslims in the United States* (Westport, CT: Greenwood Press, 2006), 96.
10. Gameze Cavdar, "Islamist Moderation and the Resilience of Gender: Turkey's Present Paradox", *Totalitarian Movements and Political Religions* 11 (2012): 350.
11. Cavdar, 342.

12. Jane I. Smith, "Women in Islam" in *Today's Woman in World Religions*, ed. Armand Sharma (Albany: State University of New York Press, 1994), 312.

13. Asef Bayat, "A Women's Non-Movement: What it Means to be a Muslim Activist in an Islamic State", *Comparative Studies of South Asia, Africa, and the Middle East*, 27 (2007), 161.

14. The Family Protection Law of 1967 (revised in 1975), addressed issues such as polygamy, divorce, and child custody. Most rural Iranian women were unaffected by these laws. Iran's last Shah banned the *chador* and promised increased education and economic power for women, but he did this by decree and without the direct involvement of women.

15. Harik and Marston, *Women in the Middle East*, 144. Harik and Marston also claim that only women in Iran who are married and are mothers are given the right to work without any restrictions from Shi'a Muslim clerics.

16. Anna King, "Islam, Women, and Violence", *Feminist Theology: Journal of the British and Irish School of Feminist Theology*, 11 (2009), 316.

17. Smith, 317.

18. Sally Armstrong, *Veiled Threat: The Hidden Power of the Women of Afghanistan* (New York: Four Walls Eight Windows, 2002), 67–68.

19. Initially, 433 foreigners, including 240 women were arrested for the "impudent" party in Jeddah; only 20 of those arrested were sentenced in the first round of trials. Incriminating evidence included a video that had been made at the party. [http://www.usatoday.com/news/world/2007-02-04-saudi-foreign-arrests_x.htm] (accessed February 18, 2013).

20. Muhammad Iqbal Siddiqi, *Islam Forbids Free Mixing of Men and Women* (Lahore, Pakistan: KAZI Publications, 1983), 38.

21. Siddiqi, 65. Siddiqi explains: "It is an admitted fact that eyes are the messengers who bring the messages to the minds of the onlookers. It is the full view of the fair sex's face and curves of the body which arouses the feelings of love and stirs emotions in one's heart." Women are "overpowered by sentiments and emotions rather easily. It is a familiar fact that in America and in the Western countries there is much moral degeneration and chaos. The free mixing of young boys and girls in colleges, clubs, ball-rooms and hotels provides vast opportunities of petting, necking and scandalous behavior. They indulge fearlessly and unhesitatingly in wicked pleasures. Thus free intermingling of the sexes has dragged women into the quagmire of pleasure, sensuality and luxury. By segregating the two sexes Islam has minimized the chances of moral lapses and hateful deeds to a great extent. In this way the honor of women is saved. She cannot be molested and humiliated. When veiled, her beauty or ugliness invites no criticism from the wicked-minded persons. Apart from the viewpoint of morality, women who do not wear veil have to worry a lot about their makeup and costly fashionable costumes (65–66) . . . . In the West, women are renouncing the role of women and have to pay heavily for it as it leads them finally to the negation of life itself. They are thus losing their charm and grace, sweetness and modest traits. Women are not only engaged in manly professions but dress like men and act like them which is a perverted and distorted conception of freedom. . . . The masculinized women of the West depict a distressing and disappointing state of affairs" (67).

22. Fauzia Ahmad, "Rethinking Muslim Women and the Veil: Challenging Historical and Modern Stereotypes", *American Journal of Islamic Social Sciences*, 19 (2002): 123.

23. "The Meaning of Freedom" (no author cited), *The Economist*, April 2, 2009, 63.

24. Harik and Marston, 24.

25. In October of 2009, the national courts ruled in the women's favor noting that the Kuwaiti Constitution guaranteed gender equality and freedom of choice in religious decisions. Women in Kuwait, it should be emphasized, have far greater freedoms than many other women in the Gulf States. Kuwait is also a nation that is highly literate and socially tolerant compared to some of their neighbors. Political and economic factors, such as Kuwait's overwhelming economic and military dependence on the United States should also be factored in to the consideration of why this particular decision was reached.

26. Ahmad, 123.

27. Sharon J. Ghuman, "Women's Autonomy and Child Survival: A Comparison of Muslim and Non-Muslims in Four Asian Countries", *Demography*, 40 (2003): 419.

28. Esack (2000), 114.

29. Garaudy, 56.

30. Armstrong, 67.

31. Shamsa Ali, *A Treatise on Women's Rights* (Lahore, Pakistan: Qur'anic Society, 1996), 75.

32. Harik and Marston, 78; see also 104.

33. Annelies Moors, *Women, Property, and Islam* (London: Cambridge University Press, 1995), 224.

34. The *Tribune* reported this [http//tribune.com.pk/story/682260/first-interview-after-attack-malala-backs-dialogue-with-militants] (accessed March 13, 2014).

35. Harik and Marston, 107.

36. Jan Goodwin, *Price of Honor: Muslim Women Lift the Veil of Silence on the Islamic World* (New York: Plume Publications, 2003), 65.

37. Esack (2000), 116.

38. Nimat Hafez Barazangi, *Women's Identity and the Qur'an: A New Reading* (Gainesville: University Press of Florida, 2004), 70.

39. Masoud Kazemzadeh, *Islamic Fundamentalism, Feminism and Gender Inequality in Iran Under Khomeini* (Lanham, MD: University Press of America, 2002), 84–85.

40. Kazemzadeh, 85.

41. Riffat Hassan, "Islam" in *Her Voice, Her Faith: Women Speak on World Religions*, ed. Arvind Sharma and Katherine K. Young (Cambridge, MA: Westview Press, 2003), 240.

42. The ten types of marriage cited by Syed are: 1. Permanent marriage between one man and one woman throughout life for which a dower is given to the wife. 2. The master who marries his female slaves. 3. *Nikah Al-Zainaah*, which is a form of marriage that took place when a man captured a woman in war and wanted to marry her. 4. *Zawaj Al-Badal*, which was the mutual exchange of wives between two couples. This has now been outlawed. 5. *Zawaj Al-Istibda*, which was a temporary marriage between a woman and a

man until a pregnancy with the man was made certain by his resemblance to the child. 6. Polyandry, in which one woman could be married to as many as ten men at a time. This is now forbidden under Islamic law. 7. Marrying once a pregnancy produces a male child. 8. *Nikah Al-Dayzan*, in which a son is entitled to marry his father's wives in the event of the father's death. 9. *Zawaj Al-Shigar*, which is similar to the first and normative marriage pattern although a dowry is not required, and 10. *Muta*, or temporary marriages, permitted for a specific period of time before being formally dissolved. Muta marriages are still practiced in parts of the Shi'a world but are not allowed in most Muslim countries. Some have tried to use this kind of marriage to justify their trysts with prostitutes or other women who are not their wives on an on-going basis. See Muhammad Ali Syed, *The Position of Women in Islam: A Progressive View* (New York: State University of New York Press, 2004), 29–31.

43. Syed, 33.
44. Hassan, 231.
45. Barbara Freyer Stowasser, *Women in the Qur'an, Traditions, and Interpretation* (New York: Oxford University Press, 1994), 25.
46. Hassan, "Islam" 229. Hassan recounts: "There is strictly speaking, no 'Fall' in the Qur'an. What the Qur'anic narrative focuses on is the moral choice that humanity is required to make when confronted by the alternatives presented to them by God and the Shaytan."
47. Arthur Frederick Ide, *The Qur'an on Women, Marriage, Birth Control and Divorce* (Las Colinas, TX: Tangelwuld Press, 1996), 25.
48. Earliest pagans in Europe did not believe that sexuality was only for procreation. Paleolithic bone-etchings from Isturitz (south-western), France illustrate this attitude. Anees states that viewing sexuality as something negative begins as an attitude espoused in Greece and by some ancient Roman philosophers before the advent of Christianity. The Genesis narrative shows that Early Judaism taught that there was a "first" and "second" gender in terms of created order and that Eve led Adam into sin. Menstruating women were impure (Lev. 15:19). Some Orthodox Jews taught that women existed for the pleasure of men and may not even have had a soul. An oft-quoted prayer that was recited was, "Blessed art Thou, Lord that thou hast not made me a woman." In spite of these historic attitudes, Jewish views toward sexuality usually (note the Essenes) developed in a much more affirming way than within Christianity. St Clement, for example, taught that women should "blush" for being female, and St Thomas Aquinas taught that women were "defective males". Early Christian writers, raised in this worldview, often cited Neo-Platonists and Neo-Pythagoreans who were critical of the pursuit of sexual pleasure. Luther renounced celibacy, but did suggest, according to Anees, that intercourse be restricted to twice a week only. The use of contraception was illegal in the United States before 1938; the Church of England was officially opposed to contraception until the Lambeth Conference of 1930. See Munawar Ahmad Anees, "Islamic Values and Western Science: A Case Study of Reproductive Biology", in *The Touch of Midas: Science, Values and Environment in Islam and the West*, ed., Ziauddin Sardar (Dover, NH: Manchester University Press, 1984), 91–120.

49. Anees, "Islamic Values", 101. Al-Ghazali said that what was most important in this regard was the intention of the act. He argued that a child was not only the mechanistic product of the male sperm but was to be appreciated in terms of the entire process and also in terms of Divine destiny.

50. Ide, 26–27.

51. Anees, 101.

52. Carla Makhlouf, *Changing Veils* (Austin: University of Texas Press, 1979), 38.

53. The term *nafs* can also be used to describe God (Q. 3:28; 5:119; 6:12; 20:41). It is also used to describe "gods" (Q. 25:3). It is usually used to describe the human soul (Q. 6:93; 64:16; 59:9 and 79:40). The soul is a place where evil can reside (Q. 12:53), but it can also be a place of tranquility (Q. 89:27). Another term to describe human life in the Qur'an is the generic "person" or self (Q. 3:61). The spirit (*ruah*) is from God (Q. 9:171; 21:91) and is the breath of life. The spirit is the place of knowledge (Q. 17:85) and a place that relates to angels (Q. 97:4; 78:38; 19:17; 16:102) who give inspiration from God. The main idea of these passages is that the human being is not simply a biological creature but a complex creation of God.

54. The National Muslim HIV/AIDS Initiative, one such program, is hosted by the Bronx Community College of the City University of New York (552 Southern Boulevard, Bronx, New York, 10455).

55. Lebacqz, 21.

56. Esack (2000), 126.

57. According to the BBC, reportage of incidences of rape to local police authorities is "suspiciously low" among a number of communities in the UK. This may relate to fears that, if reported, the guilty parties will not be prosecuted successfully and brought to justice [http://www.bbc.co.uk/news/uk-25975485] [http://www.bbc.uk/news/co.uk-25964991] (accessed March 13, 2013).

58. Yusuf Ali, commentary on the English translation of the Qur'an, from note number 547 on 220.

59. Abu Dawud, 2:2127.

60. Khaled El Fadl, *And God Knows the Soldiers: The Authoritative and the Authoritarian in Islamic Discourses* (Lanham, MD: University Press of America, 2001), 69.

61. Huda Shaarawi, *Harem Years: The Memoires of an Egyptian Feminist (1879–1924)*, trans. Margot Badran (New York: Feminist Press, 1986). Twelfth-century Europeans employed "chastity belts" to ensure that women would not have sex before marriage. See Albert Classen, *The Medieval Chastity Belt: A Myth-Making Process* (New York: Palgrave MacMillan, 2007), 4.

62. John Duffy, "Clitoridectomy: A Nineteenth Century Answer to Masturbation", The Female Genital Cutting Education and Networking Project website, [http://www.fgmnetwork.org] (accessed January 15, 2013).

63. One study from the World Health Organization (WHO) in 1993 suggested that as many as 10,000 girls were at risk of FGM in the United Kingdom, and, worldwide, at least 100–140 million women are estimated to have undergone FGM with 2 million more at risk every year. The WHO defines FGM as "all procedures involving partial or total removal of the external female genitalia or other injury to the female genital organs whether for

cultural, religious, or other non-therapeutic reasons." FGM most often happens to girls between the ages of 4 and 7 but has taken place anywhere from infancy up to puberty. In 2014, the first court case against FGM was successfully prosecuted [http://www.globalpost.com/dispatch/news/regions/europe/united-kingdom/140321/britain-prosecutes-first-female-genital-mutilatio] (accessed March 31, 2014).

64. Efua Dorkenoo, *Cutting the Rose: Female Genital Mutilation — The Practice and Its Prevention* (London: Minority Rights Institute, 1994), 8. According to Haifaa A. Jawad, a senior lecturer in Middle Eastern and Islamic Studies at Westhill College in Birmingham, UK, the three most commonly practiced forms of FGM are circumcision, excision, and infibulations. Jawad writes that circumcision is the mildest form and consists of cutting the hood of the clitoris. The second form of mutilation is excision; the removal of the clitoris and either the entire labia minora or part of it. The most inhumane form is called infibulation where all of the clitoris, the labia minora and parts of the labia majora are removed. The two sides of the vulva are then stitched together leaving a small hole for the discharge of fluids. From Haifaa A. Jawad, *The Rights of Women in Islam: An Authentic Approach* (New York: Palgrave Press, 1998), 54.

65. Imad-ad-Dean Ahmad, *Female Genital Mutilation: An Islamic Perspective* (Bethesda, MD: Minaret of Freedom Institute, 2000), 1.

66. Ahmad, 2.

67. Jawad, 55–56.

68. There is an increased risk of STI's (HSV2) which is often the precursor to AIDS.

69. Hughes, 91.

70. Harik and Marston, 104.

71. Kimball (1965), 142.

72. Saudi Arabia passed a series of laws against homosexuals in July of 1991. Article 110 states that a judge will decide the specific punishment that is to be enforced which has usually meant five to six years of prison and as many as 2,000 lashes spaced throughout that period of incarceration. There have also been reports that one penalty prescribed has been to throw homosexuals from buildings that are taller than three stories. All of these punishments, it is stated, are designed to discourage those in the community rather than to explicitly "punish" those who are guilty of being gay. In spite of these penalties, homosexuality is widespread in most, if not all, Muslim-majority nations. Some fathers have even contracted-out their sons for sexual use and other boys have been trained to be "dancers" and male prostitutes who often assume specific dress in order to be easily identified (Morocco: *hassas*; Turkey: *kocek*; Oman: *khanith*.) Article 131 of the 1991 Saudi laws focus on lesbianism; not generally treated as harshly as male homosexuality. Some women have been placed in "poor houses" "managed" by men whose task is to "turn them to the right way".

73. [http://www.amnesty.org/en/news/nigeria-halt-homophobic-witch-hunt-under-oppressive-new-law] (accessed April 10, 2014).

74. The Guardian reported this [http://www.theguardian.com/world/2014/feb/24/uganda-president-signs-anti-gay-laws] (accessed March 18, 2014).

75. In July of 2005 in Mashad, Iran, two homosexual teenagers were hanged in the public square with graphic pictures subsequently being released throughout the country in the government media in order to warn others. Before being hanged, the two youth were jailed for almost two years during which time they received 228 floggings as required by the sentence of the court: Doug Ireland, "Politics and Media", [http://www.direland.typepad.com/direland/2005/07/iran_executes_2html] (accessed February 25, 2007).

76. Annisa Helie from [http://www.newint.org/issue328/holy.htm] (accessed January 14, 2013).

77. Boellstorff defines "homo-sexism" as the belief that heterosexuality is the only natural and "moral sexuality". According to this definition, a government or religious law against homosexuality would be homo-sexist but, because a law does not attack personhood, it cannot be called "homophobic." See Tom Boellstorff, "The Emergence of Political Homophobia in Indonesia: Masculinity and National Belonging", *Ethnos*, 69 (2004), 472.

78. For example, St Augustine taught that homosexuality should always be punished. Aquinas said that homosexuality was injurious to both the sinner and the community. Luther considered both the prevalence and tolerance of homosexuality practices among the clergy as one of the worst symptoms of decay in the church. Billy Graham commented that homosexuality was the product of a reprobate mind. On the other hand, Mark A. Pike notes: "The Muslim, Jewish and Christian teachers believe that a duty incumbent upon them is to follow the teachings of their sacred texts. While all three of these religions respect close friendships and love between people of the same sex (both David and Jonathan as well as Ruth and Naomi are inspiring examples) they are unambiguous in their rejection of homosexual practice." *Mere Education: C.S. Lewis as Teacher for our Time* (Cambridge, UK: The Lutterworth Press, 2013), p.74.

79. As mentioned earlier, the use of dress as sexual advertisement has many names in different Muslim-majority countries. Sometimes, a man's hair will be worn back, as opposed to forward, to connote sexual preference.

80. Stephen O. Murray and Will Roscoe, *Islamic Homosexualities: Culture, History and Literature* (New York: New York University Press, 1997), 14.

81. Sharful Islam Khan, "Men Who Have Sex with Men and their Sexual Relations with Women in Bangladesh", *Culture, Health and Sexuality*, 7 (2005), 159–160.

82. The term, for that matter, may not have been found in any culture before the nineteenth century. Khalil El-Rouyaheb contends that the term was coined in the 1860s by the Austro-Hungarian writer Karl Maria Kertbeny, with the term first appearing in English 20 years later (Khalil el-Rouyaheb, *Before Homosexuality in the Arab-Islamic World, 1500-1800* [Chicago: University of Chicago Press, 2005], 5). Previous to the usage of this term there were two distinct terms in Arabic, and these two terms underscore the distinction between a pederast (*luti*) who commits anal sexuality (*liwat*) and homoerotic lovers (*mukhannath* or *ma'bun* or the colloquial term *'ilq*). Conjecture about the prohibition of anal sex may relate to a number of folk stories which say that anal sex is forbidden in order to ensure that men will continue to have vaginal sex (Khan, 160).

83. Vern L. Bullough, "Before Homosexuality in the Arab-Islamic World", *American Historical Review* 111 (2006), 1286.

84. El-Rouyaheb, 1–5. One of the most noted poets of homoerotic verse was Shabrawi, Shaykh of the Al-Azhar in Cairo.
85. Omar Minwalla, "Identity Experience among Progressive Gay Muslims in North America: A Qualitative Survey within Al-Fatiha", *Culture, Health, and Sexuality*, 7 (2005), 114.
86. The first Hadith citation is from Abu Dawud, 38:4448; the second is from Al-Tirmidhi.
87. Everett Rowson, "Homosexuality", in *Encyclopedia of the Qur'an* (Leiden, the Netherlands: E.J. Brill, 2002), 444. Rowson also cites Qur'an 4:15–16 to describe women who are guilty of this "abomination" (*fahisha*) although it is not really clear exactly what these passages are describing. The "two" in the verse can grammatically refer to either two men or to two women. This has led Muslim commentators to exegete that this passage refers to illicit heterosexual relations (*zina*). One of the earliest descriptions of this passage to refer to two women might come from the Mu'tazilite exegete Abu Muslim al-Isfahani (254–322/868–934). This view was cited by both Muhammad Rashid Rida and Sayyid Qutb.
88. Sabine Schmidtke, "Homoeroticism and Homosexuality in Islam: A Review Article", *Bulletin of the School of Oriental and African Studies*, 62 (1999), 260.
89. "Queen Jihad was founded in 1997 as an internet community by an individual named "Suleyman X" who eventually renounced Islam. The site provides stories of individual Muslim gays who have done *jihad* in order to maintain their lifestyle. Interestingly, their site equates prejudice and discrimination with terrorism. [http://www.well.com/user/queerjhd/index.htm] (accessed April 10, 2013). Another organization, based in New York, is called the Gay and Lesbian Arabic Society. GLAS focuses on promoting a positive image of gay and lesbian Arabs. Lastly, "Queer-Net" offers a gay and lesbian Muslim mailing list.
90. Minwalla, 114.
91. This *fatwa* states, "The very existence of Al-*Fatiha* is illegitimate and the members of this organization are apostates. Never will such an organization be tolerated in Islam, and never will the disease that it calls for be affiliated with a true Islamic society or individual. The Islamic ruling for such acts is death. It is a duty of all Muslims to prevent such evil conceptions from being voiced in the public or private arena" (Minwalla, 116).
92. Minwalla, 124.
93. Cavdar, 355.
94. This issue is at the heart of the debate between Michael Merry and Mark Halstead in the March 2005 issue of the *Journal of Moral Education* (34, 1, 19–36; 37–42). Merry argues that a simply neutral portrayal of homosexual choices in a Muslim educational context will fail if not also accompanied by stories that foster empathy towards practicing gays and lesbians. Merry also feels that Halstead's portrayal of Muslim views about homosexuality are far too monolithic and notes that many Muslims are looking at the Qur'an with fresh interpretations which are not homophobic. Halstead counters that it is unfair to accuse Muslims of homophobia simply because they believe that homosexual practice is not permissible in the same way that gays and lesbians should be free to criticize Islamic teachings without being categorized as being Islamaphobic. Both academicians are arguing for the same end: the

promotion of tolerance between peoples of differing backgrounds. It must be remembered, however, that these discussions are in a context where people are being imprisoned, and even killed, for homosexual acts.

95. Sonya Fernandez, "The Crusade over the Bodies of Women", *Patterns of Prejudice*, 43 (2009), 270.
96. Fernandez, "Crusade", 271.
97. Goodwin, 29–30.

9. Islamic Stewardship and Responses to Environmental Degradation

1. Fazlun Khalid and Joanne O'Brien, eds, *Islam and Ecology* (New York: Cassell Publishers, 1992), 2.
2. Khalid and O'Brien, 12.
3. Khalid and O'Brien, 13
4. Khalid and O'Brien, 110.
5. Izzi Dien, *The Environmental Dimensions of Islam* (Cambridge: The Lutterworth Press, 2000), introduction.
6. Chandra Muzaffar, *Rights, Religion and Reform* (London: Routledge Curzon Press, 2002), 84.
7. S. Parvez Manzoour, "Environment and Values: The Islamic Perspective", in Sardar, ed., *Touch of Midas*, 130.
8. The Nowruz Field platform spill of February 4, 1983, saw over 80 million gallons spill into the Persian Gulf. From January 23–27, 1991, Iraq deliberately released between 240–260 million gallons of oil into the Persian Gulf about ten miles off the coast of Kuwait. Between five and ten million gallons of oil were spilled at the Jieh Coast Power Station of Lebanon in the Mediterranean after it was bombed by the Israeli Navy: Cited from "Oil Spills and Disasters" *Pearson Education, Inc. 2007*, [http://www.infoplease.com/ipa/A0001451.html] (accessed January 16, 2013).
9. Muslims are like those of many faiths who have only recently confronted their role in these socially-based environmental problems. Many Muslim communities have simply imported European and North American technologies along with the assumptions implicit in their use.
10. Lloyd Timberlake, "The Emergence of Environmental Awareness in the West", in Sardar, ed., *Touch of Midas*, 132.
11. Esack (2000), 15.
12. These include Surah *Naml* (ants), Surah *Ankabut* (spider), Surah *Nahl* (bees) and Surah *Baqara* (cow).
13. M. Husain Sadr, "Science and Islam: Is There a Conflict?" in Sardar, ed., *Touch of Midas*, 20.
14. Akutaruddin Ahmad, *Islam and the Environmental Crisis* (London: Ta-Ha Publishers Ltd., 1997), 56.
15. Manzoour, 162.
16. Manzoour, 161.
17. Ahmad, 26.
18. If water is absent, soil can be used as a means of purification (*tayammum*). This is because the earth and its contents are property of Allah and are pure for that reason.

19. Dien, 137.
20. Muhammad Saleh Farsy, *Islam and Hygiene* (Leiden, the Netherlands: E.J. Brill, 1964), 6.
21. Dien, 32.
22. John Alden Williams, *The World of Islam* (Austin: University of Texas Press, 1994), 36.
23. Khalid and O'Brien, 87.
24. Abu-Bakr Ahmed Bageder, *et al.* "Environmental Protection in Islam" IUCN (World Conservation Union) Environmental Policy and Law Paper, Riyadh, Saudi Arabia, number 20, 2.
25. [http://www.theiranproject.com/blog/2014/02/26] (accessed March 17, 2014).
26. Ahmad, 31.
27. Khalid and O'Brien, 12.
28. Khalid and O'Brien, 18.
29. Khalid and O'Brien 12.
30. [http://www.speednet.com.au/-keysar/ecology.htm], (accessed January 22, 2013).
31. Paul Lunde, "Science: The Islamic Legacy", *Saudi Aramco World*, 33 (1982), 14–19.
32. See [http://www.abc.net.au/religion/articles/2013/10/15/3869365.htm] (accessed March 13, 2014).
33. Fazlun Khalid "Guardians of the Natural Order", *Our Planet*, 8 (1996), 1.
34. The Alliance of Religions and Conservation (ARC) was founded in 1995 by Prince Phillip, Duke of Edinburgh. This group currently works with eleven different world religious traditions to encourage environmental conservation. Its strategy is two-fold: to help faith communities to be proactive in recognizing specific environmental problems that are emerging in their specific contexts and to help religious groups partner with non-religious, secular organizations committed to resolving environmental problems as they arise. The IUCN is the oldest and largest conservation network and is focused on promoting the protection of sustainable living resources in various contexts. The IUCN does this by linking governments, private organizations and citizens in order to raise environmental awareness.
35. Dien, 157.
36. Bageder, 1.
37. Ahmad, 53.
38. Reza Aslan, *No God but God* (New York: Random House, 2005), 162.
39. Williams, *The World of Islam*, 35. Williams cites laws from the Maliki School of jurisprudence which state, "whatever causes harm to the water is a cause for banning and in the case of a drinking-well, any cause that impedes drinking from the drinking-well is banned" (35).
40. Dien, 37.
41. Dien, 42.
42. Dien, 420.
43. The *Daily Mail* newspaper reported this [http://www.dailymail.co.uk/news/article-2226642/Muslim-clerics-say-Sandy-Gods-way-punishing-America-anti-Muhammed-film.html] (accessed March 17, 2014).
44. Bageder, 3.
45. Manzoour, 176.

46. Ziauddin Sardar, *Islamic Futures: The Shape of Things to Come* (London: Mansell Publishing, 1985), 226.

47. This proverb was related during a meal that I shared with a Muslim friend, Sa Li Lin, in Yunnan, China (1990).

48. Ahmad, *Islam and the Environmental Crisis*, 172.

49. Harfiyah Abdel Haleem, ed., *Islam and the Environment* (London: Ta Ha Publishers, 1998), 137.

10. Creating Multifaith Social Justice Partnerships

1. See [http://www.tartarus.org/martin/essays/burkequote2.html] (accessed February 19, 2013).

2. See [http://www.spiritualityandpractice.com/days/features.php?id=16446] (accessed April 14, 2013).

3. Martin Forward, *Interreligious Dialogue: A Short Introduction* (Oxford: One World Press, 2001), 121.

4. Thomas Simons, Jr., *Islam in a Globalizing World* (Stanford, CA: Stanford University Press, 2003), 1.

5. Sheila McDonough, *Gandhi's Response to Islam* (Delhi, India: DK Printworld, 1994), 114.

6. McDonough, 2.

7. McDonough, 110.

8. McDonough, 113.

9. Nilufer Gole, "Contemporary Islamist Movements and New Sources for Religious Tolerance", *Journal of Human Rights*, 2 (2003), 18.

10. Peter Gomes, *The Good Book: Reading the Bible with Mind and Heart* (New York: William Morrow, 1996), 45.

11. Conversation with Dr Blake Burleson, Department of Religion, Baylor University (April 2, 2009).

12. Kimball (1965), 203–204. The document, entitled the "Declaration on Relations of the Church to Non-Christian Religions", was published on October 28, 1965.

13. Kimball (1965), 214.

14. Kimball (1965), 214. The English title of this document is "Light to the Gentiles".

15. El-Fadl, 17.

16. Bahman Baktiari and Augustus Norton, "Voices from Within Islam: Four Perspectives on Tolerance and Diversity", *Current History*, 104 (2005), 45.

17. Report to the United States Congress, "Annual Report on International Religious Freedom, 2005", 109th Congress of the United States, Second Session, published April 2006. These numbers are based on a census taken in 2000 and may or may not be accurate for a host of reasons. Some adherents, for example, might describe themselves as both Muslims and Christians. See Abamfo Atiemo, "Zetheal Mission and Ghana: Christians and Muslims Worshipping Together?" *Exchange*, 32 (2003), 15.

18. Miroslav Volf, "Living with the Other", in *Muslim and Christian Reflections on Peace: Divine and Human Dimensions*, ed. J. Dudley Woodberry, Osman Zumrut, and Mustafa Koylu (Lanham, MD: University Press of America, 2005), 16–17.

19. Yemeni scholar Mohammed Bahumdun maintains that the Arabs actually originate from two tribes in Yemen (the *adnan* and the *qahtan*) and migrated northwards once their water-supplies were damaged when the dam at the city of Marib was broken. These Yemeni tribesmen "Arabized" others as they went north. Ishmael, son of Father Abraham is one of those "Arabized Arabs" who became "Arabized".
20. Jonathan Edward Culver, "The Ishmael Promises: A Bridge for Mutual Respect", in Woodberry, Zumrut, and Koylu, eds, 71.
21. Khan, 89.
22. Andrew Cuomo was Secretary of Housing and Urban Development when this program was inaugurated (1998). Cuomo chose Father Joseph Hascala, a Jesuit priest, to serve as the first director of the center.
23. This aid included hygiene kits, medical supplies, and a host of practical basic necessities such as powdered milk, hand soap, and baby formula. Islamic Relief, which has also worked with victims of the South Asian tsunami, Hurricane Katrina, and the earthquakes in Indonesia and Pakistan have consistently worked with various Christian aid organizations.

Conclusion

1. Esack (2000), 43.
2. Esack (2000), 5.
3. Lebacqz, 55.
4. David Shenk, *Journeys of the Muslim Nation and the Christian Church: Exploring the Mission of Two Communities* (Scottdale, PA: Herald Press, 2003), 240.
5. Lebowitz and Orfield, 170.
6. Kimball (1965), 189.
7. Saritoprak, 414–415.
8. Fettulah Gulen is a Turkish Muslim scholar who, like Nursi, preaches non-violent activism. Gulen began as a preacher employed by the Turkish government. He has always promoted interfaith cooperation and religious freedom. Gulen established the *Journalists and Writers Foundation* with the intention that the group would bring people of differing backgrounds together in order to discuss social reconciliation. In 2004, he taught a course at Johns Hopkins University on the compatibility between Islam and Democracy. He is the spiritual leader of a neo-Sufi Islamic organization committed to establishing educational institutions that combine modern science with Islamic ethics and Sufi spirituality. In speaking of how to present Islam in the modern world, Gulen states, "We must be as if we are 'handless' to those who hit us, and 'tongueless' to those who curse us. If they try and break us 50 times, we are going to remain unbroken and embrace everyone with love and compassion. With love toward one another we will talk and walk towards tomorrow" (Saritoprak, 424).
9. Esack (2000), 60.
10. Wilfred Cantwell Smith, "Comparative Religion — Whither and Why?" in *History of Religions: Essays in Methodology*, ed. Mircea Eliade and J.M. Kitagawa (Chicago: University of Chicago Press, 1959), 34.

Glossaries

Glossary of Terminology

Allah: Literally, *God*. Name for the one and only omnipresent, just, and merciful, God.

Almsgiving: *Sadaqah*. It is one of the Five Pillars of Islam and can be given in cash or in other gifts in kind.

Apostasy: *Irtidad*. Apostasy is forbidden in Islamic law. The Kharijites, an early radical sect, proclaimed apostates (*murtadd*) all Muslims who would not accept their interpretation of Islam. A male apostate could be killed, unless he was a minor or otherwise disabled.

Ayatollah (Persian): Literally, *sign* or miracle of God. Title is given to the most eminent Twelver Shi'ite legal experts. Shi'ite *Mujtahid* (jurists) in Iran, first used in the fourrteenth century and adopted the term during the Qajar dynasty (1779–1924) (Arab-speaking Shi'ites use the title Imam). The term has been used since the nineteenth century more specifically for senior clerics within Shi'ite Islam. Since the 1979 revolution, the term is used as an honorary title for the highest ranking religious scholar-jurists.

BCE: Abbreviation for "Before the Common Era". It replaces "BC" (Before Christ).

Burqa (Arabic): Veil worn by conservative Muslim women in traditional Muslim societies. The burqa is a voluminous head-covering with a mesh grid over the eyes.

Caliph: The anglicized term for *khalifa* or the religious leader of the *ummah* who assumed power after Prophet Muhammad's death.

Caliphate: The anglicized term for *khalafat* (caliphate) or rule by a *khalifa* (caliph).

CE: Abbreviation for Common Era; an alternative is AD (*Anno Domini*).

Day of Judgment: Muslims believe in the resurrection of the body and the Day of Judgment when God will reward or punish men according to their deeds. Surah 18:49.

Eid: Celebration or feast.

Fatwah (**Fatwa**, Persian, **Fatva** or **Fetva**): Authoritative religious decree pronounced by a *Mujtahid*. Can also be a formal legal opinion by a mufti, or canon lawyer, in answer to a question of a judge, *Khadi*, or private individual.

Fundamentalism: A term initially used for nineteenth century American Protestants who emphasized the literal interpretation and absolute inerrancy of the Bible as fundamental to Christianity. In the second half of the twentieth century, the Western mass media and scholarly community popularized the term to signify a religio-political movement of any religious group that is traditionalist, orthodox, conservative, radical, revolutionary, or zealous in its orientation.

Fundamentalist: The term has been popularized in the West to describe a member of any religion which believes in the literal interpretation of his/her infallible or inerrant scriptures. A fundamentalist believes that his faith is God-given, pure, and right.

Hamas: Acronym for a Palestinian revivalist movement, the Movement of Islamic Resistance (*Harakat al-Muqawamah al-Islamiyah*).

Hadith (Arabic): Prophet Muhammad's recorded sayings that were memorized and written down by members of his extended family and close companions and later compiled into various collections. The most popular of these compilations are the Sahih Bukhari and Sahih Muslim. It has been defined as "the story of a particular occurrence".

Hezbollah (Arabic, **Hisba Allah**): Literally, *The Party of Allah*, a term which was adopted by Shi'ite Islamist parties in Iran and Lebanon. In Iran, Hezbollah rose as a revolutionary movement in the late 1970s when it contributed to the downfall of the Shah and became a vanguard of the Islamic Republican Party.

Hijab (Persian, **Hejab**): Literally, *cover* or *veil*. This is one of many terms for the veil. Can also simply be the term used to describe the covering of women. A long veil that covers from head to foot is also called a *chador*. A simple wide scarf that only covers the head is called a *rusari* or a *maqne'a* if it refers to headgear that is tied under the chin and covers the shoulders revealing only the middle of the face.

Imam (Persian, **Emam**): Leader who stands in front (*amana*) of the congregation at prayer. He "who is in the forefront" and serves as a guide (notably for prayer). In Iran the term *Emam Jom'a* is used to specify the official leader of the Friday prayers and sermons as appointed by local religious authorities.

Islam (Arabic): Derived from the Arabic root *s*, *l*, *m* and literally means "submission" or "surrender". Those who believe in Islam are called Muslims. For Muslims, Islam is the final and perfect religion of God.

Islamic Jihad: Pro-Iranian Shi'ite group, founded in Lebanon in 1982.

Islamism: It can be viewed as the ideologization of Islam, whereby Islam becomes a comprehensive political ideology, the generic term for the phenomenon of Islamic authoritarian and revisionist revivals that are occurring around the Muslim world.

Islamist: A term used generically in the literature on Islamic revivalism to refer to any participant in an Islamic revival. However it is more specifically used for prominent Islamic revivalists who make a significant contribution to bringing about an Islamic revival. In propagating their perception of the "true Islam", all Islamic revivalists frequently, but not necessarily, promote the creation of an Islamic state by teaching, preaching, and/or writing, and, on rare occasions, even by the force of arms.

Isma'ili: A term which refers to that branch of Shi'ism which follows the leadership of Isma'il, a son of Ja'far al-Sadiq, and his descendants. The two largest Isma'ili branches in existence are the Dawoodi Bohra and the Agha Khan sects.

Jihad (Arabic): Literally, "to strive" or "to struggle." It means "to struggle in the way of God." A *jihad*, when used in the military sense, is to be fought against aggressors and tyrants. It also refers to the spiritual struggle waged against one's own baser instincts.

Jizya: Poll tax formerly levied on non-Muslim monotheists who were possessors of a scripture, the Peoples of the Book (*ahl al-kitab*, such as Christians and Jews).

Kurds, Kurdistan (Carduchi, Cyrth): In Iran, the Kurds live in the Northwest bordering Iraq. There are also a large number of Kurds in Iraq, Turkey, Russia, Syria, and spread throughout many other countries of the world. They speak two main languages.

Madrasah (Arabic): A school, college, seminary, or academy where the primary emphasis is on a broad spectrum of classical Islamic disciplines. Students also learn such subjects as Arabic, astronomy, mathematics, medicine, literature, philosophy, and metaphysics.

Masjid (French, **Mosque**): A place where one prostrates oneself (*sajadah*) five times a day in prayer. The masjid has been a center for social and political life. It is a court of law, a center of education, and a place where social services are provided to the poor.

Mongol Invasion: Mongol invaders of the Islamic world who wreaked destruction. According to some sources, the 'Abbasid Caliph sought the help of Chingiz Khan against the neighboring state of the Khwarizmi Shahs, and, for a short time, Baghdad was safe. But after the death of Chingiz (1241), his grandson Hulagu moved West. He defeated the Isma'ili assassins (1258), captured Baghdad and established the Ilkhanid dynasty, which ruled the Middle East from 1256 to 1353.

Muslim Brotherhood (al-Ikhwan al-Muslimin): A religio-political organization, founded in Egypt in 1928 by Hasan al-Banna. It is the first Islamic revivalist movement in modern times, which spread throughout the Islamic world and inspired similar groups in Egypt and elsewhere.

Orientalists: Non-Muslim Western scholars who have studied, researched, interpreted, and written about the Orient (the East), and non-Western cultures in a generalizing and/or disparaging manner. Islamists believe that orientalists have undermined the Qur'an's integrity, the Prophet Muhammad's personal character, and the authenticity of the Hadith. Many Muslims believe that Orientalists have distorted the concept of *jihad* to mean only aggressive holy war, have over-emphasized Islam's conditional permission of polygamy, the veiling and segregation of women and the second-class status of Muslim women, have exaggerated the barbarity of Islamic punishments, have overstated the schism, heresies, and fanaticism in Islam, and denigrated the perceived backwardness of Islamic culture.

Ottoman: The name given to the Turkish ruling dynasty, descended from Uthman (Turkish, Osman, d. 1324), which ruled over a multinational empire beginning in the fourteenth century. At its height (the early sixteenth century), the Ottoman Empire ruled much of the Middle East, the Balkan Peninsula, and a large part of Caucasus region.

Ottoman Empire (1350-1918): After the end of the Seljuk Dynasty the Ottomans absorbed all neighboring states and captured Constantinople in 1453 ending the Byzantine Empire. The Ottoman Empire was a major enemy of various Persian kings.

Pan-Islamism: Refers to the concept of political unification in the Islamic world to gain strength for defense against European imperialism. The ideas were propounded by Sayyid Jamal al-Din Afghani and Muhammad Abdu in the late nineteenth century. They advocated reforming Islam by borrowing Western technology, and administration.

People of the Book: People of the Book (*ahl al-Kitab* also called *dhimmi*) are adherents of monotheistic religions with revealed scriptures such as Christians and Jews.

Polygamy: Although permitted in Islam, the Holy Qur'an limited previously unlimited polygamy to a maximum of four wives. The Holy Qur'an states, "Marry women of your choice, two, three, or four; but if ye fear that ye shall not be able to deal justly [with them], then only one, or that which your hand possesses [a slave]" (Q. 4:3).

Qur'an (Arabic): Literally, "recitation". According to Muslims, the Holy Qur'an is the collection of revelations sent by God to Muhammad through the agency of the Archangel Gabriel, who recited them to the Prophet Muhammad in Arabic. The Prophet Muhammad, in turn, recited these revelations to his companions, who wrote them down and recited them to others. The name "Qur'an" was later given to the holy book containing these revelations. According to Muslims, the Qur'an is the last of all holy books.

Ramadan (Arabic): The ninth month of the Islamic calendar. The name *Ramadan* is derived from *ramz* which means "to burn". Therefore, fasting from dawn to dusk during the month of Ramadan is said to burn away one's sins. It was in the month of Ramadan that God revealed the Holy Qur'an to the Prophet Muhammad.

Revolutionary Islamists: Muslims who are revolutionary and often puritanical in their religious and political orientation. They usually believe in *ijtihad* and are extremely critical of Western ideas. They often have a passionate desire to establish an Islamic state based on the comprehensive and rigorous application of *shariah* law.

Secularism: A government that promotes secularism clearly separates the Church/Masjid from the State, refuses to act as the promoter and defender of a particular faith, and rejects religious ideas as the basis of its political legitimacy.

Secularists: Those who believe that religion should not enter into the conduct of government affairs or those who promote secularization.

Shah (Persian): Farsi term meaning *king*. In this book, the term, the *Shah* usually refers to Mohammad Reza Pahlavi, who was the last Pahlavi monarch overthrown in 1979.

Shamanism: The animistic religion of certain peoples of Asia and the Americas in which mediation between the visible and spirit worlds is affected by shamans.

Shariah (Arabic, also **Shari'a, Shari'at** or even **Charia**): From *shar*, "the path leading to the water hole" is God-given and a prescription for the right life in this world and for salvation in the world to come. The Qur'an is the basis of law for all Muslims, although various sects hold different interpretations. When no conclusive guidance was found in the Qur'an, the Hadith and Sunnah of the Prophet were consulted. There are six "correct" books of Sunni Traditions, compiled by al-Bukh ari, Muslim ibn al-Hajjaj, Abu Daud al-Sijistani, Muhammad ibn Isa al-Tirmidhi, Abu 'Abd Allah Ibn Maja, and Ahmad al-Nasa'i. Shi 'ites of the Twelver Usuli school of jurisprudence find their sources of law in the Qur'an and the Traditions (*Sunnah*), the statements, deeds, and tacit consent of the Prophet and the imams, as well as the consensus (*ijma'*) of the Shi'ite jurists, and the application of reason (*'aql*). In the absence of the Hidden Imam, the qualified scholars (*Mujtahid*) of the Twelver Shi'ites are permitted to legislate on the basis of *ijtihad*.

Shaykh (Arabic): Literally, "an elder" or "wise man". It is often used for tribal chieftains, members of the educated elite, Sufi teachers in brotherhoods, and generally for men enjoying positions of authority in a Muslim society; also written as *sheikh*.

Sufism: A body of Islamic beliefs and practices, which tends to promote the spiritual union between self and God through religious discipline and mystical experience.

Surah: A chapter in the Qur'an. There are 114 chapters arranged roughly according to length, beginning with the longest, except for *fatiha*, the "opener", which is a short Surah.

Taliban: A neo-fundamentalist movement recruited from students of mosque schools and madrasahs, who were organized into a military force and captured most of Afghanistan. The term literally means "students" or "disciples".

Ummah (Persian, **Oumma**): Medina community that included Muslims and Jews, but was subsequently the term for the Islamic community, the Islamic *nation*. The term is used generally to refer to the transnational community of all true believers.

Yazidi: A minor religious group in Iran, Iraq, and Syria which mixes Zoroastrianism, Christianity, Islam, Judaism and Manichaeism. They are over 100,000 Yazidis.

Zakat: Legal alms that all Shi'ite Muslims have to pay once a year at the same time as the *khoms* which is the annual taxation on excess revenue 20% and discovered profits (treasures or inheritances) that pay for the clergy and their expenses. These funds are collected by an authorized tax agent known as the *marja' al-taqlid*.

Glossary of Arabic and Persian Terms

'Adl (Arabic): Equity, fairness, justice, balance, and equilibrium. In Islam, it is often interpreted as justice, an attempt to give everyone his due and the hallmark of a devout Muslim. It is the fundamental value governing all social behavior and forming the basis of all social dealings and Islamic legal frameworks.

Al-Dunya (Arabic): Literally, "this world." Life in this world is contrasted with the life in *al-akhira* (the hereafter or the next world).

Allahu Akbar (Arabic): Literally, "God is Great". Many Muslims interpret it as "God is Most Great", or "God is the Greatest."

Ansar (Arabic): Plural of *nasir*, which means "helper" or "supporter". In Islamic history, the *ansar* were residents of Medina who gave asylum to Muhammad and actively supported him when he emigrated from Mecca in 622.

Bid' a (Arabic): Literally, "innovation". Some Islamists consider any innovation in the purity of Islamic beliefs and practices of the *aslaf* as *bid'a*, or an "unworthy innovation", and thus reprehensible.

Chardor or **Chador** (Persian): Literally, *tent* or portable dwelling. Also the traditional garment covering a woman from head to toe. In some Muslim countries this is obligatory. It is a *Farsi* (Persian language) term referring to an all-encompassing shapeless cloth for women that covers head to toe and only leaves face and hands uncovered. See also *Hijab*.

Dajjal, Al-: Literally, "False". Al-Dajjal is a false messiah or Anti-Christ who will come before the appearance of Christ to lead people into disbelief.

Da'wah (Arabic): The call, invitation, or summons to acknowledge religious truth and join a religious community, missionary movement, or religious organization; it can also mean missionary activity or the propagation of Islam.

Du'a (Arabic): Literally, "to call"; refers to the call of an individual to God in informal prayer. It can also be a prayer that is offered on special occasions, for example, at the birth of a child or a visit to a grave.

Dhimmi (Arabic): Derives from the Arabic term *dhimma* (an agreement of protection). It is often applied to free non-Muslims (especially 'People of the Book,' namely, Christians and Jews) who lived in Muslim countries and are guaranteed freedom of worship and government protection. *Dhimmi* pay no *zakah* but pay a tax called *jizya* for the state protection guaranteed them and for not bearing the responsibility of defending the *dar al-Islam* in times of war.

Dar al-Harb: Literally, *Abode of War*; part of the world where Islam does not prevail.

Dar al-Islam: Literally, *Abode of Islam;* defines that part of the world ruled by a Muslim and where the edicts of Islam have been fully promulgated.

Darwish (Persian, **Darvish**, **Dervish**): From the word for *poor* which refers to the member of a Sufi brotherhood; in English, *dervish*. One who renounces worldly goods for the sake of a mystical contemplation of existence and compassion for others.

Da'wah: Literally, *call*. Appeal to conversion by missionary activity instead of *jihad*.

Dhikr (Persian, **Zikr**): Literally, *remembrance*. In Sufism, *dhikr* is the remembrance of God, his commands, death, and the Day of Judgment.

Du'a: The *prayer of the heart*. Can also refer to any individual, informal prayer offered on special occasions, e.g., at the birth of a child or visit to a grave.

Emir: From the Arabic *amara*, meaning, "To command." It is the title of a military commander, a nobleman, chief, prince, and ruler. Amir is also a common name.

Feqh (Arabic, **Fiqh**): Practical jurisprudence or *understanding* (comprehension). The science of knowledge and interpretation of law, both civil and religious, it encompasses all branches of Islamic studies.

Hadd (Persian, **Hudd**; plural, **Hudud**): Mandatory punishments imposed in classical Islamic law in cases of adultery, fornication, and false accusation of adultery, as well as for theft, highway robbery, apostasy, and drunkenness.

Hajj (Arabic): Literally, "pilgrimage". Adult Muslims of sound mind and body have been enjoined to undertake the *hajj*, the spiritual journey to Mecca, once in their lifetime, if they can afford it. *Hajj* is the Fifth Pillar of Islam and is formally undertaken between the seventh and tenth days of *dhul-Hajj*, the last month in the Islamic calendar.

Hajji (Arabic): A pilgrim to Mecca who has performed the *hajj* during the annual season; also a title assumed by someone who has successfully completed the pilgrimage.

Halal: Religiously lawful. Contrasted by something which is *haram*; unlawful.

Haram: Religiously unlawful. Contrasted by something this is *hallal*, or lawful.

Houri: A beautiful, paradisiacal virgin.

'Ibadat: Refers to God's commands concerning worship and ritual.

Iblis: Devil (*shaytan*) and a fallen angel (or rebellious *jinn*) who refused to bow before Adam and tempted Eve to eat from the tree of immortality; therefore, was expelled from paradise and given the power to lead astray all who are not true servants of God.

Ijma (Arabic): Literally, "agreement", unanimity, or consensus. It is considered to be the third source of Islamic law. The consensus can be that of the first generation of Muslims, of al-Ghazali, the great theologian-jurist of Medieval era of Islam, the *ummah* scattered all over the world, or even an entire nation.

Ijtihad (Persian, **Ejtehad**): Literally, *exertion* or independent judgment in the interpretation of law that is practiced by a *Mujtahid* to clarify religious law through using the principles of jurisprudence (*osul al-feqh*). The effort of interpretation and the exercise of personal reasoning and private judgment or "informed opinion" (*ra'y*) and reasoning by analogy (*qiyas*) in questions of Shari'ah not expressly explained in the Qur'an and Hadith. An example of this is the prohibition of all intoxicants, not just wine, mentioned in the Qur'an. Shi'ites have always accepted the *ijtihad* of qualified doctors (*Mujtahid*).

Ijtihad (Arabic): The word *ijtihad* derives from the same Arabic root as *jihad* and literally means "to exert oneself". Technically, *ijtihad* implies a Muslim jurist exercising his personal, independent reasoning, knowledge, and judgment to give his opinion on a legal issue where there is no specific order in the Qur'an. The term now commonly implies the independent interpretation or reinterpretation of Islamic laws.

Kafir, al-: Literally, *unbeliever*. A *kafir* (adjective form of one who practices *kufr*) is an infidel, one who denies the existence of God or gives partners to God (a polytheist). The term was first applied to unbelieving Meccans who rejected Muhammad's message and denounced him. The term has also been used for non-Muslims, enemies of Islam, and Muslims as well as for apostates, polytheists, infidels, hypocrites, and non-practicing Muslims.

Kalam (Arabic): Literally, "speech" or "dialect." It is applied to Islamic theology, which is the study of God's words, the subject that attempts to give rational proofs for religious beliefs, deals with the problems of God's oneness, His attributes and human free will and self-determination, among other philosophical issues.

Khalifa: Office of the *Khalifah* (Caliph): literally, *deputy* (of God's Prophet).

Madrasah: Literally, *place of study*. It is a general name for the secondary school that functions as a theological seminary, law school, and a mosque that trains religious functionaries in Islamic sciences and law.

Mahdi (Arabic): Literally, "the divinely guided one", the "expected deliverer", the "redeemer", or the "savior". The doctrine of the Mahdi first originated in Shi'ism and their belief that the hidden Twelfth Imam sent by God to establish the "true Islam".

Muezzin (Mu'adhdhin): Term used to describe an Islamic functionary who delivers the call for prayer from either a minaret or the door of a mosque.

Mufti (Arabic): Title given to an expert on Islamic theology and jurisprudence; a *mufti* might also claim the authority to not only interpret Islamic law but also to issue a *fatwa*.

Qadi (Khadi, Kazi, Qadhi): Literally, "judge". He should be a person of good reputation who is versed in Islamic jurisprudence and acts as a judge in civil and criminal matters. Also the term is used to describe a court that is directed by a Qadi, as in a "Qadi Court".

Sadaqah (Arabic): The voluntary charitable contribution of money or food for the sake of acquiring merit with Allah. It is often criticized by Sunni Fundamentalists.

Shaykh (English, **Sheikh**): Literally, *Old Man*. In pre-Islamic times the title of a Bedouin chief who earned dignity through bravery, generosity, and leadership of his tribe in warfare. In Africa the term is often used for tribal chieftains, members of the educated elite, Sufi teachers in brotherhoods, and generally for men enjoying positions of authority in a Muslim society.

Shi'ism: The sect of the partisans of 'Ali developed a doctrinal basis only gradually. The party began as an Arab political movement that was strongly supported by non-Arab converts and eventually developed into a sect.

Shirk: Literally, *polytheism*. It is an unforgivable sin. Islam espouses a strict monotheism that rejects "giving partners to God."

Sirat: A narrow bridge across hell which souls must cross, according to Hadith.

Sunnah (Arabic): In Islam it is understood as Prophet Muhammad's "trodden path", "way", "custom", or "tradition". The Sunnah comprising the Prophet's sayings and deeds complements the Holy Qur'an as the major source of Islamic faith and practice.

Taqlid: Following a senior religious authority in matters of Islamic law.

Ta'asob: Literally, *fanaticism*. A person who is a fanatic is viewed favorably because they have a strongly motivated commitment.

Tawhid (Arabic): Signifies the unity and oneness of God and His sovereignty. This is the most important tenet of Islam and it is the "frame" for all other theological formulations.

'Ulema (Arabic, **Ulama**): Collective term for the doctors of Islamic sciences. An 'alim (plural, *ulema*) is "one who possesses the quality of *'ilm*, knowledge, or learning, of the Islamic traditions and the resultant canon law and theology". An *'alim* is the product of a religious institution of higher education. A term for mid-ranking (to high ranking) clerics.

Waqf (Arabic, plural, **auqaf**): An Arabic term for an Islamic endowment (usually of landed property) established for pious charitable purposes.

Glossary of Names and Events

'Abbasid Caliphate (749–1258): The dynasty that succeeded the Umayyad Caliphate. The revolution to destroy the Umayyads was led by the Khorasanian leader Abu Muslim (d. 755). He captured Marv in 747. The third and last caliphates, originating from the family of Muhammad's uncle; the Abbasid capital was Baghdad, 750-1258.

'Abd Al-Wahhab, Muhammad Ibn (1703–1792): 'Abd al-Wahhab studied theology with his father and then traveled widely in Arabia, Iran, and Iraq, before going to Medina to study Islamic law and theology. He became active in the fight against British colonial rule in Egypt and became the founder of the movement known as "Wahhabism".

Abu Bakr (573–639): First of the "Rightly Guided Caliphs" and father of 'Aisha, the favorite wife of Muhammad. He was one of the earliest converts to Islam. Prophet Muhammad's close companion (r. 632–639).

Abu Hanifah, Al-Num'Man Ibn Thabit (ca. 700–767): Great Sunni jurist and founder of the Hanafi school of law, the largest of four orthodox schools and the dominant school in the Ottoman Empire (1281–1924). He was born in Kufah and died in a Baghdad prison because he was a supporter of a revolt.

'Ali Ibn Abu Talib (r. 656–661): The fourth of the Rightly Guided Caliphs and the first imam of Shi'ite Islam. He was a cousin of Muhammad and his son-in-law, after his marriage to Fatimah. First convert after Khadija, Muhammad's wife. The partisans of 'Ali (shi'atu 'ali) maintained that 'Ali had a divine right to succession, to be continued through his sons Hasan and Hoseyn (Hussein), and repudiated the first three Sunni Caliphs as usurpers. 'Ali moved his capital to Kufah. He was assassinated by a Kharajite during Morning Prayer in 661. His tomb in Najaf, in present-day Iraq, is one of the most important places of Shi'ite pilgrimage. He is considered by the Shia (along with his descendants) to be the only legitimate ruler of the Muslim world.

Agha Khan: Imam of the Nizari branch of the Isma'ili' s. Iranian Qajar rulers at times bestowed this title on notables. In 1818 Fath 'Ali Shah gave the title Agha Khan I to Abu al-Hasan 'Ali Shah Mahallati (1800–1881), governor of Kerman province. He fled Iran after an unsuccessful revolt in 1841 and settled in Bombay.

Ahmadis: an offshoot of Sunni Islam that was founded by Mirza Ghulam Ahmad (1837–1908), who was born in a village in the Indian Punjab called Qadian. Thus, Ahmadis are also called Quadianis. Other Muslims view them as having moved beyond the pale of Islam because of some of their beliefs.

'Aisha (613–678): "Mother of the Believers" (*Umm al-Mu'minin*), the favorite wife of the Prophet Muhammad and daughter of Abu Bakr. She was given in marriage to Muhammad when she was six years old after his wife Khadija died, but the marriage was consummated a number of years later.

Al-Ansari, Abd Allah (1005–1089): Islamic theologian, commentator on the Qur'an, mystic from Herat, and author of a commentary on Sufi theory. He wrote both in Arabic and Persian; his Arabic collection is said to contain more than 6,000 couplets, and his Persian poetry is said to amount to about 14,000 verses.

Al-Farabi, Abu Nasr (ca. 870–950): One of the greatest Muslim philosophers who published in the fields of logic, politics, ethics, natural science, psychology, mathematics, music theory, and other subjects. He was of Turkic origin, born in Farab, Turkestan, and studied in Baghdad and other cities of the Islamic world and finally settled in Aleppo, Syria.

Al-Ghazali, Abu Hamid Muhammad (1058–1111): Jurist of the Shafi'ite school, philosopher, theologian, mystic, and one of the most influential thinkers. He was born at Tus, near the present city of Mashhad in eastern Iran and educated in Nishapur. He was instrumental in reconciling Sufism with orthodox Islam.

Badr, Battle of: First military victory of the Muslim community of Medina against a superior force of Meccans in the year 624.

Bedouin: Nomadic Arabs who originally inhabited desert areas of the Middle East. Less than 2% of the Arab World today is inhabited by Bedouins (most of whom are Muslim).

Ibn Khaldun, 'Abd Al Rahman Ibn Muhammad (1332–1406): Arab philosopher of history. He was born in Tunis where he worked as a secretary. In Fez, he was the chief judge. In Oran, he wrote the famous *Muqaddima* (*Prolegomena*), the introduction to his book on the origins of the Arabs, Berbers, and Persians.

ibn Sina, Abu 'Ali Al-Husain ibn 'abd Allah (Avicenna), 980–1037: Born near Bukhara of Persian parents, Ibn Sina traveled to study with famous doctors. "At the age of ten years, he was a perfect master of the Qur'an and general literature, and had attained a certain degree of information in dogmatic theology, the Indian calculus (arithmetic), and algebra. . . . In the sixteenth year of his age, physicians on the highest eminence came to read, under his tuition the works which treat of the different branches of medicine and learn from him those modes of treatment which he had discovered by his practice" (Ibn Khallikan, I, 440). Known in the West as Avicenna, he was a philosopher, physician and author of the *al-qanun fi tibb* (Canon of medicine) which made him famous in Europe.

Ibn Taymiyyah, Taqui Al-Din (1263–1328 CE): A Syrian-born theologian-jurist who spent his life sharing his teachings in puritanical writings and sermons. He rejected *taqlid* (legal conformity), and *ijma* (consensus), insisting upon the literal interpretation of the Qur'an and Sunnah.

Jama'at-I Islami: Name of a Pakistani political organization founded by Maulana Abu'l-'ala Mawdudi (1903–1979) in 1941 that advocates the establishment of an Islamic state patterned after the early Islamic community. It is pan-Islamic and looks at the Muslim community as one nation (*ummah*) and rejects nationalism as contrary to Islam.

Jesus (Arabic, **Isa**): Jesus is recognized in Islam as a prophet (19:30, 34), messenger (4:171), messiah, and the only creature, besides Adam, who has no father (3:52, 59). He is an apostle, but not God (5:72). Many Persian and Arab Christians reject the name *Isa*.

Khadija (d. 619): First wife of the Prophet Muhammad.

Kharijites (Khawardij): Originally followers of Caliph 'Ali who deserted him when he agreed to arbitration with the Caliph over a dispute with Mu'awiyah at Adhruh. These rebels turned against 'Ali and became a source of rebellions during the Umayyad and early 'Abbasid periods.

Khomeini, Ayatollah Ruhollah Al-Musavi al (1900–1989): Born in Khomeyn, a town about 270 kilometers south of Tehran, Khomeini received a traditional madrassah education until 1922. In 1944, he published a book entitled *Kashf al-Asrar* (*Discovery of Secrets*) in which he condemned the government of Rida Shah, stated that a monarchy should be limited by the provisions of the Shari'a as interpreted by mujtahids and hinted that government by mujtahids was preferable. During the leadership of Ayatollah Burujirdi, Khomeini remained quiet politically (in keeping with Burujirdi's leadership). But from about 1960 onwards, when Burujirdi's himself took a more politically active line (and particularly after Burujirdi's death) Khomeini's lectures at Qom on ethics began to be openly critical of the government. Arrested 25 January, 1963, 5 June 1963, and 5 November, 1963; arrested and exile to Bursa, Turkey, in November 1964. In the Constitution inaugurated in December of 1979, he became the *Rahbar* (Leader) of the Revolution. After living in Qom on his return, he moved to Jamaran, near Teheran.

Persia: The name given Iran by the ancient Greeks, Iran was called Persia until 1935, when the name was changed by Reza Khan (r. 1921–1941).

Qutb, Sayyid (1906–1966): Qutb was a leading member of the Muslim Brotherhood who was eventually disowned by that group and who went on to become one of the "Founding Fathers" of the modern Islamist movement.

Al-Razi, Abu Bakr (865–925): Physician, philosopher, and universal thinker from Persia. Al-Razi was known in Medieval Europe as *Rhazes*. He published works on various diseases and their symptoms which were translated into Latin, Greek, and other European languages. His first medical book, dedicated to the Samanid Prince al-Mansur (*kitab al-mansuri*), established him as a medical authority.

Rumi, Jalal Al-din, Maulana (1207–1273): Considered by many the greatest of all mystical Sufi poets, called Shaykh al-Akbar, the *Great Master* (or *Mawlana*, by his supporters. Born in Balkh, in present-day Afghanistan, he moved with his father to Konya in Turkey, called Rum at the time; hence his name Rumi.

Shi'a (Arabic): Members of this minority sect are "partisans" or "followers" of 'Ali ibn-i-Abu Talib and believe that God and Muhammad wanted 'Ali to be Islam's first caliph. They, like the Sunnis, believe in the fundamentals of Islam, the Holy Qur'an, the five pillars, Muhammad's Hadith, and Sirah.

Sulayman: *Suleiman*, Solomon. Wise Jewish King mentioned in the Bible and Qur'an.

Sufis: The term Sufi was derived from early Muslim ascetics and pious mystics who wore simple clothes made out of suf (coarse wool). Sufis became lax in their observance of the *shariah* and devoted their lives to meditation and proselytization. They emphasize the spiritual rather than the literal interpretation of the Holy Qur'an and the Sunnah.

Sunni (Arabic): Refers to the majority Islamic sect (approximately 80% of the Muslim world) as well as to the members of that sect. Sunnis and Shi'a follow the Sunnah or "the way", "the path", or the "road' shown by Prophet Muhammad.

Tijaniya: A Sufi movement that arose in West Africa in the eighteenth century that was named after the founder, Ahmad al-Tijani.

Umayyad: Descendants of Umayyah within the Quraish tribe. They were one of the most influential families at the time of Muhammad and established the first hereditary caliphate in 661.

Wahhabis: Followers of Muhammad ibn Abd Al Wahhab (1703–1792). They belong to the Hanbali School of jurisprudence and are now concentrated in Saudi Arabia and Qatar, where royal families in both Kingdoms have adopted Wahhabism. Wahhabis dislike this term assigned to them by Westerners, claiming that the term *Wahhabi* implies that they venerated Muhammad ibn Abd al-Wahhab. In actuality, they venerate no one but God. They prefer to be known as *al-Muwahhidum,* which literally means monotheists.

Selected Bibliography

Aba-Namay, Rasheed, "The Recent Constitutional Reforms in Saudi Arabia", *The International and Comparative Law Quarterly*, 42 (1993): 295–331.

Abashiya, Chris Shu'aibu and Ayuba Jalaba Ulea, *Christianity and Islam: A Plea for Understanding and Tolerance*, Jos, Nigeria: Holman Limited, 1991.

Abd-el-Kader, Deina, *Social Justice in Islam*, Herndon, VA: International Institute of Islamic Thought, 2000.

Al-Abdin, al-Tayib Zein, "Zakat and Alleviation of Poverty in the Muslim World", *Hamdard Islamicus*, 20 (1997): 65–82.

Aboul-Enin, Youssef H., and Sherifa Zuhur, *Islamic Rulings on Warfare*, Carlisle, PA: Strategic Studies Institute Publishing, 2004.

Abu-Arqub, Mamoun, and Isabel Phillips, *A Brief History of Humanitarianism in the Muslim World*, Birmingham, UK: Islamic Relief Worldwide, 2009.

Abu-Lughod, Lila, *Veiled Sentiments: Honor and Piety in a Bedouin Society*, Berkeley: University of California Press, 2004.

Abu-Nimer, Muhammad, "Conflict Resolution in an Islamic Context: Some Contextual Questions", *Peace and Change*, 21 (1996): 22–40.

— *Nonviolence and Peace Building in Islam: Theory and Practice*, Gainesville: University Press of Florida, 2003.

Abu-Sinnah, Ahmad Fahim, "*Nazariyyat al-Haqq* [Theory of Rights]", In *Al-Fiqh al-Islami*, ed. Muhammad Tawfiq 'Uwaydah, 175–235, Cairo: Matabi'al-Ahram al-Tijariyyah, 1971.

Accad, Fouad Elias, *Building Bridges: Christianity and Islam*, Colorado Springs, CO: Navpress, 1997.

Adas, Emin B., "The Making of Entrepreneurial Islam and the Islamic Spirit of Capitalism", *Journal for Cultural Research*, 10, no. 2 (2006): 113–137.

Adeney, Miriam, *Daughters of Islam: Building Bridges with Muslim Women*, Downers Grove, IL: Intervarsity Press, 2002.

Afkhami, Mahnaz, and Haleh Vaziri, *Claiming Our Rights: A Manual for Women's Human Rights Education in Muslim Societies*, Bethesda, MD: Sisterhood Is Global Institute, 1996.

Afshari, Reza, "Egalitarian Islam and Misogynist Islamic Tradition: A Critique of the Feminist Reinterpretation of Islamic History and Heritage", *Critique: Journal of Critical Studies of Iran and the Middle East*, 4 (1994): 13–34.

Aftab, Safiya, Naved Hamid, and Safdar Parvez, *Poverty in Pakistan: Issues, Causes, and Institutional Responses*, Islamabad, Pakistan: Asian Development Bank, 2002.

Aghnides, Nicolas P., *Mohammedan Theories of Finance*, Lahore, Pakistan: Premier Book House, 1961.

Agwan, A.R., *The Environmental Concern of Islam*, New Delhi: Institute of Objective Studies, 1992.

Ahmad, Akutaruddin, *Islam and the Environmental Crisis*, London: Ta-Ha Publishers, 1997.

Ahmad, Ali, "Islamic Water Law as an Antidote for Maintaining Water Quality", *University of Denver Water Law Review*, 2 (1999): 170–188.

Ahmad, Fauzia, "Rethinking Muslim Women and the Veil: Challenging Historical and Modern Stereotypes", *The American Journal of Islamic Social Sciences*, 19 (2002): 118–123.

Ahmad, Hazrat Mirza Tahir, *Murder in the Name of Allah*, trans. Syed Barakat Ahmad, Cambridge: The Lutterworth Press, 1990.

Ahmad, Imad-ad-Dean, *Female Genital Mutilation: An Islamic Perspective*, Bethesda, MD: Minaret of Freedom Institute, 2000.

— The Islamic View of Adoption and Caring for Homeless Children", In *Adoption Fact Book III*, 245–46, Washington, DC: National Council for Adoption, 1999.

Ahmad, Leila, *Women and Gender in Islam: Historical Roots of a Modern Debate*, New Haven, CT: Yale University Press, 1992.

Ahmad, Shaikh Mahmud, *Social Justice in Islam*, Lahore, Pakistan: Institute of Islamic Culture, 1975.

Ahmed, Akbar, *Post-Modernism in Islam: Predicament and Promise*, New York: Routledge Press, 1992.

Akiner, Shirin, *Political and Economic Trends in Central Asia*, London: British Academic Press, 1994.

Akthar, Shabbir, *The Final Imperative: An Islamic Theology of Liberation*, London: Bellew Publishing, 1991.

Ali, Ayaan Hirsi, *The Caged Virgin: An Emancipation Proclamation for Women and Islam*, New York: Free Press, 2006.

Ali, Basheer M., "Fatwa and War: On the Allegiance of the American Muslim Soldiers in the Aftermath of September 11th", *Islamic Law and Society*, 11 (2004): 78–116.

Ali, Keicia, *Sexual Ethics and Islam*, Oxford: One World Publications, 2006.

Ali, Moulavi Chiragh, "War and Peace: Popular Jihad", In *Modernist and Fundamentalist Debates in Islam*, ed.Mansour Moaddel and Kamran Talattof, 71–94, New York: Palgrave MacMillan, 2002.

Ali, Shamsa, *A Treatise on Women's Rights*, Lahore, Pakistan: Qur'anic Society, 1996.

Ali, Souad T., *A Religion, Not a State: Ali Abd al-Raziq's Islamic Justification of Political Secularism*, Salt Lake City: University of Utah Press, 2009.

Ali, Syed Muhammad, *The Position of Women in Islam: A Progressive View*, New York: New York University Press, 2004.

Ali, Yusuf, The *Holy Qur'an: English Translation of the Meanings and Commentary*, Medina, Saudi Arabia: King Fahd, 1413 A.H.

Al-Alwani, Taha Jabir, *The Ethics of Disagreement in Islam*, Herndon, VA: International Institute of Islamic Thought, 1993.

Amirahmadi, Hooshgang, *Revolution and Economic Transition: the Iranian Experience*, Albany: State University of New York Press, 1990.

An-Naim, 'Abdullah Ahmed and Francis M. Deng, *Human Rights in Africa: Cross Cultural Perspectives*, Washington, DC: Brookings Institute, 1990.

Anees, Munawar A., "Islamic Values and Western Science: A Case Study of

Reproductive Biology", In *The Touch of Midas: Science, Values and Environment in Islam and the West*, ed. Ziauddin Sardar, 91–120, Dover, NH: Manchester University Press, 1984.

— "Salvation and Suicide: What Does Islamic Theology Say?" *Dialog: A Journal of Theology*, 45 (2006): 275–79.

— Syed Z. Abedin and Ziauddin Sardar, *Christian-Muslim Relations: Yesterday, Today, Tomorrow*, London: Grey Seal Books, 1991.

Anzulovic, Branimir, *Heavenly Serbia: From Myth to Genocide*, New York: New York University Press, 1999.

Aras, Bulent, "Turkish Islam's Moderate Face", *Middle East Quarterly*, 5 (1998): 23–30.

Armanini, A.J., *Politics and Economics of Central Asia*, New York: Novinka Books, 2002.

Armour, Rollin, *Islam, Christianity and the West: A Troubled History*, Maryknoll, NY: Orbis Books, 2002.

Armstrong, Karen, *The Battle for God: Fundamentalism in Judaism, Christianity and Islam*, London: Harper Collins, 2000.

— *Muhammad: A Biography of the Prophet*, San Francisco: Harper San Francisco, 1992.

Armstrong, Sally, *Veiled Threat: The Hidden Power of the Women of Afghanistan*, New York: Four Walls Eight Windows, 2002.

Ascha, Ghassan, *Du statut inférieur de la femme en Islam*, Paris: L'Harmattan, 1987.

Ashgar, Muzaffar Iqbal, *Islam and Science*, Burlington, VT: Ashgate Publishers, 2002.

El-Ashker, Ahmad, *The Islamic Business Enterprise*, London: Croom Helm, 1987.

Ashraf, Imran, and Abu Nasir, "Zakat as a Social Safety Net: Exploring the Impact on Household Welfare in Pakistan", *Pakistan Economic and Social Review*, 42 (2004): 87–102.

Aslan, Reza, *No God but God*, New York: Random House, 2005.

Asmal, Abdul Cader, and Mohammed Asmal, "An Islamic Perspective", In *Consumption, Population, and Sustainability: Perspectives from Science and Religion*, ed. Audrey Chapman, Rodney Peterson, and Barbara Smith-Moran, 157–165, Washington, DC: Island Press, 2000.

Ateek, Naim Stifan, *Justice and Only Justice: A Palestinian Theology of Liberation*, Maryknoll, NY: Orbis Books, 1989.

Al-Attas, Syed Muhammad Naquib, *Islam, Secularism, and the Philosophy of the Future*, London: Mansell, 1985.

Al-Awadi, Hesham, *In Pursuit of Legitimacy: The Muslim Brothers and Mubarak, 1982–2000*, London: Tauris Academic Studies, 2005.

Al-'Awwa, Muhammad S., *Punishment in Islamic Law*, Indianapolis: American Trust Publications, 1982.

Ayoub, Mohammed, "Deciphering Islam's Multiple Voices", *Middle East Policy*, 12 (2005): 79–90.

Ayoub, Mahmoud, "Islam and Christianity: Between Tolerance and Acceptance", *Islam and Christian-Muslim Relations*, 2 (1991): 171–81.

— "Martyrdom in Christianity and Islam", In *Religious Resurgence: Contemporary Cases in Islam, Christianity, and Judaism*, ed. R.T. Antoun and M.E. Hegland, 67–77, Syracuse, NY: Syracuse University Press, 1987.

— *A Muslim View of Christianity: Essays on Dialogue*, Maryknoll, NY: Orbis Books, 2007.

Ba Kader, Abou Bakr Ahmed, *Environmental Protection in Islam*, Washington, DC: Island Press, 1995.

Ba-Yunus, Ilyas and Kassim Kone, *Muslims in the United States*, Westport, CT: Greenwood Press, 2006.

Badran, Margot, *Feminism and Islam: Secular and Religious Convergences*, Oxford: One World Publications, 2009.

Bahrani, Zaynab, *Rituals of War: The Body and Violence in Mesopotamia*, New York: Zone Books, 2008.

Bailey, Betty Jane and J. Martin Bailey, *Who Are the Christians in the Middle East?* Grand Rapids, MI: Eerdmans Publishing, 2003.

Balakian, Peter, *Black Dog of Fate: An American Son Discovers His Armenian Past*, New York: Doubleday Books, 1998.

Banuazizi, Ali and Myron Weiner, *The State, Religion, and Ethnic Politics: Afghanistan, Iran, and Pakistan*, Syracuse, NY: Syracuse University Press, 1986.

Barazangi, Nimat Hafez, *Women's Identity and the Qur'an: A New Reading*, Gainesville: University Press of Florida, 2004.

— M. Raquibuz Zaman, and Omar Afzal, eds, *Islamic Identity and the Struggle for Justice*, Gainesville: University Press of Florida, 1996.

Bargach, Jamilah, "Adoption and Wardship (Kafala) in Morocco", *Recht Van De Islam*, 18 (2001): 77–98.

— *Orphans of Islam: Family, Abandonment, and Secret Adoption in Morocco*, Lanham, MD: Rowman and Littlefield, 2002.

Baumgartner, Winfried, *Imperialism: The Idea and Reality of British and French Colonial Expansion, 1880–1914*, New York: Oxford University Press, 1982.

Bayat, Asef, "A Women's Non-Movement: What it Means to be a Muslim Activist in an Islamic State", *Comparative Studies of South Asia, Africa, and the Middle East*, 27 (2007): 160–172.

Bayman, Henry, *The Secret of Islam: Love and Law in the Religion of Ethics*, Berkeley, CA: North Atlantic Books, 2003.

Bayoumi, Moustafa, *How Does It Feel to Be A Problem? Being Young and Arab in America*, New York: Penguin Books, 2008.

Bennett, Clinton and Geros Kunkel, "The Concept of Violence, War, and Jihad in Islam", *Dialogue and Alliance*, 18 (2004): 31–51.

Benthall, Jonathan, "Islamic Aid in a North Malian Enclave", *Anthropology Today*, 22 (2006): 19–21.

Berman, Ian, and Paul Michael Wihbey, "The New Water Politics of the Middle East", *Strategic Review*, 27 (1999): 45–52.

Berryman, Phillip, *The Religious Roots of Rebellion: Christians in Central American Revolutions*, Maryknoll, NY: Orbis Books, 1984.

Beverley, James A., "Islam a Religion of Peace?" *Christianity Today*, 46 (2002): 32–42.

Bielefeldt, Heiner, "Muslim Voices in the Human Rights Debate", *Human Rights Quarterly*, 17 (1995): 587–617.

Binder, Leonard, *Islamic Liberalism: A Critique of Development Ideologies*, Chicago: University of Chicago Press, 1988.

Blackburn, Robin, "The Old World Background to European Colonial Slavery", *The William and Mary Quarterly*, 54, no., 1 (1997): 65–102.

Blyden, Edward, *Christianity, Islam, and the Negro Race*, Edinburgh: Edinburgh University Press, 1887.

Bonner, Michael, "The *Kitab Al-Kasb* Attributed to Al-Shaybani: Poverty, Surplus, and the Circulation of Wealth", *Journal of the American Oriental Society*, 121, no. 3 (2001): 410–427.

— "Poverty and Economics in the Qur'an", *Journal of Interdisciplinary History*, 35, no. 3 (2005): 391–406.

Bourdieu, Pierre, *Sociology as a Martial Art: Political Writings*, ed. Gisele Sapiro, New York: The New Press, 2010.

Boyle, Elizabeth Herger, *Female Genital Cutting: A Myth-Making Process*, New York: Palgrave McMillan, 2007.

Bradley, John R., "Iran's Ethnic Tinderbox", *Washington Quarterly*, 30 (2006): 181–190.

Brockopp, Jonathan, ed., *Islamic Ethics of Life: Abortion, War, and Euthanasia*, Columbia, S.C: University of South Carolina Press, 2003.

Brown, Nathan J. and Amr Hamzawy, *Between Religion and Politics*, Washington, DC: Carnegie Endowment for International Peace, 2010.

Bucar, Elizabeth M. and Barbara Barnett, eds, *Does Human Rights Need God?* Grand Rapids, MI: Eerdmans Publishers, 2005.

Buckley, Mary, ed., *Post-Soviet Women: From the Baltic to Central Asia*, New York: Cambridge University Press, 1997.

Bullough, Vern S., "Before Homosexuality in the Arab-Islamic World", *American Historical Review*, 111 (2006): 1286–1296.

Burke, Edmund and Ira M. Lapidus, *Islam, Politics and Social Movements*, Berkeley: University of California Press, 1988.

Burrell, R. Michael, *Islamic Fundamentalism*, London: Royal Asiatic Society, 1989.

Cabestrero, Teofilo, *Blood of the Innocents*, Maryknoll, NY: Orbis Books, 1985.

Caetura, Linda Brandi, ed., *Voices of American Muslims*, New York: Hippocrene Books, 2005.

Çapan, Ergün, *Terror and Suicide Attacks: An Islamic Perspective*, trans. Nagihan Haliloğlu and Mükerrem Faniküçükmehmetoglu, Somerset, NJ: The Light, 2004.

Carmody, Denise Lardner, *Women and World Religions*, Englewood Cliffs, NJ: Prentice Hall, 1989.

Cavdar, Ganze, "Islamist Moderation and the Resilience of Gender: Turkey's Persistent Paradox", *Totalitarian Movements and Political Religions*, 11 (2012): 341–357.

Chapra, M. Umar, "Is It Necessary to Have Islamic Economics?" *The Journal of Socio-Economics*, 29 (2000): 21–37.

Charnay, Jean-Paul, *Islamic Culture and Socio-Economic Change*, Leiden, the Netherlands: E.J. Brill, 1971.

Chittick, William, "God Surrounds All Things: An Islamic Perspective on the Environment", *The World and I*, 1 (1986): 671–78.

Choudhury, Masudul Alam, *The Principles of Islamic Political Economy*, London: MacMillan Publishers, 1992.

Choudhury, A.B.M. Sultanul Alam, "The Problem of Representation in the Muslim Law of Inheritance", *Islamic Studies*, 3 (1964): 375–391.

Christian Mission and Islamic Da'wah: Proceedings of the Chambesy Dialogue Consultation, London: Islamic Foundation, 1982.

Clarence-Smith, William Gervase, *Islam and the Abolition of Slavery*, New York: Oxford University Press, 2006.

Clark, Elizabeth, and Herbert Richardson, *Women and Religion: A Feminist Sourcebook of Christian Thought*, New York: Harper and Row, 1977.

Classen, Albert, *The Medieval Chastity Belt: A Myth-Making Process*, New York: Palgrave MacMillan, 2007.

Cook, David, *Understanding Jihad*, Los Angeles: University of California Press, 2005.

Cook, M.A., *Commanding Right and Forbidding the Wrong in Islamic Thought*, Cambridge: Cambridge University Press, 2000.

Coward, Harold and Gordon S. Smith, eds, *Religion and Peace building*, Ithaca: State University of New York Press, 2004.

Cragg, Kenneth, *Counsels in Contemporary Islam*, Edinburgh: Edinburgh University Press, 1965.

Culver, Jonathan Edward, "The Ishmael Promises: A Bridge for Mutual Respect", In *Muslim and Christian Reflections on Peace: Divine and Human Dimensions*, ed. J. Dudley Woodberry, Osman Zumrut, and Mustafa Koylu, 67–80, Lanham, MD: University Press of America, 2005.

Curiel, Jonathan, *Al'America: Travels Through America's Arab and Islamic Roots*, New York: New Press, 2008.

Dadrian, Vahakn N., *Warrant for Genocide: Key Elements of Turko-Armenian Conflict*, New Brunswick, NJ: Transaction Publishers, 1999.

Dakake, David, "The Myth of Militant Islam", in *Islam, Fundamentalism, and the Betrayal of Tradition: Essays by Western Muslim Scholars*, ed. Joseph E.B. Lumbard, 3–38, Indianapolis, IN: World Wisdom Press, 2004.

Daniels, Timothy, *Islamic Spectrum in Java*, Surrey, UK: Ashgate Publishing, 2009.

Davidson, Lawrence, *Islamic Fundamentalism: An Introduction*, Westport, CT: Greenwood Press, 2003.

Davies, Meryl Wynn and Ziauddin Sardur, *Distorted Imagination: Lessons from the Rushdie Affair*, London: Grey Seal Books, 1990.

Davis, Robert C., *Christian Slaves, Muslim Masters: White Slavery in the Mediterranean, the Barbary Coast, and Italy, 1500–1800*, New York: Palgrave MacMillan, 2003.

Davis, Scott G., *Religion and Justice in the War over Bosnia*, London: Routledge Press, 1996.

Dean, Hartley, and Zahar Khan, "Muslim Perspective on Welfare", *Journal of Social Policy*, 26 (1997): 193–210.

Deeb, Lara, *An Enchanted Modern: Gender and Public Piety in Shi'a Lebanon*, Princeton, NJ: Princeton University Press, 2006.

Degorge, Barbara, "Modern Day Slavery in the United Arab Emirates", *European Legacy*, 11 (2006): 657–66.

Denny, Frederick M., "Islam and Ecology: A Bestowed Trust Inviting Balanced Stewardship", *Earth Ethics*, 10 (1998): 10–11.

DeWolf, Antenor, "Modern Condottieri in Iraq: Privatizing War from the Perspective of International and Human Rights Law", *Indiana Journal of Global Legal Studies*, 13 (2006): 315–356.

Dien, Izzi, *The Environmental Dimensions of Islam*, Cambridge: The Lutterworth Press, 2000.

Diouf, Sylvain, *Servants of Allah: African Muslims Enslaved in the Americas*, New York: New York University Press, 1998.

Donahue, John J. and John L. Esposito, *Islam in Transition: Muslim Perspectives*, New York: Oxford University Press, 1982.

Dorkenoo, Efua, *Cutting the Rose: Female Genital Mutilation — The Practice and Its Prevention*, London: Minority Rights Publications, 1994.

Easwaran, Eknath, *Nonviolent Soldier of Islam: Badshah Khan, A Man to Match His Mountains*, Tomales, CA: Nilgiri Press, 2002.

Ebrahim, Abul Fadl Mohsin, *Organ Transplantation, Euthanasia, Cloning, and Animal Experimentation: An Islamic View*, Leicester, UK: Islamic Foundation, 2001.

Eibner, John, "My Career Redeeming Slaves", *Middle East Quarterly*, 6 (1999): 3–16.

Ellens, J. Howard, "Jihad in the Qur'an Then and Now", in *The Destructive Power of Religion: Violence in Judaism, Christianity, and Islam, Volume 3*, ed. J. Howard Ellens, 150–160, Westport, CT: Praeger Publishing, 2004.

Engineer, Ashgar Ali, *The Qur'an, Women and Modern Society*, Berkshire, UK: New Dawn Publications, 2005.

— *The Rights of Women in Islam*, New York: St Martin's Press, 1992.

Erdur, Oguz, "Reappropriating the 'Green': Islamist Environmentalism", *New Perspectives on Turkey*, 17 (1997): 151–66.

Esack, Farid, "In Search of Progressive Islam Beyond 9/11", In *Progressive Muslims on Justice, Gender, and Pluralism*, ed. Omid Safi, 78–97, Oxford: One World Publications, 2003.

— *On Being a Muslim: Finding a Religious Path in the World Today*, Oxford: One World Publications, 2000.

— *Qur'an, Liberation, and Pluralism: An Islamic Perspective of Interreligious Solidarity against Oppression*, Oxford: One World Publications, 1997.

— "To Whom Shall We Give Access to our Water Holes?" *Cross Currents*, 51 (2002): 503–504.

— and Sarah Chiddy, eds, *Islam and AIDS*, Oxford: One World Publications, 2009.

Esposito, John L., *Islam and Development: Religion and Sociopolitical Change*, Syracuse, NY: Syracuse University Press, 1980.

— *Islam and Politics*, Syracuse, NY: Syracuse University Press, 1984.

— *The Islamic Threat: Myth or Reality?* New York: Oxford University Press, 1999.

— "It's the Policy, Stupid! Political Islam and the United States Foreign Policy", [http://hir.harvard.edu/articles/1453/2/] (accessed January 17, 2013).

— *Political Islam: Revolution, Radicalism, or Reform?* Boulder, CO: Lynne Rienner, 1997.

— *The Straight Path*, New York: Oxford University Press, 1991.

— *Unholy War: Terror in the Name of Islam*, New York: Oxford University Press, 2002.

— and Netana J. Delong-Bas, *Women in Muslim Family Law*, Syracuse, NY: Syracuse University Press, 2001.

— and John O. Voll, *Islam and Democracy*, New York: Oxford University Press, 1996.

Euben, Roxanne L., *Enemy in the Mirror: Islamic Fundamentalism and the Limits of Modern Rationalism — A Work of Comparative Political Theory*, Princeton, NJ: Princeton University Press, 1999.

El-Fadl, Khaled M. Abou, *And God Knows the Soldiers: The Authoritative and the Authoritarian in Islamic Discourses*, Lanham, MD: University Press of America, 2001.

— "The Human Rights Commitment in Modern Islam", In *Human Rights and Responsibilities in the World Religions*, eds, Joseph Runzo, Nancy M. Martin, and Arvind Sharma, Oxford: OneWorld Publications (2003): 301–64.

— "Islamic Law and Muslim Minorities: The Juristic Discourse on Muslim Minorities from the Second/Eighth to the Eleventh/Seventeenth Centuries", *Islamic Law and Society*, 22 (1994): 141–187.

— *The Place of Tolerance in Islam*, Boston: Beacon Press, 2002.

Faksh, Mahmud A., *The Idea of Women in Fundamentalist Islam*, Gainesville: University of Florida Press, 2003.

— and Lamina Rustum Shehadeh, *The Future of Islam in the Middle East: Fundamentalism in Egypt, Algeria, and Saudi Arabia*, Westport, CT: Praeger Press, 1997.

Farhadian, Charles E., *Christianity, Islam and Nationalism in Indonesia*, London: Routledge Press, 2005.

Farsy, Muhammad Saleh, *Islam and Hygiene*, Leiden, the Netherlands: E.J. Brill, 1964.

Ferguson, John, *War and Peace in the World's Religions*, New York: Oxford University Press, 1978.

Fernandez, Sonya, "The Crusade over the Bodies of Women", *Patterns of Prejudice*, 43 (2009): 269–286.

Fekete, Liz, *A Suitable Enemy: Racism, Migration, and Islamophobia in Europe*, New York: Pluto Press, 2009.

Firestone, Reuven, "Disparity and Resolution in the Qur'anic Teachings on War", *Journal of Near Eastern Studies*, 56 (1997): 1–19.

Fluehr-Lobban, Carolyn, *Islamic Societies in Practice*, Gainesville: University Press of Florida, 2004.

Foltz, Richard C., *Animals in Islamic Tradition and in Muslim Cultures*, Oxford: One World Publications, 2006.

Forche, Carolyn, ed., *Against Forgetting: Twentieth Century Poetry of Witness*, New York: W.W. Norton and Company, 1993.

Forward, Martin, *Interreligious Dialogue: A Short Introduction*, Oxford: One World Press, 2001.

Fregosi, Paul, *Jihad in the West: Muslim Conquests from the 7th to the 21st Centuries*, Amherst, NY: Prometheus Books, 1998.

Friedman, Thomas L., *From Beirut to Jerusalem*, New York: Farrar, Straus and Giroux, 1989.

Friedmann, Yohann, *Toleration and Coercion in Islam: Interfaith Relations in the Muslim Tradition*, Cambridge: Cambridge University Press, 2003.

Frisk, Sylva, *Submitting to God: Women and Islam in Urban Malaysia*, Seattle: University of Washington Press, 2009.

Fuller, Graham E., *The Future of Political Islam*, New York: Palgrave MacMillan, 2003.

Funk, Nathan C., and Abdul Aziz Said, *Islam and Peacemaking in the Middle East*, Boulder, CO: Lynn Rienner Publishers, 2009.

Gaimani, Aaron, "The 'Orphans' Decree' in Yemen: Two New Episodes", *Middle Eastern Studies*, 40 (2004): 171–84.

Garaudy, Roger, "Human Rights and Islam: Foundation, Tradition, Violation", In *The Ethics of World Religions and Human Rights*, Concilium 1990/2, ed. Hans Küng and Jürgen Moltmann, London: SCM Press (1990): 46–60.

Gautier, Francois, *Rewriting Indian History*, New Delhi, India: Vikas Publishers, 1996.

Geaves, Ron, *Aspects of Islam*, Washington, DC: Georgetown University Press, 2005.

— Theodore Gabriel, Yvonne Haddad and Jane Idleman Smith, eds, *Islam and the West Post 9/11*, Burlington, VT: Ashgate Publishing, 2004.

Ghadbian, Najib, *Democratization and the Islamist Challenge in the Arab World*, Boulder, CO: Westview Press, 1997.

Ghanea Bassari, Kambiz, *A History of Islam in America: From the New World to the New World Order*, Cambridge: Cambridge University Press, 2010.

Gil, Moshe, "The Earliest Waqf Foundations", *Journal of Near Eastern Studies*, 57 (1998): 125–140.

Gilsenan, Michael, *Recognizing Islam: Religion and Society in the Modern Middle East*, London: I.B. Tauris, 2000.

Ginat, Joseph, *Women in Muslim Rural Society: Status and Role in Family and Community*, Brunswick, NJ: Transaction Books, 1982.

Glaser, Ida and Napoleon John, *Partners or Prisoners? Christians Thinking About Women and Islam*, Carlisle, UK: Solvay Publications, 1998.

Glover, Jonathan, *Humanity: A Moral History of the 20th Century*, New Haven, CT: Yale University Press, 2001.

Goldenberg, David M., *The Curse of Ham: Race and Slavery in Early Judaism, Christianity and Islam*, Princeton, NJ: Princeton University Press, 2003.

Gole, Nilufer, "Contemporary Islamist Movements and New Sources for Religious Tolerance", *Journal of Human Rights*, 2 (2003): 17–30.

Gomes, Peter, *The Good Book: Reading the Bible with Mind and Heart*, New York: William Morrow, 1996.

Gomez, Michael A, "Muslims in Early America", *The Journal of Southern History*, 60 (1994): 671–710.

Goodson, Larry P., *Afghanistan's Endless War: State Failure, Regional Politics, and the Rise of the Taliban*, Seattle: University of Washington Press, 2001.

Goodwin, Jan, *Price of Honor: Muslim Women Lift the Veil of Silence on the Islamic World*, New York: Plume Publishing, 2003.

Gopin, Marc, *Holy War, Holy Peace: How Religion Can Bring Peace to the Middle East*, New York: Oxford University Press, 2002.

Gordon, Barry, *The Economic Problem in Biblical and Patristic Thought*, Leiden, the Netherlands: E.J. Brill, 1989.

El-Guindi, Fadwa, *Veil, Modesty, Privacy, and Resistance*, New York: Berg Publishing, 1999.

Engineer, Ashgar Ali, "On Developing Liberation Theology in Islam" (394-403), in *Voices from the Margin: Interpreting the Bible in the Third World*, ed. R.S. Sugirtharajah, Maryknoll, NY: Orbis Books, 1995.

Gusau, Sule Ahmed, "The Prophet Muhammad (PBH) and the Problem of Poverty and Distress", *Hamdard Islamicus* 16 (1993): 19–37.

Gusfield, Joseph R, "Tradition and Modernity: Misplaced Polarities in the Study of Social Change", *American Journal of Sociology*, 72 (1967): 351–362.

Haar, Gerrie and James J. Busuttil, eds, *The Freedom to Do God's Will: Religious Fundamentalism and Social Change*, New York: Routledge Press, 2003.

Haddad, Yvonne Yazbeck, Byron Haines, and Ellison Findlay, eds, *The Islamic Impact*, Syracuse, NY: Syracuse University Press, 1984.

— and Barbara Freyer Stowasser, *Islamic Law and the Challenges of Modernity*, Walnut Creek, CA: Altamira Publishers, 2004.

Haghayeghi, Mehrdad, *Islam and Politics in Central Asia*, New York: St Martin's Press, 1995.

Haleem, Harfiyah Abdel, ed., *Islam and Environment*, London: Ta-Ha Publishers, 1998.

Hallaq, Wael B., ed., *The Formation of Islamic Law*, Burlington, VT: Ashgate Publishers, 2004.

— *A History of Islamic Legal Theories*, Cambridge: Cambridge University Press, 1999.

— *The Origin and Evolution of Islamic Law*, Cambridge: Cambridge University Press, 2005.

Halliday, Fred, "Anti-Arab Prejudice in the UK: The Kilroy-Silk Affair and the BBC Response", in *Muslims and the News Media*, eds, Elizabeth Poole and John E. Richardson, 24–34, London: I.B. Tauris, 2006.

Halstead, J. Mark, "Islam, Homophobia, and Education: A Reply to Michael Merry", *Journal of Moral Education*, 34 (2005): 37–42.

Hamid, Abdul Ali, ed. and trans., *Moral Teachings of Islam: Prophetic Traditions from al-Adab al-Mufrad by Imam al-Bukhari*, Walnut Creek, CA: Altamira, 2002.

Hamidullah Muhammad, *The Muslim Conduct of State*, seventh edition, Lahore, Pakistan: Islamic Foundation, 2004.

Haneef, Suzanne, *What Everyone Should Know About Islam and Muslims*, Chicago: Kazi Publications, 1982.

Harik, Ramsay M. and Elsa Marston, *Women in the Middle East: Tradition and Change*, New York: Franklin Watts, 1996.

Al-Harran, Saad, *Islamic Finance: Partnership Financing*, Selangor, Malaysia: Pelanduk Publishing, 1993.

Hasan, Asman Gull, *American Muslims: The New Generation*, New York: Continuum International Publishers, 2002.

Hashmi, Sohail H., "Saving and Taking Life in War: Three Modern Muslim Views", *Muslim World*, 89 (1999): 158–180.

Hassan, Riaz, *Muslim Conceptions of Islam and Society*, Oxford: Oxford University Press, 2002.

Heath, Jennifer, *The Scimitar and the Veil: Extraordinary Women of Islam*, Mahwah, NJ: Hidden Spring Press, 2004.

Heggy, Tareek, *The Arab Mind Bound*, London: Valentine Mitchell, 2011.

Hekmat, Anwar, *Women and the Koran: The Status of Women in Islam*, New York: Prometheus Books, 1997.

Heyneman, Stephen P. and Alan J. DeYoung, *The Challenge of Education in Central Asia*, Greenwich, CT: Information Age Publishing, Inc., 2004.

Hourani, George F., *Reason and Tradition in Islamic Ethics*, Cambridge: Cambridge University Press, 1985.

Houston, Christopher, *Islam, Kurds, and the Turkish National State*, New York: Berg Publishing, 2001.

Howell, Leon, "Muslim Leaders Urge Ban on Secret Evidence", *The Christian Century*, 117 (2001): 749.

Hoyland, Robert G., *Seeing Islam as Others See It*, Princeton, NJ: Darwin Press, 1997.

Hughes, Aaron, *Theorizing Islam: Disciplinary Deconstruction and Reconstruction*, Sheffield, UK: Equinox Publishers, 2012.

Hunt, Arnold, Marie T., Crotty, and Robert B. Crotty, eds, *Ethics of World Religions*, San Diego: Greenhaven Press, 1991.

Hunt, Lynn, *Inventing Human Rights: A History*, New York: Norton and Norton Company, 2007.

Hunt, Robert A., and Yüksel A. Aslandoğan, eds, *Muslim Citizens of the Globalized World: Contributions of the Gülen Movement*, Somerset, NJ: IID Press, 2007.

Husain, Mir Zohair, *Global Islamic Politics*, New York: Longman Publishers, 2003.

Husaini, S. Waqar Ahmad, *Islamic Environmental Systems Engineering*, London: Macmillan, 1980.

Hussain, Asaf, *Beyond Islamic Fundamentalism: The Sociology of Faith and Action*, Leicester, UK: Volcano Press, 1992.

— *Western Conflicts with Islam: Surveys of the Anti-Islamic Tradition*, Leicester, UK: Volcano Press, 1990.

Içduygu, Ahmet, and Sule Toktas, "How Do Smuggling and Trafficking Operate Via Irregular Border Crossings in the Middle East? Evidence from Fieldwork in Turkey", *International Migration*, 40, no. 6 (2002): 25–54.

Ide, Arthur Frederick, *The Qur'an on Women, Marriage, Birth Control and Divorce*, Las Colinas, TX: Tangelwuld Press, 1996.

Iqbal, Munawar, ed, *Distributive Justice and Need Fulfillment in an Islamic Economy*, Leicester, UK: Islamic Foundation, 1988.

Iqbal, Muhammad, *The Reconstruction of Religious Thought in Islam*, Lahore, Pakistan: Ashraf Publications, 1960.

Ishaq, Ibn, *Sirat Rasul Allah*, trans. Alexandre Guillaume, Karachi, Pakistan: Oxford University Press, 1998.

Islahi, Amin Ahsan, *Islamic Law: Concept and Codification*, Lahore, Pakistan: Islamic Publications, 1979.

Ismael, Tariq Y. and Jacqueline S. Ismael, eds, *Government and Politics in Islam*, New York: St Martin's Press, 1985.

Izetbegovic, Alija Ali, *Islam between East and West*, second edition, Indianapolis, IN: American Trust Publications, 1989.

Jahanbakhsh, Forough, *Islam, Democracy, and Religious Modernism in Iran (1953–2000)*, Leiden, the Netherlands: E.J. Brill, 2001.

Jansen, G.H., *Militant Islam*, London: Pan Books, 1979.

Jawad, Haifaa A., *The Rights of Women in Islam: An Authentic Approach*, New York: Palgrave Publishers, 1998.

Jenkins, Philip, *Laying Down the Sword: Why We Can't Ignore the Bible's Violent Verses*, New York: Harper Collins Publishers, 2011.

Johnson-Davies, D., *The Island of Animals, Adapted from an Arabic Fable*, Austin: University of Texas Press, 1994.

Kamali, Muhammad Hashim, *Freedom of Expression in Islam*, Cambridge: Islamic Texts Society, 1997.

Karim, Karim H., "American Media Coverage of Muslims: The Historical Roots of Contemporary Portrayals", in *Muslims and the News Media*, eds, Elizabeth Poole and John E. Richardson, 116–27, London: I.B. Tauris, 2006.

Kazemzadeh, Masoud, *Islamic Fundamentalism, Feminism and Gender Inequality in Iran under Khomeini*, Lanham, MD: University Press of America, 2002.

Kechichian, Joseph A., "The Role of the Ulama in the Politics of an Islamic State: The Case of Saudi Arabia", *International Journal of Middle East Studies*, 18 (1986): 53–71.

Kellenberger, J., *Moral Relativism, Moral Diversity, and Human Relationships*, Philadelphia: Pennsylvania State University Press, 2001.

Keller, Nuh Ha Mim, "The Concept of Bid'a in the Islamic *Shariah*", [http://www.masud.co.uk/ISLAM/nuh/bida.htm] (accessed January 5, 2013).

Kettani, A. Ali, *Muslim Minorities in the World Today*, London: Mansell Publishing, 1986.

Khadduri, Majid, *The Islamic Conception of Justice*, Baltimore: Johns Hopkins Press, 1984.

— *War and Peace in the Law of Islam*, Baltimore: Johns Hopkins Press, 1955.

Khalid, Asma, "Lifting the Veil: Muslim Women Explain Their Choice", *National Public Radio*, April 21, 2011, [http://www.npr.org/2011/04/21/135523680/lifting-the-veil-muslim-women-explain-their-choice] (accessed January 29, 2012)

Khalid, Fazlun, "Guardians of the Natural Order", *Our Planet*, 8 (1996): 8–12.

— *Qur'an: Creation and Conservation*, Birmingham, UK: IFEES, 1999.

— and Joanne O'Brien, eds, *Islam and Ecology*, London: Cassel Publishing, 1992.

Khan, Aalia Sohail, "Islam: A Religion of Peace and Tolerance", *Hamdard Islamicus*, 20 (1997): 87–89.

Khan, Maulana Wahiduddin, *Islam: The Voice of Nature*, trans. Farida Khanam, New Delhi: Islamic Centre, 1995.

Khan, Muhammad Shabbir, *Islam: Social and Economic Structure*, New Delhi, India: Punjabi Bagh, 1956.

Khan, Sajjad, "Global Poverty: A Perspective from Islamic Political Economy", *Globalizations*, 3 (2006): 251–254.

Khashan, Hilal, "Collective Palestinian Frustration and Suicide Bombings", *Third World Quarterly*, 24 (2003): 1049–1067.

Kimball, Charles A., *Striving Together: A Way Forward in Christian-Muslim Relations*, Maryknoll, NY: Orbis Books, 1991.

— *When Religion Becomes Evil: Five Warning Signs*, New York: Harper and Row, 2002.

King, Anna "Islam, Women, and Violence", *Feminist Theology: Journal of the British and Irish School of Feminist Theology*, 17 (2009): 292–328.

King, Martin Luther, Jr, *Why We Can't Wait*, New York: New American Library, 1964.

Kucukcan, Talip, "Encountering the Victims of Genocide: Observations of a Traveler", *Journal of Muslim Minority Affairs*, 16 (1996): 317–318.

Kumar, Deepa, *Islamophobia and the Politics of Empire*, Chicago: Haymarket Books, 2012.

Küng, Hans and Jürgen Moltmann, eds, *The Ethics of World Religions and Human Rights*, Concilium 1990/2, London: SCM, 1990.

— *Islam: A Challenge for Christianity*, Maryknoll, NY: Orbis Books, 1994.

Kuran, Timur, "The Genesis of Islamic Economics: A Chapter in the Politics of Muslim Identity", *Social Research*, 64 (1997): 301–331.

— "On the Notion of Economic Justice in Contemporary Islamic Thought", *International Journal of Middle East Studies*, 21 (1989): 171–191.

Laher, Suheil, "Indiscriminate Killings in Light of Islamic Sacred Texts", In *The State We are In: Identity, Terror, and the Law of Jihad*, ed., Aftab Ahmad Malik, 41–54, Bristol, UK: Amal Press, 2006.

Landau-Tasseron, Ella, "Adoption, Acknowledgement of Paternity and False Genealogical Claims in Arabian and Islamic Societies", *Bulletin of the School of Oriental and African Studies*, University of London, 66 (2003): 169–192.

— "Jihad", In *The Encyclopedia of the Qur'an: Volume Three (J–O)*, ed. Jane Dammen McAuliffe, Leiden, the Netherlands: E.J. Brill, 2003.

Lanternari, Vittorio, *The Religions of the Oppressed: A Study of Modern Messianic Cults*, trans. Lisa Sergio, New York: Mentor Books, 1965.

Larzeg, Marnia, *The Emergence of Classes in Algeria: A Study of Colonialism and Socio-Political Change*, Boulder, CO: Westview Press, 1976.

Lawrence, Bruce B., *Defenders of God: The Fundamentalist Revolt against the Modern Age*, San Francisco: Harper and Row Publishers, 1989.

Layachi, Azzedine, "The Berbers in Algeria: Politicization of Ethnicity and Ethnicization of Politics", In *Nationalism and Minority Identities in Islamic Societies*, ed. Maya Shatzmiller, 193–228, Montreal: McGill-Queen's University Press, 2005.

Leahy, M. and D. Cohn-Sherbok, eds, *The Liberation Debate: Rights at Issue*, London: Routledge, 1996.

Lean, Nathan, *The Islamophobia Industry: How the Right Manufactures Fear of Muslims*, New York: Pluto Press, 2012.

Lebacqz, Karen, *Justice in an Unjust World: Foundations for a Christian Approach to Justice*, Minneapolis, MN: Augsburg Press, 1987.

Lebowitz, Holly J. and Gary Orfield, eds, *Religion, Race and Justice in a Changing America*, New York: Century Foundation Press, 1999.

Lefebure, Leo D., *Revelation, the Religions, and Violence*, Maryknoll, NY: Orbis Books, 2000.

Lev, Yaacov, *Charity, Endowments, and Charitable Institutions in Medieval Islam*, Gainesville: University Press of Florida, 2005.

Lewis, Bernard, *The Crisis of Islam*, New York: Random House, 2003.

— *Islam: From the Prophet Muhammad to the Capture of Constantinople, Volume 1: Politics and War*, Oxford: Oxford University Press, 1974.

— "On Revolutions in Early Islam", *Studia Islamica*, 32 (1970): 215–231.

— *Race and Color in Islam*, New York: Harper and Row, 1971.

— *Race and Slavery in the Middle East: An Historical Enquiry*, New York: Oxford University Press, 1990.

— *What Went Wrong? The Clash between Islam and Modernity in the Middle East*, New York: Oxford University Press, 2002.

Lewis, Reiy, *Rethinking Orientalism: Women, Travel, and the Ottoman Harem*, London: I.B. Tauris, 2004,

Lindholm T. and K. Vogt, eds, *Islamic Law Reform and Human Rights: Challenges and Rejoinders*, Oslo, Norway: Nordic Human Rights Publications, 1993.

Little, David, John Kelsay, and Abdulaziz A. Sachedina, *Human Rights and the Conflict of Cultures: Western and Islamic Perspectives on Religious Liberty*, Columbia: University of South Carolina Press, 1988.

Llewellyn, Othman, "Desert Reclamation and Conservation in Islamic Law", *The Muslim Scientist*, 11 (1982): 9–29.

Lo, Mbaye, "Seeking the Roots of Terrorism: An Islamic Traditional Perspective", *Journal of Religion and Popular Culture*, 10 (2005): 1–13.

Lovejoy, Paul, Behnaz Mirzai, and Ismael Musah Montana, eds, *Slavery, Islam and Diaspora*, Trenton, NJ: Africa World Press, 2009.

Lunde, Paul, "Science: The Islamic Legacy", *Saudi Aramco World*, 33 (1982): 14–19.

Lyall, Francis, *Slaves, Citizens, Sons: Legal Metaphors in the Epistles*, Grand Rapids, MI: Academic Books, 1984.

Mackey, Virginia, "Punishment in the Scripture and Tradition of Judaism, Christianity, and Islam", In *Crime, Values, and Religion*, ed. James Day and William Laufer, 23–110, New York: Ablex Publishing Company, 1987.

Madani, Mohammad Asrar, *Verdict of Islamic Law on Blasphemy and Apostasy*, Lahore, Pakistan: Idara-E-Islamiat, 1994.

Maddy-Weitzman, Bruce and Efraim Inbar, eds, *Religious Radicalism in the Greater Middle East*, London: Frank Cass Publishers, 1997.

Majid, Anouar, The Politics of Feminism in Islam", *Signs*, 23 (1998), 321–361.

Makhlouf, Carla, *Changing Veils*, Austin: University of Texas Press, 1979.

Mandeville, Peter, *Transnational Muslim Politics: Reimagining the Ummah*, London: Routledge Press, 2001.

Manzoour, S. Parvez, "Environment and Values: The Islamic Perspective", In *The Touch of Midas: Science, Values and Environment in Islam and the West*, ed. Ziauddin Sardar, 150–69, Manchester, UK: Manchester University Press, 1984.

Marlow, Louise, *Hierarchy and Egalitarianism in Islamic Thought*, Cambridge Studies in Islamic Civilization, New York: Cambridge University Press, 1997.

Marmon, Shaun E., *Eunuchs and the Sacred Boundaries in Islamic Societies*, Oxford: Oxford University Press, 1995.

— *Slavery in the Islamic Middle East*, Princeton, NJ: Markus Wiener Publishers, 1999.

Martinson, Paul Varo, ed., *Islam: An Introduction for Christians*, Minneapolis, MN: Augsburg, 1994.

Maumoon, Dunya, "Islamism and Gender Activism: Muslim Women's Quest for Autonomy", *Journal of Muslim Minority Affairs*, 30 (1999): 425–435.

Al-Mawdudi, Abdul, "Human Rights in Islam: Enemies Rights in War", *Al-Tawhid Journal*, 4 (1987) pp.59–89.

Mayer, Ann Elizabeth, *Islam and Human Rights: Tradition and Politics*, Boulder, CO: Westview Press, 1991.

Mazrui, Ali A., *Muslims' Place in the American Public Square*, New York: Altamira Press, 2004.

McAuliffe, Jane Dammen, ed., *Encyclopedia of the Qur'an*, Five Volumes, Leiden: Brill, 2001–2006.

McCloud, Aminah Beverly, *African American Islam*, London: Routledge Press, 1995.

McDonough, Sheila, *Gandhi's Responses to Islam*, Delhi, India: DK Printworld, 1994.

— *Muslim Ethics and Modernity: A Comparative Study of the Ethical Thought of Sayyid Ahmed Khan and Mawlana Mawdudi*, Waterloo, ON: Wilfred Laurier Press, 1984.

Meddeb, Abdel Wahhab, *The Malady of Islam*, New York: Basic Books, 2003.

Megahead, Hamid A., and Sandra Cesario, "Family Foster Care, Kinship Networks, and Residential Care of Abandoned Infants in Egypt", *Journal of Family Social Work*, 11 (2008): 463–477.

Mernissi, Fatima, *Islam and Democracy: Fear of the Modern World*, trans. Mary Jo Lakeland, Cambridge, MA: Perseus Books, 1992.

— *Women and Islam: An Historical and Theological Inquiry*, Oxford: Blackwell Press, 1991.

Merry, Michael S., "Should Educators Accommodate Intolerance? Mark Halstead, Homosexuality, and the Islamic Case", *Journal of Moral Education*, 34 (2005): 19–36.

Minai, Naila, *Women in Islam: Tradition and Transition in the Middle East*, New York: Seaview Books, 1981.

Mirbagheri, S.M. Farid, *War and Peace in Islam: A Critique of Islamic/ist Political Discourses*, New York: Palgrave Macmillan, 2012.

Moaveni, Azadeh, *Lipstick Jihad: A Memoir of Growing Up Iranian in America and American in Iran*, New York: Public Affairs, 2005.

Modirzadeh, Naz, "Taking Islamic Law Seriously: INGOs and the Battle for Muslim Hearts and Minds", *Harvard Human Rights Journal*, 19 (2006): 191–234.

Moezzi, Melody, *War on Error: Real Stories of American Muslims*, Fayetteville: University of Arkansas Press, 2007.

Mohammadi, Ali, "The Culture and Politics of Human Rights in the Context of Islam", In *Islam Encountering Globalization*, ed. Ali Mohammadi, 111–130, London: Routledge Curzon Press, 2002.

Moors, Annelies, *Women, Property, and Islam*, New York: Cambridge University Press, 1995.

More, Elizabeth, "The Universal Declaration of Human Rights in Today's World", *Journal of International Communications*, 11 (2007): 27–45.

Morgan, Keith, and Almut Scheppler, eds, *Human Rights Have No Borders: Voices of Irish Prophets*, Dublin: Marino Books, 1998.

Moucarry, Chawkat, *The Prophet and the Messiah: An Arab Christian Perspective on Islam and Christianity*, Downers Grove, IL: Intervarsity Press, 2001.

Moussalli, Ahmed S., *The Islamic Quest for Democracy, Pluralism, and Human Rights*, Gainesville: University Press of Florida, 2001.

Muhaiyadden, M.R., Bawa, *Islam and World Peace: Explanations of a Sufi*, Philadelphia: Fellowship Press, 1987.

Murphy, Carlyle, *Passion for Islam: Shaping the Modern Middle East: The Egyptian Experience*, London: Scribner, 2002.

Murray, Stephen O., and Will Roscoe, *Islamic Homosexualities: Culture, History and Literature*, New York: New York University Press, 1997.

Muzaffar, Chandra, *Rights, Religion and Reform*, London: Routledge Curzon Press, 2002.

Naqvi, Sayed Nawab Haider, *Islam, Economics and Society*, London: Kegan Paul, 1994.

Nasseef, 'Abdullah Omar, "The Muslim Declaration on Nature", *Environmental Policy and Law*, 17 (1987): 47.

— *Today's Problems, Tomorrow's Solutions*, London: Mansell Publishing, 1988.

Nasr, Seyyed Hossein, *Islam, Religion, History and Civilization*, New York: Harper Collins, 2003.

Nazir-Ali, Michael, *Islam: A Christian Perspective*, Philadelphia: Westminster Press, 1983.

Netton, Ian Richard, *Islam, Christianity, and Tradition: A Comparative Explanation*, Edinburgh: Edinburgh University Press, 2006.

Niazi, Kausar, *Mirror of Trinity*, Lahore, Pakistan: Shah Muhammad Ashraf, 1991.

Nojumi, Nimatullahi, *The Rise of the Taliban in Afghanistan: Mass Mobilization, Civil War and the Future of the Region*, New York: Palgrave, 2002.

Noorani, A.G., *Islam and Jihad: Prejudice versus Reality*, London: ZED Books, 2002.

Northrop, Douglas, *Veiled Empire: Gender & Power in Stalinist Central Asia*, Ithaca, NY: Cornell University Press, 2004.

Noyon, Jennifer, *Islam, Politics and Pluralism: Theory and Practice in Jordan, Tunisia and Algeria*, London: Royal Institute for International Affairs, 2003.

Ochsenwald, William, "Saudi Arabia and the Islamic Revival", *International Journal of Middle East Studies*, 13 (1981): 271–286.

Omar, A. Rasheed, "Islam and Violence", in *The Ecumenical Review*, 55, no. 2, April 2003, pp.158–163.

O'Shaughnessy, Thomas J., "The Qur'anic View of Youth and Old Age", *Zeitschrift der Deutschen Morgenländischen Gesellschaft*, 141 (1991): 33–51.

Oweiss, Ibrahim M., *The Political Economy of Contemporary Egypt*, Washington, DC: Center for Contemporary Arab Studies, Georgetown University, 1990.

Paidar, Parvin, *Women and the Political Process in Twentieth-Century Iran*, Cambridge: Cambridge University Press, 1995.

Parenti, Michael, *Against Empire*, San Francisco: City Lights Books, 1995.

Parshall, Phil and Julie, *Lifting the Veil: The World of Muslim Women*, Waynesboro, GA: Gabriel Publishing, 2002.

Partner, Peter, *God of Battles: Holy Wars of Christianity and Islam*, London: Harper Collins, 1997.

Pearl, David, *A Textbook on Muslim Law*, London: Croom Helm Ltd., 1979.

Peters, Rudolph, *Crime and Punishment in Islamic Law*, Cambridge: Cambridge University Press, 2005.

— *Jihad in Classical and Modern Islam*, Princeton, NJ: Markus Wiener Publishers, 1996.

— and Gert J.J. DeVries, "Apostasy in Islam", *Die Welt des Islams*, 17 (1976–1977): 1–25.

Philips, Jonathan, *The Crusades, 1095–1197*, New York: Longmans Publishing, 2002.

Pipes, Daniel, *In the Path of God: Islam and Political Power*, New York: Basic Books, 1983.
— *Militant Islam Reaches America*, New York: W.W. Norton and Company, 2002.
— *Slave Soldiers and Islam: The Genesis of a Military System*, New Haven: Yale University Press, 1981.
Poole, Elizabeth, and John E. Richardson, eds, *Muslims and the News Media*, London: I.B. Tauris, 2006.
Power, Samantha, *A Problem from Hell: America and the Age of Genocide*, New York: Basic Books, 2002.
Powers, David S., *Muhammad Is Not the Father of Any of Your Men*, Philadelphia: University of Pennsylvania Press, 2009.
Preston, Ronald, *Religion and the Ambiguities of Capitalism*, London: SCM Press, 1991.
Prins, Baukje, "Sympathetic Distrust: Liberalism and the Sexual Autonomy of Women", *Social Theory and Practice*, 34 (2008): 243–270.
Qutb, Sayyid, *Milestones*, second edition, trans. S. Badrul Hasan, Delhi: Markazi Maktaba Islami, 1988.
— *Social Justice in Islam*, trans. John B. Hardie, New York: Islamic Publications International, 1953.
— "War, Peace, and Islamic Jihad", In *Modernist and Fundamentalist Debates in Islam*, ed. Mansour Moaddel and Kamran Talattof, 223–246, New York: Palgrave MacMillan, 2002.
Radoncic, Seki, *A Fatal Freedom*, The Hague, the Netherlands: Humanitarian Law Center, 2005.
Rahbar, Daud, *God of Justice: A Study of the Ethical Doctrine of the Qur'an*, Leiden, the Netherlands: E.J. Brill, 1960.
Rahman, Fazlur, *Islam and Christianity in the Modern World*, Delhi, India: Noor Publishing House, 1992.
— *Major Themes of the Qur'an*, Minneapolis: Bibliotheca Islamica, 1980.
Rahman, M.K., "Environmental Awareness in Islam", *MAAS Journal of Islamic Science*, 2 (1986): 99–106.
Ramadan, Tariq, *Western Muslims and the Future of Islam*, Oxford: Oxford University Press, 2004.
Ramage, Douglas E., *Politics in Indonesia: Democracy, Islam and the Ideology of Tolerance*, London: Routledge Press, 1995.
Rana, Junaid, *Terrifying Muslims: Race and Labor in the South Asian Diaspora*, Durham, NC: Duke University Press, 2011.
Raschke, Carl, *Postmodernism and the Revolution in Religious Theory: Toward a Semiotics of the Event*, Charlottesville: University of Virginia Press, 2012.
Rashid, Ahmed, *Taliban: Militant Islam, Oil and Fundamentalism in Central Asia*, New Haven, CT: Yale University Press, 2000.
Read, Jen'an Ghazal, "The Sources of Gender Role Attitudes among Christian and Muslim Arab-American Women", *Sociology of Religion*, 64 (2003): 207–222.
Reeves, Minou, *Female Warriors of Allah: Women and the Islamic Revolution*, New York: E.P. Dutton, 1989.
Richardson, Gail, "Islamic Law and Zakat: Waqf Resources in Pakistan", In *Islam and Social Policy*, ed. Stephen P. Heyneman, 156–180, Nashville: Vanderbilt University Press, 2004.

Rifkin, Ira, *Spiritual Perspectives on Globalization: Making Sense of Economic and Cultural Upheaval*, second edition, Woodstock, VT: Sky Light Paths, 2004.

Ron, James, and Oskar Thoms, "Do Human Rights Violations Cause Internal Conflict?" *Human Rights Quarterly*, 29 (2007): 674–705.

Rosen, Lawrence, *Varieties of Muslim Experiences: Encounters with Arab Political and Cultural Life*, Chicago: University of Chicago Press, 2011.

Rouner, Leroy S., ed., *Human Rights and the World's Religions*, Notre Dame, IN: University of Notre Dame Press, 1988.

Rowson, Everett K., "Homosexuality", In *Encyclopedia of Islam and the Muslim World*, New York: Thomson Gale, 2004.

El-Rouyaheb, Khalil, *Before Homosexuality in the Arab-Islamic World, 1500–1800*, Chicago: University of Chicago Press, 2005.

Roy, Oliver, *Globalized Islam: The Search for a New Ummah*, New York: Columbia University Press, 2004.

Rubenstein, Richard L., *The Cunning of History: The Holocaust and the American Future*, New York: Perennial Books, 1978.

Rubin, Barry, *Islamic Fundamentalism in Egyptian Politics*, New York: Palgrave Macmillan, 2002.

Rugh, Andrea B., "Orphanages in Egypt: Contradiction or Affirmation in a Family-Oriented Society", In *Children in the Muslim Middle East*, ed. Elizabeth Warnock Furnea, 124–141, Austin: University of Texas Press, 1995.

Runzo, Joseph, Nancy Martin and Arvind Sharma, eds, *Human Rights and Responsibilities in the World Religions*, Oxford: One World Publications, 2003.

El-Saadawi, Nawal, *Woman at Point Zero*, trans. Sheriff Hetata, London: ZED Books, 1975.

Sabra, Adam, *Poverty and Charity in Medieval Islam*, New York: Cambridge University Press, 2000.

Sachedina, Abdulaziz, *The Islamic Roots of Democratic Pluralism*, Oxford: Oxford University Press, 2001.

Sachiko, Murata and William C. Chittick, *The Vision of Islam*, St Paul, MN: Paragon House, 1994.

Sadiq, Abul Hasan M., "Waqf, Perpetual Charity and Poverty Alleviation", *International Journal of Social Economics*, 29 (2002): 135–151.

Sadiki, Larbi, *The Search for Arab Democracy: Discourses and Counter Discourses*, New York: Columbia University Press, 2004.

Sadr, M. Husain, "Science and Islam: Is There a Conflict?" In *The Touch of Midas: Science, Values and Environment in Islam and the West*, ed. Ziauddin Sardar, 15–25, Manchester, UK: Manchester University Press, 1984.

Saeed, Abdullah and Hassan Saeed, *Freedom of Religion, Apostasy, and Islam*, Aldershot, UK: Ashgate Publishing, 2004.

Safi, Omid, ed., *Progressive Muslims: On Justice, Gender, and Pluralism*, Oxford: One World Publications, 2003.

— *Voices of American Muslims*, New York: Hippocrene Books, 2005.

Said, Abdul Aziz, ed., *Peace and Conflict Resolution in Islam: Precept and Practice*, New York: University Press of America, 2001.

— "Precept and Practice of Human Rights in Islam", *Universal Human Rights*, 1 (1979): 63–79.

— and Meena Sharify-Funk, eds, *Cultural Diversity and Islam*, Lanham, MD: University Press of America, 2003.

Said, Edward, *Covering Islam: How the Media and the Experts Determine How We See the Rest of the World*, New York: Vintage Books, 1997.

Saleh, Nabil A., *Unlawful Gain and Legitimate Profit in Islamic Law*, New York: Cambridge University Press, 1986.

Salvatore, Armando and Dale F. Eickelman, eds, *Public Islam and the Common Good*, Leiden, the Netherlands: E.J., Brill, 2004.

Sardar, Ziauddin, *Desperately Seeking Paradise: Journeys of a Skeptical Muslim*, London: Granta Books, 2004.

— *Islam, Postmodernism and Other Futures: A Ziauddin Sardar Reader*, ed. Sohail Inayatullah and Gail Boxwell, London: Pluto Press, 2003.

— *Islamic Futures: The Shape of Things to Come*, London: Mansell Publishing, 1985.

— ed., *The Touch of Midas: Science, Values and Environment in Islam and the West*, Manchester, UK: Manchester University Press, 1984.

Saritoprak, Zeki, "An Islamic Approach to Peace and Nonviolence: A Turkish Experience", *Muslim World*, 95 (2005): 413–27.

Satloff, Robert, *Among the Righteous: Lost Stories from the Holocaust's Long Reach into Arab Lands*, New York: Public Affairs, 2006.

Savage, Timothy, "Europe and Islam: Crescent Waxing, Cultures Clashing", *Washington Quarterly*, 27 (2004): 25–50

Schacht, Joseph, *An Introduction to Islamic Law*, Oxford: Clarendon Press, 1964.

Schmidtke, Sabine, "Homoeroticism and Homosexuality in Islam: A Review Article", *Bulletin of the School of Oriental and African Studies*, 62 (1999): 260–266.

Segal, Ronald, *Islam's Black Slaves: The Other Black Diaspora*, New York: Farrar, Strauss and Giroux, 2001.

Selengut, Charles, *Sacred Fury: Understanding Religious Violence*, Walnut Creek, CA: AltaMaria Press, 2003.

Sells, Michael, *The Bridge Betrayed: Religion and Genocide in Bosnia*, Berkeley: University of California Press, 1996.

Senturk, Omer Faruk, *Charity in Islam: A Comprehensive Guide to Zakat*, Somerset, NJ: Light Publications, 2007.

Serajzadeh, Seyyed Hussein, *Islam and Crime: The Moral Community of Muslims*, Teheran, Iran: Teheran Teacher Training University Publications, 2006.

Shaarawi, Huda, *Harem Years: The Memoirs of an Egyptian Feminist (1879–1924)*, trans. Margot Badran, New York: Feminist Press, 1986.

Shabon, Anwar M. and Isik U. Zeytinoglu, *The Political, Economic and Labor Climate in Turkey*, Philadelphia: University of Pennsylvania, 1985.

Shadid, W.A.R., and P.S. van Koningsveld, eds, *Political Responses to the Presence of Islam in Western Europe*, Kampen, the Netherlands: Pharos, 1996.

Shahabuddin, Syed, "Comments on Yoginder Sikand's Article on Dalit Muslims", *Journal of Muslim Minority Affairs*, 22 (2002): 479–81.

Sharma, Arvind, *Today's Woman in World Religions*, New York: State University of New York Press, 1994.

— and Katherine Young, eds, *"Her Voice, Her Faith": Women Speak on the World's Religions*, Cambridge, MA: Westview Press, 2003

Shatzmiller, Maya, *Nationalism and Minority Identities in Islamic Societies*, Montreal: McGill-Queen's University Press, 2005.

Shaw, John A. and David E. Long, *Saudi Arabian Modernization: The Impact of Change on Stability*, New York: Praeger, 1982.

Al-Sheha, Abdul Rahman, *Woman in the Shade of Islam*, trans. Mohammed Said Dabas, Riyadh, Saudi Arabia: Islamic Educational Center, no date.

Shehadeh, Lamina Rustum, *Islamic Fundamentalism*, Westport, CT: Praeger Press, 1996.

Shenk, David W., *God's Call to Mission*, Scottdale, PA: Herald Press, 1994.

— *Journeys of the Muslim Nation and the Christian Church: Exploring the Mission of Two Communities*, Scottdale, PA: Herald Press, 2003.

Shepard, William E., *Sayyid Qutb and Islamic Activism: A Translation and Critical Analysis of Social Justice in Islam*, Leiden, the Netherlands: E.J. Brill, 1996.

Shirazi, Faegheh, *The Veil Unveiled: The Hijab in Modern Culture*, Gainesville: University Press of Florida, 2003.

Shukri, Ahmed, *Muslim Law of Marriage and Divorce*, Piscataway, NJ: Gorgias Press, 2009.

Siddiqi, Abdul Hamid, ed., *Sahih Muslim*, Lahore, Pakistan: Hafez Press, 1976.

Siddiqi, Muhammad Iqbal, *Islam Forbids Free Mixing of Men and Women*, Lahore, Pakistan: Kazi Publications, 1983.

— *Why Islam Forbids Intoxicants and Gambling*, Lahore, Pakistan: Kazi Publications, 1981.

Siddiqi, Muhammad Nejatullah, *Muslim Economic Thinking: A Survey of Contemporary Literature*, Leicester, UK: Islamic Foundation, 1981.

Sikainga, Ahmad A., "Shari'a Courts and the Manumission of Female Slaves in the Sudan, 1898–1939", *The International Journal of African Historical Studies*, 28, (1995): 1–24.

Simons, Jr., Thomas W., *Islam in a Globalizing World*, Stanford, CA: Stanford University Press, 2003.

Simone, T., Abdou Maliqalim, *In Whose Image? Political and Urban Practices in the Sudan*, Chicago: University of Chicago Press, 1994.

Singer, Amy, *Charity in Islamic Societies*, Cambridge: Cambridge University Press, 2008.

Sisk, Timothy D., *Islam and Democracy: Religion, Politics and Power in the Middle East*, Washington, DC: United States Institute of Peace, 1992.

Slackman, Michael, "Scholarly Cleric Wields Religion to Pierce the Foundation of Iran's Theocracy", *New York Times*, November 25, 2009, A8.

Smith, Jane I, *Women in Contemporary Muslim Societies*, Lewisburg, PA: Bucknell University Press, 1980.

— "Women in Islam", In *Today's Woman in World Religions*, ed. Armand Sharma, 303–25, Albany: State University of New York Press, 1994.

Smith, Wilfred Cantwell, "Comparative Religion — Whither and Why?", in *History of Religions: Essays in Methodology*, ed. Mircea Eliade and J.M. Kitagawa, 31–58, Chicago: University of Chicago Press, 1959.

Soffan, Linda Ursa, *The Women of the United Arab Emirates*, London: Croom Helm, 1980.

Soguk, Nevzat, *Globalization and Islamism: Beyond Fundamentalism*, Lanham, MD: Rowan and Littlefield, 2011.

Stassen, Glen, ed., *Just Peacemaking: Ten Practices for Abolishing War*, New York: Pilgrim Press, 1998.

Stillman, Norman A., "Charity and Social Service in Medieval Islam", *Societas*, 5 (1975): 105–115.

Stivers, Robert L., ed., *Reformed Faith and Economics*, Lanham, MD: University Press of America, 1989.

Stowasser, Barbara Freyer, *Women in the Qur'an, Traditions, and Interpretation*, New York: Oxford University Press, 1994.

Sullivan, Denis J., and Sana Abed-Kitab, *Islam in Contemporary Egypt: Civil Society vs, the State*, Boulder, CO: Lynne Rienner Publishers, 1999.

Swidler, Arlene, ed., *Human Rights in the Religious Traditions*, New York: Pilgrim Press, 1982.

Swidler, Leonard, ed., *Muslims in Dialogue: The Evolution of a Dialogue*, Lewiston, NY: Edwin Mellen Press, 1992.

Syed, Muhammad Ali, *The Position of Women in Islam: A Progressive View*, Albany: State University of New York Press, 2004.

Taha, Mahmoud Mohamed, *The Second Message of Islam*, Syracuse, NY: Syracuse University Press, 1987.

Taji-Farouki, Suha, ed., *Modern Muslim Intellectuals and the Qur'an*, Oxford: Oxford University Press, 2004.

Tal, Nachman, *Radical Islam in Egypt and Jordan*, Brighton, UK: Sussex Academy Press, 2005.

Talabany, Nouri, "Who Owns Kirkuk? The Kurdish Case", *Middle East Quarterly*, 14, (2007): 75–78.

Tanthhowi, Pramano U., *Muslims and Tolerance: Non-Muslim Minorities under Shariah in Indonesia*, Chang Mai, Thailand: Silkworm Press, 2008.

Taspinar, Omer, *Kurdish Nationalism and Political Islam in Turkey: Kemalist Identity in Transition*, London: Routledge Press, 2005.

Taylor, Alan R., *The Islamic Question in Middle East Politics*, Boulder, CO: Westview Press, 1988.

Teitelbaum, Joshua, *Holier Than Thou: Saudi Arabia's Islamic Opposition*, Washington, DC: The Washington Institute for Near East Policy, 2000.

Tennent, Timothy C., *Christianity at the Religious Roundtable: Evangelicalism in Conversation with Hinduism, Buddhism, and Islam*, Grand Rapids, MI: Baker Academic Books, 2002.

Tibi, Bassam, *Islam and the Cultural Accommodation of Social Change*, Boulder, CO: Westview Press, 1990.

Timberlake, Lloyd, "The Emergence of Environmental Awareness in the West", In *The Touch of Midas: Science, Values and Environment in Islam and the West*, ed. Ziauddin Sardar, 123–133, Manchester: Manchester University Press, 1984.

Toledano, Ehud R., *As If Silent and Absent: Bonds of Enslavement in the Islamic Middle East*, New Haven: Yale University Press, 2007.

Totten, Samuel and William S. Parsons, eds, *Century of Genocide: Critical Essays and Eyewitness Accounts*, New York: Routledge Press, 2009 (1995).

Turner, Bryan S., "Islam, Capitalism and the Weber Theses", *The British Journal of Sociology*, 25 (1974): 230–43.

Tutu, Desmond, "Freedom Fighters or Terrorists?", in *Theology and Violence: The*

South African Debate, ed. Charles Villa-Vicencio, 71–78, Grand Rapids, MI: Eerdmans Press, 1987.

Van Doorn-Harder, Pieternella, *Women Shaping Islam: Reading the Qur'an in Indonesia,* Chicago: University of Illinois Press, 2006.

Van Gorder, A. Christian, *Muslim-Christian Relations in Central Asia,* London: Routledge Press, 2008.

— *No God but God: A Path to Muslim-Christian Dialogue on God's Nature,* Maryknoll, NY: Orbis Books, 2003.

— *Violence in God's Name: Muslim and Christian Relations in Nigeria,* Baltimore: African Diaspora Press, 2012.

Vikor, Knut S., *Between God and the Sultan: A History of Islamic Law,* London: Hurst and Company, 2005.

Villa-Vicencio, Charles, ed., *Theology and Violence: The South Africa Debate,* Grand Rapids, MI: Eerdmans Publishing, 1987.

Viorst, Milton, *The Shadow of the Prophet: The Struggle for the Soul of Islam,* Boulder, CO: Westview Press, 2001.

Volf, Miroslav, "Living with the Other", In *Muslim and Christian Reflections on Peace: Divine and Human Dimensions,* ed. J, Dudley Woodberry, Osman Zumrut, and Mustafa Koylu, 3–22, Lanham, MD: University Press of America, 2005.

Voll, John Obert, *Islam: Continuity and Change in the Modern World,* Syracuse, NY: Syracuse University Press, 1994.

Wadud, Amina, *Inside the Gender Jihad: Women's Reform in Islam,* Oxford: One World Press, 2006.

— *Qur'an and Woman: Rereading the Sacred Text from a Woman's Perspective,* New York: Oxford University Press, 1999.

Waines, David, *Introduction to Islam,* Cambridge: Cambridge University Press, 2003.

Ward, Keith, *Religion and Human Nature,* Oxford: Clarendon Press, 1998.

Warraq, Ibn, ed., *What the Koran Really Says: Language, Text and Commentary,* Amherst, NY: Prometheus Books, 2002.

Wicker, Brian, ed., *Witness to Faith? Martyrdom in Christianity and Islam,* Burlington, VT: Ashgate Publishers, 2006.

Wiktorowicz, Quintan, *Radical Islam Rising: Muslim Extremism in the West,* Lanham, MD: Rowan and Littlefield, 2005.

Wilkinson, John C., "Muslim Land and Water Law", *Journal of Islamic Studies,* 1 (1990): 54–72.

Williams, John Alden, *The World of Islam,* Austin: University of Texas Press, 1994.

Willis, John Ralph, *Slaves and Slavery in Muslim Africa: Volume One: Islam and the Ideology of Enslavement,* London: Frank Cass, 1986.

— *Slaves and Slavery in Muslim Africa: Volume Two: The Servile Estate,* London: Frank Cass, 1986.

Wills, Lawrence M., *Not God's People: Insiders and Outsiders in the Biblical World,* Lanham, MD: Rowman and Littlefield, 2007.

Wilson, Rodney, *Economics, Ethics, and Religion: Jewish, Christian and Muslim Economic Thought,* New York: New York University Press, 1997.

Wogman, J. Philip, *Economics and Ethics: A Christian Enquiry,* London: SCM Press, 1986.

Woodberry, J. Dudley, ed., *Muslims and Christians on the Emmaus Road*, Pasadena, CA: MARC Publications, 1990.

Wright, Robin, *Sacred Rage: The Wrath of Militant Islam*, New York: Touchstone Books, 1986.

Yazbeck, Mahmoud, "Muslim Orphans and the Shari'a in Ottoman Palestine According to Sijill Records", *Journal of the Economic and Social History of the Orient*, 44 (2001): 123–140.

Ye'or, Bat, *The Dhimmi: Jews and Christians under Islam*, trans. Paul Fenton, David Littman, and David Maisel, Philadelphia: Fairleigh Dickinson University Press, 1985.

Yilmaz, Ihsan, "State, Law, Civil Society and Islam in Contemporary Turkey", *Muslim World*, 95 (2005): 385–411.

Zagorin, Perez, *How the Idea of Religious Toleration Came to the West*, Princeton, NJ: Princeton University Press, 2003.

Zakaria, Rafiq, *The Struggle within Islam: The Conflict between Religion and Politics*, New York: Penguin Books, 1989.

El-Zayat, Ahmed Hassan, "How Islam Tackles Poverty", *Maqalat Al-Azhar*, 31 (1960): 153–157.

Zeidan, David, *Sword of Allah: Islamic Fundamentalism from an Evangelical Perspective*, Waynesboro, GA: Gabriel Publishing, 2003.

Zein, M. Farouk, *Christianity, Islam, and Orientalism*, London: Saqi Books, 2003.

Ziaullah, Mohammad, *The Islamic Concept of God*, Boston: Kegan Paul International, 1984.

Zubaida, Sami, *Islam: The People and the State — Political Ideas and Movements in the Middle East*, London: I.B. Tauris, 1993.

Index